Program Administrator's Guide to Early Childhood Special Education

Program Administrator's Guide to Early Childhood Special Education

Leadership,
Development,
& Supervision

Edited by

Janeen McCracken Taylor, Ph.D.
James R. McGowan, Ph.D.

The Johns Hopkins University School of Education
Baltimore, Maryland

Toni Linder, Ed.D.

College of Education
University of Colorado, Denver

·P·A·U·L·H·
BROOKES
PUBLISHING CO.®

Baltimore • London • Sydney

Paul H. Brookes Publishing Co.
Post Office Box 10624
Baltimore, Maryland 21285-0624
USA

www.brookespublishing.com

Typeset by Integrated Publishing Solutions, Grand Rapids, Michigan.
Manufactured in the United States of America by Sheridan Books, Inc.,
Chelsea, Michigan.

The individuals described in this book are composites or real people whose
situations are masked and are based on the authors' experiences. In all instances,
names and identifying details have been changed to protect confidentiality.

Library of Congress Cataloging-in-Publication Data
Taylor, Janeen McCracken, 1946–
    Program administrator's guide to early childhood special education : leadership,
development, and supervision / Janeen McCracken Taylor, James R. McGowan,
Toni Linder.
        p.   cm.
    Includes index.
    ISBN-13: 978-1-55766-805-9 (pbk.)
    ISBN-10: 1-55766-805-1
    1. Children with disabilities—Education (Early childhood)—United States.
I. McGowan, James R.   II. Linder, Toni, 1946–   III. Title.
    LC4019.3.T39   2009
    379.1'12–dc22   2008054810

British Library Cataloguing in Publication data are available from the British Library.

2013   2012   2011   2010   2009
10   9   8   7   6   5   4   3   2   1

Contents

About the Editors

Janeen McCracken Taylor, Ph.D., Consultant, Private Practice, 4749 East Donington Drive, Bloomington, IN 47401

Dr. Taylor started working with children who were disabled when she was 16 years old and an employee of the Maryland Parks and Recreation Department. After earning a degree in physical education from the University of Maryland in 1968, she taught young men with disabilities in Raleigh, North Carolina. A move to Albuquerque, New Mexico, brought time to study for an M.S. degree in Special Education, which led to her first job as a preschool special education teacher. For 10 years, Dr. Taylor taught children from birth to 5 years of age and started the first family education program at her school. She earned her Ph.D. degree from the University of New Mexico while a research assistant at the Parent Involvement Center there. After graduation, Dr. Taylor moved to Maryland and became the Maryland State Department of Education's specialist for infants, toddlers, and preschoolers with special needs. She then spent 3 years at George Washington University directing a post-masters program. The next 5–6 years were spent at the Maryland Infants and Toddlers Program coordinating higher education efforts on behalf of young children with disabilities. In 1993, Dr. Taylor accepted a faculty position at The Johns Hopkins University in what is now the College of Education and coordinated early childhood special education teacher preparation until her retirement in 2006. She is currently consulting, writing, and traveling.

Toni Linder, Ed.D., Professor and Coordinator of Early Childhood Special Education Graduate Studies Program, Administrator, Family Connections, College of Education, University of Denver, University Park Denver, CO 80210

Dr. Linder is a professor in the Child, Family, and School Psychology program in the Morgridge College of Education at the University of Denver. She has been a leader in the development of authentic assessment for young children and is nationally and internationally known for her work on *Transdisciplinary Play-Based Assessment* and *Transdisciplinary Play-Based Intervention.* In addition, she developed *Read, Play, and Learn!® Storybook Activities for Young Children: The Transdisciplinary Play-Based Curriculum* (Paul H. Brookes Publishing Co., 1999), an inclusive literature- and play-based curriculum for preschool and kindergarten learning and development. Dr. Linder also is the Director of the Play and Learning Assessment for the Young (PLAY) Clinic at the University of Denver, where professional and student teams conduct transdisciplinary play-based assessments for young children and their families. She consults widely on assessment, intervention, early childhood education, and family involvement issues. Dr. Linder has conducted research on a variety of topics, including transdisciplinary influences on development, parent–child interaction, curriculum outcomes, and the use of technology for professional development in rural areas.

James R. McGowan, Ph.D., Instructor, The Johns Hopkins University, 6740 Alexander Bell Drive, Columbia, MD 21046

Dr. McGowan has served as an educator in the public schools for 30 years. For 28 of those years, he served as an assistant principal, principal, and director of high schools in a highly successful suburban school district. For 12 of the 28 years, Dr. McGowan was employed as the associate superintendent in the same district, where he was responsible for providing leadership to instructional programs, including special education. During Dr. McGowan's entire public education experience, he taught courses for the University of Maryland, Loyola College of Baltimore, and The Johns Hopkins University. Upon retirement from the public school system, Dr. McGowan assumed the responsibility of coordinating a program at The Johns Hopkins University for the training and development of educational leaders, which he has done for 10 years.

About the Contributors

Amy Aloi, B.S., M.A., Teacher, Howard County Public School System, 8200 Savage Guilford Road, Jessup, MD 20794

Ms. Aloi has been a preschool teacher for 20 years, first in Head Start, then in Special Education. She is an innovative and creative veteran early childhood special educator and serves as a mentor of novice teachers.

Carol Ann Baglin, Ed.D., Assistant State Superintendent, Division of Special Education/Early Intervention Services, Maryland State Department of Education, 200 West Baltimore Street, 9th Floor, Baltimore, MD 21201

Dr. Baglin has a background in Special Education and Marriage and Family Counseling. She has extensive experience with specialized educational, social, and health services; state and federal statutes and regulations and public/private funding mechanisms for programs and services for children with disabilities as well as their families.

Haidee Kaye Bernstein, Ph.D., Westat, 1650 Research Boulevard, Rockville, MD 20850

Dr. Bernstein is a Senior Study Director at Westat, an employee-owned research company, with almost 20 years of experience in special education research and program management, public policy analysis, and program policy evaluation. Prior to Westat, she taught a variety of age levels from preschool through high school in New Orleans, Louisiana; Tampico, Mexico; New York City; and Washington, D.C., and graduate school courses at Hood College in Maryland, She also worked as a program specialist for the Office of Special Education Programs (OSEP) Part C Program.

Deborah T. Carran, Ph.D., Associate Professor, Johns Hopkins University, 6740 Alexander Bell Drive, Columbia, MD 21046

Dr. Carran is a professor in the School of Education at The Johns Hopkins University (JHU) in Baltimore. She received her doctorate in Developmental Psychology from the University of Miami and then was a postdoctoral fellow in Psychiatric Epidemiology in the Department of Mental Hygiene at The Johns Hopkins School of Hygiene and Public Health. She has been on the faculty at JHU for nearly 20 years, with areas of specialization in research design, statistical analysis, and evaluation. Current areas of interest include longitudinal database linkage and tracking. program evaluation methodologies, and risk analysis.

John Castellani, Ph.D., Associate Professor, The Johns Hopkins University, 6740 Alexander Bell Drive, Columbia, MD 21046

Dr. Castellani received his Doctor of Philosophy degree in Instructional Technology from George Mason University in 1997. He is a national and international presenter, researcher, and writer. His areas of expertise are assistive and instructional technology and data-driven decision making. He currently coordinates the Technology for Educators program at The Johns Hopkins University.

Margaret R. Gossner, B.A, M.S., Special Educator, 2201 Wisconsin Avenue N.W., Washington, D.C. 20007

Ms. Gossner has worked for 4 years as a special educator in Montgomery County, Maryland. She currently teaches a K–1 class at a public special education learning center in Rockville, Maryland. She graduated from Franklin & Marshall College in 2003 with a B.A. degree in government and from The Johns Hopkins University in 2006 with an M.S. degree in Special Education, Early Childhood Special Education (Infancy–Grade 3)

Sheldon Greenberg, Ph.D., M.Ed., Associate Dean, School of Education, and Director, Division of Public Safety Leadership, The Johns Hopkins University, 6747 Alexander Bell Drive, Suite 350, Columbia MD 21046

For 2 years, Dr. Greenberg served as Associate Dean and Director of The Johns Hopkins University (JHU) Division of Business and Management (currently Carey School of Business). Prior to joining JHU, he served as Associate Director of the Police Executive Research Forum (PERF) in Washington, D.C., a nationally renowned law enforcement think tank and center for research. Dr. Greenberg began his career as an officer in the Howard County, Maryland, Police Department (HCPD). During his tenure with HCPD, he served as a patrol officer, investigator, supervisor, director of the police academy, and commander of the administrative services bureau. He has served on national task forces on violence in public schools, race-based profiling, police response to people who have mental illness, police recruiting, highway safety, military call-up of law enforcement personnel, and homeland defense. Dr. Greenberg is the author of several books, including *Stress and the Helping Professions* (Paul H. Brookes Publishing Co., 1980), *Stress and the Teaching Profession* (Paul H. Brookes Publishing Co., 1984), and *On the Dotted Line* (Police Executive Research Forum, 1992), a guide to hiring and retaining police executives.

Mary S. Hendricks, Ph.D., Resource Teacher, Office of Early Intervention, Howard County Public Schools, 10598 Marble Faun Court, Columbia, MD 21043

Dr. Hendricks has been teaching for 31 years in public schools in Maryland. She currently teaches in the Early Childhood Special Education graduate division at The Johns Hopkins University.

Anne Hickey, B.S., M.A., Instructional Facilitator, Office of Early Intervention Services, Department of Special Education, Howard County Public School System, Faulkner Ridge Center, 10598 Marble Faun Court, Columbia, MD 21044

For the past 5 years, Ms. Hickey has been the program director for the Howard County Infants and Toddlers Program, and Supervisor for Birth to Five Services with the Howard County Public School System in Maryland. She was an adjunct instructor at The Johns Hopkins University Early Childhood Special Education department for 7 years, teaching courses in both early intervention and assessment for children ages birth to 5 years. She was a parent–infant educator for 11 years and a preschool special education teacher for 3 years in Maryland and the District of Columbia.

Brenda T. Hussey-Gardner, Ph.D., M.P.H., Assistant Professor, University of Maryland School of Medicine, 29 South Greene Street, Suite 110, Baltimore, MD 21201

Dr. Hussey-Gardner has more than 20 years of experience working with infants and toddlers in the neonatal intensive care unit (NICU) and in early intervention programs. She is an assistant professor with the Department of Pediatrics, Division of Neonatology at the University of Maryland School of Medicine and holds adjunct professor positions with the Department of Psychology at University of Maryland, Baltimore County, and the Department of Special Education at University of Maryland, College Park. She has written several books for parents that are used by early intervention programs across the country and is the author of several journal articles.

Cynthia A. Johnson, M.S., Project Facilitator, Howard County Public School System, Faulkner Ridge Center, 10598 Marble Faun Court, Columbia, MD 21044

Ms. Johnson is a speech-language pathologist employed by the Howard County Public School System as a project facilitator for the Office of Early Intervention Services. She has designed and provided professional development for professionals and families on a wide variety of topics, including implementation of assistive technology and best practices in early childhood special education.

Frank J. Masci, Ph.D., Associate Professor, The Johns Hopkins University, Montgomery County Campus, 9601 Medical Center Drive, Rockville, MD 20850

Dr. Masci has been a secondary education teacher, assistant principal, and middle and high school principal in schools with extensive special education programs. He currently works as coordinator of a graduate-level teacher preparation program for The Johns Hopkins University.

Kevin J. McCracken, M.S., M.B.A., CEO, Red Oak Industries, 720 North Marr Road, Columbus, IN 47201

Mr. McCracken has more than 13 years of experience working for and managing not-for-profit agencies. He currently directs Red Oak Industries, a not-for-profit corporation that provides competitive employment to persons with a disability by providing high-quality products and services to businesses in the Midwest. He is also a licensed mental health counselor.

Andrew W. Nussbaum, J.D., Attorney, Knight, Manzi, Nussbaum & La Placa, P.A., 14440 Old Mill Road, Upper Marlboro, MD 20772

Mr. Nussbaum is a partner at the law firm of Knight, Manzi, Nussbaum & La Placa. His law practice concentrates in the area of public school law and he represents public school systems in Maryland. He also teaches School Law at The Johns Hopkins University and at McDaniel College in Westminster, Maryland. He received his undergraduate degree from Stanford University and his Juris Doctor degree from George Washington University.

William Scott Taylor, M.D., Medical Director, Council for Ideal Obstetrical Care, MedStar Health, Inc.; Assistant Clinical Professor, Department of Obstetrics and Gynecology, University of Maryland School of Medicine, 4749 East Donington Drive, Bloomington, IN 47401

Dr. Taylor has contributed to the discipline of obstetrics and gynecology for almost 40 years. His work has ranged from private general practice to specialized work in obstetrical ultrasound to teaching, research, and in recent years, work in improving maternal and infant outcomes. His experiences in the settings of traditional private practice, HMOs, military medicine, and hospital-based practice have been invaluable to his work.

Linda A. Tsantis, Ed.D., Associate Professor, Johns Hopkins University, 6740 Alexander Bell Drive, Columbia, MD 21046

Dr. Tsantis is the coordinator of the Technology for Educators graduate program at The Johns Hopkins University (JHU). She received her Ed.D. degree in early childhood/special education at George Washington University, where she taught in the graduate program for 14 years, and has completed postdoctoral research at Harvard University. Following a sabbatical assignment in IBM Academic Systems, She was recruited to direct IBM innovative study projects involving the application of computer and communications technology in special education and early childhood education. In 1991 Dr. Tsantis joined two colleagues to form a small company providing information and technology consulting services to educators and education associations. In 1996, Linda became the Director of Academic Affairs at the American Speech-Language-Hearing Association (ASHA). She joined the faculty of JHU in November 1997. Her current interests include the design of distributed learning graduate courses that combine the mentoring possibilities of online communications with the data mining possibilities of deep information resources. Dr. Tsantis served on the technology committee of the National Association for the Education of Young Children and was a board member of the East Coast Migrant Head Start Project. She has written two book chapters on applications of technology in learning and is on the international advisory board of New Horizons for Learning and the National Learning Foundation. Dr. Tsantis also served on the White House Task Force on Innovative Teaching. She has won awards from the Council for Exceptional Children Teacher Education Division and the U.S. Department of Education Office of Special Education Programs for the development of innovative teaching programs.

Naomi Chowdhuri Tyler, Ph.D., Research Assistant Professor of Special Education, Vanderbilt University, Peabody College Box 160, Nashville, TN 37203

Dr. Tyler is a research assistant professor at Peabody College of Education at Vanderbilt University. She is Co-Director of the IRIS Center for Training Enhancements, a federally funded center that provides online resources regarding working with students with disabilities in inclusive settings. During her career, she has co-written proposals totaling more than $20 million in external grant funding. Several of these funded projects provided proposal writing and grant management training to others, from which a great deal of the content for Chapter 13 was drawn.

Preface

In 2002, Marisa Conner (former specialist for Early Childhood Special Education [ECSE] efforts in Maryland's Baltimore County School System) brought together Toni Linder (University of Denver), Janeen Taylor (The Johns Hopkins University [JHU]), and Melissa Behm (Paul H. Brookes Publishing Co.). Dr. Linder was in Maryland to work with professionals at Brookes Publishing on several of her publications and Baltimore County Public School System's ECSE teachers who were using the *Read, Play, and Learn!*® curriculum materials (Linder, 1999). Marisa Conner was the organizer of professional development for Baltimore County preschool teachers and thought a quiet lunch would provide the perfect break for Dr. Linder, who had multiple meetings and teacher development activities.

During lunch, after updating each other regarding personal and professional activities, Dr. Linder mentioned that she wished she had the time to update her first book related to administration of ECSE programs (Linder, 1983). Her book has served as a desk reference for ECSE teacher educators, administrators, teachers, therapists, leaders, families, and others interested in young children and their families.

With changes in ECSE theory, policy, research findings, and practice, it was time to incorporate these changes into a new text related to ECSE leadership and administration. Dr. Taylor volunteered to collaborate with Dr. Linder to update and expand her ECSE administration book. Later in the afternoon, Dr. James R. McGowan quickly signed on to provide additional expertise in education leadership and program administration.

Dr. Linder's original text regarding ECSE administration has been helpful for many years to both novice and experienced ECSE leaders and practitioners. It provided an overview of ECSE history, theoretical models of ECSE, suggestions for ECSE practice, ideas for ECSE-related grant preparation/management, strategies for ECSE program leadership, and program evaluation tactics.

The updated text offers an update on historical and contemporary issues and events related to ECSE. Skilled practitioners from the highly regarded Howard County Public School System's (HCPSS) ECSE program (i.e., including the local infants and toddlers program) put pen to paper in order to share their collective experiences with family-centered ECSE screening, evaluation, assessment, programming, and professional development. The excellent preparation, practical experience, and extensive professional development of Mary Hendricks (Chapter 4), Anne Hickey (Chapter 5), Amy Aloi (Chapter 6), and Cynthia A. Johnson (Chapter 9) provide the perfect combination of knowledge and skills for realistic overviews and suggestions for ECSE practitioners who are committed to family-centered programs. They are active in ECSE organizations, teacher preparation, policy planning, policy implementation, and practice. For many years, each has proven her ability to work collaboratively with colleagues and families to provide effective ECSE.

Dr. McGowan and his colleague at JHU, Dr. Frank J. Masci (Chapters 2 and 10), have served in a variety of educational roles from novice teachers to experienced systemwide leaders. They share more than 60 years of education, experience, and wisdom in direct service, administration, and teacher preparation. These roles provide a superb background for their chapters related to effective leadership and supervision.

Interagency collaboration, a critical component of an effective ECSE system, is addressed by a nationally prominent state director of special education. After a number of years teaching special education, Dr. Carol Ann Baglin (Chapter 3) became one of the youngest local directors of special education in California. Within a few years, Dr. Baglin was hired as the first director of Maryland's Infants and Toddlers Program. With her leadership, Maryland provided one of the first models for a seamless system of early intervention and preschool services in the United States. In the late 1990s, Dr. Baglin became director of special education and early intervention in Maryland. Dr. Baglin has spent many years developing and implementing interagency collaboration and agreements on behalf of children with disabilities and their families. In Chapter 3, Dr. Baglin provides theories and models of interagency collaboration in a practical and replicable manner.

Drs. Linda A. Tsantis and John Castellani of JHU offer innovative ways to examine the technology needs of an ECSE program (Chapter 7). Once needs are determined, Drs. Tsantis and Castellani provide an excellent overview of strategies for implementing a technology plan in either an individual program or an ECSE local or state system. Drs. Tsantis and Castellani are both involved in national ECSE and technology organizations. They have consulted with local, state, national, and international programs regarding uses of technology for serving infants, toddlers, young children, and their families.

Dr. William Scott Taylor (Chapter 11), a retired physician, offers clear ideas on how to minimize the spread of communicable diseases in settings for young children, Both adults and children in such settings can be vulnerable to infectious disease(s), but Dr. Taylor's sage advice provides a concrete foundation for health-related practices in ECSE settings.

Kevin J. McCracken (Chapter 12), president of a nonprofit organization for individuals with disabilities, has graduate degrees in psychology and business from Indiana University. Financial accountability and business savvy are two skill sets that many ECSE leaders lack. With Mr. McCracken's educational background and many years of experience in the mental health system of Indiana, he offers a unique perspective on the financial and business aspects of nonprofits program leadership.

Drs. Brenda T. Hussey-Gardner and Haidee Kaye Bernstein (Chapter 8) of the Division of Pediatrics at the University of Maryland Medical Center work with high-risk infants and their families. As such, they have become experts at service coordination. They provide a range of information related to service coordination for a variety of health care, social work, physical therapy, and educational professionals and paraprofessionals. As with financial aspects of program leadership, service coordination is also an overlooked area of personnel preparation. Drs. Hussey-Gardner and Bernstein provide important guidance regarding the form and function of service coordination for young children and their families.

Since September 11, 2001, we have developed a heightened awareness of safety in both public and private settings. Dr. Sheldon Greenberg, who authored the chapter on safety in educational settings (Chapter 16), is an international expert on public safety issues and directs the Public Safety Leadership Division at JHU. Prior to joining the faculty at JHU, Dr. Greenberg was Associate Director of the Police Executive Research Forum (PERF) in Washington, D.C. and provided technical assistance to police agencies in the United States and abroad. Dr. Greenberg began his career as a police officer and was one of the founding members and past president of the Maryland Crime Prevention Association.

Mr. Andrew W. Nussbaum (Chapter 14), a partner in the Maryland law firm of Knight, Manzi, Nussbaum and La Placa, addresses the legal issues that might arise in an ECSE setting. Mr. Nussbaum has practiced law for more than 20 years and has provided professional development to legal and education professionals and para-professionals at a variety of conferences throughout the United States. Mr. Nussbaum is a member of the Council of School Attorneys of the National School Boards Association and one focus of his practice is education law.

Last, but definitely not least, Dr. Deborah T. Carran (Chapter 15) provides practical advice regarding program evaluation. Dr. Carran is a Professor of Education at JHU and has consulted with educational programs on evaluative efforts in numerous states. Dr. Carran has an extensive list of publications related to program evaluation and is an authority on the use of relational databases for evaluative purposes. In an era of data-based decision making (Schoenbrodt, Carran, & Preis, 2007), Dr. Carren stands out as a leader in the arena of program evaluation.

The goal of this book is to provide a practical handbook for ECSE professionals and others interested in family-centered services for young children with disabilities and their families. Today's ECSE programs and systems are complex, and policy decisions must be made in the context of contemporary laws, regulations, policies, customs, and, most important, children (i.e., within a family context). It is the hope of all contributors that we have met this goal and made the readers' professional lives a little less complex and more rewarding. Please enjoy this book, your job, and your life outside of work.

Janeen McCracken Taylor

REFERENCES

Linder, T.W. (1983). *Early childhood special education: Program development and administration*. Baltimore: Paul H. Brookes Publishing Co.

Linder, T.W. (1999). *Read, Play, and Learn!® Storybook activities for young children: The Transdisciplinary Play-Based Curriculum*. Baltimore: Paul H. Brookes Publishing Co.

Schoenbrodt, L., Carran, D.T., & Preis, J. (2007). A study to evaluate the language development of post-institutionalised children adopted from eastern European countries. *Language, Culture, and Curriculum, 20*(1), 52–69.

Acknowledgments

The folks at Paul H. Brookes Publishing Company have been professional, persistent, and supportive throughout the inception, preparation, and completion of this book. Thanks to all of you and a special thanks to Melissa Behm, Heather Shrestha, Janet Krejci, Johanna Cantler, and Laurel Craven. Their hard work and good counsel have enriched the form and content of this project. Others who have made this book possible include our professional families, including Ralph Fessler, Gloria Lane, and Cheri Nicodemus; our extended families (i.e., our precious grandchildren who enrich our lives and are an endless source of joy and learning); and our friends (e.g., "First Fridays"), who encouraged us and kept us in good spirits.

Most important, thank you to the men and women of the armed services who keep us safe while putting themselves in harm's way. Because of these brave people, we can pursue our academic endeavors. Thank you for your service to our country.

*To our families
and to all of the children with disabilities
and their families
who have touched our lives.*

Something Old, Something Newer

Janeen McCracken Taylor, Toni Linder, and Margaret R. Gossner

The flavor with which you scent vessels when new remains in them.
Quintilian, Marcus Fabius (c. 35–95 A.D.)

What If? Beth David has just accepted the position of Director of the local Office of Early Intervention Services. She has 4 weeks to make the transition from her current role as a classroom teacher of preschool children with disabilities to her new role as program leader. She is worried that fulfilling such new roles as personnel supervisor; curriculum specialist; board liaison; fiscal manager; and general advocate for children, staff, and families will be stressful. Although Beth's professional development during the past few years has focused on leadership knowledge and skills (e.g., she has taken workshops related to current laws affecting children with disabilities, paraprofessional support in the classroom, and interagency coordination of services), she is looking for information that can help her with her new responsibilities.

CHAPTER OVERVIEW

In this chapter we describe the evolution of early childhood special education (ECSE) and give an introduction to contemporary standards in ECSE. We also explore the relationship of standards to high-quality programs for young children with disabilities and their families. A description of the essential components of an outstanding ECSE program or system is summarized as an introduction to subsequent chapters.

CHAPTER OBJECTIVES

After reviewing this chapter, the reader will

- Understand historical, philosophical, and legislative influences on ECSE
- Understand the sources of standards and practices in contemporary ECSE
- Know the essential components of excellent programs or systems of programs for young children with disabilities and their families
- Be aware of the Child Reporting Outcomes requirements of the U.S. Department of Education

There was a time when people interested in ECSE could review and absorb the majority of research and literature related to young children with disabilities and their families in a reasonable amount of time (e.g., Ball, 1971; Kanner, 1964). Familiarity with these materials facilitated the application of research findings and theories to settings for the early care and education of children (Allen, Holm, & Schiefelbusch, 1978; Fewell & Vadasy, 1983; Meisels, 1979; Morrison, 1988). Since the 1960s there has been an explosion of print and, more recently, on-line information relative to the education of young children and their families (e.g., Johnson, LaMontagne, Elgas, & Bauer, 1998). At present, the body of literature focusing on interventions for young children and their families has enormous depth and breadth (e.g., Chandler, et al., 2008; Dunlap, 1997; Gonzales-Mena & Stonehouse, 2007; Harry, 2008; Johnson et al., 1994; Lerner, Lowenthal, & Egan, 2003; Meisels & Shonkoff, 1990; Purcell, Horn, & Palmer, 2007). Unfortunately, despite this increase in resources related to early education (e.g., Roopnarine & Johnson, 1993; Thurman & Widerstrom, 1990), there is a dearth of information describing the complex tasks associated with providing leadership and direction for programs and systems of ECSE. This chapter offers a context for the development of contemporary standards and practices associated with high-quality services for young children with disabilities and their families and a framework for providing leadership for such programs and services.

Following this chapter, ECSE and general education leaders, many of whom have been in the field for decades, provide insights and practical suggestions with regard to guiding services for young children and their families. Discussions of such issues as effective leadership, interagency collaboration, child evaluation/assessment, programming, technology, transitions, and service coordination are followed by specific suggestions for professional development, supervision, management of health issues, budget design/implementation, grant funding, legal issues, program evaluation, and safety considerations. This text is designed to support professional development and serve as a resource in times of crisis and contemplation.

ACKNOWLEDGING OUR PAST

To understand the importance of ECSE, it is important to explore historical and theoretical foundations of the early childhood field. Historical trends continue to influence contemporary practice, and theoretical paradigms profoundly affect research and subsequent performance (Clarke & Clarke, 1977; Isenberg & Jalongo, 1997; Kanner, 1964; Safford & Safford, 1996).

Acknowledging the historical roots of a field is necessary for a number of reasons, including learning from past errors so as to avoid repeating them and being better informed (Linder, 1983). Young children have been viewed in a great variety of ways over time. At one time, infants were viewed as screaming, messy creatures in need of structure and training to become productive and respectful citizens (Weeks, 1914). Early philosophers variously described children as *tabulae rasae* (i.e., blank slates), as trees in need of pruning, and as little adults (Shannon, 1917). There have been wide swings in the pendulum of perception and treatment of young children throughout history. Strict authoritarianism has been the norm for some periods of time in the United States; in other eras, more child-friendly educational practices have been in vogue (Gallagher & Ramey, 1987).

In the 1800s, newborns with noticeable disabilities were typically placed in one of the many large institutions for children, youth, and adults with disabilities. This was seen as preferable to the prior practice of placing children with disabilities in asylums for criminals, people with mental illness, people with no financial resources, and others who were in unfortunate circumstances (Association of Medical Officers of American Institutions for Idiotic and Feeble-Minded Persons, 1877).

With the advent of such events as Seguin's (1866) education of a child in Paris who was feral and who possibly had an intellectual disability (i.e., Victor) and the development of Montessori's instructional strategies for use with children with intellectual disabilities in Italy, a new era of enlightened thinking about early education began (Montessori, 1914/1964). Schools for children with intellectual disabilities, hearing impairments, and/or blindness were established in the basements of churches, synagogues, and other community venues, but few formal curricula existed for these children, and little funding was available for qualified special education teachers. Families, volunteers, and a handful of paid professionals paved the way for more formal systems of special education (Turnbull, Turnbull, & Wehmeyer, 2007).

Researchers reached a milestone in understanding the importance of relationships and interaction when they compared the outcomes of children who were adopted or who were cared for by residents of an institution for individuals with intellectual disabilities with the outcomes of children raised in orphanages in which adult–child interactions were severely restricted. Children who were adopted and children who experienced abundant caregiver contact in an institution (i.e., children cared for by individuals with intellectual disabilities) had significantly better cognitive and functional outcomes than those who were left in orphanages in which social interaction was limited (Skeels, 1941, 1966; Skeels & Dye, 1939; Skeels, Updegraff, Wellman, & Williams, 1938; Skodak & Skeels, 1949). The pioneering work of Skeels and his colleagues demonstrated that children need social interaction and environmental stimulation in the earliest years to avoid acquired disabilities or for the effects of congenital conditions to be minimized. This understanding furnished an important foundation for providing intervention in the early years to prevent disabilities or to ameliorate the effects of disabilities.

As a logical consequence of the research efforts of Skeels and his colleagues, infant stimulation, parent–child interaction, and parent education programs were developed. This led to the creation of such parent–child programs as the Portage Project, in which parent education fostered child development (Bluma, Shearer, Frohman, & Hillard, 1976). Another pilot project, the Carolina Abecedarian Project, focused primarily on children born into low-income, multirisk families, but the positive outcomes bolstered efforts to provide services for children with disabilities as well (Feldman, 2004).

Behavioral programs were very popular in the early days of special education and continue to offer valid approaches to encouraging positive child outcomes (Bijou, 1993; Wolery, 2000). Skinner (1953) and other behaviorists believed that "behavior was a result of one's physiology, learning history, and current situation" (Wolery, 2000, p. 181). More recently, ecological, resource-based, eclectic, and response to intervention approaches have become accepted models of intervention (Haager, Klingner, & Vaughn, 2007; Shonkoff & Meisels, 2000).

Numerous past federal laws laid the foundation for relatively newer laws pertaining to services for young children with disabilities and their families. Multiple authors and sources offer overviews of early legislation related to special education and ECSE (A 25-Year History of the IDEA, n.d.; Adam, 2005; Ballard, Ramirez, & Weintraub, 1982; Department of Health, Education and Welfare, 1968; Gallagher, Trohanis, & Clifford, 1989; Heward, 2006; Kirk, Gallagher, & Anastasiow, 2000; Martin,

Table 1.1. Early federal legislation affecting early childhood special education (ECSE)

Year of enactment	Title	Purpose	Public Law number
1958	The National Defense Act	First federal involvement of elementary and secondary education	PL 85-864
1958	The Captioned Films Act	Support for a lending library of captioned films for individuals with hearing impairments	PL 85-905
1958	An Act to Encourage Expansion of Teaching Retarded Children Through Grants to Institutions of Higher Learning and State Education Agencies	Support for training of teachers of children with intellectual difficulties	PL 85-926
1959	Training of Professional Personnel Act	Grants to higher education for training teachers of children with intellectual disabilities	PL 86-158
1961	The Teachers of the Deaf Act	Support for training instructional personnel for children who were deaf or hearing impaired	PL 87-276
1963	The Mental Retardation Facilities and Community Mental Health Centers Construction Act	Extended federal support for preparing teachers of all children with disabilities	PL 88-164
1965	Elementary and Secondary Education Act (ESEA)	Funding for states and local jurisdictions to develop programs for children who were economically disadvantaged or who had disabilities	PL 98-10
1966	Amendments to Title I of the ESEA	Additional funding for state-supported institutional and other programs for children with disabilities	PL 89-313
1966	ESEA Act Amendments	Creation of the Bureau of the Education of the Handicapped*	PL 89-750

*Known today as the Office of Special Education and Rehabilitative Services, which provides oversight of programs affecting children, youth, and adults with disabilities.

Martin, & Terman; 1996). Starting in 1958, the U.S. Congress began providing federal funding for general and special education personnel preparation, the education of children with specific kinds of disabilities, and the education of all children with disabilities. For a partial listing of foundational federal laws for ECSE, see Table 1.1.

The positive effects of intervention services in children's early years were substantiated through President Lyndon B. Johnson's Head Start program, which was "designed to be a part of the War on Poverty" (Gallagher, 2000, p. 2). Head Start was established in 1965, and subsequent evaluation studies showed that participants demonstrated "gains in social and academic performance" (Gallagher, 2000, p. 2). This interest on the part of the federal government in children from families who were economically disadvantaged strengthened arguments for funding ECSE efforts.

Despite the encouraging results from Head Start, President Johnson froze spending for this program because of increasing involvement by the United States in the Vietnam War. This decision bothered many members of Congress who had supported early services through Head Start. In response, the BEH developed a program for preschool age children to provide funds for exemplary programs and demonstrate the gains young children with disabilities could make (Gallagher, 2000). This program was passed as the Handicapped Children's Early Education Assistance Act of 1968 (PL 90-538) and eventually became the Handicapped Children's Early Education Program (HCEEP). Thus, the establishment of Head Start spurred expansion of ECSE through public awareness that early education could prevent problems and improve outcomes for children from economically disadvantaged backgrounds (Zigler & Styfco, 2004).

Head Start continued to provide innovative models of services for young children, and in 1970, the Economic Opportunity Act required at least 10 percent of all children enrolled in Head Start programs to have disabilities (Bailey, 1989). This legislation was enacted to give young children with disabilities access to early education services. According to Bailey, this period sparked the beginning of a movement "based on a single fundamental assumption: By providing early supportive services for handicapped children and their families, the debilitating effects of handicapped conditions could be lessened, and the subsequent costs of providing care for handicapped individuals could be reduced" (1989, p. 64).

Bailey's belief was supported by Congress's passage of the Education for All Handicapped Children Act (EHC; PL 94-142) in 1975. EHC mandated a free appropriate public education (FAPE) in the least restrictive environment (LRE) for students with disabilities ages 6–21 years of age. Although some states opted to include younger children in their system of special education services, most did not (Dunlap, 1997).

Through the Education of the Handicapped Act Amendments of 1983 (PL 98-199), Congress amended the law "to expand incentives for preschool special education programs, early intervention, and transitions programs" ("Attention!!" 1996, p. 7). States received grants "to plan, develop, or implement a comprehensive system of services for handicapped children from birth to 5 years" (Gallagher, 2000, p. 5). This was the first federal law to address infants and toddlers regarding special education; however, the law did not state specific requirements for these children. It was not until the passage of the Education of the Handicapped Act Amendments of 1986 (PL 99-457) that services for infants, toddlers, and preschool children were given adequate attention (Gallagher, Trohanis, & Clifford, 1989).

According to Florian, this law introduced "a national policy that created the conditions for further advancement in the interest of children with disabilities" (1995, p. 36). It did so by 1) lowering the age of eligibility for special education and related services for all children with disabilities to 3 years, 2) establishing the Handicapped Infants and Toddlers Program (Part H), and 3) focusing on the developmental needs of children within a family context. "PL 99-457 fundamentally altered the provision of early services for the youngest children with disabilities and their families" (Brown & Conroy, 1999) and advanced the development of services and programs for infants, toddlers, and children ages 3–5.

The driving motivation behind the development of the Education of the Handicapped Act Amendments of 1986 was to ensure that states provided FAPE for children ages 3–21. Although EHC did mandate FAPE for this age group, states did not have to provide it if the "provision of services...was inconsistent with state law" (Florian, 1995, p. 29). Thus, the Education of the Handicapped Act Amendments of 1986 was designed to fix this loophole.

To support state compliance, regulations for the Education of the Handicapped Act Amendments of 1986 created a "grant program containing the minimum components of a statewide system of early intervention" (Florian, 1995, p. 20). States were given a 4-year phase-in period to provide such services as individualized family service plans (IFSPs), case management services, a comprehensive system for identifying eligible children, a comprehensive system for personnel development, procedural safeguards for the timely resolution of complaints, a single line of responsibility for state-level administration and coordination of programs, an Interagency Coordinating Council (ICC), and multidisciplinary evaluations of children.

The EHC was renamed in 1990 with passage of the Individuals with Disabilities Education Act (IDEA; PL 101-476). In addition to the existing categories of disabilities, autism and traumatic brain injury were included in IDEA. This change was in response to advocacy by families and others interested in the education of children with disabilities.

Early intervention (EI) and preschool special education services received another boost with the passage of IDEA 1997 (PL 105-17), which focused on services directly related to EI (Part C, formerly Part H) and preschool special education (Part B). These parts of the law explicitly delineated provisions for program services for EI (for children birth to age 3 years) and special education (for children ages 3–5 years) (Heward, 2006).

Under President George W. Bush, the No Child Left Behind (NCLB) Act of 2001 (PL 107-110) was enacted. NCLB did not specifically address children and youth with disabilities but did include a goal stating that all children would be proficient in essential subject matter from the general curriculum by 2014, that children in all school districts would make adequate yearly progress toward the proficiency goal, and that all children would be taught by highly qualified teachers. The implications of this legislation for children with disabilities have been hotly debated as states have struggled to meet timelines and requirements (Heward, 2006) outlined in the law.

The Office of Special Education and Rehabilitative Services (OSERS) in the U.S. Department of Education (DOE) has prepared a variety of documents that cover high-interest topics related to current federal statues and regulations affecting young children with disabilities. (See Table 8.1 for the DOE web site address.) A major issue in ECSE is support for states interested in a seamless system of services from birth to age 5. The IFSP, the form documenting services and other details of EI services for infants and toddlers, may also be used (i.e., at the discretion of states and trust territories) after the age of 3 up to kindergarten age (see Appendix A for a sample IFSP).

PROGRAM STANDARDS FOR EARLY CHILDHOOD SPECIAL EDUCATION

The groundwork for program standards in all of special education was laid by the Council for Exceptional Children (Bowe, 2000; CEC, n.d.). CEC "is the largest international professional organization dedicated to improving educational outcomes for individuals with exceptionalities, students with disabilities, and/or the gifted" (CEC, n.d.). CEC publishes standards for personnel in special education and updates them regularly (CEC, 2003). These guidelines serve as special education teacher training program accreditation criteria for colleges and universities throughout the United States and Canada. CEC has numerous special interest divisions, including the Division for Early Childhood (DEC). DEC's purpose is to promote policies and evidence-based practices that support the development of young children with disabilities (and those at risk for disabilities) and their families (DEC, n.d.).

Prior to the early 1990s, there were no standards for practice in ECSE. Sandall, McLean, and Smith (2000, p. 1) noted that in the early 1990s,

Several members of DEC undertook a project to identify recommended practices in early intervention/early childhood special education. The practices were compiled in two products: a DEC document first published in 1993 (DEC Task Force on Recommended Practices, 1993) and a book that extended the underlying concepts (Odom & McLean, 1996).

In 1998, DEC members and staff undertook a revision of the 1993 version of recommended practices for professionals serving young children with disabilities and their families. More than 1,000 articles from 48 scientific journals were reviewed to generate a preliminary list of recommended practices. This literature review was followed by input garnered from expert/scientific and stakeholder focus groups. A list of recommended practices was synthesized from all of these sources. The resultant list of practices was then validated at field sites and ultimately published as a set of recommended practices for EI and ECSE.

The resulting publication, *DEC Recommended Practices in Early Intervention/Early Childhood Special Education* (Sandall et al., 2000), served as the basis for program standards. It also spawned several publications and media materials designed to clarify policy and practice with regard to services for young children with disabilities and their families and the preparation of professionals in EI and ECSE (e.g., Dinnebeil, Miller, & Stayton, 2002; Hemmeter, Smith, Sandall, & Askew, 2005; Sandall, 2001; Sandall, Giacomini, Smith, & Hemmeter, 2006; Sandall, Hemmeter, Smith, & McLean, 2005).

Evolution of Standards for Early Childhood and Early Childhood Special Education Programs

Although this section focuses on programs and settings for young children with disabilities and their families, descriptions of recommended practices and attributes of high-quality environments presume familiarity with guidelines developed by the National Association for the Education of Young Children (NAEYC; Bredekamp & Copple, 1997). NAEYC has long been a leader in development of standards for settings serving young children, and many DEC leaders collaborated with NAEYC leaders to develop DEC's recommendations for practice (Bredekamp, 1987; Bredekamp & Rosegrant, 1992, 1995; Sandall et al., 2000). NAEYC and DEC representatives maintain an ongoing collaboration with regard to services and program standards for young children with disabilities and their families (e.g., Johnson et al., 1998; Smith, Miller, & Bredekamp, 1998). More recently, states and local programs are involved with collecting and transmitting baseline data to meet federal requirements for child outcomes (Early Childhood Outcomes Center, n.d.). Child outcomes that must be reported to the U.S. Department of Education include 1) positive social-emotional skills, including social relationships; 2) acquisition and use of knowledge and skills, including language/communication, and early literacy for preschoolers; and 3) use of appropriate behavior to meet needs. A scale for qualitative judgments regarding child progress is used to measure each outcome. Family outcomes need not be reported at this time, but include 1) knowledge of basic rights regarding early intervention and preschool special education rights; 2) ability to effectively communicate children's needs; and 3) ability of the families to help their child[ren] develop and learn (Early Childhood Outcomes Center, n.d.; National Early Childhood Technical Assistance Center, n.d.). For further information, please see the web sites for the National Early Childhood Technical Assistance Center (NECTAC; http://www.nectac.org) and the Early Childhood Outcomes Center (ECO; http://www.fpg.unc.edu/~eco).

Division of Early Childhood Program Standards

With standards set by DEC for programs serving young children with disabilities and their families, essential features of high-quality programs as well as additional issues that have been identified since the publication of the first DEC set of recommended practices in 2000 follow (Hemmeter, Joseph, Smith, & Sandall, 2001; Sandall et al., 2005; Sandall et al., 2000).

Interdisciplinary Services

When setting a vision for a program serving young children with disabilities and their families, it is critical to recognize the interdependence of family members and multiple service providers in the development and implementation of ECSE services (Allen et al., 1978; Briggs, 1997). Families, professionals, and paraprofessionals build partnerships to influence child development within a family context. Although Chapter 3 addresses issues of collaboration in detail, it is important to note here that given human differences in functioning and style, ongoing professional development relative to team building and functioning to promote positive outcomes for children and families is an essential aspect of any ECSE program. Team collaboration is critical to such activities as 1) development and implementation of outcomes as documented in IFSPs and individualized education programs (IEPs), 2) service delivery in the child's natural environment (i.e., the environment in which a child would typically spend time if he or she did not have a disability), and 3) monitoring of child and family progress (Hemmeter et al., 2001).

Family-Centered Practices

Epps and Jackson noted that "the ability of both of these parties [family members and providers] to develop collaborative partnership is a key factor in successful early intervention" (2000, p. 131). Supporting families in their role as caregivers is a long-standing tradition in special education and is critical to ECSE as well (Bowe, 2000; Turnbull et al., 2007). Families can bring a wealth of resources to the intervention process. Families may express concerns that are unique and require innovative intervention strategies. Individualizing ECSE services for each child and family is a hallmark of a high-quality program. Family-centered practices should be woven into the following aspects of programs:

- Evaluating the child's developmental status

- Determining child and family strengths, resources, and concerns

- Identifying intervention priorities within a family context

- Creating advisory groups

- Developing program activities (e.g., newsletters, informational meetings)

- Providing support activities

- Preparing and sharing program materials

- Conducting program evaluation

- Providing professional development opportunities (Hemmeter et al., 2001)

Evaluation and Assessment

Evaluation (i.e., determination of developmental status at a single point in time) and assessment (i.e., ongoing monitoring of a child's developmental progress) are important components of an ECSE program. Evaluation assists in identifying a child's disability, eligibility for services, developmental strengths, developmental needs, and appropriate interventions. Assessment information is used to monitor a child's progress in a program, make adjustments to the amount and type of intervention, and determine when a child-related outcome is met. Both evaluation and assessment techniques involve collaborating with families, gathering information, sharing information, meeting practice standards, following legal and procedural guidelines, and evaluating program efficacy. Hemmeter et al. (2001) offered greater detail on issues related to evaluation and assessment as components of program evaluation. Sandall et al. (2005) provided specific suggestions for practical applications of DEC-recommended practices for evaluation and assessment.

Child-Focused Interventions

In the earliest years of a child's life, interventions tend to be home or community based (e.g., at a child care center). As a child reaches the age of 3 years, services shift to educational settings in accordance with a child's IFSP or plan for making the transition to services beyond EI. These settings may be preschool special education classrooms, community preschool programs, Head Start, or other community-based programs. Although services continue to be family centered, the educational focus shifts somewhat to child-focused teaching (Hemmeter et al., 2001).

"Teaching is helping children learn and making sure that they are learning" (Hemmeter et al., 2001, p. 41). Teaching involves a child's active engagement and participation in learning. Such environmental aspects of learning as space, equipment, materials, lighting, and learning centers can be extremely important in supporting children as they become independent learners and socially competent individuals. Individual activities should be planned in combination with group activities to encourage social interaction and communication. While building on a child's strengths, specific educational strategies address each child's learning needs. For a more thorough treatment of intervention options, please see Chapter 6, which addresses preschool programming options.

Additional Attributes of High-Quality Early Childhood Special Education Programs

Important components of excellent programs for young children are addressed in subsequent chapters in this book. These components have been derived from previously cited federal legislation, federal policy, findings of research institutes, professional organizations, input from stakeholders, and other relevant sources (e.g., Bailey et al., 2006; CEC, n.d.; DEC, n.d.; National Child Care Information Center, n.d.; NAEYC, n.d.). Key topics to be covered include

- Evaluation and assessment

- Family-centered interventions for infants and toddlers

- Family-centered interventions for preschool children

- Technology considerations in ECSE

- Transitions in ECSE

- Service coordination

- Interagency collaboration

- Professional development

- Health and safety

- Leadership

- Supervision

These topics represent critical components of high-quality early childhood education programs for infants, toddlers, and preschoolers with disabilities and their families and are worth careful review. To support program improvement, a chapter on program evaluation provides specific strategies for overall evaluation of program effectiveness. Because most program leaders must deal with fiscal issues, a chapter on budget and finance for nonprofit programs (see Chapter 15) has been included that offers information on topics seldom addressed in educational texts. In recognition of post-9/11 issues related to safety, a chapter on building a safe program is timely (see Chapter 16).

CONCLUSIONS

ECSE programs and systems continue to evolve and expand. From the early days of limited educational opportunities for young children with disabilities to contemporary community-based systems of intervention, services for young children with disabilities and their families are increasingly responsive to family and community values. As interventions become more family and child friendly, researchers are working hard to find ways to validate or modify existing practices and incorporate emerging research findings into current standards. ECSE leaders must look to national professional organizations (e.g., CEC, DEC, NAEYC) and research centers (e.g., University of North Carolina's FPG Child Development Institute, Beach Center on Disability at the University of Kansas) for guidance relative to recommended practices.

REFERENCES

A 25 Year History of the IDEA. (n.d.). Retrieved April 5, 2008, from http://www.ed.gov/policy/speced/leg/idea/history.html/

Adam, A.R. (2005). *The elusive ideal: Equal educational opportunity and the federal role in Boston's Public Schools, 1950–1985.* Chicago: The University of Chicago Press.

Allen, K.E., Holm, V.A., & Schiefelbusch, R.L. (1978). *Early intervention: A team approach.* Baltimore: University Park Press.

Association of Medical Officers of American Institutions for Idiotic and Feeble-Minded Persons. (1877). *Proceedings of the Association of Medical Officers of American Institutions for Idiotic and Feeble-Minded Persons.* Philadelphia: J.B. Lippincott.

Attention!! The laws are changing!! (1996). *NICHCY News Digest 15,* 1–13.

Bailey, D.B. (1989). Early schooling for children with special needs. *Theory in Practice, 28,* 64–69.

Bailey, D.B., Bruder, M.B., Heebeler, K., Carta, J. Defoosset, M., Greenwood, C., et al. (2006). Recommended outcomes for families of young children with disabilities. *Journal of Early Intervention, 28*(4), 227–251.

Ball, T.S. (1971). *Itard, Seguin, and Kephart: Sensory education—A learning interpretation.* Columbus, OH: Charles E. Merrill.

Ballard, J., Ramirez, B.A., & Weintraub, F.J. (Eds.). (1982). *Special education in America: Its legal and governmental foundations.* Reston, VA: Council for Exceptional Children.

Bijou, S.W. (1993). *Behavior analysis of child development* (2nd rev. sub. ed.). Reno, NV: Context Press.

Bluma, S., Shearer, M., Frohman, A., & Hillard, J. (1976). *Portage guide to early education.* Portage, WI: Cooperative Educational Service Agency #12.

Bowe, F.G. (2000). *Birth to five: Early childhood special education* (2nd ed.). Albany, NY: Delmar.

Bredekamp, S. (Ed.). (1987). *Developmentally appropriate practice in early childhood programs serving children from birth through age 8* (Exp. Ed.). Washington, DC: National Association for the Education of Young Children.

Bredekamp, S., & Copple, C. (1997). *Developmentally appropriate practice in early childhood programs.* Washington, DC: National Association for the Education of Young Children.

Bredekamp, S., & Rosegrant, T. (Eds.). (1992). *Reaching potentials: Appropriate curriculum and assessment for young children* (Vol. 1). Washington, DC: National Association for the Education of Young Children.

Bredekamp, S., & Rosegrant, T. (Eds.). (1995). *Reaching potentials: Appropriate curriculum and assessment for young children* (Vol. 2). Washington, DC: National Association for the Education of Young Children.

Briggs, M.H. (Ed.). (1997). *Building early intervention teams: Working together for children and families.* Gaithersburg, MD: Aspen.

Brown, W., & Conroy, M. (1999). Entitled to what? Public policy and the responsibilities of early intervention. *Infants & Young Children, 11*(3), 27–36.

Chandler, L., Young, R., Nylander, D., Dhields, L., Ash, J., Bauman, B., et al. (2008). Promoting early literacy skills within daily activities and routines in preschool classrooms. *Young Exceptional Children, 11*(2), 2–16.

Clarke, A.M., & Clarke, A.D.B. (1977). *Early experience: Myth and evidence.* New York: The Free Press.

Council for Exceptional Children. (n.d.). *About CEC.* Retrieved April 9, 2007, from http://www.cec.sped.org/AM/Template.cfm?Section=About_CEC

Council for Exceptional Children. (2003). *What every special educator must know: Ethics, standards and guidelines for special educators* (5th ed.). Arlington, VA: Author.

Department of Health, Education and Welfare. (1968). *A summary of selected legislation relating to the handicapped (1963–1967).* Washington, D.C.: U. S. Government Printing Office.

Dinnebeil, L., Miller, P., & Stayton, V. (2002). *Personnel preparation in early childhood special education: Implementing the DEC recommended practices.* Longmont, CO: Sopris West.

Division for Early Childhood. (n.d.). *About us.* Retrieved April 9, 2008, from http://www.dec-sped.org/aboutdec.html

Division for Early Childhood Task Force on Recommended Practices. (1993). *DEC recommended practices: Indicators of quality programs for infants and young children with special needs.* Reston, VA: Council for Exceptional Children.

Dunlap, L.L. (Ed.). (1997). *An introduction to early childhood special education.* Boston: Allyn & Bacon.

Early Childhood Outcomes (ECO) Center. (n.d.). *OSEP's revised child outcomes reporting requirements for Part C and Part B/619 Programs: What the changes mean for states.* Retrieved April 9, 2008 from http://www.fpg.unc.edu/~eco/faqs.cfm

Education for All Handicapped Children Act of 1975, PL 94-142, 20 U.S.C. §§ 1400 *et seq.*

Education of the Handicapped Act Amendments of 1983, PL 98-199, 20 U.S.C. §§ 1400 *et seq.*, Stat. 1357.

Education of the Handicapped Act Amendments of 1986, PL 99-457, 20 U.S.C. §§ 1400 *et seq.*

Elementary and Secondary Education Act Amendments of 1966, PL 89-750, 80 Stat. 1191, 20 U.S.C. §§ 873 *et seq.*

Elementary and Secondary Education Act of 1965, PL 89-10, 20 U.S.C. §§ 241 *et seq.*

Epps, S., & Jackson, B.J. (2000). *Empowered families, successful children: Early intervention programs that work.* Washington, DC: American Psychological Association.

Feldman, M.A. (Ed.). (2004). *Early intervention: The essential readings.* Malden, MA: Blackwell.

Fewell, R.R., & Vadasy, P.F. (1983). *Learning through play: A resource manual for teachers and parents.* Hingham, MA: Teaching Resources.

Florian, L. (1995). Part H early intervention program: Legislative history and intent of the law. *Topics in Early Childhood Special Education, 15*(3), 247–263.

Gallagher, J.J. (2000). The beginnings of federal help for young children with disabilities. *Topics in Early Childhood Special Education, 20*(1), 3–7.

Gallagher, J.J., & Ramey, C.T. (1987). *The malleability of children.* Baltimore: Paul H. Brookes Publishing Co.

Gallagher, J.J., Trohanis, P.L., & Clifford, R.M. (1989). *Policy implementation and PL 99-457: Planning for young children with special needs.* Baltimore: Paul H. Brookes Publishing Co.

Gonzales-Mena, J., & Stonehouse, A. (2007). *Making links: A collaborative approach to planning and practice in early childhood.* New York: Teachers College Press.

Haager, D., Klingner, J., & Vaughn, S. (Eds.). (2007). *Evidence-based reading practices for Response to Intervention.* Baltimore: Paul H. Brookes Publishing Co.

Handicapped Children's Early Education Assistance Act of 1968, PL 90-538, 20 U.S.C. §§ 621 *et seq.*

Harry, B. (2008). Collaboration with culturally and linguistically diverse families: Ideal versus reality. *Exceptional Children, 74*(3), 372–351.

Hemmeter, M.L., Joseph, G.E., Smith, B.J., & Sandal, S. (2001). *DEC recommended practices: Program assessment: Improving practices for young children with special needs and their families.* Longmont, CO: Sopris West.

Hemmeter, M.L., Smith, B.J., Sandall, S., & Askew, L. (2005). *DEC recommended practices workbook.* Longmont, CO: Sopris West.

Heward, W.L. (2006). *Exceptional children: An introduction to special education* (8th ed.). Upper Saddle River, NJ: Pearson/Merrill/Prentice Hall.

Individuals with Disabilities Education Act Amendments (IDEA) of 1997, PL 105-17, 20 U.S.C. §§ 1400 *et seq.*

Individuals with Disabilities Education Act (IDEA) of 1990, PL 101-476, 20 U.S.C. §§ 1400 *et seq.*

Isenberg, J.P., & Jalongo, M.R. (1997). *Major trends and issues in early childhood education: Challenges, controversies, and insights.* New York: Teachers College Press.

Johnson, L.J., Gallagher, R.J., LaMontagne, M.L., Jordan, J.B., Gallagher, J.J., Hutinger, P.L., et al. (Eds.). (1994). *Meeting early intervention challenges: Issues from birth to three* (2nd ed.). Baltimore: Paul H. Brookes Publishing Co.

Johnson, L.J., LaMontagne, M.J., Elgas, P.M., & Bauer, A.M. (1998). *Early childhood education: Blending theory, blending practice.* Baltimore: Paul H. Brookes Publishing Co.

Kanner, L. (1964). *A history of the care and study of the mentally retarded.* Springfield, IL: Charles C Thomas.

Kirk, S.A., Gallagher, J.J., & Anastasiow, N.J. (2000). *Educating exceptional children* (9th ed.). Boston: Houghton Mifflin.

Lerner, J.S., Lowenthal, B., & Egan, R. (2003). *Preschool children with special needs: Children at risk and children with disabilities* (2nd ed.). Boston: Allyn & Bacon.

Linder, T.W. (1983). *Early childhood special education: Program development and administration.* Baltimore: Paul H. Brookes Publishing Co.

Martin, E.W., Martin, R., & Terman, D.L. (1996). The legislative and litigation history of special education. *Special Education for Students with Disabilities, 6*(1), 25–39.

Meisels, S. (Ed.). (1979). *Special education and development: Perspectives on young children with special needs.* Austin, TX: PRO-ED.

Meisels, S.J., & Shonkoff, J.P. (Eds.). (1990). *Handbook of early childhood intervention.* New York: Cambridge University Press.

Montessori, M. (1964). *Dr. Montessori's own handbook.* Cambridge, MA: Robert Bentley. (Original work published 1914)

Morrison, G.S. (1988). *Early childhood education today* (4th ed.).Columbus, OH: Merrill.

National Association for the Education of Young Children (NAEYC). (n.d.). Retrieved April 9, 2008 from http://www.naeyc.org/

No Child Left Behind Act of 2001, PL 107-110, 115 Stat. 1425, 20 U.S.C. §§ 6301 *et seq.*

Odom, S.L., & McLean, M.E. (Eds.). (1996). *Early intervention/early childhood special education: Recommended practices.* Austin, TX: PRO-ED.

Purcell, M., Horn, E., & Palmer, S. (2007) . A qualitative study of the initiation and continuation of preschool inclusion programs. *Exceptional Children, 74*(1), 85–99.

Roopnarine, J.L., & Johnson, J.E. (1993). *Approaches to early childhood education* (2nd ed.). New York: Macmillan.

Safford, P.L., & Safford, E.J. (1996). *A history of childhood and disability.* New York: Teachers College Press.

Sandall, S. (2001). *DEC recommended practices video.* Longmont, CO: Sopris West.

Sandall, S., Giacomini, J., Smith, B.J., & Hemmeter, M.L. (2006). *DEC recommended practices toolkit: Interactive tools to improve practices for young children with special needs and their families* [CD]. Longmont, CO: Sopris West.

Sandall, S., Hemmeter, M.L., Smith, B.J., & McLean, M.E. (2005). *DEC recommended practices: A comprehensive guide for practical application in early intervention/early childhood special education.* Longmont, CO: Sopris West.

Sandall, S., McLean, M.E., & Smith, B.J. (2000). *DEC recommended practices in early intervention/early childhood special education.* Longmont, CO: Sopris West.

Seguin, E. (1866). *Idiocy and its treatment by the physiological method.* New York: W. Wood.

Shannon, T.W. (1917). *Eugenics.* Marietta, OH: S.A. Mullikin.

Shonkoff, J.P., & Meisels, S.J. (Eds.). (2000). *Handbook of early childhood intervention* (2nd ed.). Cambridge, UK: Cambridge University Press.

Skeels, H.M. (1941). A study of the effects of differential stimulation on mentally retarded children: A follow-up report. *American Journal of Mental Deficiency, 46,* 340–350.

Skeels, H.M. (1966). Adult status of children from contrasting early life experiences: A follow-up study. *Monographs of the Society for Research in Child Development, 31*(3, Serial No. 105).

Skeels, H.M., & Dye, H.B. (1939). A study of the effects of differential stimulation on mentally retarded children. *Proceedings and Addresses of the Sixty-Third Annual Session of the American Association on Mental Deficiency, 44*(1), 114–36.

Skeels, H.M., Updegraff, R., Wellman, B.L., & Williams, H.M. (1938). A study of environmental stimulation: An orphanage preschool project. *University of Iowa Studies in Child Welfare, 15*(4), 1–191.

Skinner, B.F. (1953). *Science and human behavior.* New York: Macmillan.

Skodak, M., & Skeels, H.M. (1949). A final follow-up study of one hundred adopted children. *Journal of Genetic Psychology, 75,* 85–125.

Smith, B.J., Miller, O., & Bredekamp, S. (1998). Sharing responsibility: DEC-, NAEYC-, and Vygotsky-based practices for quality inclusion. *Young Exceptional Children, 2*(1), 11–20.

Thurman, S.K., & Widerstrom, A.H. (1990). *Infants and young children with special needs: A developmental and ecological approach* (2nd ed.). Baltimore: Paul H. Brookes Publishing Co.

Turnbull, A., Turnbull, R., & Wehmeyer, M.L. (2007). *Exceptional lives: Special education in today's schools.* Upper Saddle River, NJ: Pearson.

Weeks, M.H. (1914). *Parents and their problems: Child welfare in home, school, church and state.* Washington, DC: National Congress of Mothers and Parent–Teacher Associations.

Wolery, M. (2000). Behavioral approaches to early intervention. In J.P. Shonkoff & S.J. Meisels (Eds.), *Handbook of early intervention* (2nd ed.). Cambridge, UK: Cambridge University Press.

Zigler, E., & Styfco, S.J. (Eds.). (2004). *The Head Start debates.* Baltimore: Paul H. Brookes Publishing Co.

Effective Leadership

Frank J. Masci and James R. McGowan

Only in growth, reform, and change, paradoxically enough, is true security found.
Anne Morrow Lindbergh

What If?   You are the director of an inclusive preschool for children ages 2–5 years. There are 50 children at the center along with 8 full-time staff and 6 part-time personnel. Staff members' education levels range from high school equivalency certificates to graduate degrees. There are also approximately 10 part-time volunteers.

You collaborate closely with families, local school system personnel, community program representatives, and staff from other relevant agencies to provide outstanding early childhood and early childhood special education (ECSE) services to children and their families. Special education representatives of the state board of education have communicated to all programs serving children with disabilities that a new type of testing will be implemented in about 3 months. You must work with your staff to develop a plan for incorporating this new layer of testing into your program's already crowded schedule. Where do you start?

CHAPTER OVERVIEW

This chapter presents a look at what makes an effective leader. First, we briefly examine the history of recent leadership theory; we then turn to the effect of the standards-based movement on leadership. Next, we explore the importance of developing and maintaining a school vision and mission, creating a climate of trust and purpose, and using data. We examine practical elements of management, collaboration, and professional development within the context of an ethical and a multicultural framework. Finally, we present implications for future research and clinical/educational practice.

CHAPTER OBJECTIVES

After reviewing this chapter, the reader will

- Understand the historical influences and the effect of the standards-based movement on leadership

- Understand how to develop a school vision and mission

- Know the practical elements of education and administration management

- Understand the importance of data collection and how to interpret data

LEADERSHIP IN EARLY CHILDHOOD SPECIAL EDUCATION

Most people would readily identify effective leadership as an important component of effective schools; considerable research conducted over the past decade supports this assertion (Lezotte, 1997, 1999). As educational leaders, ECSE administrators play a critical role in school success, exercising considerable influence over student achievement, staff motivation and competence, and staff morale—all of which contribute to the school and school system's effectiveness and reputation in the community. In the context of educational leadership, the ECSE administrator will be expected to assume the roles of instructional leader, manager, supervisor, public relations agent, personnel/human relations specialist, evaluator, and staff developer.

A SELECTED HISTORY OF 20TH- AND 21ST-CENTURY LEADERSHIP THEORY

Are we headed in the right direction? Are students learning? Are we meeting the expectations of students, parents, business, and society in general for the education of our students? Bennis and Nanus (1985) stated that "the problem with many organizations, and especially ones that are failing, is that they tend to be over managed and under led. They may excel in the ability to handle the daily routine, yet never question whether the routine should be done at all" (p. 26).

Traditional

Some of these tendencies to overmanage are rooted in the history of modern management theory. Taylor and his associates (1991) tended to view the worker as a nonthinking cog in the wheel of the organization. The worker was to be managed, not led. This thinking meshed with Weber's concept of bureaucracy, in which people were forced into specialties (Jacobs, 1971). Both of these theoretical bases involved a desire to increase routinization and efficiency. *Normal schools,* developed for the training of teachers in the mid-19th century, seem to have incorporated a similar concept of routinization in that the procedures to be followed by teachers were highly prescribed by supervisors. However, according to Wright (1930), a focus on the needs of students and on increased teacher professionalism were important normal school innovations.

Taylor's and Weber's notion that people should be placed in prescribed roles rather than be seen as having the infinite possibilities offered by human potential was also congruent with a concern that Oakes raised about tracking in schools. In Chapter 2, Oakes (1985) fully discusses the impact that factors such as the development of intelligence testing, the belief in Social Darwinism, and the industrialization of the country had on thoughts about the purpose and process of education in the United States. In essence, according to Oakes, there was now a process and reason for deciding who would receive what kind of education. Some students would be prepared for higher level opportunities, while others would be prepared to perform menial tasks. Students with disabilities were early victims of tracking as well as unconscionable experimentation resulting from the eugenics movement in the United States in the early 20th century. Children and adults with special needs were all too often subjected to sterilization and other medical procedures designed to keep the gene pool "pure." It is worth noting that Hitler and his regime were influenced by the principles and practice of eugenics, with horrific and tragic results.

Human Relations

In the late 1980s and early 1990s, educators gave much attention to some form of participative management, where teachers and other stakeholders were included in fundamental decisions with respect to the education of students and the management of educational institutions. A great deal of research was reported in educational journals on this subject. Numerous attempts were made to implement these strategies (David, 1989; Hill & Bonan, 1991). However, the initial work on the effects of employees participating in decision making, which also served as the basis for future educational management theory, was established in business-related research. This seminal work is described further as follows. Mayo (1945) and Roethlisberger (1941) conducted the early research that led to greater roles in decision making. They are credited with the finding that human concern rather than economic gain influences individual commitment to an organization. Jacobs (1971) noted that this finding, often included in what has been termed the *human relations movement,* indicates that "workers can and will contribute meaningfully to the development of more effective decisions and methods if allowed." The human relations movement was important because it introduced the idea that a leader must consider the needs of staff members. Maslow (as cited in Hersey & Blanchard, 1993) theorized that people's motivation, in very simple terms, is linear. Basic human needs must be in place prior to meeting any higher order needs. Figure 2.1 illustrates Maslow's hierarchy of needs.

Figure 2.1. Maslow's hierarchy of needs. (From Hersey P., & Blanchard, K. [1993]. *Management of organizational behavior: Utilizing human resources* [6th ed., p. 37]. Englewood Cliffs, NJ: Simon & Schuster.)

Hygiene Factors	**Motivational Factors**
(if not present, lead to dissatisfaction)	(if present, provide motivation)

Interpersonal relationships with supervisors	Achievement
Interpersonal relationships with peers	Recognition
Technical supervision	Work itself
Company policy and administration	Responsibility
Working conditions	Advancement
Personal life	

Figure 2.2. Frederick Herzberg's two-factor hygiene and motivation theory. (From Jacobs, T.O. [1971]. *Leadership and exchange in formal organizations* [p. 130]. Alexandria, VA: Human Resources Research Organization.)

Hertzberg's work (cited in Jacobs, 1971) contributed to an increased understanding of what motivates people. His research yielded two distinct categories of factors that affect worker performance. Figure 2.2 provides a description of these factors. One set of factors, called the *hygiene factor,* describes preventive and environmental elements in the workplace that must be present to avoid employee dissatisfaction. The second set of factors are those that enable employees to grow and to become motivated and more satisfied with work.

The issue of motivation was also addressed through the work of the Institute for Social Research of the University of Michigan (Jacobs, 1971). This extensive body of work focused on organizational structure and the degree to which workers are involved in making decisions regarding organizational goals (Jacobs, 1971).

The work of Hackman and Oldham (1975) also shed light on people in the workplace and conditions that affect their motivation. Figure 2.3 presents the model developed by Hackman and Oldham. This model posits specific psychological states that must be addressed in order for a worker to be motivated. On close examination of these psychological states, one can reach the conclusion that each is within the control of leadership. This thinking aligns with a comment by Stogdill (1974) on the work of Ackerson in which he stated,

> The findings suggest that leadership is not a matter of passive status, or of the mere possession of some combination of traits. It appears rather to be a working relationship among members of a group, in which the leader acquires status through active participation and demonstration of the capacity for carrying on cooperative tasks through completion. (p. 68).

At about the same time the motivation studies were being done at the University of Michigan, similar studies began at Ohio State University that yielded additional insight into leadership. The findings at Ohio State indicated that a leader has the twin responsibilities of achieving organizational goals and satisfying group members' needs. The model developed by Blake and Mouton (1964), two Ohio State researchers, is presented in Figure 2.4 and gives a clear representation of these twin responsibilities, by providing a simple, graphical method of gauging leadership characteristics. The vertical axis of the grid measures concern for people (or relationship-orientation); the horizontal axis measures concern for performance (or task-orientation). Using this model, a predominantly task-oriented person, who ignored people, would be described as a "9, 1 leader," that is, one who put a high priority on performance but who cared little for the people involved. This leadership style is seen as authoritarian. A leader who is a "1,9 leader" is one who ignores performance and

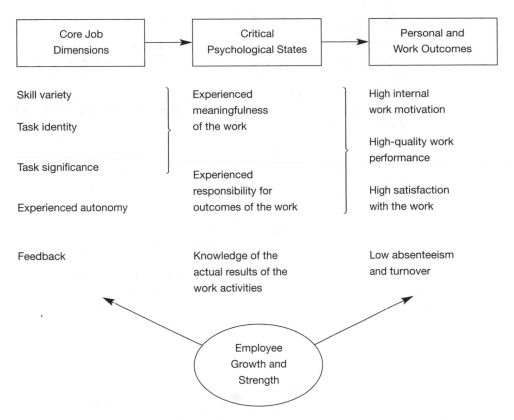

Figure 2.3. The Job Diagnostic Survey: A theoretical model relating the core job dimensions, the critical psychological states, and on-the-job outcomes (as moderated by employee growth and strength). (From Hackman, R., & Oldham, G.R. [1975]. Development of the Job Diagnostic Survey. *Journal of Applied Psychology, 60*[2], 161.)

concentrates on people. This leadership style is sometimes referred to as the "country club" style. The "9,9 leader" is the most desirable in the model. This leader places strong emphasis on performance and people, and the model predicts that this style will be the most effective in both production and employee satisfaction. The "1,1 leader" fails to place emphasis on either people or performance. One could argue that this is not leadership at all.

Contemporary

It is important to note that this discussion has moved from concern for how the worker fits into the organizational structure to a more expansive set of considerations involved in leading an organization. As the work of management and leadership researchers and commentators continues, it is important to stress that contemporary understanding of the leadership role is highly complex and involves many different facets. The rest of this historical section provides only a very brief survey of current concepts and authors who are building on the work that has been done already. Much of this recent work is concerned primarily with preparedness of leaders.

The work of Stephen Covey (1991) conveys the importance of a person developing certain habits that are associated with a highly effective person. These habits are presented in Figure 2.5. In the figure, there is a growth cycle from Dependence through Independence to Interdependence. Growth in the first three habits leads one to become

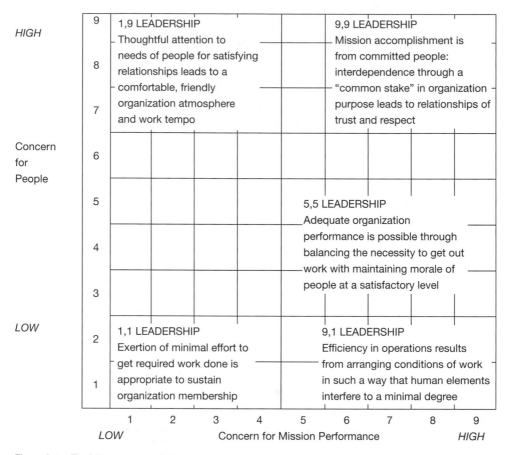

Figure 2.4. The Military Leadership Grid. (Adapted from Blake, R.R., & Mouton, J.S. [1964]. *The Management Grid* [p. 10]. Houston, TX: Gulf Publishing. Reproduced by permission.)

independent. Growth in habits 4 through 6 leads one to interdependence and the realization that true effectiveness is accomplished through the ability to be highly effective in working with others. Last, habit 7, if practiced, leads one to continuous growth. These habits, when combined with Covey's overall concept of preparing one's spirit in order to lead effectively, offer a powerful argument for the importance of the psychological and spiritual components of leadership. In similar fashion, Deal and Bolman (2001) wrote extensively about the importance of caring for the spirit.

Another major concern of leadership is creating and sustaining changes in ineffective strategies. Numerous authors in the business field have focused on organizational change; their insights can also be considered for application to educational settings in general and to ECSE settings in particular. A few of these authors are discussed here.

Kotter (1999) clearly focused on the need for a leader to make changes in the status quo. He also pointed out the need for a leader to anticipate and to address resistance to change. The leader needs to develop an attitude of anticipation instead of reaction. Lack of trust is one of the main reasons people resist change. Kotter stated that "people also resist change when they do not understand its implications and perceive that it might cost them much more than they will gain" (p. 33).

Leaders must also be well prepared to communicate clearly with those they are leading. Fullan (1993, 1999) has written a series of books on change. He suggested

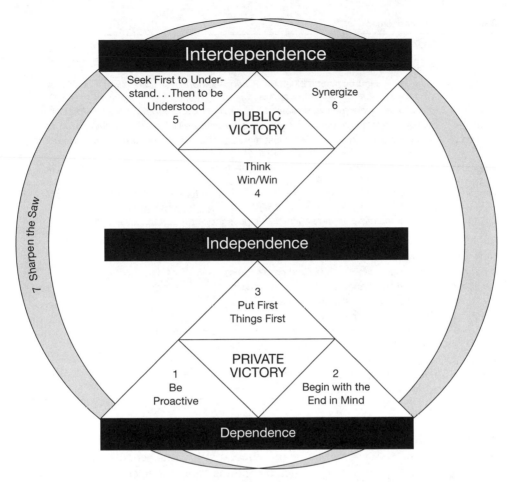

Figure 2.5. The seven habits—An overview. (From Covey, S. [1991]. *Principle-centered leadership* [p. 41]. New York: Summit Books; reprinted with permission.)

that there is basic learning that a leader must master in order to manage change. As Fullan's work has progressed, he has modified his ideas to reflect recent research. Of importance is the idea that the prospective leader must fully understand the human side of change. Table 2.1 presents two sets of observations made by Fullan (1999) about change. Although the items presented under the First Change Forces still hold true, the items under the New Change Forces provided a fuller presentation of the complexity of forces affecting the understanding of change. When comparing the First Change Forces with the New Change Forces, it seems obvious that the New Change Forces are based on deeper consideration of moral, ethical, psychological, and sociological factors.

Senge (1990) made another important contribution to leadership theory with his suggestion that a leader must understand the five disciplines of an organization. These elements are presented in Table 2.2.

When all of the previously discussed elements are examined together, the concept of the learning organization emerges. A leader must understand that situations are constantly changing and that those changes are not isolated but rather are systemic. The leader must work with colleagues to learn from the organization and its surroundings and to make suitable adjustments, knowing that changes can have far-

Table 2.1. Change forces

First Change Forces

Lesson 1   You can't mandate what matters. (*The more complex the change, the less you can force it.*)

Lesson 2   Change is a journey, not a blueprint. (*Change is nonlinear, loaded with uncertainty and excitement, and sometimes perverse.*)

Lesson 3   Problems are our friends. (*Problems are inevitable, and you can't learn without them.*)

Lesson 4   Vision and strategic planning come later. (*Premature visions and planning blind.*)

Lesson 5   Individualism and collectivism must have equal power. (*There are no one-sided solutions to isolation and groupthink.*)

Lesson 6   Neither centralization nor decentralization works. (*Both top-down and bottom-up strategies are necessary.*)

Lesson 7   Connection with the wider environment is critical for success. (*The best organizations learn externally as well as internally.*)

Lesson 8   Every person is a change agent. (*Change is too important to leave to the experts; personal mind set and mastery is the ultimate protection.*)

New Change Forces

Lesson 1   Moral purpose is complex and problematic.

Lesson 2   Theories of change and theories of education need each other.

Lesson 3   Conflict and diversity are our friends.

Lesson 4   Understand the meaning of operating on the edge of chaos.

Lesson 5   Emotional intelligence is anxiety provoking and anxiety containing.

Lesson 6   Collaborative cultures are anxiety provoking and anxiety containing.

Lesson 7   Attack incoherence: Connectedness and knowledge creation are critical.

Lesson 8   There is no single solution: Craft your own theories and actions by being a critical consumer.

reaching effects on the organization and its members. Educational leaders, especially, must understand the systemic nature of school districts and schools; even the smallest school is a complex system of often competing constituencies.

In concluding this section, we turn to Bennis and Nanus (1985), who stressed the importance of differentiating between the actions that involve leadership and those that involve management. They pointed out the need for leaders to create a direction for the organization, stating that "to choose a direction, a leader must first have developed a mental model of a possible and desirable future state of the organization" (p. 89). The leader must know where he or she stands, which requires the effective leader to be especially honest and self-critical. We turn now to a discussion of the importance of developing a vision and mission for the school and/or school district.

Table 2.2. The five disciplines of an organization

Building shared vision: the practice of unearthing shared "pictures of the future" that foster genuine commitment

Personal mastery: the skill of continually clarifying and deepening our personal vision

Mental models: the ability to unearth our internal pictures of the world, to scrutinize them, and to make them open to the influence of others

Team learning: the capacity to "think together," which is gained by mastering the practice of dialogue and discussion

Systems thinking: the discipline that integrates the others, fusing them into a coherent body of theory and practice

From Senge, P.M. (1990). *The fifth discipline: The art and practice of the learning organization* (pp. 6–10). New York: Currency Doubleday; reprinted with permission.

VISION AND MISSION

Any organization, especially a school or school district, needs to be able to identify and articulate its core beliefs. These beliefs should then form the basis of the myriad programs and practices that characterize and guide the organization. The statement of an organization's core beliefs is known as its *vision*; an expansion of these beliefs into operational terms is called its *mission statement*. In this section we examine how vision and mission statements are created, implemented, disseminated, and monitored for effectiveness.

Creating Vision and Mission Statements

Nanus (1992) defined vision as "...a realistic, creditable, attractive future for your organization" (p. 8). He interpreted mission, on the other hand, as a statement of the organization's purpose (p. 31). Applied to education, a vision states what special educators hope to attain; the mission statement describes the means of attainment. (See Chapter 2 Appendix for a sample vision and mission statement.)

Senge (1990) noted that shared visions, that is, those accepted by the members of an organization, derive first from individual or personal visions. He also distinguished between the personal visions of those in leadership roles and those in subordinate roles. Although it more often happens that leaders have strong ideas of what is best for the organization, we admit to a bias here: The most effective visions are those that, regardless of the source, are embraced and owned by the entire organization. This is especially challenging for special education administrators, whose programs represent only a small part of the total organization. The key question becomes this: How do special education administrators, in their particular setting, create a realistic yet inspirational vision, make it come to life through a well-crafted mission statement, and ensure enthusiastic acceptance by all stakeholders? The key word is *participation*. All members, or at least a representative sample of them, must be directly involved in the visioning process. Steps for creating a vision and mission statement for a school follow.

Determine the Organization's Core Values   As a first step in creating a vision and mission statement, the special education administrator should convene a meeting of all staff to begin the visioning process. The entire school staff, both faculty and support staff, should be invited to the meeting, as should representatives from other stakeholder groups, such as parents, business partners, and district supervisors. A few weeks before the meeting, all participants should receive a written overview that defines the terms *vision* and *mission* and explains the visioning process. At the meeting, either in a large group or in small groups, participants brainstorm the school or school district's core values in response to the following question (or a similar question): "What are the most important things we do here at school (or in this office or district)?" The administrator should lead the session and ask a staff member to record responses.

Establish a Small Group of Staff to Create Draft Vision and Mission Statements   At the conclusion of the brainstorming session, the administrator should ask for volunteers to serve on a committee to craft the actual vision and mission statements. It is important that at least one person on the committee write well—an obvious but often overlooked consideration. The administrator should decide if he or she wants to be part of the committee. If so, it is probably best that the administrator not be the chair so that the members feel ownership for the group's product. The administrator then gives the committee a reasonable deadline for creating the draft statements. If the administrator elects not to be part of the committee, he or she needs to follow the deliberations of the committee closely. All committee members should be encouraged to solicit input from their constituencies.

Reconvene the Entire Faculty and Staff   Once the draft statement is written and reviewed by the administrator, copies are distributed to all participants prior to the meeting at which it is to be presented to give them time to examine it. At this meeting, the administrator strives to achieve consensus on elements of the statement; voting should not be employed unless absolutely necessary. If the group has difficulty reaching consensus, it may be helpful to return to the original core belief statements. After reaching consensus, the entire group sets realistic timelines for periodically checking progress on implementing the vision and mission.

Implementing the Vision and Mission

Once the school or school district staff and stakeholder representatives agree on the vision and mission statement, it is necessary to determine how it will be implemented. After consultation with their constituencies, members of the committee take responsibility for its various elements; they then report back to the large group with their ideas for implementation.

Spreading the Word: Disseminating the Vision and Mission

Schools and school districts across the country have disseminated their vision and mission statements in a variety of creative ways. Most use web sites as the chief means of informing the public of their aspirations. Many schools extract a motto from the vision statement and include this in publications and on stationery. Newsletters for both staff and parents should include initial information about the visioning process as well as the final product. The initial visioning committee or larger faculty/staff/ stakeholder group can also provide additional ideas and strategies for dissemination.

Monitoring the Vision and Mission

The people who have taken responsibility for implementing the various parts of the vision and mission statements will also need to assist in monitoring them. This is best done as a continuous process; the administrator can facilitate this process by asking selected people to report on the status of their area of responsibility throughout the year, adhering to the timeline initially established by the whole group. One suggestion is to make it a standing item on the faculty meeting agenda. The summer planning meetings scheduled by many schools and districts are also a good time to review the effectiveness of the vision and mission statements. Organizations and their needs change; the vision and mission statements should be flexible enough to reflect this.

CREATING A CULTURE OF TEACHING AND LEARNING

There are many definitions of culture. A simple one is this: Culture consists of the rules by which people live. The purpose of culture is to put into place a formal and informal framework by which the culture's inhabitants live. Deal and Kennedy (1982) explored culture by looking at several elements, which are presented in Table 2.3.

Table 2.3. Elements of culture

Environment: What are the conditions in which educators function with respect to competition, technology, politics, economy, and law?

Values: What are our values?

Heroes: Who are the people both past and present who are spoken of with reverence? What is important about their stance?

Rites and rituals: What and how do we celebrate?

Cultural network: Who are the priests and priestesses, the spies, the whisperers, the storytellers, and gossips? What functions do they play?

From Deal, T.E., & Kennedy, A.A. (1982). *Corporate cultures* (pp. 13–15). New York: Addison-Wesley; reprinted with permission.

Educators in many societies today emphasize putting the child first. This is a statement of value and belief about what is important. One way to fully understand how deep this belief is in a culture is to examine it using Deal and Kennedy's Elements of Culture. As you read the next several sections of this chapter, keep these elements in mind and consider how they relate to the organization in which you work.

Trust

Another aspect of current management literature deals with trust. Trust is fundamental to leadership in all organizations and at all levels. The last several decades have seen glaring examples on a national scale of how presidents' actions contributed to a widespread distrust of leadership: Richard Nixon's Watergate debacle, Ronald Reagan's Iran Contra scandal, and Bill Clinton's dissembling about his relationship with a White House intern. Nor are educators immune from scrutiny: The press has raised concerns about the consulting work of various superintendents of schools and their receipt of personal benefits as a result of granting contracts to certain purveyors. Campbell (1996) stated,

> To build trusting relationships, we need to communicate with the intent to learn from others, not control them. Trust is the glue that makes effective collaboration and teamwork possible. Without trust, people can become competitive or defensive, and communication is distorted and unreliable. (p. 137)

Leaders must work continually to earn the trust of those with whom they work. This can only happen when they tell the truth, act as they said they would, sincerely seek input, and avoid inappropriate situations.

Some cultures permit or at least overlook bribery and may also tolerate varying degrees of deception. This is not typically true of the United States, whose culture neither expects nor allows cheating while performing tasks in the public interest. Trust is one of the most important elements of leadership, because it is very difficult for employees to take risks and to explore new ways of doing things if they are unable to trust their leaders. The work of an organization is only accomplished through its members. This implies that the members need to communicate with each other. If this communication is inaccurate or even incomplete, and if this problem stems from the actions of a leader, resentment, fear, anxiety, and sabotage will often be directed toward the organization and its leaders. DuFour and Eaker (1998) have suggested, like Senge (1990), that a learning organization (e.g., a business) is a promising vehicle for dealing with the challenges facing education today. And communication is at the heart of the learning organization model. Teachers and administrators need to know that they are working in the best interests of both the students and the organization.

If anything occurs to weaken this belief, trust will be damaged, and the organization will cease to be seen as one concerned with learning.

Kouzes and Posner (1995) further indicated the importance of trust. In their research members of an organization were asked to rank certain leadership elements in terms of importance. They found that honesty, a trait closely related to trust or trustworthiness, always ranked as one of the top four items. Clearly, a leader needs to seriously consider ways of building trust. This is especially true of leaders in special education. The complexity of federal mandates and the importance of documentation, time-sensitive responses, and communication with parents, staff, and related agencies requires that the special education administrator earn and retain the trust of all involved.

How does one inspire trust or become trustworthy? This is not a simple task. Those who have written about trust seem to conclude that no single action ensures that a leader will be perceived as trustworthy; it depends instead on the leader's lifetime record. Leaders must act with integrity and moral conviction in all aspects of their lives. Covey (1991) talked of setting the compass to due north, in other words, creating a life that is guided by conviction and honesty. The following questions may help clarify Covey's major points and encourage reflection on one's own actions with regard to honesty and trustworthiness: Do I tell the truth even when it may cost me money or recognition? Do I always do what I said I would do? Do I accept recognition for others' work? Do I try to take advantage of others' weaknesses?

Empowerment

Empowerment, shared decision making, and *site-based management* are terms that reflect the value of employees' contributions to an organization. In the 1990s, various initiatives designed to empower educational employees failed due to a variety of factors: lack of commitment by boards of education, lack of training, time restraints, and the failure to focus on areas that make a difference. However, staff members often greatly appreciate having an administrator attempt to give them a voice in decision making. Although some teachers may not want the increased level of responsibility that comes with empowerment, they usually appreciate being asked for their opinion. Whenever possible, the special education administrator should at least try to solicit staff input; there is a great deal of untapped expertise in classrooms.

Standards

The role and importance of standards in contemporary educational practice cannot be overstated. On a national level, the meeting of student achievement standards is a major component of the No Child Left Behind (NCLB; 2001) legislation; general education graduates in many colleges and universities must demonstrate mastery of the Interstate New Teacher and Support Consortium (INTASC) Principles (Council of Chief State School Officers, 2002); special education administrators are expected to be knowledgeable of the standards developed by the Council for Exceptional Children (CEC; 2003); and all school administrators are informed by the standards of the Interstate School Leaders Licensure Consortium (ISLLC; Council of Chief State School Officers, 1996).

Because readers of this book, as special educators and school administrators, will be most concerned with the CEC and ISLLC standards, those two sets of standards are presented here.

CEC Standards for Beginning Teachers

- Standard 1: Foundations

- Standard 2: Development and Characteristics of Learners

- Standard 3: Individual Learning Differences

- Standard 4: Instructional Strategies (no knowledge and skills listed)

- Standard 5: Learning Environments and Social Interactions (no knowledge and skills listed)

- Standard 6: Communication (no knowledge and skills listed)

- Standard 7: Instructional Planning

- Standard 8: Assessment

- Standard 9: Professional and Ethical Practice

- Standard 10: Collaboration

ISLLC Standards
A school administrator is an educational leader who promotes the success of all students by

- Standard 1: Facilitating the development, articulation, implementation, and stewardship of a vision of learning that is shared and supported by the school community

- Standard 2: Advocating, nurturing, and sustaining a school culture and instructional program conducive to student learning and staff professional growth

- Standard 3: Ensuring management of the organization, operations, and resources for a safe, efficient, and effective learning environment

- Standard 4: Collaborating with families and community members, responding to diverse community interests and needs, and mobilizing community resources

- Standard 5: Acting with integrity, fairness, and in an ethical manner

- Standard 6: Understanding, responding to, and influencing the larger political, social, economic, legal, and cultural context

A comparison of the various standards in use today reveals several common elements. Table 2.4 illustrates areas of commonality between the CEC and ISLLC standards. It can be readily seen from this table that the two standards have a great deal in common. From a practical standpoint, this serves as assurance for the special education administrator that current thinking by special and general educators on teaching, learning, and leadership are in essential accord. This also means that special education administrators, as instructional leaders, can, within the framework of these standards, develop, implement, and evaluate policies and procedures at the local school or district level with confidence that there exists a body of complementary standards that supports their efforts.

The standards presented are also useful in two far more practical ways. First, they provide direction for action. The special education administrator would do well to compare existing practice to the standards; any aspect of school and district functioning ought to be examined in their light. Any contemplated change in program or

Table 2.4.   Comparison of CEC beginning administrator standards and ISLLC standards

CEC standards[a]	ISLLC standards					
	1: Vision	2: School culture and instruction	3: Management	4: Collaboration and communication	5: Ethics	6: Larger context
#1: Foundations		X	X		X	X
#2: Development and characteristics of learners		X				
#3: Individual learning differences		X				
#7: Instructional planning		X	X			
#8: Assessment	X	X				
#9: Professional and ethical practice	X	X		X	X	
#10: Collaboration		X	X	X		X

[a]Only those standards with identified knowledge and/or skill components are listed.

practice should likewise be compatible with the standards. Second, adherence to the standards provides reassurance that actions taken are in concert with recommended practice and renders these actions all the more defensible.

Practical Management Issues

Although they may seem rather pedestrian, managing time and conducting effective meetings often have a profound effect on organizational functioning. They also can reflect significantly on staff perception of a leader's effectiveness. Careless attention by the leader to either of these may also leave staff with the impression that the leader does not understand or is not respectful of their job and its time constraints.

Managing Time   One of the most difficult aspects of leadership is finding enough time to achieve everything that is required and expected of those in the position. For school administrators to survive and be effective, they must become both organized and efficient. There are a number of excellent sources that provide detailed, extensive information on this topic, including Covey (1994) and McGee-Cooper (1993). Here, we suggest a few ways for special education administrators to manage their time effectively.

Perhaps the most basic way to begin to manage time effectively is to create and frequently consult a detailed calendar. This can be either a traditional paper calendar or an electronic version supported by a computer and a personal digital assistant (PDA).

During the summer the administrator should set aside a few hours to set up his or her personal calendar. The first step should be to include the school district's

calendar dates: all holidays, professional and in-service days, marking period information, districtwide meetings, and special events. Then the district's deadlines for
submitting reports and staff evaluation forms should be added; any district- or statewide testing dates should also be included. Next, the school's regularly scheduled
meetings (faculty/staff, department or team, and committee meetings) are placed on
the calendar. Finally, after determining the staff observation and conference schedule
(see Chapter 10), these dates should be added. This process will result in the creation
of a reasonably comprehensive calendar for the coming school year. For it to be used
effectively, however, it must be consulted several times each day. This last step will
impose an appropriate level of organization on daily activities and will ensure meeting all obligations. Moreover, it should effectively eliminate the embarrassing possibility of missed appointments.

Organization is only half the solution to managing time: Efficiency is critical. A
surprising number of people are highly organized but woefully inefficient. The successful leader needs to be open to processes that promote efficiency simply because,
at the risk of sounding clichéd, there really are not enough hours in the day to accomplish the job. On an overall school basis, the special education administrator needs to
eliminate any overlapping functions and focus on the required tasks. Are all those
committees necessary? Does the administrator really need to attend every meeting?
Is it possible to delegate responsibility for certain tasks and functions? The administrator should consult the school or school district's vision and mission statements
and prioritize activities in their light.

Efficiency also requires frequent monitoring. In addition to checking the calendar on a regular basis, the administrator must set time limits for meetings and activities and adhere to them whenever possible; consistently solicit staff input to ensure
that their perceptions of the worthwhile use of their time matches the administrator's; respect and include support staff and ensure that their time is used wisely; and
find ways to combine tasks. An example of the latter suggestion, which will be expanded on in Chapter 10, is for the administrator to set aside a few minutes during
observation of a teacher's lesson to begin analyzing the data collected. Waiting to
conduct the analysis after the observation opens up the possibility of interruption
and even failure to complete this critical task.

Conducting Productive Meetings   Few activities provoke more consterna-
tion on the part of teachers than disorganized, lengthy meetings of questionable purpose. As special education administrators chair many school-based meetings, it is
important for them to develop an overall structure for each meeting, keep participants on task, and end the meeting on time. Efficient, productive meetings are especially crucial in special education, as many of these meetings are mandated by law
and are subject to precise deadlines—for instance, those associated with the Individuals with Disabilities Education Act (IDEA). Those responsible for other meetings
must first make sure that they are clearly necessary. Often it is possible to communicate through e-mail or memoranda and thus eliminate a meeting. Most staff will appreciate an administrator's efforts to curtail the number of meetings; this signals that
staff planning time is valuable and should not be wasted. For more detailed ideas on
conducting effective meetings, see *How to Run Better Business Meetings: A Reference
Guide for Managers* (The 3M Management Team, 1987).

IDEA-prescribed meetings require specific participants, timelines, and agendas.
Most importantly, the special education administrator must know the purpose of
each meeting: Will it be, for example, an annual review of the child's individualized

family service plan (IFSP) or a triennial reevaluation meeting to determine the appropriateness of additional testing? It is beyond the scope of this chapter to discuss the range of meeting types; Turnbull and Turnbull (2001) and written district procedures provide valuable information on this topic.

A written agenda is probably the best way to structure and provide organization for all other types of meetings. Ideally, the administrator should contact the participants well before the meeting to solicit input and agenda items; e-mail makes this a relatively easy task (a deadline should be specified for submitting information). Once input is received, the administrator creates two written agendas. One is distributed to all participants and lists the topics to be covered in the meeting. A second agenda, for the chair's use only, includes approximate times to be spent on each topic. Some chairs distribute an agenda containing topic times to everyone, but they risk staff displeasure if the times are not rigidly observed. The chair should also determine in advance who will keep minutes for the meeting. For IDEA-prescribed meetings, responsibility for completing the required forms must also be assigned.

The goal to conducting a successful meeting is to ensure that each person present has the opportunity to express his or her views. Occasionally, a participant will speak for an unnecessarily long period. It takes a great deal of skill for the chair to diplomatically terminate this type of speech. One tactic for managing this type of situation would be for the chair to ask, "Could you summarize what you've said, so we can hear from others?" This often helps bring the speaker to closure. The special education administrator also needs to develop an awareness of the various roles people play in meetings (Campbell, 1996). In many ways, running a meeting is like supervising a classroom discussion: The chair tries to allow as many people as possible to share their views while managing the timing and appropriateness of the comments.

Finally, it is critical to watch the clock. Everyone appreciates a meeting that ends on time or, preferably, a little early. Again, the message sent when this occurs is that staff time is valuable.

Supervising, Observing, and Evaluating Staff   One of the most important responsibilities of the special education administrator is the supervision of teachers and support staff. This function is so crucial that it warrants a separate chapter; please see Chapter 10 for a detailed description of staff supervision.

Using Data in the Age of Accountability

In this age of accountability, every school or district-based administrator must be able to generate, analyze, interpret, and explain a vast variety of data. These data provide vital information about individual children, the school, and the school system. Although the special education administrator is no stranger to testing, recent provisions in the NCLB legislation require substantial testing of youngsters, and nothing less than each school's success as an educational institution is at stake.

Although it is not possible to provide detailed how-to information on data analysis in this section, we hope to at least alert the special education administrator to some general areas of required expertise. Another useful source of information on data analysis is the administrator's state department or commission of education. Personal contact with the division responsible for data collection or a visit to its web site may provide invaluable assistance.

Generating Data   All administrators must become proficient in the use of databases, such as Microsoft Excel and Access. In larger school districts data may be collected centrally; it is imperative that the administrator master the program(s) used by the district. It may also be necessary for the administrator to collect additional data or to categorize the data in ways that are more useful at the school or, if possible, the individual level. Obviously, this requires more than a cursory knowledge of the use of databases. Although working with existing databases, or creating new ones, requires a considerable degree of skill, the information provided can be invaluable. One caution: Some standardized test data are intended for program rather than individual evaluation; the administrator must make sure that he or she knows the purpose of the data in question.

Analyzing and Interpreting Data   Those who are cynical claim that data can be used to prove almost anything. As the administrator's task is to ensure an accurate, ethical analysis, he or she should not be afraid to seek help. Unless the administrator's background includes extensive coursework and/or experience in mathematics and statistics, it is unlikely that his or her initial analytical forays will feel completely comfortable. In addition to the state-level resources mentioned above, there are also experts in the school, at the district level, or in university partnerships who can be of assistance. The special education administrator would do well to keep in mind that there are at least two overall purposes of data analysis: ensuring that the organization is true to its vision and mission and that assessments of children are appropriate and occur in a timely manner.

Once the administrator is adept at the process of analysis and interpretation, he or she will need to determine the purpose, scope, and use of the analysis. Individual student data will invariably become part of a child's record and will be used to decide on appropriate programming, placement, and even the extent of the child's academic success. Programwide data (such as that which describes the degree of success for all special education students in the school) will assist the administrator and special educators in making decisions that will affect the delivery format, structure of the various programs, and the curriculum.

Explaining Data   The school staff should be the first beneficiaries of the data analysis. This step is imperative if staff members are to incorporate the results and implications of the data in their teaching. It may be necessary to meet individually with staff to explain relevant findings, although in larger settings it may make more sense to meet with all the special educators in the school. In mandated meetings with parents, individual student data must be shared and interpreted. Moreover, the meeting chair should solicit parental input and work to incorporate the relevant input into program decisions for their child. Finally, the school and school district must communicate the results of school- and districtwide data analysis, respectively, to the community. This can be difficult, as the analyses must be presented in ways that are understandable to the general population. If the analyses reveal shortcomings, these should be presented honestly and openly.

Collaboration

People generally collaborate in two ways: internally and externally. Internal collaboration in an educational setting occurs among groups within a given unit (school, district office), whereas external collaboration occurs with groups outside the school. Both forms of collaboration involve cooperation and heightened communication between and among these groups.

At the school or district office level, initial collaboration is most likely to occur exclusively between special educators. Proximity to one another, common educational goals, and similar issues and problems are some of the more obvious reasons special educators communicate frequently. Administrators should participate in and encourage this type of collaboration as it is a chief way of improving instruction and student achievement. Often, teachers seek one another out and share ideas, materials, and strategies. If this does not occur, the administrator should create structures that facilitate communication, such as regular meetings, less formal sharing sessions, individual directives given during post-observations conferences, and focused in-service activities.

Unfortunately, in many educational settings special and general educators continue to operate independently of each other, with little or no evidence of collaborative activity. This situation presents the special education administrator with a real opportunity to effect positive change. Depending on the number of special and general educators involved, the special education administrator can introduce a number of strategies designed to encourage communication. Consider the following possibilities: scheduling preliminary meetings between those special and general educators who seem most open to establishing a dialogue; encouraging co-teaching; requesting that a future in-service activity be devoted to a simulation of disabilities or to providing accommodations for students who receive special education services and are placed in general education classes; or creating a committee (or using an existing staff development committee) to develop additional activities that will promote collaboration. One of the most important things the administrator can do is provide constant encouragement; it is certainly in the best interests of all staff to hold productive conversations so that whatever barriers or misunderstandings exist between special and general educators can be removed and instruction for all students can be enhanced.

Cooperative communication with individuals and groups in the community is an essential function of the special education administrator, and is especially critical in early childhood settings. It is neither wise nor sufficient for the school or district leadership to wait to be approached by individuals or groups in the community; the administrator must encourage the development of a plan for collaboration. This plan should first attempt to identify the individuals and groups who are the school's or school district's stakeholders. These could include (but are not limited to) parents of students in general and special education, parent organizations, special education interest groups, private agencies that provide special education services, community support groups, state and local politicians, the special education division of the state department/commission of education, and the U.S. Department of Education. Special education administrators must expect that some stakeholders will require a significant degree of education about the needs of children in early childhood programs and the nature of these programs.

Just contacting the appropriate liaison for each of these groups signals a willingness to enter into dialogue. Better still would be convening a meeting of group representatives to solicit input and explore avenues for possible agency support of the school or school district's ECSE programs. If possible, a standing committee could be created to ensure ongoing communication. For additional information on external collaboration, see Chapter 3.

Diversity and Multicultural Issues

It is critical that special education administrators be aware of and sensitive to the complex multicultural issues that confront schools and school districts. One of the most important of these issues involves the overrepresentation of children who are African American or Hispanic, especially males, in special education classes and the persistent achievement gap between white children and black children. It is imperative that special educators address these issues in a sincere and forthright manner; these are certainly appropriate areas to be included in the types of community involvement described earlier.

The special education administrator must also ensure, through effective staff supervision, that classroom teachers are sensitive to multicultural issues. Curricula should celebrate and be representative of the range of heritages of the children in the school and district. Lewis (2004) pointed out the superficiality of typical multicultural attempts and the often hostile attitude toward even these attempts on the part of some parents. Schools can and must do better.

More subtle issues, especially the attitudes and biases that many teachers bring to the classroom, also need to be examined and, if necessary, confronted. Delpit (1995) reminded teachers that many so-called liberal beliefs may actually be destructive to black children. She argued persuasively for teachers to be aware of and respect the cultural norms found in their students' homes and adjust their classroom practices accordingly. She provided many telling examples, but perhaps the one most likely to upset the well-meaning, constructivist-oriented teacher is her contention that many African American children are best served through direct instruction. Delpit also maintains that African American children from disadvantaged backgrounds are often unaware of the white "codes" that exist in many classrooms. Thus, when a teacher, in an attempt to be pleasant and nonconfrontational, suggests rather than directs, some African American children, who are used to a more direct approach at home, may ignore the request or interpret it as a sign of teacher weakness, with resulting negative consequences.

Given the persistent overrepresentation of children of minority background in special education classrooms, the above are cautionary tales for special education administrators. The mandate is clear: The special education administrator, at any level, has an obligation to ensure that all children, their families, and their heritages are respected and celebrated.

Ethics

Today's educational leaders live in a world that demands increased student performance, concern for the manner in which students are instructed, safe schools, increased accountability for all, and increased accountability for all. All of these can present leaders with ethical dilemmas. Rather than speak to general ethics issues, this section will address an issue that is perhaps on nearly every special educational leader's agenda: the ethical issues presented by advocate groups competing for resources.

There appears to be an increasing number of advocacy groups representing a variety of concerns, especially for children with special needs. Each group's primary purpose is to secure the best possible education for the children they represent. This is a noble cause; however, this advocacy is not without its problems. As groups grow stronger, often a differential arises in their ability to advocate. Power differentials become obvious as these groups ultimately try to secure resources.

The primary issue for the special educational administrator may appear to be one of budgeting and managing resources. In fact, the issue is much larger and involves the ethical treatment of students. As seen in the section of this chapter on standards, each of the ISLLC standards begins with the statement "An administrator is an educational leader who promotes the success of all students by. . ." Additionally, ISLLC Standard 5 and CEC Standard 9 address ethics directly. In essence, leaders are charged with a moral responsibility. Fullan (2003) stated,

> Moral purpose of the highest order is having a system where all students learn
> and the gaps between high and low performing becomes greatly reduced and
> what people learn enables them to be successful citizens and workers in a
> morally based knowledge society. (p. 29).

When this moral obligation to do what is in the best interest of all is juxtaposed with the drive of certain groups to secure the best and most for their group, sometimes at the expense of others, the educational leader is left on the horns of an ethical dilemma. The deepest, most important of questions must be asked: "Do I do what will cause the least trouble?" Nieto and Sinclair (1991) stressed the moral obligation of providing equal and quality education to all.

This leads to another question: "How do I, as a special education administrator, prepare for the political and ethical dilemma of addressing the issues presented by advocacy groups and the obligation to serve all equally?" Unfortunately, there is no easy answer. One must first be truly competent in all aspects of leadership. One must, as noted elsewhere in this chapter, be able to create a shared vision that includes all, understand instructional issues and their implementation, be very aware of the legal aspects of education, and be able to work with all parties in the educational community. All the elements of competency are far too numerous to note here, but we single out one: the need for the special education administrator to adopt a moral and ethical philosophy that is so personally ingrained that it is visible in every action taken.

John Stuart Mill was an advocate of a philosophical view known as *utilitarianism.* In essence, this philosophy espouses acting in a way that produces the greatest good for the greatest number. This viewpoint is provided to illustrate the type of thinking that leads one to do what is best for all children, as the ISLLC and CEC standards suggest. The special education administrator needs to act in an ethical way that is consistent with the ISLLC and CEC Standards and to serve as a model to others. Preparing oneself to act in an ethical and a moral manner is a lifelong pursuit. A number of authors, Deal and Bolman (2001) and Covey (1991) among them, have spoken of the need to prepare one's spirit. Their works can be used as a point of further study on the continued ethical development of the leader.

During the past decade, schools across the country have adopted the principles of "Character Counts" (Josephson Institute of Ethics, 1992), which specifically include "Six Pillars of Character: trustworthiness, respect, responsibility, fairness, caring, and citizenship." Preparing oneself for ethical leadership may be as simple as adopting a life course consistent with the meaning behind these words!

Professional Development

Although many professions place considerable emphasis on training and professional development, this is still not the case in education. Funding for professional development activities has often been placed near the end of the list of budget priorities; when critical issues such as class size and salary increases are in jeopardy, professional development is usually among the first items cut. Recently, however, many school districts have begun to place more emphasis on professional development, often by providing assistance to beginning teachers in an attempt to improve retention and by providing release time for in-service activities. For more detailed information, see Chapter 9.

The special education administrator needs to encourage and, sometimes, assume responsibility for professional development activities, even if funding is less than adequate. The continued education of all staff is a critical enterprise; after all, lifelong learning is something educators should be modeling for students.

Because many staff members may be discouraged by and become cynical about professional development through bad experiences with ineffective in-service activities, providing a meaningful, truly helpful program of professional development is especially challenging. For this reason alone it makes sense for the special education administrator to keep initial efforts simple and the audience specific. One tactic would be to have the audience be the special education staff and confine in-service efforts to this audience. Creating a committee to assist in the overall, ongoing delivery of professional development activities is also a good early step in the process. The committee's first task should be to develop and administer a brief needs assessment instrument to find out what staff members know and what they would like to know across a broad range of topics. On analysis of the results of the needs assessment, the initial focus of professional development should become apparent; it will also be necessary to include school- or districtwide mandates.

Once the topics for professional development are identified, it is imperative that a systematic, comprehensive delivery system be created. The most effective in-service activities are those explored over several sessions, with opportunities for staff to try out what they have learned in the sessions in their own classrooms. Staff should always be given the opportunity to report back their experiences honestly and candidly in subsequent sessions. And, just as in effective teaching, the effective administrator should make changes to the sessions and reteach as appropriate. A brief evaluation form administered at the end of each session can be especially helpful in assessing the effectiveness of the activities.

Professional development can also be a nonthreatening contact point between special education and general education staff. Frankly, it will probably be up to the special education administrator to make general educators aware of their need for this collaboration, although increasingly, inclusion efforts and required accommodations for students may make this task easier. An effective first attempt at connecting with the general education staff could be an activity designed to simulate disabilities. Once general educators have experienced what many students with disabilities contend with daily, they usually become much more sympathetic to students' needs and are more open to providing meaningful accommodations.

Many school districts require teachers to maintain professional development plans. These can be useful tools, as they provide identification and documentation of the training needs of each staff member. Often, staff members are required to respond to specific initiatives of the school or school district in their individual plans. Special education administrators should attempt to ensure that appropriate and timely issues critical to the needs of students in special education be incorporated into these special initiatives. They should also work closely with individual staff to make sure that their plans are reflective of the needs of all the children.

Finally, the role of reflection, as part of an effective program of professional development, cannot be understated. Whether done as part of journal writing, periodic discussion in large- or small-groups, or post-observation conferences, reflection is vital to the process of continuous improvement and should be encouraged by the special education administrator whenever possible.

IMPLICATIONS FOR FUTURE RESEARCH

As most of the topics discussed in this chapter would probably benefit from additional research, we will confine our recommendations to those topics we believe are most critical or those for which the research base is inadequate.

Most would agree that having a clear vision and sense of mission is critical to the functioning of schools, school districts, and organizations in general. The body of research on effective schools is considerable, but the direct bearing that vision and mission statements and activities associated with these statements have on school success needs to be explored further.

The effective use of data is another area that needs to be researched more fully. Given the current public and governmental insistence on accountability, extensive reliance on data will be a given for the foreseeable future. But data do not always represent the total picture: Children and their achievement cannot be quantified that easily. As every special educator knows, affective components must be considered in addition to hard facts. The emphasis on testing, mandated by NCLB, can cause real damage to children who may possess the requisite knowledge but who do not always perform well on tests. Currently, many state testing programs focus exclusively on results and do not credit improvement, which is another real issue for special educators. Data generated by testing is important, but they should not constitute the only source of evaluation. Testing and the preparation for testing should also not be so pervasive that they compromise instructional time.

Special education administrators should always question the efficacy of their actions. Are there too many meetings? Is there too much unnecessary paperwork? Is the instructional program too rigid? Future research needs to more fully address these and the many other questions that arise from administrative practice. Frequent, honest reflection on the part of the administrator will also prove useful in ensuring that administrative practice is supportive of teachers and students.

Probably the most critical area that begs research is that of the relationship between the myriad administrative and instructional practices that are daily occurrences in schools and school districts and the actual effect these practices have on student achievement. This sounds like a relatively simple undertaking, but few have conducted meaningful research due to the sheer immensity and complexity of the issues involved.

Finally, although it is our firm belief that ECSE programs and the children they serve will benefit from collaboration with general educators, more research needs to be done to confirm the specific value of general–special education collaboration.

IMPLICATIONS FOR CLINICAL/EDUCATIONAL PRACTICE

Because of the enormous demands placed on special education teachers and administrators by state and federal mandates, as well as the extraordinarily complex nature of individualized instruction, teachers and administrators struggle to keep up with the research. The special education administrator should strive to develop ways to read and selectively disseminate current research among the special education and general education faculty. Perhaps time could be set aside at each faculty meeting to present synopses of relevant research; a research study group could also be created for staff to share successful practices based on what they have read in the literature. As pointed out previously, the special education administrator should not have to function in isolation: he or she should approach potentially interested staff members and solicit their input and assistance.

Ideally, the practice of reviewing and attempting to create instructional strategies based on current research will lead naturally to sharing these practices with other special and general educators. Such collaboration could certainly result in the development of age-appropriate integrated and interdisciplinary curricula and could also foster and facilitate inclusion.

Finally, beyond the school and even school district, it may well be necessary to lobby for testing that is meaningful and appropriate for young children with special needs. No piece of legislation is perfect, and it becomes the responsibility of the experts—ECSE administrators and teachers—to educate politicians and policymakers about what is best for young children.

CONCLUSIONS

Effective educational leaders lead by example. They strive to develop consensus. Like effective teachers, they encourage, inspire, and assist rather than criticize, demean, and demand. Effective leaders support their staff even while requiring improvement. Effective leaders have a clear and consistent vision for their staff and organization and assist in implementation and periodic assessment of this vision. They ensure that instructional practices are informed by the local, state, and national standards that govern early childhood education, and they keep current with not only district and federal mandates but also cutting-edge research. Through meaningful and appropriate professional development, effective leaders strive for the twin goals of continuous individual and organizational improvement.

Above all, effective leaders earn the trust of the teaching and support staff and constantly validate their positive effort and performance. This, ideally, will result in the development of an esprit de corps that will encourage cooperation, excellence, pride, and profound concern for all students.

REFERENCES

The 3M Management Team. (1987). *How to run better business meetings: A reference guide for managers.* New York: McGraw-Hill.

Bennis, W., & Nanus, B. (1985). *Leader: the strategies for taking charge.* New York: Harper & Row.

Blake, R.R., & Mouton, J.S. (1964). *The Management Grid.* Houston, TX: Gulf Publishing.

Campbell, S. (1996). *From chaos to confidence.* New York: Fireside.

Council for Exceptional Children. (2003). *CEC knowledge and skill base for all beginning special education administrators.* Arlington, VA: Author.

Council of Chief State School Officers. (1996). *Interstate school leaders licensure consortium (ISLLC) standards for school leaders.* Washington, DC: Author.

Council of Chief State School Officers. (2002). *Interstate new teacher assessment and support consortium (INTASC) principles.* Washington, DC: Author.

Covey, S.R. (1991). *Principle-centered leadership.* New York: Summit Books.

Covey, S.R. (1994). *First things first.* New York: Fireside.

David, J. (1989). Synthesis of research on school-based management. *Educational Research Journal, 46*(8), 45–53.

Deal, T.E., & Bolman, L.G. (2001). *Leading with soul.* San Francisco: Jossey-Bass.

Deal, T.E., & Kennedy, A.A. (1982). *Corporate cultures.* New York: Addison-Wesley.

Delpit, L. (1995). *Other people's children: Cultural conflict in the classroom.* New York: The New Press.

DuFour, R., & Eaker, R. (1998). *Professional learning communities at work.* Bloomington, IN: National Education Service.

Fullan, M. (1993). *Change forces: Probing the depths of educational reform.* Philadelphia: Falmer Press.

Fullan, M. (1999). *Change forces: The sequel.* Philadelphia: Falmer Press.

Fullan, M. (2003). *The moral imperative of school leadership.* Thousand Oaks, CA: Corwin Press.

Hackman, R., & Oldham, G.R. (1975). Development of the job diagnostic survey. *Journal of Applied Psychology, 60*(2), 159–170.

Hersey, P., & Blanchard, K. (1993). *Management of organizational behavior: Utilizing human resources* (6th ed.). Englewood Cliffs, NJ: Simon & Schuster.

Hill, P.T., & Bonan, J. (1991). *Decentralization and accountability in public education.* Santa Monica, CA: RAND.

Jacobs, T.O. (1971). *Leadership and exchange in formal organizations.* Alexandria, VA: Human Resources Research Organization.

Josephson Institute of Ethics. (1992). *The six pillars of character.* Retrieved March 30, 2005, from http://www.charactercounts.org

Kotter, J. (1999). *What leaders really do.* Cambridge, MA: HBS Press.

Kouzes, J.M., & Posner, B.Z. (1995). *The leadership challenge.* San Francisco: Jossey-Bass.

Lewis, A.E. (2004). *Race in the schoolyard: Negotiating the color line in classrooms and communities.* New Brunswick, NJ: Rutgers University Press.

Lezotte, L.W. (1997). *Learning for all.* Okemos, MI: Effective Schools Products.

Lezotte, L.W. (1999). *The effective school: A proven path to learning for all.* Okemos, MI: Effective Schools Products.

Mayo, E. (1945). *The social problem of an industrialized civilization.* Cambridge, MA: Harvard University, Graduate School of Business Administration.

McGee-Cooper, A. (1993). *Time management for unmanageable people.* New York: Bantam Books.

Nanus, B. (1992). *Visionary leadership.* San Francisco: Jossey-Bass.

Nieto, S., & Sinclair, R.L. (1991). Leadership and the expanded environment for learning. In B.G. Barnett, F.O. McQuarrie, & C.J. Norris (Eds.), *The moral imperative of leadership: A focus on human decency.* Memphis, TN: National Policy Board for Educational Administration.

No Child Left Behind Act of 2001, PL 107-110, 115 Stat. 1425, 20 U.S.C. §§ 6301 *et seq.*

Oakes, J. (1985). *Keeping track.* New Haven: Yale University Press.

Roethlisberger, F.J. (1941). *Management and morale.* Cambridge, MA: Harvard University Press.

Senge, P.M. (1990). *The fifth discipline: The art and practice of the learning organization.* New York: Currency Doubleday.

Stogdill, R.M. (1974). *Handbook of leadership.* New York: The Free Press.

Turnbull, A., & Turnbull, R. (2001). *Families, professionals, and exceptionality: Collaborating for empowerment.* Upper Saddle River, NJ: Merrill/Prentice Hall.

Wright, F.W. (1930). The evolution of the normal schools. *The Elementary School Journal, 30*(5), 363–371.

Chapter 2 Appendix

Sample Vision and Mission Statement

Howard County (Maryland) Early Intervention Program

HOWARD COUNTY PUBLIC SCHOOL SYSTEM
OFFICE OF EARLY INTERVENTION SERVICES

MISSION: To foster learning and development in young children through excellence in early education and partnerships with staff, families, and community members.

VISION: We envision Early Intervention Services that reflect our core values of focus on instruction, partnerships, and continuous improvement.
- Family members and professionals collaborate in the evaluation and intervention process to develop personalized programs for young children.
- Personalized programs for children address each child's unique strengths and needs, include involvement in early childhood curriculum, reflect sound principles of child development and intervention, and result in children being active learners of real-life skills.
- Children with disabilities and typically developing peers learn together and develop friendships.
- Family members participate in education and support activities.
- All service providers collaborate for continuous program improvement and HAVE FUN!

GOALS OF THE PROGRAM—To ensure that children
- Develop skills that meet or exceed rigorous performance standards in the areas of personal and social development, communication, literacy, mathematical thinking, scientific thinking, social studies, the arts, and physical development and health through research-based early childhood curriculum
- Engage and interact appropriately with adults, peers, and materials
- Display appropriate behavior and self-management in the home, school, and community environments
- Develop self-help skills needed for independent functioning

Early Intervention Services Targets for 2004–2005:
- Accelerate academic achievement as measured by Early Childhood Assessment (WSS) data
- Increase opportunities for preschoolers with disabilities to learn successfully in regular early childhood settings
- Decrease the proportion of children identified with the disability of developmental delay who are African American by at least 1%.

Providing Leadership and Support for Interagency Collaborative Efforts

Carol Ann Baglin

*Education takes place in the combination of the home,
the community, the school, and the receptive mind.*
Harry Edwards

What If? Cheri Mead, a 2-year-old child with developmental disabilities, and her family have complex service needs. Cheri lives with her mother and grandmother. Her mother is a clerk at the local supermarket during the day. Cheri's grandmother provides child care but will be starting a new full-time job in 2 weeks. Transportation, child care, therapy, health care, and a variety of social services are needed by Cheri and her family to support Cheri's development. How will Cheri's mother obtain the needed services, coordinate their delivery, and figure out how to pay for them?

CHAPTER OVERVIEW

In this chapter, an introduction to interagency collaboration is followed by a brief history, including trends, of interagency collaboration. Interagency collaborative processes are then explored, followed by an explanation of how to use interagency agreements as a tool to achieve the end goal: the provision of appropriate and useful services to children and families.

CHAPTER OBJECTIVES

After reviewing this chapter, the reader will

- Understand the historical trends in interagency collaboration
- Understand the possible interagency collaborative processes

- Understand the importance of early intervention (EI) services in the interagency context

- Identify barriers to successful interagency collaboration

- Understand how to use interagency agreements

THE NEED FOR INTERAGENCY COLLABORATION

Each year the federal government spends billions of dollars on programs for young children and their families. In 1997 alone almost $14 billion supported programs that provide early childhood services, health care, and social services (Government Accounting Office [GAO], 2000; Shaul, 1999). These programs are administered by multiple agencies and address the diverse concerns of children and families, creating issues of cost effectiveness and service delivery efficiency. In spite of these substantial government initiatives, many children who are at risk or who have disabilities, although eligible for multiple programs, may not receive services due to lack of accessibility, not meeting financial criteria, overlap of eligibility, or long waiting lists. Although these programs may serve multiple child-centered and other goals, fragmentation and duplication render the outcomes useless for many families in need of assistance and support. Each public crisis prompts the government to create yet another focused effort to address the needs of children with disabilities; however, this is often done without regard to existing programs, which, if fully funded or expanded to include the target group or address the issue of the moment, might better meet children's and families' needs than new initiatives.

Interagency efforts at all levels of government are often just that—efforts, leaving the need for tangible results unmet and ongoing. Too often, there is a nominal satisfaction with the design of the program and little concern for results. Established measurements of success are process oriented rather than outcome based, resulting in the proliferation of programs with few measurable outcomes and effective interventions. It is clear that state interagency efforts need to provide direction and leadership for the coordination of EI services. Local policies and procedures need to facilitate community-based planning to provide a workable environment for practitioners and service providers to deliver services. This may require agency personnel to adjust service roles, job definitions, and the service delivery process.

In one vision of family-centered service delivery, parents have a greater role in negotiating the necessary services for their child and family. The availability of services and allocation of resources are based on the likelihood of their benefit to young children and their families. To reach those children most likely to benefit from EI, state policies need to be continually reviewed, based on current research, and aligned with contemporary standards. Effective, meaningful coordination of child- and family-centered services can have a pervasive impact on the family. These services can provide parents with the support services needed to enhance coping skills, which will allow families to utilize their own strengths, ultimately resulting in a higher quality of life for families as well as financial savings at all levels of government (Baglin, 1992).

Interagency coordination is an institutional process, yet it is influenced by personal attitudes and agency loyalties. To be effective, interagency coordination must be ongoing and include operationalized agreements that lead to solutions for difficult and persistent problems. Professionals involved in interagency activities designed to improve service delivery cannot operate independently but must seek to work together as a team.

For those working in EI, the early identification of children's developmental difficulties can help focus appropriate funding and services. The challenge for administrators is how to identify those children most in need of services. Siegel (1985) developed a risk index to predict aspects of cognitive and language development in children at 2 years of age. She found that it was possible to predict intellectual performance with some precision and to specify which children were likely to develop difficulties. Although inherited variables were found to correlate moderately with development, environmental factors were also demonstrated to be important. Although research has established a statistically reliable link between low birth weight (LBW) and disabling conditions, it has not quantified the risk of educational disabilities among these medically high-risk children compared with their normal birth weight (NBW) peers (Carran, Scott, Shaw, & Beydouin, 1989). Many very low birth weight (VLBW) children do have special learning needs and lower test scores than NBW children; many also experience additional related family issues. Based on the results of numerous studies, the Institute of Medicine (Abel, 1997) cited LBW as a major determinant of infant mortality. The studies in this area support the importance of detecting academic risk early on (Schmidt & Wedig, 1990) and highlight the need for interagency coordination.

There is a scarcity of research on the long-term outcomes of children exposed to drugs in utero, including cocaine, marijuana, heroin, and multiple drugs (Frank et al., 2002). Interagency intervention efforts based primarily on knowledge of a child's intrauterine exposure to such drugs, although somewhat supported by research, are limited in effectiveness. Access to this information is frequently limited due to confidentiality issues and social stigma associated with drug use, particularly in middle- and upper-class families. National estimates of drug use by women who are pregnant are not readily available.

Another group not frequently followed is composed of infants born to abused women. As with children with intrauterine drug exposure, issues of confidentiality and stigma limit families' access to interagency interventions on behalf of the mother or the infant. In addition, these women may try to avoid detection by abusers and so do not seek help. Estimates of the prevalence of maternal abuse range from 0.9% to 20.1% (McFarlane & Soeken, 1999). This population, although at risk, is unlikely to be routinely identified or available for intervention, regardless of the agency point of contact; identifying maternal abuse would be by self-report or hospital emergency room visits.

Nonmedical factors, such as socioeconomic status, social class, education, race, pre- and postnatal care, and social support, have been examined in relationship to birth weight, with a particular emphasis on VLBW and LBW. Longo et al. (1999) found that socioeconomic factors along with medical factors were more closely associated with birth outcomes than medical factors alone, highlighting a continuing need for social service supports.

Children living in poverty are at particularly high risk for developmental delays. Baxter and Kahn (1996) investigated the needs, supports, and stresses of inner-city minority families of children enrolled in EI programs. They found that when basic survival needs are not met, families will concentrate on these needs rather than on future developmental issues related to their children. This often results in later rather than earlier identification of children's needs.

INTERAGENCY COLLABORATION

The interagency collaboration process, by definition, involves more than one agency. This process allows the achieving of mutual outcomes by collaboration among connected and mutually dependent agencies. It is an ongoing process and, when successful, can lead to effective solutions on behalf of children and families. There are no limits to the possibilities for collaboration. Sometimes collaborative issues are superficial, such as the co-location of services targeting families with young children; other issues may be more complex and involve integrated funding and multiple program eligibility.

Many children with disabilities have complex multiple needs requiring the involvement of many agencies over a long period of time. These agencies' variations in definitions of client eligibility, required paperwork, and complex eligibility criteria often interfere with their collaboration regarding children, resulting in little effective communication between providers and bureaucracies. Anderson (2000) observed that over the previous 15 years there was a growth in the number of multiagency programs within a community; these are referred to as *systems of care,* having a positive impact on delivery and quality of care.

Effective models of interagency intervention, used early on in a child's life, may help reduce the impact of prenatal insult, poverty, and disability. Efforts have focused on developing strategies to improve the overall quality of early childhood experiences for young children by 1) improving the quality of early child care and education experiences, 2) increasing access to early childhood education experiences, 3) supporting families with young children, and 4) increasing access to early childhood health screening and care. Many of these efforts have also targeted personnel improvements through the development of a credentialing system for family child care providers and an accreditation program for preschool programs. Health initiatives that will indirectly result in reductions in childhood disability have included 1) the expansion of programs to increase health coverage for young children up to 300% of the federal poverty level; 2) expansion of substance abuse prevention and treatment programs, including a pilot program for mothers of infants born addicted to drugs; 3) lead paint prevention and treatment programs; and 4) universal infant hearing screening (Maryland Infants and Toddlers Program, 2000; Subcabinet for Children, Youth, and Families, 2000).

Using a model of preventive EI and providing these varied services may result in a reduction in the number of students with disabilities in need of costly special education services (Berman & Urion, 2003; Ramey & Ramey, 1992). There are limited data on direct spending by social service and health agencies. The last national study of spending for students in special education (Moore, 1988, as cited in Chambers, Parrish, Lieberman, & Wolman, 1998) was conducted almost 20 years ago and estimated the total expenditures for the average student in special education to be 2.3 times that of the average general education student. It is estimated, however, that state and local governments provide more than half of the fiscal resources required to support early intervention and special education programs (Parrish, O'Reilly, Duenas, & Wolman, 1997).

The availability of services and allocation of resources should be based on the likelihood of benefit to young children and their families. Although there are identified windows of learning opportunity in early childhood when some skills are more easily developed than at other times (Ramey & Ramey, 1999), many children face uncertain outcomes due to biological and environmental risk factors (Baxter & Kahn, 1996; Bricker, 1996; Hershberger, 1996; O'Brien, Rice, & Roy, 1996; Sandieson & Gorodzinsky, 1998). State policies need to be continually reviewed, based on current research and knowledge, to identify the children within these groups who are most likely to benefit from EI services.

Team planning creates a uniquely focused approach to working with families, and its benefits are numerous. This process can minimize the differences across programs and help professionals forge a relationship so that all can work together to understand the uniqueness of each system. Also, through this process the natural community supports of families can be activated.

Increasing the Cost Effectiveness of Collaboration

Selecting models based on effective program outcomes remains the goal. Realistically, costs drive the focus of coordination efforts. Although there is some evidence (Escobar, Barnett, & Goetze, 1994; Ramey & Ramey, 1992; Warfield, 1995) of the cost effectiveness of EI for at-risk populations compared with intervention for children with disabilities, there is a need to identify the most effective models of services for the specific target populations likely to receive the most benefit. Warfield found that the factors with the greatest impact on cost were program model, frequency of service intervention, duration (measured in hours and minutes per week), intensity of services (staff–child ratio), geographic location, and resources. The least expensive programs were those providing a high number of service hours in a center-based setting serving preschoolers. The highest costs per hour were found in home-based programs.

Trends Through the Decades

Interest in young children with disabilities can be characterized as a series of broad trends at the federal level, beginning with a growing awareness and gradual maturing of the social consciousness in American society coupled with a sense of responsibility for its citizens (Gallagher, 2000). Chapter 1 presented a detailed look at the history of initiatives and legislation dealing with the education of young children with special needs; some highlights relevant to agency collaboration will be discussed here.

Federal Policy and Support Services for young children developed largely as a reaction to societal needs, such as the infant schools and the early efforts for social reform in the early 1900s related to immigration and industrialization (Gallagher, Clifford, & Maxwell, 2004). Many of these services were crisis oriented, resulting in service systems that were not well planned or coordinated with related family interventions.

The field of early childhood intervention was initially assisted by the establishment of the Children's Bureau in 1912 and through governmental support of maternal and child health and practices designed to promote the well-being of all children. In 1930 the White House Conference on Child Health and Protection recommended that programs for "crippled children" be made available. In 1935 the Social Security Act established Maternal and Child Health Services, which specifically included children with disabilities (Weintraub, Abeson, Ballard, & LaVor, 1976).

Modern efforts on behalf of young children began in the 1960s as part of an overall concern by society with becoming more socially responsible. The Head Start program was significant in that it targeted young children, included an emphasis on the central role of parents, and eventually required that enrollment be composed of at least 10% of children with disabilities (Gallagher, 2000; Hebbeler, Smith, & Black, 1991). The Handicapped Children's Early Education Program (HCEEP), established by the Handicapped Children's Early Education Assistance Act of 1968 (PL 90-538), was the first federal special education program exclusively for young children with disabilities (Hebbeler et al., 1991). It provided funding for exemplary programs to demonstrate that early intervention could work. Beginning with HCEEP, initial efforts at intervention were focused at the local level to stimulate community-oriented models that would be replicable. As these programs were funded throughout the nation, interest in expansion and support for providing services to children with disabilities increased, and by the 1970s the focus shifted to the state level and increased regulation and program requirements. The Education of the Handicapped Act Amendments of 1974 (EHA; PL 93-380) established a program of grants to assist in the provision of educational services and required a state plan to support local educational agencies.

The Education for All Handicapped Children Act of 1975 (PL 94-142), although a landmark piece of education, did not include children birth to 3 years of age, and it placed certain limitations on the provision of services for young children with disabilities ages 3–5 (Gallagher, 2000). Consequently, early childhood services were unevenly available and funding was not provided to expand services to all children with disabilities prior to the age of school entry. This decade did, however, see the development of equal access to services for individuals with disabilities and their families and the expansion of health-related support services, such as physical therapy and occupational therapy. These services had not been previously included in educational programs.

In addition to the role of federal legislation in special education, the courts played a significant role in a number of cases involving special education throughout these decades. These included *Brown v. Board of Education* in 1954, *PARC v. Commonwealth of Pennsylvania* in 1972, and *Mills v. Board of Education* in 1973.

The 1980s saw a continued progression of federal legislation and funding that would first encourage and then require states to provide services to young children with disabilities. Passage of the Education of the Handicapped Act Amendments of 1983 (PL 98-199) and 1986 (PL 99-457) created a comprehensive, interagency system of service delivery for children with disabilities from birth to age 3 and a seamless set of educational services for children and youth ages 3–21.

With the consolidation of programs into block grants and the dwindling resources due to budgetary and personnel cuts, the challenge in the 1980s and 1990s was for governments to provide coordinated, collaborative, and cost-effective services in health, human services, and education. The 1990s marked an approach in which services for young children and their families emphasized the whole child. This focus reinforced the need for coordination, communication, and collaboration among a variety of disciplines to meet the needs of young children with disabilities.

As this history illustrates, early childhood special education (ECSE) evolved as a natural product of the interface between early childhood education and the right to special education. As both of these fields matured, access for young children with disabilities to education became guaranteed through legal mechanisms and supported through research findings that demonstrated the importance and long-term benefits of early education for young children (see Table 3.1).

Table 3.1.   Federal legislation supporting early childhood special education

Year	Legislation	Function
1965	Amendments to Title I of the Elementary and Secondary Education Act (ESEA; PL 89-313)	Gave payments to states for educating children birth through age 20 with disabilities in state-owned and state-operated programs
1968	Handicapped Children's Early Education Assistance Act (PL 90-538)	Established the Handicapped Children's Early Education Program (HCEEP)
1970	Education of the Handicapped Act (EHA; PL 91-230)	Consolidated other federal special education programs; provided direct financial support to states for programs for children ages 3–5
1974	Education Amendments (PL 93-380)	Enacted new requirements for special education for preschool, elementary, and secondary students; increased authorization levels for the basic state grant program
1975	Education for All Handicapped Children Act (PL 94-142)	Established free appropriate public education for ages 6–18; established Preschool Incentive Grants; awarded state monies based on child count, including 3- to 5-year-olds
1983	Education of the Handicapped Act Amendments (PL 98-199)	Established State Planning Grants for children with disabilities from birth through age 5; broadened use of funds to include children from birth through age 5
1986	Education of the Handicapped Act Amendments (EHA; PL 99-457), Handicapped Infants and Toddlers Program (Part H)	Provided services for infants and toddlers with developmental disabilities and their families; extended the mandate for full services under Part B to 3-year-olds and increased funding
1990	Individuals with Disabilities Education Act (IDEA; PL 101-476)	Reauthorized EHA
1997	Individuals with Disabilities Education Act Amendments (PL 105-17)	Redefined special education to be a service for support of student achievement rather than a place; ensured access to the general curriculum
2004	Individuals with Disabilities Education Improvement Act (PL 108-446)	Consensus bill to reauthorize services; did not provide for full funding; aligned with No Child Left Behind; reduced parents' rights; required effective early interventions that are scientifically based

Sources: Hebbeler et al. (1991) and Gallagher (2000).

The Current State of Services for Young Children   Currently, there is broad federal support for education and other services for young children with disabilities, which has resulted in a combination of mandates, regulations, incentives, and complex program and funding initiatives. National efforts to develop and implement legislation for young children have led to the development of many community-based systems whose goal is to coordinate existing services and identify federal, state, and local initiatives. The EI system in each state is operated largely locally within the federal and state requirements for implementation. EI services include the variety of services that have traditionally been available (e.g., physical, occupational, speech-language therapy), as well as certain family-oriented support services such as respite care, specialized child care, and in-home aides. Outcomes of a coordinated EI system include a statewide organization of services for infants, toddlers, and their families, using combinations of existing services, family outreach systems, innovative funding patterns, and specialized services to fill the gaps in the service delivery system.

Although there have been improvements in the range and quality of programs for young children with disabilities, challenges remain that will be resolved only through the application of research and program outcomes, specifically in identifying those populations that might benefit the most from EI services. There is wide variation across states in eligibility for EI and ECSE programs, resulting in uneven services and research that has limited the reliability of study findings. These variances influence the types of children receiving services, the types of services and models provided, and the ultimate cost of EI systems and their effectiveness in reducing the need for later special education (Shackelford, 2000).

Professionals and families have long recognized the divisions that exist among the traditionally autonomous medical, human services, and education communities. These disciplines have maintained that their basic responsibilities to children with disabilities and developmental problems are separate and distinct. In reality, the services available over the last several decades through a wide variety of governmental programs for children and their families have blurred distinctions among these disciplines. Mandated services to children with special needs of all ages now transcend many of the traditional boundaries of established service systems.

Along with this change, a broadening perception of child and family needs has emerged. Executive Order 12606 in 1987 required that federal agencies recognize the role of the family as the primary force in a child's life. Systems of comprehensive care today must rely heavily on the family as the primary provider of services.

The Importance of Early Intervention
Services in an Interagency Context

Research continues to expand the application of multiple agency coordination for younger children and their families. Every agency, in addition to the family, has a significant influence on the developing child. The foundation for learning and school readiness lies in the development of a healthy brain and early and rewarding life experiences. Preparation for early learning begins in the womb and depends on a healthy and nurturing environment, with good nutrition and avoidance of teratogens.

When the nation adopted as its first national goal "By the year 2000, all children in America will start school ready to learn" (U.S. Department of Education, 1999), a strong belief was expressed that from the time of birth, all children are ready to learn. Bredekamp, Knuth, Kunesh, and Shulman (1992) suggested the following strategies to support early development and learning:

- Active, hands-on learning

- Conceptual learning that leads to understanding along with acquisition of basic skills

- Meaningful, relevant learning experiences

- Interactive teaching and cooperative learning

Congress enacted Part H (now Part C) in 1986 to address the needs of infants and toddlers with developmental delay and their families, recognizing that they required comprehensive services that were unlikely to be fully available through a single public or private agency. Interestingly, although the Federal Interagency Coordinating Council was established to coordinate programs and early intervention strategies on behalf of young children with disabilities and their families, this strategy that was once considered vital to model the coordination of services for young children was deleted in the Individuals with Disabilities Education Improvement Act (IDEA) amendments of 2004.

Service Integration: Focusing on the Outcomes

The policy of the federal government since the 1980s has been to provide assistance to states to develop and implement coordinated and integrated systems of care (Park & Turnbull, 2003). Throughout the past decades the focus on integration of services has been defined by both the process and the outcomes. Much of the literature references service coordination, a more superficial linkage of service agencies and functions, on a continuum to service integration, a more intense process linked to quantifiable outcomes (Konrad, as cited in Park & Turnbull, 2003).

Professionals and families continue to assert the need for improving integration and planning of education, health, and human services within their local communities (Salisbury, Crawford, Marlowe, & Husband, 2003). Early childhood interagency programs that are coordinated through services plans contribute to improved health outcomes, positive early development, and increased economic self-sufficiency for families (Harbin et al., 2004).

State and local agencies providing services for young children share a similar goal of providing cost-effective and efficient EI services; however, it is necessary to understand the different nuances in the approach of these agencies. Each agency has developed specialized language, intervention techniques, and training plans. The trend toward specialization has contributed significantly to the polarity among these service communities, often resulting in duplication as well as gaps in services. The individualized family service plan (IFSP) has been viewed as a useful cross-agency planning tool to enhance coordination; however, the IFSP is inconsistently implemented (Salisbury et al., 2003), limiting its usefulness in this regard.

Some of the differences in agency approaches are due to legislative mandates. For example, state and local education agencies have mandated free services for children, requiring the delivery of all necessary special education and related services, without regard to funding levels. Health agencies also may have legislative mandates (e.g., health departments are required to assist in school health programs), but they generally have a more specific service orientation and a finite budget. Services may be paid for through private providers or clinic fees, income maintenance, or a targeted grant program. A variety of human services are available according to specific age and disability, in combination with income eligibility. Eligibility criteria for health and human services include age, disease diagnosis, financial need, geographic area, and targeted areas of need. Eligibility criteria vary from program to program and may be based on agency mandates, policies, state and local priorities, and limitations on resources.

There are also differences in the structure of services provided by education, health, and human service agencies. State departments of education primarily provide management services, such as administration, monitoring, technical assistance, and fund distribution to local educational agencies (LEAs). State health and human service agencies frequently provide direct services through state-operated local agencies. These services may include medical evaluation and treatment services, therapy, counseling, recreation, income maintenance, and a variety of support services to children and families.

Education, health, and human service agencies all may operate through a categorical approach to service delivery. Following some type of screening and diagnosis, specific probable services are indicated. Services by health and human service agencies often are provided based on income eligibility, court-related issues, or handicapping conditions with definitions that may differ from those used by educational agencies.

To meet the interagency goal of cost-effective, efficient EI services, education, health, and human service providers have to make a specific commitment to the team approach of working in family-centered care. Service planners must work toward the development and management of comprehensive service systems to ensure long-term coordinated approaches. Young children and their families often need access to a variety of specialized EI services within their communities. Education, health, and human service agencies, although they may provide different avenues for obtaining services, must examine methods for coordination through a single IFSP. Although legislative mandates and agency structures may differ, common EI service goals among the programs can be identified and woven into a responsive system. Education, health, and human service programs for young children may be provided through the public or private sectors and may be state or locally funded, large or small, generic or highly specialized, but they must be coordinated to fulfill legislative expectations.

Changes in each of these disciplines have occurred that are in line with a more cross-disciplinary approach. For instance, human service agencies have adapted their systems to incorporate the physical health and developmental status of children into planning for the psychosocial and economic well-being of the whole family. The emphasis in recent years has been on wraparound family support systems and interventions based on each family's identified needs.

The major change in health services has been a new emphasis on preventing disease by promoting health in the family. These health initiatives have resulted from the coordinated efforts of public agencies, the private sector, and individual professionals representing a wide variety of disciplines. Among the areas targeted for prevention activities are those directly related to consumers, such as pregnancy prevention and prenatal and postnatal care, including immunizations.

EI has seen a change in focus from traditional home-based models to those that are family-focused. Although studies of traditional home-based models showed weak effects on children's development (Halpern, 1984; LeLaurin, 1992), studies of combined family-focused and child intervention models (Ramey & Ramey, 1992) support the efficacy and long-term benefits of EI with at-risk infants and toddlers (see Table 3.2 for a list of child and family services). The family-focused education intervention model was implemented with families having infants with moderate or severe disabilities (Caro & Derevensky, 1991). Parents perceived significant progress in the ability of their families to meet the challenges of caring for young children with disabilities. Fewell and Oelwein (1991) studied the effectiveness of an intervention program for young children enrolled in outreach sites of a program for children with Down syndrome and other developmental delays. The rate of development during intervention was higher than the rate of development at pretest. Ramey and Ramey (1992) summarized findings related to the prevention of intellectual disabilities in children of mothers with low IQ scores, who were at risk for poor outcomes. The positive outcomes of EI in the first 5 years of life lasted until early adolescence. EI was associated with an almost 50% reduction in the rate of failing a grade in school and a reduction

Table 3.2. Child and family services

Child services	Family services
Special instruction	Identification of strengths and needs
Speech pathology and audiology	Family training and counseling
Occupational therapy	Home visits
Physical therapy	Respite care
Psychological services	Transportation
Service coordination (previously known as case management services); provided to each child and family	Homemaker services
	Service coordination
	Financial counseling
Medical services (for diagnosis or evaluation only)	Protection and advocacy
	Family education
Early identification, screening, and assessment	Parent networks and support
Health services (to enable child to benefit from other EI services)	Interdisciplinary team services
	Interpreters
Alternative living arrangements	Legal services
Specialized child care	
Transportation	
Special equipment	
Health services	
Nursing services	
Recreation/adaptive physical education	
Nutrition services	
Dental services	
Specialized foster care	
Immunizations	

in borderline functioning from 44% for the control group to 13% for children receiving intervention.

The provision of related services for young children with disabilities continues to pose a significant challenge for educators, pediatricians, and families. The main challenges remain how to integrate the definitions of educational services into a comprehensive interagency focus on the young child in a community setting, and how to coordinate planning. IDEA provides a definition of related services, seen in Table 3.3. Definitions of related services are not considered exhaustive. The 2004 reauthorization of IDEA expanded the list to include school health and interpreter services. Any

Table 3.3. IDEA definition of related services for children with disabilities

(26) RELATED SERVICES—

    (A) IN GENERAL—The term "related services" means transportation, and such developmental, corrective, and other supportive services (including speech-language pathology and audiology services, interpreting services, psychological services, physical and occupational therapy, recreation, including therapeutic recreation, social work services, school nurse services) designed to enable a child with a disability to receive a free appropriate public education as described in the individualized education program of the child, counseling services, including rehabilitation counseling, orientation and mobility services, and medical services, except that such medical services shall be for diagnostic and evaluation purposes only as may be required to assist a child with a disability to benefit from special education, and includes the early identification and assessment of disabling conditions in children.

    (B) EXCEPTION—The term does not include a medical device that is surgically implanted, or the replacement of such device.

IDEA, A Sec. 602. Definitions. 26

Table 3.4. Students covered under 504 plans

Eligibility

Very broad

    Covers many different types of disabilities

    Based on the definition of disability, not on categories

    Schools required to locate students who may be eligible

Qualified student

    Has a physical or mental impairment[a] that substantially limits one or more of such person's major life activities

    Has a record of such an impairment, or is regarded as having such an impairment

    Of an age during which persons without disabilities are provided such services

    Of an age during which it is mandatory under state law to provide such services to students with disabilities; or

    For whom a state is required to provide a free appropriate public education under IDEA

[a]The Americans with Disabilities Act (ADA) of 1990 defines a physical or mental impairment as

Any physiological disorder or condition, cosmetic disfigurement, or anatomical loss affecting one or more of the following body systems: neurological; musculoskeletal; special sense organs; respiratory, including speech organs; cardiovascular; reproductive; digestive; genitourinary; hemic and lymphatic; skin; and endocrine; or any mental or psychological disorder, such as mental retardation, organic brain syndrome, emotional or mental illness, and specific learning disabilities. (28 C.F.R. § 35.104)

service that is necessary to benefit from special education is required to be provided to the student.

Students who do not require special education but who may need related services may be eligible under Section 504 of the Rehabilitation Act of 1973 (PL 93-112), which covers many children not eligible for services under IDEA (see Table 3.4).

Service Coordination for All Children

Often a family may be eligible for services and programs from multiple agencies. One strategy for deciding how best to serve a family in this situation is to determine which child or family need is the key to the best outcome for the child. Knowing whether that need is mostly related to health, education, or family function will help identify which program can primarily serve the child and family. Many of the programs designed for improving services coordination require identification of current service delivery options and directing the family into the option that will most effectively meet the child's and family's needs.

Coordination Mechanisms   All levels of government need to be involved in agency coordination efforts. To ensure long-term collaborative approaches, formal arrangements should be made for interagency commitments, assignment of financial responsibilities, and service agreements. Although informal coordination activities have been conducted among professionals in many communities, the lack of formal, written policies and procedures can disrupt continuity of activities when the personnel central to the coordination process are no longer employed by their respective agencies. Turnover in personnel at the state and local level can disrupt even the most successful coordination efforts if those efforts have been based solely on informal interactions among existing personnel.

The major goals of interagency collaboration are to

- Identify services and programs for infants and toddlers with disabilities

- Promote awareness of specific agency and program mandates and responsibilities

- Ensure exchange of information and ideas among professionals

- Facilitate coordinated service delivery at state and local levels through integration of services and policies

- Maximize use of existing resources

- Reduce gaps and eliminate unnecessary duplication of services

- Increase the cost effectiveness of service delivery plans

- Facilitate data collection efforts through interagency systems

- Improve the effectiveness of family-centered programs and EI services

- Promote a core of quality services throughout the state

Young children with disabilities often have a variety of education, health, and social service difficulties. Prior to the passage of PL 99-457, states approached service delivery based on the agency where services originated. With the passage of legislative requirements for interagency service delivery, states have begun to examine several methods for approaching system design across agencies and programs: through 1) a single agency only, 2) a dominant single agency coordinating services, 3) a single agency in the leadership capacity, and 4) distinct interagency units (Harbin & Terry, 1991). Many states have struggled with determining the most relevant profession to function as service coordinator, particularly when identifying the responsibilities inherent in acting on behalf of the lead agency and the family.

State Progress in Use of Interagency Agreements   In the Twenty-Seventh Annual Report to Congress on the Implementation of the Individuals with Disabilities Education Act (U.S. Department of Education, 2005), the Office for Special Education Programs noted that during the previous 20 years, many states made progress in working toward interagency collaboration. The focus at the state level is to provide more comprehensive, cost-effective, and streamlined services to children with disabilities. This process has continued with each of the reauthorizations of IDEA, which have required interagency collaboration to strengthen special education services. The National Association of State Directors of Special Education (2004) has developed guiding principles to assist states with coordinating services in order to be effective and cost efficient in delivery (see Table 3.5). The federal focus is on whether or not states' interagency agreements address the administrative spectrum of services for students with disabilities, including school-to-work transition activities, data sharing, coordinated EI and preschool services, expanded health services access for children, eligibility for Medicaid, and collaboration on multiagency professional personnel development.

Policy Considerations: Administering and Coordinating Interagency Services   Interagency coordination and collaboration require time, patience, and communication at all levels. Agency personnel should be prepared to make appropriate modifications as their needs change with changes in client eligibility and funding patterns. All professionals must carefully examine and reexamine their roles in this process, and every effort should be made to facilitate rather than hinder the flow of services and information. The first step is to document the client needs and expected outcomes and target the interagency process focus. The parameters of the target populations must be defined, including the definition of the family to be used for

Table 3.5.   National Association of State Directors of Special Education (NASDSE) Goals

NASDSE members, supported by NASDSE staff, will

• Improve educational results for children with disabilities through education reform
• Bring about aligned, continuously improving educational services
• Promote educational equity for all children
• Strengthen ongoing professional development
• Design efficient, cost-effective, flexible administrative systems and practices
• Nuture partnership-based, whole-systems collaboration
• Create school environments conducive to learning
• Build effective family-school partnerships
• Advance public engagement in educational reform efforts that support high achievement for all children

From National Association of State Directors of Special Education, Inc. (2008).

the parameters of service delivery. Also, all agencies and programs serving the target population should be identified. The needs of the target populations, in this case infants and toddlers and their families, should be clearly delineated.

The organization and authority for interagency decision making must also be established. It may be a council composed of consumers, local providers, and state agency representatives, or a separate state authority or agency. It may also be principally an advisory group or a board with decision-making powers.

Systems of Change

Once these considerations have been acted upon, strategies for implementing program changes should then be determined. State and local planners need to choose the most effective techniques for changing the way agencies and professionals relate to each other in the provision of services to the target population. A last step in the process, which should be ongoing, is to ensure the implementation of program changes at the service delivery level. This step includes state and local involvement in management, education, technical assistance, quality assurance, follow-up, and program evaluation.

The overall goal of interagency coordination and planning is to provide quality services to children and their families through collaboration. Interdependence is central to a functional relationship among professional and families. The challenges for administrators and community planners initially focus on identifying services and programs. Many become absorbed in promoting awareness of agency roles and mandates for specific target populations. Usually the exchange of information among professionals and whether it is appropriate is a significant obstacle to progress.

Facilitating coordinated services delivery through integration of policies and programs is the most effective strategy to maximize the use of existing resources and improve program effectiveness. This will reduce gaps and eliminate duplication of services, thereby increasing cost effectiveness. Inherent in these efforts is the need to facilitate data collection among agencies not co-located, which will be discussed later in this chapter.

Innovative Professional Development Practices   Effective early childhood intervention requires well-prepared early childhood professionals trained to deliver a wide range of education, health, and social services. Professional preparation is a renewable resource that must be continually and effectively provided to enhance the skill base of those on the front lines. These early childhood education learning communities increase collaboration among multiple interagency partners at state and local levels, enhance sensitivity to diversity issues, and promote family involvement in personnel preparation (Winton, 2000).

Parents and other family members, too, need opportunities for building their own capacity to assist children in achieving developmental and societal outcomes. Unique strategies must be undertaken to provide innovative approaches for families, including web-based instruction, family support groups, and community activities.

Professional Development: Cross-Discipline Competencies In-service training and education represent opportunities to further supplement the skills of a wide range of professionals in the field of early care and education (see Figure 3.1). Those in leadership need a definitive approach for developing in-service plans to capture meaningful content and learning opportunities (Trohanis, 1994). Educational programs targeting adults require high-interest, multimedia approaches to effectively engage participants in acquiring new information and applying research in their professional capacities. According to Trohanis, six assumptions should be integrated into any in-service plan:

- Training needs to be an integral part of the program.

- Participants need to be treated as adults and respected.

- Participants should be involved in many aspects of the in-service.

- An ongoing planning approach needs to be directed toward maintaining quality work and facilitating change or improvement.

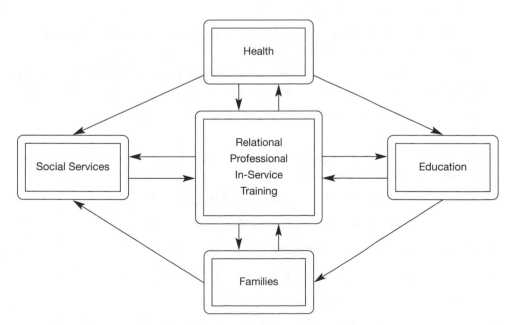

Figure 3.1. Professional development: Cross-discipline competencies.

- Individual and organizational readiness and commitments to learning, changing, and growing should be fostered.

- A conducive learning environment and high-quality pathways to learning need to be available.

The creation of a conducive environment for adult learning requires a complex combination of needs assessment, organizational planning, leadership, and adequate funding. Paramount to successful implementation of in-service activities is the commitment of personnel to improve their skills and knowledge, both for self-development and for the benefit of children.

Barriers to Interagency Collaboration

The federal government has been visionary in designing programs to address the integration and coordination of multiple programs on behalf of children. In spite of these efforts, the GAO (2000) has identified barriers to interagency work that have continued to surface. These barriers include

- Missions that are not mutually reinforcing or those that may even conflict

- Lack of consensus on strategies and priorities, practices, and program priorities

- Territorial and control issues over resources among agencies

- Incompatible procedures, processes, and data and computer systems

- Competition for funding between similar services/programs

- Categorical programming for target populations within the family structure

- Different approaches inherent in specialization

- Absence of the holistic approach to the family and narrow focus of agencies on the problem rather than the child or family

- Lack of communication among professionals and terminology and languages that accompany specialized knowledge

- Lack of understanding of roles of other professionals or agency policies and procedures

- Differences in program eligibility requirements, which create confusion and contribute to incomplete service plans

- Discouragement of additional intervention through another agency

- Perceived threats to an agency's autonomy

- Increase in professionals' workloads

- Varying agency priorities, mandates, and responsibilities

- Conflicting organizational frameworks

- Perceived confidentiality issues, which limit information sharing

Interagency Agreements as a Tool

Negotiating specific interagency agreements between service providers to improve interagency coordination is a key step in the coordination process. Some programs that serve children with disabilities are required by federal law to develop cooperative agreements. The purpose of these agreements is to ensure that the services provided under state plans are coordinated with other public and private agencies providing services to children. Interagency agreements also help in identifying and using existing resources and obtaining appropriate financial support from other agencies.

Interagency agreements may include a wide range of creative options but are systematically negotiated and written to facilitate an effective systemic intervention for children. Initially, an agreement may seek to establish common standards for similar programs. For instance, an agreement between agencies may establish specific criteria for identifying young children for assessment or extended program eligibility. Other agreements might address the allocation of agency resources for accomplishing mutual objectives, such as an agreement between local agencies and local health entities that the health agency will serve as the location for screening eligible infants and toddlers by using an neonatal intensive care unit (NICU) admission as an automatic eligibility determination. Some agreements may focus on providing uniform procedures, forms, and activities by agencies offering EI services. Such an agreement might specify that Child Find personnel and community providers will use the same standard form for screening infants and exchanging information (Bender & Baglin, 1992).

Coordination and collaboration are dependent on the commitment of key decision makers, staff, and administrative officials. Ensuring the institutionalization of key agreements requires that they be articulated in formal, written form. Agreements should include a purpose statement, clarify program mandates, clearly indicate each program's responsibilities, identify key processes for each agency, and contain closing components, including a termination clause (Wischnowski, Fowler, & McCollum, 2000; Wischnowski, Pfluke, & Twining, 2003).

Funding Considerations

Decisions on local funding for services should be based on the best interests of the family and the community, as well as the types of resources available. For example, professionals in a community with many private nonprofit agencies may want to involve these agencies in funding agreements and ensure that they provide a share of the required services.

One consideration in the development of joint funding agreements is whether the resources of the participating agencies are adequate to pay for all required services. It may be necessary to develop collaborative agreements with additional resources to supplement agency budgets. To avoid difficulties, professionals should become aware of all major funding sources, including educational, health, human service, other state and local, and private resources.

Because no single system works equally well in all communities, funding agreements may be generic or individual for a specific child and family. A generic agreement usually describes the specific population by age, target problems, or other factors and specifies which services will be provided by which agency. An individual case agreement specifies which agency will pay for a given service to a particular child. State and local agencies must decide on the most appropriate form for their agreements based on local needs and available services.

Additional considerations in joint funding include maximizing each source of funds to the state and community, maximizing services to the child and family, and distributing the cost of service provision equitably among all appropriate service agencies. These are key issues in a time of limited resources.

Interagency Data Collection

Assessment is a systematic process of evaluation that measures an infant's or a toddler's physical, social, or emotional status by established developmental standards. The result is a description of the child's strengths and weaknesses, behavioral patterns, and level of functioning in a variety of areas. Assessment provides information to document the nature of developmental delays and other conditions and supports recommendations for appropriate intervention. Interagency cooperation during the evaluation process helps ensure the accuracy of the diagnosis/assessment and promotes smooth transition to family-centered program planning.

A centralized record system for storage and retrieval of information can be limited to the information an agency needs in order to coordinate service delivery and to fulfill reporting requirements. Initially, professionals will need to identify the data elements that should be included in a record file to ensure that the file is accessible to each agency needing the information. These elements include 1) a unique child identifier, 2) names of the service agencies involved, 3) services provided, and 4) assessment information.

An identifier for each child is required because data will be added from a variety of programs and agencies, which may be in different locations. A number of state and program systems have determined methods of establishing a unique identifier. The majority of these methods fall into several categories:

- Those generated by participating agencies from an individual child's personal characteristics, such as name and date of birth. This enables all participating agencies to establish a number that is easily derived and would be consistent among all service agencies.

- Those created externally, such as the child's Social Security number or birth certificate number. This can be problematic because not every child has a Social Security number; and for those who do, frequently the numbers are not known or would need to be verified with the Social Security Administration.

- Those created and controlled centrally to assure uniqueness and validity. This system must be consistently maintained, updated, and expanded.

The goal of interagency data collection is to improve services, encourage coordination, and reduce duplication through access to a centralized source of data on families being served or evaluated by any public agency or system. Data elements that describe information about the child that is not likely to change or need updating should be included to enable the system to match on a combination of fields to eliminate the duplication that results from even the most carefully constructed unique identifier. Next, each agency needs to identify the significant issues in developing an interagency data system, including the input process, access, and interagency confidentiality policies.

The following factors should be considered in predicting the validity of interagency data collection: 1) adjustments for duplication within and across agencies, 2) analysis of expected annual intake per program, and 3) length of time a record remains open when a child is no longer receiving services from any program (Bender & Baglin, 1992).

CONCLUSIONS

Meaningful interagency collaboration is complex to define and remarkably elusive to strategically measure. It can be proposed through legislation and policy at the federal, state, and local levels, but it takes place on the community level. As a tool to improve service delivery, it can be evaluated by assessing accessibility, family satisfaction, cost effectiveness, staff knowledge, and personnel retention. Government agencies tend to view its success through budget allocations, cost effectiveness, and political support.

The most effective measure of the success of interagency efforts is the positive impact on children and families. Measuring family satisfaction with EI services remains a challenge for the field.

REFERENCES

Abel, M.H. (1997). Low birth weight and interactions between traditional risk factors. *Journal of Genetic Psychology, 158,* 443–454.

Americans with Disabilities Act (ADA) of 1990, PL 101-336, 42 U.S.C. §§ 12101 *et seq.*

Anderson, J.A. (2000). The need for interagency collaboration for children with emotional and behavioral disabilities and their families. Retrieved December 29, 2004, from www.highbeam.com/library/doc3.asp?ctrlInfo=Round9c%AProd%3ADOC%3AP

Baglin, C.A. (1992). Managing interagency resources. In M. Bender & C.A. Baglin (Eds.), *Infants and toddlers: A resource guide for practitioners* (pp. 125–152). San Diego: Singular Publishing Group.

Baxter, A., & Kahn, J.V. (1996). Effective early intervention for inner-city infants and toddlers: Assessing social supports, needs, and stress. *Infant-Toddler Intervention: The Transdisciplinary Journal, 6*(3), 197–211.

Bender, M., & Baglin, C.A. (Eds.). (1992). *Infants and toddlers: A resource guide for practitioners.* San Diego: Singular Publishing Group.

Berman, S.H., & Urion, D.K. (2003, March). The misdiagnosis of special education costs. *The School Administrator.* American Association of School Administrators. Retrieved April 25, 2008, from http://www.aasa.org/publications/saarticledetail.cfm?ItemNumber=2548

Bredekamp, S., Knuth, R.A., Kunesh, L.G., & Shulman, D.D. (1992). *What does research say about early childhood education?* Retrieved September 25, 2005, from http://www.ncrel.org/sdrs/areas/stw_esys/5erly_ch.htm

Bricker, D. (1996). The goal: Prediction or prevention? *Journal of Early Intervention, 20*(4), 294–296.

Caro, P., & Derevensky, J.L. (1991). Family-focused intervention model: Implementation and research findings. *Topics in Early Childhood Special Education, 11*(3), 66–80.

Carran, D.T., Scott, K.G., Shaw, K., & Beydouin, S. (1989). The relative risk of educational handicaps in two birth cohorts of normal and low birthweight disadvantaged children. *Topics in Early Childhood Special Education, 9*(1), 14–31.

Chambers, J.G., Parrish, T.B., Lieberman, J.C., & Wolman, J.M. (1998, February). What are we spending on special education in the U.S.? *CSEF Brief, 8,* 1–4.

Education for All Handicapped Children Act of 1975, PL 94-142, 20 U.S.C. §§ 1400 *et seq.*

Education of the Handicapped Act (EHA) of 1970, PL 91-230, 84 Stat. 121-154, 20 U.S.C. §§ 1400 *et seq.*

Education of the Handicapped Act Amendments of 1974, PL 93-380, 88 Stat. 576.

Education of the Handicapped Act Amendments of 1983, PL 98-199, 20 U.S.C. §§ 1400 *et seq.*, 97 Stat.1357.

Education of the Handicapped Act Amendments of 1986, PL 99-457, 20 U.S.C. §§ 1400 *et seq.*

Escobar, C.M., Barnett, W.S., & Goetze, L.D. (1994). Cost analysis in early intervention. *Journal of Early Intervention, 18*(1), 48–63.

Fewell, R.R., & Oelwein, P.L. (1991). Effective early intervention: Results from the model preschool program for children with Down syndrome and other developmental delays. *Topics in Early Childhood Special Education, 11*(1), 56–68.

Frank, D.A., Jacobs, R.R., Beeghly, M., Augustyn, M., Bellinger, D., Cabral, H., & Heeren, T. (2002). Level of prenatal cocaine exposure and scores on the Bayley Scales of Infant Development: Modifying effects of caregiver, early intervention, and birth weight. *Pediatrics, 110*(6), 1143–1152.

Gallagher, J.J. (2000). The beginnings of federal help for young children with disabilities. *Topics in Early Childhood Special Education, 20*(1), 3–6.

Gallagher, J.J., Clifford, R.M., & Maxwell, K. (2004). Getting from here to there: To an ideal early preschool system. *Early Childhood Research & Practice, 6*(1), 1–23.

Government Accounting Office. (2000). *Managing for results: Barriers to interagency coordination* (GAO/GGD-00-106). Washington, DC: U.S. Government Printing Office.

Halpern, R. (1984). Lack of effects of home-based early intervention? Some possible explanations. *American Journal of Orthopsychiatry, 54,* 33–42.

Handicapped Children's Early Education Assistance Act of 1968, PL 90-538, 20 U.S.C. §§ 621 *et seq.*

Harbin, G., Bruder, M.B., Adams, C., Mazzarella, C., Whitbread, K., Gabbard, G., et al. (2004). Early intervention service coordination policies: National policy infrastructure. *Topics in Early Childhood Special Education, 24*(2), 89–97.

Harbin, G.L., & Terry, D.V. (1991). *Interagency service coordination: Initial findings from six states.* Carolina Policy Studies Program. Chapel Hill, NC: FPG Child Development Institute.

Hebbeler, K.M., Smith, B.J., & Black, T.L. (1991). Federal early childhood special education policy: A model for the improvement of services for children with disabilities. *Exceptional Children, 58*(2), 104–112.

Hershberger, P. (1996). The relationship of medical and family characteristics to language development skills of low birthweight children at three years of age. *Infant-Toddler Intervention: The Transdisciplinary Journal, 6*(1), 75–85.

Individuals with Disabilities Education Act Amendments (IDEA) of 1997, PL 105-17, 20 U.S.C. §§ 1400 *et seq.*

Individuals with Disabilities Education Act (IDEA) of 1990, PL 101-476, 20 U.S.C. §§ 1400 *et seq.*

Individuals with Disabilities Education Improvement Act (IDEA) of 2004, PL 108-446, 20 U.S.C. §§ 1400 *et seq.*

LeLaurin, K. (1992). Infant and toddler models of service delivery: Are they detrimental for some children and families? *Topics in Early Childhood Special Education, 12*(1), 82–104.

Longo, D.R., Kruse, R.L., LeFevre, M.L., Schramm, W.R., Stockbauer, J.W., & Howell, V. (1999). An investigation of social and class differences in very-low-birth-weight outcomes: A continuing public health concern. *Journal of Health Care Finance, 25,* 75–89.

Maryland Infants and Toddlers Program. (2000). *Maryland's statewide early intervention system under Part C of IDEA annual performance report: July 1, 1999-September 30, 2000.* Baltimore: Maryland State Department of Education.

McFarlane, J., & Soeken, K. (1999). Weight pattern of infants, age birth to 12 months, born to abused women. *Pediatric Nursing, 25*(1), 19–23.

National Association of State Directors of Special Education, Inc. (2004). *Interagency coordination.* Retrieved August 10, 2004, from www.nasdse.org

National Association of State Directors of Special Education, Inc. (2008). *Mission statement.* Retrieved October 28, 2008, from www.nasdse.org/AboutNASDSE/MissionStatement/tabid/405/Default.aspx

O'Brien, M., Rice, M., & Roy, C. (1996). Defining eligibility criteria for preventive early intervention in an NICU population. *Journal of Early Intervention, 20*(4), 283–293.

Park, J., & Turnbull, A.P. (2003). Service integration in early intervention: Determining interpersonal and structural factors for its success. *Infants & Young Children, 16*(1), 48–58.

Parrish, T.B., O'Reilly, R., Duenas, I.E., & Wolman, J. (1997). *State special education finance systems, 1994–95.* Palo Alto, CA: American Institutes for Research, Center for Special Education Finance.

Ramey, C.T., & Ramey, S.L. (1992). Effective early intervention. *Mental Retardation, 30*(6), 337–345.

Ramey, C.T., & Ramey, S.L. (1999). *Right from birth: Building your child's foundation for life.* New York: Goddard Press.

Rehabilitation Act of 1973, PL 93-112, 29 U.S.C. §§ 701 *et seq.*

Salisbury, C.L., Crawford, W., Marlowe, D., & Husband, P. (2003). Integrating education and human service plans: The interagency planning and support project. *Journal of Early Intervention, 26*(1), 59–75.

Sandieson, R., & Gorodzinsky, F. (1998). The psycho-educational outcomes of children with very low birthweight. *Physical Disabilities: Education and Related Services, XVII*(1), 5–61.

Schmidt, R.E., & Wedig, K.E. (1990). Very low birth weight infants: Education outcome at school age from parental questionnaire. *Clinical Pediatrics, 29*(11), 649–651.

Shackelford, J. (2000). State and jurisdictional eligibility definitions for infants and toddlers with disabilities under IDEA. *NECTAS Notes, 5* (rev.), 1–14.

Shaul, M. (1999) *Multiple program coordination in early childhood education. Congressional testimony: 3/25/1999.* Retrieved December 29, 2004, from www.highbeam.com/library/doc3.asp?ctrlInfo=Round9c%Aprod%3ASOC%3AP

Siegel, L.S. (1985). Biological and environmental variables as predictors of intellectual functioning at 6 years of age. In S. Harel & N.J. Anastasiow (Eds.), *The at-risk infant* (pp. 65–73). Baltimore: Paul H. Brookes Publishing Co.

Social Security Act of 1935, PL 74-271, 42 U.S.C. §§ 301 *et seq.*

Subcabinet for Children, Youth, and Families. (2000, October). Presentation to the Joint Committee on Children, Youth, and Families October 11, 2000. Annapolis, MD: Author.

Trohanis, P.L. (1994). *Planning for successful inservice education for local early childhood programs.* Retrieved November 28, 2004, from www.highbeam.com/library/doc3.asp?ctrlInfo=Round9b%3AProd%3ADOC%3APrint&DOCID=1P1:2859132&print=yes

U.S. Department of Education. (1999). The national education goals report. Retrieved May 4, 2008, from http://www.ed.gov/pubs/goals/summary/goals.html

U.S. Department of Education. (2005). Twenty-seventh annual report to Congress on the implementation of the Individuals with Disabilities Education Act. Retrieved September 3, 2007, from http://www.ed.gov/about/reports/annual/osep/2005/parts-b-c/index.html

Warfield, M.E. (1995). The cost-effectiveness of home visiting versus group services in early intervention. *Journal of Early Intervention, 19*(2), 130–148.

Weintraub, J., Abeson, A., Ballard, J., & LaVor, M.L. (Eds.). (1976). *Public policy and the education of exceptional children.* Reston, VA: Council for Exceptional Children.

Winton, P.J. (2000). Early childhood intervention personnel preparation: Backward mapping for future planning. *Topics in Early Childhood Special Education, 20*(2), 87–94.

Wischnowski, M.W., Fowler, S.A., & McCollum, J.A. (2000). Supports and barriers to writing an interagency agreement on the preschool transition. *Journal of Early Intervention, 23*, 294–307.

Wischnowski, M.W., Pfluke, J., & Twining, D. (2003). Head Start and school district collaborations: Writing an interagency agreement. *Young Exceptional Children, 6*(4), 11–17.

Screening, Evaluation, and Assessment in Early Childhood Special Education

Mary S. Hendricks and Janeen McCracken Taylor

*Respect all of the reasonable forms of activity in which
the child engages and try to understand them.*
Maria Montessori

What If?   You and the physical therapist have an appointment in a week with a young child, her mother, and grandmother. The 2-year-old girl is suspected of having a developmental delay and was referred by a community health nurse to your early intervention (EI) program. You spoke to her mother, a single teenager, on the phone and she seemed surprised that you thought her daughter might have a "problem." In preparing for the visit you wonder how you should approach your conversation with this mother and which test or tests would be appropriate to administer. If there are family literacy issues, how can you best communicate the results of your testing to this young mother? Where can you turn for help in addressing these issues?

CHAPTER OVERVIEW

This chapter presents a description of the history of screening, evaluation, and assessment, followed by detailed discussions. The chapter closes by describing team models, including the role of the family within the team, and giving a brief description of assessment.

CHAPTER OBJECTIVES

After reviewing this chapter, the reader will

- Understand the Individuals with Disabilities Education Act (IDEA), particularly Part B and Part C

- Know about several recommended screening, evaluation, and assessment instruments

- Understand the differences between formal and informal evaluation and assessment tools and the components of each

- Understand select team models for conducting screening, evaluation, and assessment

- Understand how evaluation differs from assessment

SCREENING, EVALUATION, AND ASSESSMENT UNDER THE INDIVIDUALS WITH DISABILITIES EDUCATION ACT

Bagnato, Neisworth, and Munson (1997) defined early childhood special education (ECSE) assessment as a flexible, collaborative decision making process in which teams of families and professionals periodically reach consensus about the changing developmental needs of young children and their families. This philosophy provides the framework for this chapter. Screening, evaluation, and assessment of young children have changed dramatically since the 1950s (i.e., the initial days of ECSE). Parents are equal, respected partners in the process, illustrating, as Kjerland and Kovach (1990) indicated, the central role families play in the lives of their child. ECSE practitioners have always been cognizant of the ever-changing processes young children go through and thus are aware that evaluation and assessment, too, is an ongoing, dynamic process (Boone & Crais, 2000).

IDEA requires each state to develop a system for identifying children who are at risk for delay or are experiencing a delay in development; this identification is for the purpose of providing intervention at the earliest possible time. The requirements for this process differ under Part C (i.e., for children from birth to 3 years) and Part B (i.e., for children from 3 to 5 years) of the law.

Part C is the portion of IDEA supporting EI systems for children from birth to age 3 years. It is sometimes referred to as the *infants and toddlers program* or the *early intervention system*. EI systems must include policies and procedures for screening, assessing, and evaluating referred infants and toddlers. The process for doing so must be timely, comprehensive, and multidisciplinary (Fewell, 2000). In addition, the evaluation must identify a child's developmental strengths and needs.

Part B of IDEA, the portion relating to children older than 3 years of age, is referred to as the special education section. The upper age limit for Part B services is determined by each state. Children deemed eligible for services under the special education provision of IDEA must meet the requirements of one of the federal disability categories (see Table 4.1 for a list of these categories). The evaluation must be sufficiently comprehensive to identify all of the child's needs for special education (i.e., instruction) and related services (e.g., physical therapy, occupational therapy, speech therapy). The reauthorization of IDEA in 2004 strengthened the role of the family in the screening, evaluation, and assessment processes (Bailey, Hebbler, Scarborough, Spiker, & Mallik, 2004). Terms such as *family friendly, family centered, family directed,* and *family driven* were once common terms used in Part C, and now in Part B procedures (Hansen, 2003). This chapter will focus on the family's role throughout the screening, evaluation, and assessment process.

Table 4.1. Federal disability categories under IDEA 2004

Autism
Deaf-blindness
Deafness
Emotional disturbance
Hearing impairment
Intellectual disability
An orthopedic impairment
Other health impairment
A specific learning disability
A speech or language impairment
Traumatic brain injury
A visual impairment including blindness
Multiple disabilities

SCREENING

Screening can be defined as the process of gathering information to determine the need for further evaluation (Fewell, 2000). In other words, once basic information is gathered (screening), a multidisciplinary team then determines that a child will be eligible for services under either Part C or Part B of IDEA.

The initial referral for screening is typically made when someone knowledgeable about the child and child development notices a potential delay in development. This person may be considered the primary or secondary referral source and could be a pediatrician, child care provider, parent, or other person of significance to a child.

Effective screening tests or procedures identify all eligible children and those children with a high likelihood of eligibility. Because screening is conducted with a larger number of children than is the more expensive evaluation process, screening should be relatively quick, easy to administer, and inexpensive. Some children who are screened will not be eligible for EI or special education services. Given the expense of a full developmental or educational evaluation, it is important that screening identify children who are eligible and as few additional children (i.e., those who are not eligible) as possible.

Screening should also be child and family friendly. Minimizing child and family anxiety and stress is important for ethical reasons as well as for ensuring accurate test results (Fewell, 2000). Choosing tests that are child and family friendly starts the collaborative relationship with families in a positive manner. Both children and their families are more likely to fully engage in the screening process if a test or procedure is enjoyable and nonthreatening (Hanson & Lynch, 2003).

Screening may be conducted by highly educated practitioners or by paraprofessionals with minimal training in child development (Dunst & Trivette, 2004). To facilitate screening of all children suspected of having developmental or learning problems, test instruments or procedures should be easily learnable by a broad spectrum of EI and special education personnel. Training of screeners should be relatively quick and inexpensive to ensure that all personnel are appropriately trained. The ideal training scenario would involve clear, brief instruction in the use of the instrument or procedure with as many staff members as possible who are qualified to conduct the training. Having people on staff who can conduct training minimizes the costs of professional development, supports consistency of results, and minimizes the disruption when there is staff turnover (McLean, Bailey, & Wolery, 2003).

Under Part C of IDEA, the information yielded from the screening may be used to determine the need for an evaluation if the information suggests that the child has a 25% delay in one or more of the developmental domains, is exhibiting atypical development, or has evidence of a diagnosed medical condition that suggest a high probability of developmental delay.

Under Part B of the law, the screening information should provide documentation of a suspected disability under the federal categories (see Table 4.1). For either Part C or Part B, screenings should be comprehensive and multidimensional. A variety of sources, including family members, teachers, child care providers, pediatricians, and others familiar with the child should provide information related to all aspects of the child's development, which is then incorporated into the screening results.

Screening Instruments

A variety of instruments have been designed to provide information to EI teams for determining the need for further evaluation. Factors to consider when selecting a screening instrument include its reliability and validity, ease of use, cultural sensitivity, and ability to incorporate family information (Sand et al., 2005). Another important consideration in choosing a screening instrument or procedure is minimizing the transmission of communicable disease among children, family members, and practitioners. Therefore, the instrument(s) used for screening should be washable or disposable after each administration. Manipulative materials or toys used by a child should be thoroughly cleaned between test administrations. Health care representatives (e.g., local or state health department representatives) can provide specific guidelines for disinfecting toys and other materials (Taylor & Taylor, 1989).

Table 4.2 lists the three screening instruments discussed in this section. Although other screening instruments exist, those described here allow for the consideration of skills across multiple domains and consider the use of caregiver information to be valid and authentic.

Denver II   The Denver Developmental Screening Test (Frankenburg & Dodds, 1969) was first developed for use by health care providers. It was revised to be more comprehensive and was normed on a larger group. The author describes the tool as a screening tool, not an IQ test, and it is used to determine the need for further evaluation. Caregivers' reports are encouraged as part of the information collection and are considered valid information for the screening.

The Denver II (Frankenburg et al., 1992) looks at development in four domains (i.e., personal/social, fine motor adaptive, language, and gross motor), with 125 items across all domains. The age indicators allow for a designation of the percentage of the norm sample that passed the items at that age range, thus allowing for young children's variability in skill acquisition. The scoring procedures allow the observer to determine the need for rescreening or referral for further evaluation.

The Ages & Stages Questionnaires®   The Ages & Stages Questionnaires® (ASQ; Bricker & Squires, 1999) is a parent-completed child monitoring system. ASQ

Table 4.2. Screening instruments

Name of instrument	Publisher	Age range	Domains	Outcomes
Denver II	Denver Developmental Materials, Inc.	2 weeks– 6 years	Personal/social Fine motor adaptive Language Gross motor	Normal Suspect Untestable Refer
ASQ	Paul H. Brookes Publishing Co.	Birth– 60 months	Communication Gross motor Fine motor Problem-solving Personal-social skills	Numerical score indicates "may need further evaluation"
DIAL-3	Pearson Education	2–6 years	Motor Concepts Language Behavioral observations	Potential Problems OK Potential Advanced

Key: ASQ, Ages and Stages Questionnaires®; DIAL-3, Developmental Indicators for the Assessment of Learning–Revised

was first developed by Squires, Potter, and Bricker in 1995, and a revised edition was published in 1999. The authors describe the questionnaire as a comprehensive, first-level developmental screening tool for children from birth to 5 years of age. ASQ is available in both English and Spanish and allows the omission of items that are culturally biased. The questionnaire provides 30 developmental items per age level and is written at a fourth- to sixth-grade reading level. The questionnaire can be completed by either a parent or a caregiver, and it takes approximately 10–20 minutes to administer. A series of questions related to development across five domains are asked (communication, gross motor, fine motor, problem solving, and personal-social skills). Parents are asked to answer *yes, sometimes,* or *not yet* to each question. A professional then scores the questionnaire and rates the child as either developmentally at age level or in need of further evaluation.

DIAL–Third Edition   Developmental Indicators for the Assessment of Learning–Third Edition (DIAL-3) is an individually administered screening test designed to identify young children in need of further diagnostic testing (Czudnowski & Goldenberg, 1990). Three areas are addressed in this screening: motor, concepts, and language. It is administered by a team of individuals and takes approximately 30 minutes to complete. The results may indicate that a child is delayed in development and warrants an evaluation or that a child is either developing as expected or at an advanced rate.

EVALUATION AND ASSESSMENT

An evaluation is recommended when the screening information suggests that a child may be eligible for services under the requirements of either Part C or Part B. An evaluation is completed to determine or diagnose a developmental delay.

Part C requires that the evaluation of each child (birth to 3) is timely, comprehensive, and multidisciplinary. Additionally, a family-directed identification of the needs of each child's family is needed to appropriately assist in the development of the child. Evaluation and assessment (34 C.F.R. 303.322) are considered processes that have different purposes under Part C. Evaluation is defined as the procedures used by "appropriate qualified personnel to determine a child's initial and continuing eligibility," consistent with the state definition of infants and toddlers with disabilities, and including a determination of the status of the child in each developmental area (i.e., cognitive development, physical development, including vision and hearing, communication development, social or emotional development, and adaptive development). Assessment involves ongoing procedures used by appropriate and qualified personnel throughout the period of a child's eligibility under this part to "identify the child's unique strengths and needs and services appropriate to meet those needs" (Fewell, 2000).

Unlike Part C, Part B does not define evaluation and assessment as different processes. Part B requires that "a full and individual evaluation is conducted for each child being considered for special education and related services under Part B of the Act to determine if the child is a 'child with a disability' and to 'determine the educational needs of the child'" (34 C.F.R. 300.320).

Evaluation and Assessment Tools

As described previously, screening involves the identification of children who are suspected of having developmental problems. Evaluations and assessments differ from screening in that evaluations and assessments are more extensive examinations of children's development and may be conducted simultaneously (i.e., program eligibility determined during the process of identifying a child's developmental or curricular outcomes). To provide a seamless system of services for young children with disabilities, EI and ECSE leaders must collaborate with agency or program representatives to link screening efforts with evaluation and assessment processes (Bender & Baglin, 1997). This ensures a smooth and collaborative screening, evaluation, and assessment system for children and their families.

As program leaders, it is important to choose appropriate evaluation and assessment instruments. In addition to child and family factors (e.g., cultural sensitivity, developmental appropriateness), evaluation and assessment instruments must meet federal, state, and local requirements (McLean, Wolery, & Bailey, 2003). One strategy for selecting appropriate evaluation and assessment instruments or procedures is appointment of individuals to a task force with the purpose of recommending specific evaluation and assessment strategies. This group can include administrators, practitioners, family members, consultants, or others involved in evaluation or assessment processes. A checklist of issues to consider when selecting evaluation instruments and procedures can be found in Figure 4.1. Descriptions of specific instruments and strategies for evaluation and assessment follow and are summarized in Table 4.3.

Battelle Developmental Inventory–Second Edition

The Battelle Developmental Inventory–Second Edition (BDI-2; Newborg, 2004) has a screening test in addition to the full battery (i.e., evaluation and assessment) of test items in all domains of child development. The original BDI was published in 1988 and revised in 2004. BDI-2 is available in English and Spanish. The BDI-2 addresses five domains of child development and 13 subdomains of development. The screening test takes approximately 10–30 minutes and the full BDI-2 takes from 1 to 2 hours.

Before selecting a particular instrument or procedure for developmental evaluation or assessment of young children, ask the following questions:

Yes	No	
☐	☐	Does this instrument or procedure meet federal legislative and regulatory requirements?
☐	☐	Does this instrument or procedure meet local policy requirements or guidelines?
☐	☐	Is the examiner qualified to administer this instrument or procedure?
☐	☐	Does this instrument or procedure address the relevant areas of a child's development adequately?
☐	☐	Is this instrument culturally appropriate for the child(ren) being tested?
☐	☐	Does this instrument allow for serial use (i.e., can be used repeatedly with the same child)?
☐	☐	Does this instrument have family-friendly procedures (e.g., facilitates family collaboration, does not add to family stress)?
☐	☐	Does this instrument measure qualitative (e.g., the quality of a child's movements) and/or quantitative (e.g., measurable) aspects of a child's performance?
☐	☐	Does this instrument identify developmental strengths as well as developmental needs of children being tested?
☐	☐	Does this instrument have sufficient reliability for this situation?
☐	☐	Does this instrument have sufficient validity for this situation?
☐	☐	Is this instrument developed for a population that is similar to the children who will be tested?
☐	☐	Does this instrument yield standardized scores (e.g., required in some states, systems, or programs)?
☐	☐	Can this instrument be administered and scored in a timely fashion?
☐	☐	Is this instrument available in more than one language? If yes, which language(s)?
☐	☐	Does this instrument provide adaptations for specific disabling conditions?
☐	☐	Is this instrument flexible enough to be used by individuals from a variety of disciplines?
☐	☐	Does this instrument facilitate a collaborative effort?
☐	☐	Is use of this instrument or procedure cost effective (i.e., including the cost of the instrument, materials, and examiner fees)?

From Taylor, J.M., & Fleming, J.A. (1993). Early childhood special education evaluation/assessment guide. Baltimore: Maryland State Department of Education; adapted by permission.

Figure 4.1. Checklist for selection of evaluation or assessment instruments or procedures.

Validity and reliability data are published in the examiner's manual. The BDI-2 can be administered by EI or ECSE practitioners with a bachelor's level education or by a team of practitioners. Results of the BDI-2 are reported as standard scores or age equivalents. Training is available from the publisher.

Bayley Scales of Infant and Toddler Development–Third Edition

The Bayley Scales of Infant and Toddler Development–Third Edition (BSID-3; Bayley, 2005) was first developed in the 1930s (e.g., Bayley, 1933). Eventually, Bayley published the first edition of the BSID (Bayley, 1969) and in 2005 a third edition was published (Bayley, 2005). The original, revised, and third editions of the Bayley Scales are widely used evaluation instruments. With the latest revision of this popular test, there are measures of additional aspects of child development (i.e., social-emotional development, adaptive behavior). Although requirements for administration of this test are relatively high (e.g., minimum of a master's degree in psychology, speech and language therapy, occupational therapy, physical therapy), those who have such appropriate training as early intervention practitioners, early childhood educators, child development specialists, and school psychologists may be eligible to administer this instrument. Scores are standardized and the test results can be calculated on a personal digital assistant (PDA).

Carolina Curriculum for Infants and Toddlers with Special Needs–Third Edition and the Carolina Curriculum for Preschoolers with Special Needs–Second Edition

The Carolina Curriculum or Infants and Toddlers with Special Needs–Third Edition (CCITSN-3; Johnson-Martin, Attermeier, & Hacker, 2004) and the Carolina Curriculum for Preschoolers with Special Needs–Second Edition (CCPSN-2; Johnson-Martin, Attermeier, & Hacker, 2004) are widely used curriculum referenced evaluation and assessment instruments (Hebbeler, Malik, & Kahn, 2008). Together, these instruments cover the development of children from birth to 6 years. There is an overlap between the two instruments and each is accompanied by scoring forms. Observation of children and families' reports are used to determine children's skills in five domains of development. Age ranges are based on recently normed tests and information from child development literature. Brookes Publishing provides information on these tests as compared with the Office of Special Education Programs (OSEP) child outcomes (Crosswalk for The Carolina Curriculum, 2008).

Hawaii Early Learning Profile Strands (0–3) and the Hawaii Early Learning Profile for Preschoolers Assessment Strands

The Hawaii Early Learning Profile Strands (0–3) (HELP 0–3; Parks, 2007) and the Hawaii Early Learning Profile for Preschoolers with Special Needs Strands (HELP-P; VORT Corporation, 2004) were developed from the original HELP curriculum (Furuno et al., 1984). These curriculum-referenced materials can be used to identify children's developmental needs/strengths, track children's development, and develop plans for meeting developmental outcomes and objectives. Materials are family-friendly and support documents (e.g., administration guidelines, home activities) are available for use by families and practitioners.

Learning Accomplishment Profile–Third Edition

The Learning Accomplishment Profile–Third Edition (LAP-3; Hardin, Peisner-Feinberg, & Weeks, 2005) is a norm-referenced evaluation and assessment tool that provides a systematic way to document the development of children who are functioning in the 30–72-month age range. EI and ECSE practitioners can use the LAP Diagnostic Edition (LAP-D) to provide a context of an individual child's development relative to the standardization sample. Results of the LAP-D can be used to plan and implement IFSP or IEP outcomes or objectives. The LAP-D is based on research conducted over a 2-year period (2002–2004) to provide updated norms. A Spanish version of this instrument is available.

Parent Interviews   A number of parent interview tools are available for obtaining authentic information from families on their child's behaviors.

McWilliam (1992) developed the family-centered intervention planning (FCIP) process. The primary purpose of the FCIP is for intervention planning, using a routines-based approach (RBA). The RBA interview process is used to determine a child's strengths and needs, the family's priorities and concerns, and the functional skills the child uses to be a successful member of the family. This approach emphasizes the support for the family, as the major influence on a child's development. Its adjunct use, however, is to determine the child's level of functioning, either to support or concur with standardized procedures or to profile the day-to-day functional skills the child shows within the context of the family's routines (McWilliam, 1992).

During the initial phase, an interview is conducted to gather meaningful and authentic information about the family and the child's routine within the family setting. The interviewer begins by completing an ecomap of the family's sources of support. The ecomap helps the interviewer establish a relationship with the family and determine who is involved in the child's and family's lives. An attempt is made to also establish the family's relationship within these support systems. For example, if the child is involved in a child care setting, information should be gathered from the individuals in this setting to support and document the child's strengths and needs within this setting.

Following the completion of the ecomap, the assessment continues with a discussion of the child's routine. Careful consideration is given to questioning techniques. As the interviewer (I) asks the parent (P) about the child's frequently occurring routines, he or she must carefully gauge the questioning so as to identify areas of need. Following is an example:

I: What happens for you and your child in the morning?

P: Joe wakes up and we go downstairs.

I: What does "wake up" look like? Do you wake up first, or does Joe?

P: Joe wakes me up.

I: How does he wake you up?

P: He cries and calls "Mama."

I: Does this routine work for you?

P: Most of the time it does, but sometimes I cannot come right away, and Joe gets very upset. He cries so hard, I cannot get him to stop.

This sample dialogue shows that Joe has some verbal language. It also shows that the interviewer may need to come up with some suggestions on how Joe can entertain himself if his mom cannot get to him soon enough in the morning. A guided parent interview, such as the one described by McWilliam (1992), can provide practitioners with enough information to present a realistic picture of the child's day-to-day functioning in the family. This information leads to the development of functional and more meaningful outcomes and objectives for the child.

Play-Based Evaluation   Play-based evaluation can be considered an informal tool for assessing young children. It uses their typical interactions as the basis for gathering information about the current level of skills within the context of play. The assumption is that children's play is their work and that children's evaluators will gain meaningful information about children's development as they observe their daily activities (Montessori, 1995). The work of Linder (1993) was instrumental in the use of this approach in evaluating young children. Linder (2008) focuses on children from birth to age 6. Linder's purpose is to determine a child's developmental processes and functional skills across the following domains for the purposes of planning and implementing meaningful curricula evaluating cognitive, emotional and social, language and communication, and sensorimotor. This approach is grounded in developmental and Piagetian theory. It is designed to be administered by a transdisciplinary team and always includes the child's parent(s) or caretaker. Linder's evaluation strategies can be incorporated into a child's and family's daily routines, can be used in a home or center-based environment, and does not require special toys or equipment.

Observation   One cannot dispute the importance of child observation as a powerful informal evaluation tool. Observing children in their typical settings during their typical activities can contribute a wealth of information to the evaluation process. The term *informed clinical opinion* appears in the regulatory requirements of IDEA as an important component of the evaluation process. This allows the team, including family members, to use their observations to form a more complete picture of the child than is possible with formal evaluation (Fewell & Rich, 1987).

In formal evaluations, as described by Losardo and Notari-Syverson (2001), consist of structured, systematic observations of behaviors within meaningful context-bound activities. Information is collected on an ongoing basis at different times and across multiple environments, using a broad variety of quantitative and qualitative methods. These observations by individuals familiar with typical child development and knowledgeable of the particular child's typical behavior provide a broader context of the child's strengths and needs. Observation of a child across multiple settings with a variety of people, tools, and materials provides authentic anecdotal information that may not be gathered through more formal procedures. As those who are familiar with young children know, they may not perform naturally on demand.

Procedures for observation may vary and may call for using commercial or published checklists, running records (i.e., observation notes), or verbatim samples (i.e., language samples). Key items to include in a running record are

- Purpose for the observation

- Setting and the relevance of that setting

- Activities the child participates in

- Others present during the observation

When recording observations, objective descriptors of the child's movements should be included. Table 4.4 includes a few of the qualitative descriptors used to pinpoint developmental strengths and needs.

Assessment Tools

Assessments typically refers to the use of standardized norm-referenced procedures. Since the 1960s, the use of these types of tools for young children has been challenged (Fewell, 2000). Many programs require formal diagnostic procedures for the determination of eligibility, to satisfy funding requirements, or to meet federal or state standards (McLean, Wolery, & Bailey, 2003). Those in the field of EI, however, know that variability of performance exists both among children and within children. Bagnato, Neisworth, and Munson (1997) indicated that many instruments and procedures developed through psychometric methods do not meet professional standards for use in early intervention. For example, some tests were normed on select groups and are not valid for diverse populations of children (Fewell, 2000). Flexibility in choosing instruments for developmental testing must be considered by determining the purpose for the evaluations (McLean, Wolery, & Bailey, 2003).

Criterion-referenced, curriculum-based tools provide a means to an end, a way to provide standards for evaluation without using strict standardization procedures. Most curriculum-based assessments are based on well-established developmental norms yet allow for the modifications and adaptations needed to gather meaningful information on a child's performance. A number of these instruments exist and have been modified and updated over the years. Bagnato et al. (1997) explored several of these tools and their effectiveness and meaningfulness for use in EI assessment. Their reference provides a comprehensive approach to identifying the most effective and efficient tools. See Table 4.3 for examples of assessment instruments.

Role of the Family

Typically, a family comes to an evaluation session with several questions:

- What's wrong with my child?

- What will my child's future be like?

- What can be done to help my child?

Although families may be overwhelmed at the possibility of their child's potential diagnosis, it is imperative that they be considered full members of the evaluation team. Boone and Crais (2000) stated that "parents are generally the most reliable and frequent contacts for their child. Parents know their child best. Indeed, research has documented that parents are accurate appraisers of their young child's development, especially when they are asked to make judgements about behaviors the child currently exhibits" (p. 1). Professionals should not minimize the family's role in the evaluation process because of concerns that the information may not be realistic. Families provide valuable authentic and longitudinal information about their child that is not otherwise available (Diamond & Squires, 1993). Although this information may differ from the information gathered by the rest of the team, it should not be considered any less valuable. Because of differing perspectives and contexts, professionals and families should be considered independent rather than interchangeable raters (Suen, Lu, Neisworth, & Bagnato, 2005).

Before the 1980s, the family played a more traditional role in the evaluation process. Family members were expected to provide the team of professionals with a case history and developmental information, and they might be asked to complete a family report instrument. Many times, parents were asked to leave the room during the evaluation so that the professionals could get an unbiased picture of the child. This role has dramatically changed. Typically, evaluations are now conducted at least partially in the child's natural environment, whether at home or in a child care setting. Parents are often asked to administer test items themselves or to demonstrate typical interactions with the child.

Table 4.3. Select evaluation and assessment instruments for use in determining the developmental status of young children or progress relative to their IFSPs or IEPs

Name of instrument	Publisher	Age range	Developmental domain(s)	Reported outcomes
BDI-2	Riverside Publishing	Birth to 7 years 11 months	Personal social, adaptive, motor, communication, cognitive ability	Developmental levels in each domain
Bayley-III	Pearson Assessment	Birth to 42 months	Cognitive, language, motor, social-emotional, adaptive	Standardized scores for mental and motor development plus social-emotional and adaptive behavior descriptions
CCITSN-3	Brookes Publishing	Birth to 36 months	Person-social, cognition, cognition-communication, communication, fine motor, gross motor	Status in each domain of the curriculum
CCPSN-2	Brookes Publishing	2–5 years (i.e., developmental age)	Person-social, cognition, cognition-communication, communication, fine motor, gross motor	Status in each domain of the curriculum
HELP Strands (0–3)	VORT Corporation	Birth to 36 months	Regulatory/sensory, cognitive, language, gross motor, fine motor, social-emotional, self-help	Approximate developmental age levels in each domain
HELP-P	VORT Corporation	3–6 years	Cognitive, language, gross motor, fine motor, social-emotional, self-help	Approximate developmental age levels in each domain
LAP-D3	Kaplan Early Learning Company	30–72 months	Fine motor, gross motor, cognition, language	Child's skill level in comparison to normative scores

Key: BDI-2, Battelle Developmental Inventory (2nd ed.); Bayley-III, Bayley Scales of Infant Development (2nd ed.); CCITSN-3, Carolina Curriculum for Infants and Toddlers with Special Needs (3rd ed.); CCPSN-2, Carolina Curriculum for Preschoolers with Special Needs (2nd ed.); Help Strands (0–3), Hawaii Early Learning Profile Strands (Birth to age 3 years); HELP-P, Hawaii Early Learning Profile (Preschool); LAP-D3, Learning Accomplishment Profile–Diagnostic (3rd ed.)

These changes in practice make sense. Parents are the experts on their child. Professionals are the experts in the development of children. Together they can form a whole picture of the total child so as to get a clearer idea of the child's strengths and needs. From a philosophical perspective, this approach acknowledges the importance of the information provided by the family. The information is treated as authentic, and the professionals respect the family's perspective. Ideally, this approach pro-

Table 4.4. Descriptors of child behaviors

Aspect of development	Examples of qualitative descriptors		
Activity level	Slow to warm up	High energy	Lethargic and inattentive
Persistence	Follow through with activities	Level of independence	Approach to the activity
Movements	Fluency of movements	Types of movements	
Stamina	Tires easily	Abundance of energy	
Transitions	Movement between activities	Level of assistance from adults	Prompt hierarchy
Interactions	With people	With objects	In situations

motes shared knowledge and allows the family to have a role in the decision-making process. The message sent is that the family members are valued members of the team. There is a widespread belief that decisions concerning a child's IFSP or IEP that incorporate multiple perspectives are better than decisions made by a single person from a single perspective.

Evaluation and Assessment Teams Models   Evaluation and assessment teams are formed in a variety of ways. Under both Part B and Part C of the law, the evaluation must be multidisciplinary, incorporating the results from more than one area of expertise. The way in which team members collaborate is dependent on the model chosen by the team.

Multidisciplinary Team   A multidisciplinary team comprises professionals who work independently of each other. They use instruments particular to their discipline, and their evaluation reports are separate. Some might insist that this approach is not really a team approach and that because the professionals work separately, parents may be confused by having to interpret and pull together all of the results. Traditionally, family is not necessarily a part of a multidisciplinary team.

Interdisciplinary Team   Interdisciplinary team members may work separately or in pairs. This team's primary focus is on team communication. Members rely heavily on pre-meetings and post-meetings and develop a report collaboratively. The family is always a part of this team, either in a direct or an indirect way. This approach generates a more unified evaluation report than the multidisciplinary approach, and program planning is more cohesive. However, each individual or team of professionals may have a different set of experiences with the child and family, resulting in discrepant, disjointed results. Although there is a focus on communication, there can be breakdowns in this communication because not all team members are working together as a group.

Transdisciplinary Team   The transdisciplinary team is a group of professionals who rely on shared responsibility; family members are included as central team members. The professionals may choose a primary service provider to facilitate and coordinate the evaluation. The primary idea in this model is role release. Each professional on the team needs to understand that the different disciplines and skills represented by team members interact and overlap and that, therefore, the person with the best set of skills will be the primary facilitator of the evaluation. For example, a physical therapist would lead team efforts to evaluate a child with gross motor delays. For this type of team to be successful, team members must respect this philosophy and commit to constant communication and team building. This type of team collaboration results in a cohesive, comprehensive evaluation.

Arena Evaluation

Arena evaluation is a critical part of the transdisciplinary approach. Arena evaluation can be defined as the simultaneous evaluation of the child by multiple professionals of differing disciplines (Linder, 1993; McGonigel et al., 1991). This approach is based on the philosophy that at a young age all of a child's skills are interrelated and cannot be separated by discipline or developmental area. The advantages of arena evaluation are numerous and include decreased time in actual assessment, reduced repetition of demonstration of skills that overlap developmental domains, having family members participate as full members of the team, and immediate feedback among professionals about the child's skills. Most important, team members can collaborate and come to a consensus due to having observed the child at the same time.

Typically, an arena evaluation is organized by establishing roles for the evaluation. These roles may include a primary facilitator, a family facilitator, a recorder, and a coach. One team member may be chosen to facilitate the majority of interactions with the child. This does not imply that no one else may relate with the child; it merely means that one person focuses on building rapport with the child, limiting the number of people the child needs to engage with. Another role in an arena evaluation is the family facilitator. This individual may check in periodically with the parents to gauge whether the child's performance is typical of his or her day-to-day behavior. The recorder documents the responses of the child and the family. Finally, the coach may serve as a guide to the facilitator, reminding the facilitator of strategies and items that need to be addressed.

An arena evaluation has a basic structure that is necessary for the process to be successful. The steps in an arena evaluation are

- Preevaluation planning meeting

- Structured evaluation

- Follow-up meeting

- Collaboration and reporting

These steps, however, are not exclusive to the arena evaluation process. They are useful tools for any team of professionals evaluating young children.

Preevaluation Planning Meeting   The preevaluation planning meeting is held prior to the actual evaluation. This meeting can be held with the family to review any information gathered through the screening process, identify what additional information is needed, and determine the methods and procedures that will be used to gather that information. This ensures that the evaluation meets the criteria for a multidimensional assessment: multidomain, multimeasures, and multisources. If the family is unable to attend the preevaluation meeting, information can be gathered using the form in the Chapter 4 Appendix.

Structured Evaluation   The actual evaluation may take a number of different forms depending on the child and family. However, it should always include an opportunity for the child to warm up to the team members and for the family to provide any new information. Following this, all of the activities listed below should be included in the evaluation. The order of these activities may vary based on the needs and preferences of the family and child.

- Free Play

- Snack

- Structured tasks

- Literacy/story

- Closing activities

During these activities, each evaluator needs to be aware not only of task performance but also of the approaches the child takes to learning and indicators that lead to success. Keen observation skills can provide a wealth of information about the child.

Follow-Up Meeting   The follow-up meeting may or may not include the parents. During this meeting the professionals score and discuss their observations from the evaluation session. It is a time for the team members to ensure that they all are in agreement with what was seen in the evaluation. If the evaluation was recorded, the team may review the tape or DVD during this time. Team members might also discuss the child's eligibility for services and the category that might be used to qualify the child.

As part of the collaborative effort with family members, the team may invite families to sit in on the meeting. Given the emotional nature of discussions regarding eligibility, it may be necessary to hold this meeting with only the professional team so that the team can present a unified opinion when reviewing the collaborative report with the family.

Collaboration and Reporting   The final step in the evaluation process is the completion and review of a report. The written report must provide a complete picture of the evaluation process and of the skills the child demonstrated. It must be presented in a way that is understandable to the parents, without professional jargon. The report should be useful, providing information that can lead to effective and meaningful program planning.

The following components are necessary to an evaluation report: identifying information, background information, evaluation methods, results, and recommendations.

Identifying information refers to general information about the child: name, birth date, age at the time of assessment, and gender. This section of the report my also include the reason the child was referred, as well as the name of the person who made the referral. It may include information about the family's primary concerns, their resources, and their priorities. This information is required by Part C; however, its usefulness to Part B cannot be disputed. The section may also include the names of the assessors.

The *background information* section describes the child's prior history. It reviews pertinent information related to birth and medical history, developmental history, and educational experiences. Careful consideration must be given to ensure that statements regarding prenatal and birth history are presented objectively.

The section regarding *evaluation methods* should state all screening instruments, all parent and caregiver interviews, and all observations. Dates and duration of these methods should be included as well.

The section regarding *results* is the most comprehensive portion of the report. All information, regardless of how it is obtained, should be presented as factual. Parent reports and interviews are considered to be authentic information and are valid to the evaluation process. This section may be the most challenging section to complete, as the reporter must take careful consideration in stating the performance of the child as well as the conditions under which the child's skills were observed. The results must be stated clearly and objectively.

The *recommendation* section of the report is a culmination of the evaluation. This section should state the child's strengths and needs, present level of performance, and initial suggestions for intervention and programming.

CONCLUSIONS

Screening, evaluation, and assessment procedures for young children have dramatically changed over the past years to include a strong family-focused approach. Families are now involved from the time of referral through completion of the evaluations to the assessment of the intervention's effectiveness. Although the laws governing Part C and Part B may vary, the family continues to be the primary source of authentic information on children, leading to a functional and meaningful approach to intervention.

REFERENCES

Bagnato, S.J., Neisworth, J.T., & Munson, S. (1997). *LINKing assessment and early intervention: An authentic curriculum-based approach* (3rd ed.). Baltimore: Paul H. Brookes Publishing Co.

Bailey, D.B., Hebbeler, K., Scarborough, A., Spiker, D., & Mallik, S. (2004). First experiences with early intervention: A national perspective. *Pediatrics, 113*(4), 887–896.

Bayley, N. (1933). *The California First-Year Mental Scale.* Berkeley, CA: University of California Press.

Bayley, N. (1969). *Bayley Scales of Infant Development.* San Antonio, TX: Pearson Assessment.

Bayley, N. (2003). *Bayley Scales of Infant and Toddler Development–Third Edition.* San Antonio, TX: Pearson Assessment.

Bender, M., & Baglin, C.A. (Eds.). (1992). *Infants and toddlers: A resource guide for practitioners.* San Diego: Singular.

Berman, C., & Shaw, E. (1997). *Family-directed child evaluation and assessment under IDEA: Lessons from families and programs.* Chapel Hill, NC: National Early Childhood Technical Assistance Center.

Boone, H.A., & Crais, E. (2000). Strategies for achieving family-driven assessment and intervention planning. *Young Exceptional Children 3*(1), 2-11.

Brassard, M.R., & Boehm, A.E. (2007). *Preschool assessment: Principles and practices.* New York: Guildford Press.

Bricker, D., & Squires, J. (with Mounts, L., Potter, L., Nickel, R., Twombly, E., & Farrell, J.). (1999). *Ages & Stages Questionnaires® (ASQ): A parent-completed, child-monitoring system* (2nd ed.). Baltimore: Paul H. Brookes Publishing Co.

Crosswalk for The Carolina Curriculum. (2008). Retrieved November 8, 2008, from http://www.brookespublishing.com/store/books/johnson-martin/Carolina-OSEPCrosswalk.pdf

Czudnowski, C., & Goldenberg, D. (1990). *Developmental Indicators for the Assessment of Learning-Revised.* Circle Pines, MN: American Guidance Service.

Diamond, K., & Squires, J. (1993). The role of parental report in the screening and assessment of young children. *Journal of Early Intervention, 17*(2), 107–115.

Dunst, C., & Trivette, C. (2004, August). Toward a categorization scheme of child find, referral, early identification and eligibility determination practices. *TRACELINES, 1*(2), 1–18.

Fewell, R.R. (2000). Assessment of young children with special needs. *Topics in Early Childhood Special Education, 20*(1), 38–42.

Fewell, R.R., & Rich, J.S. (1987). Play assessment as a procedure for examining cognitive, communication, and social skills in multihandicapped children. *Journal of Psychoeducational Assessment, 5*(2), 107–118.

Frankenburg, W.K., & Dodds, J.B. (1969). *The Denver Developmental Screening Test.* Denver: University of Colorado Medical Center.

Frankenburg, W.K., Dodds, J.B., Archer, P., Bresnick, B., Maschka, P., Edelman, N., et al. (1992). *Denver II* (2nd ed.). Denver, CO: Denver Developmental Materials.

Furuno, S., O'Reilly, K.A., Hosaka, C.M., Inatsuka, T.T., Zeisloft-Falbey, B., & Allman, T. (1984). *Hawaii Early Learning Profile (HELP) Checklist.* Palo Alto, CA: VORT Corporation.

Hanson, M.J. (2003). National legislation for early intervention: United States of America. In S.L. Odom, M.J. Hanson, J.A. Blackman, & K. Sudha (Eds.), *Early intervention practices around the world.* Baltimore: Paul H. Brookes Publishing Co.

Hanson, M.J., & Lynch, E.W. (2003). *Understanding families: Approaches to diversity, disability, and risk.* Baltimore: Paul H. Brookes Publishing Co.

Hardin, B.J., Peisner-Feinberg, E.S., & Weeks, S.W. (2005). *The learning Accomplishment Profile–Third Edition.* Lewisville, NC: Kaplan Early Learning Company.

Hebbeler, K., Mallik, S., & Kahn, L. (2008). *State approaches to collecting outcomes data for young children with disabilities in state early intervention and EC special education programs.* A paper presented at the Conference on Research Innovations in Early Intervention, San Diego.

Individuals with Disabilities Education Improvement Act (IDEA) of 2004, PL 108-446, 20 U.S.C. §§ 1400 *et seq.*

Johnson-Martin, N.M., Attermeier, S.M., & Hacker, B.J. (2004). *Assessment log and developmental progress charts for the Carolina Curriculum.* Baltimore: Paul H. Brookes Publishing Co.

Johnson-Martin, N.M., Attermeier, S.M., & Hacker, B.J. (2004). *The Carolina Curriculum for Infants and Toddlers with Special Needs* (3rd ed.). Baltimore: Paul H. Brookes Publishing Co.

Johnson-Martin, N.M., Attermeier, S.M., & Hacker, B.J. (2004). *The Carolina Curriculum for Preschoolers with Special Needs* (2nd ed.). Baltimore: Paul H. Brookes Publishing Co.

Kjerland, L., & Kovach, J. (1990). Family–staff collaboration for tailored infant assessment. In E.D. Gibbs & D.M. Teti (Eds.), *Interdisciplinary assessment of infants: A guide for early intervention professionals* (pp. 287–297). Baltimore: Paul H. Brookes Publishing Co.

Linder, T. (1993). *Transdisciplinary Play-Based Assessment.* Baltimore: Paul H. Brookes Publishing Company.

Linder, T. (2008). *Transdisciplinary Play-Based Assessment, Second Edition (TPBA2).* Baltimore: Paul H. Brookes Publishing Co.

Losardo, A., & Notari-Syverson, A. (2001). *Alternative approaches to assessing young children.* Baltimore: Paul H. Brookes Publishing Co.

McGonigel, M.J., Kaufmann, R.K., & Johnson, B.H. (Eds.). (1991). *Guidelines and recommended practices for the individualized family service plan.* Rockville, MD: Association for the Care of Children's Health.

McLean, M., Bailey, D.B., & Wolery, M. (1996). *Assessing infants and preschoolers with special needs.* Upper Saddle River, NJ: Prentice Hall.

McLean, M., Wolery, M., & Bailey, D.B. (2003). *Assessing infants and preschoolers with special needs* (3rd ed.). Columbus, OH: Charles E. Merrill.

McWilliam, R. (1992). *Family centered intervention planning: A routines-based approach.* Tucson, AZ: Communication Skill Builders.

Montessori, M. (1995). *The absorbent mind.* New York: Henry Holt & Company.

Newborg, J. (2004). *Battelle Developmental Inventory–Second Edition.* Rolling Meadows, IL: Riverside Publishing.

Ostrosky, M., & Horn, E. (2002). *Assessment: Gathering meaningful information* (Young Exceptional Children Monograph Series No. 4). Reston, VA: Council for Exceptional Children, The Division for Early Childhood.

Parks, S. (2007). *Hawaii Early Learning Profile (HELP) Strands (0–3).* Palo Alto, CA: VORT Corporation.

Sand, N., Silverstein, M., Glascoe, F.P., Gupta, V. B., Tonniges, T.P., & O'Connor, K.G. (2005). Pediatricians' reported practices regarding developmental screening: Do guidelines work? Do they help? *Pediatrics, 116*(1), 174–179.

Sandall, S., McLean, M., & Smith, B. (2000). *DEC recommended practices in early intervention/early childhood special education.* Longmont, CO: Sopris West.

Suen, H.K., Lu, C.H., Neisworth, J.T., & Bagnato, S.J. (2005). The authentic alternative for assessment in early intervention: An emerging evidence-based practice. *Journal of Early Intervention, 28*(1), 17–22.

Taylor, J.M., & Fleming, J. (1993). *Early childhood special education evaluation/assessment guide.* Baltimore: Maryland State Department of Education.

Taylor, J.M., & Taylor, W.S. (1989). *Communicable disease and young children in group settings.* Austin, TX: PRO-ED.

VORT Corporation. (2004). *Hawaii Early Learning Profile (HELP) for Preschoolers–Assessment Strands.* Palo Alto, CA: Author.

Chapter 4 Appendix

*Form: Information About
My Child for the Evaluation
and Assessment Process*

HOWARD COUNTY PUBLIC SCHOOL SYSTEM
Howard County, Maryland
EARLY INTERVENTION SERVICES

**Information About My Child for the
Evaluation and Assessment Process**

Date _____

To the Parent/Guardian of: _____

    Family members are important members of the assessment team. Your participation in the assessment and evaluation process is greatly encouraged and appreciated. The information that you provide will be considered by the team and may be included in the written Report of Collaborative Assessments.

    Please complete this form and return it to _____ by _____.

If you have questions, please contact _____ at _____.

Thank you for your cooperation and participation.

I would describe my child in this way:

    (Please include a description of your child's strengths.)

Evaluation Questions

    I would like this assessment to address the following questions I have about my child:

    My child's teacher or child care provider offers these questions or comments about my child:

Family concerns, priorities, and resources related to the child's development:

    I would like my child to learn or get better at:

    My family can help my child by:

    I would like help with:

    I use the following individuals or agencies as a support or resource:

Developmental Milestones (recent progress or changes I have seen in my child at home)
   Learning concepts

   Communication with adults and peers

   Playing with children and adults, sharing, expressing feelings

   Motor skills

   Self-help skills such as feeding, toileting, dressing

Functional Skills/Daily Routine
   A typical day with my child includes: (Give information about the morning routine, child care,
      preschool, meals, evening routine, and so forth)

   My child needs help with:

Learning Style, Motivators, and Reinforcers
   My child learns best when:

   My child enjoys or is interested in:

   My child does not like or avoids:

Is there any additional information which you would like us to know so that we may help your child?

_____   _____   _____
             Signature   Relationship   Date

Program Planning and Implementation for Infants and Toddlers with Disabilities and Their Families

Anne Hickey

Children are apt to live up to what you believe of them.
Lady Bird Johnson

What If? Sonia Gambretti is 2 days old, and her pediatrician has just explained to her mother, Maria, that Sonia has Down syndrome. Maria is a single mother with limited financial resources. She is a legal resident of the United States, but her English skills are somewhat limited. She is not sure where to turn for support and information on how to help Sonia. Her pediatrician gives her a pamphlet that describes the state's early intervention (EI) system and gives the phone number for the local EI program. Maria is anxious about her daughter's health and development and worried that she will not have enough money to pay for the services Sonia needs.

CHAPTER OVERVIEW

This chapter will address essential components in planning and implementing quality EI programs for children and families, including legislative requirements related to service provision for infants and toddlers and their families; identification and Child Find activities; and family-centered intervention, supports, and strategies. This chapter will also cover community and cultural considerations relating to program planning, the individual family service plan (IFSP) process, and philosophical and curricular approaches to service delivery for infants and toddlers and their families.

CHAPTER OBJECTIVES

After reviewing this chapter, the reader will

- Know the legislative requirements for program planning

- Know how to identify children in need of EI services

- Understand the importance of family-centered intervention, supports, and strategies

- Understand the importance of considering the family's community and culture when program planning

- Understand the IFSP process

- Understand a generalized model for service delivery

A COORDINATED, FAMILY-CENTERED SYSTEM OF SERVICES

Part C of the Individuals with Disabilities Education Act (IDEA) of 2004 (PL 108-446) outlines a comprehensive, interagency, multidisciplinary program of EI services. Part C is designed to provide one-stop shopping for families whose children ages birth through 2 have delays or disabilities. The law requires that public and private community agencies collaborate to develop a coordinated program of services through interagency agreements. Coordinating educational, developmental, medical, and social resources is an arduous task for EI program administrators. Varying philosophies about family support services and intervention strategies and conflicting funding structures and staffing patterns must be integrated to provide each family with an individualized plan of services. Part C services differ from other IDEA services as they are, by definition, family-centered. The family-centered nature of EI permeates all aspects of a recommended practice service delivery model and must be clearly defined for administrators, participating agency service providers, referral resources, and families. Families of young children with delays and disabilities are faced with a full range of emotions and challenges. Compassionate, empathic, and knowledgeable EI service providers are often a family's first allies, guiding the family forward until the child's delay is remedied or, more often, setting the course for a lifelong journey.

LEGISLATIVE REQUIREMENTS

Part C of IDEA outlines a program of services for eligible infants and toddlers and their families. Services are provided through service coordination and an IFSP. For eligible infants and toddlers, the initial IFSP is developed within 45 days of referral to the single point of entry. The IFSP is formally reviewed at least every 6 months and annually. Each family is entitled to a service coordinator, who may be assigned from any one of the agencies participating in the delivery of services or at the request of the parent. One agency is selected to serve in a lead role and provide program administration. This lead agency coordinates the development of a yearly plan for program implementation. Required components of the plan are

- Procedures for referral, including a public awareness plan and comprehensive Child Find system

- Procedures for evaluation, service delivery, program review, and transition

- A comprehensive system for personnel development, including personnel standards

- A central directory that includes services and resources

- Policies and procedural safeguards

- Funding and budgets

- Supervision and monitoring activities

This yearly plan outlines the role each agency will play in service provision. Due to the cross-agency nature of EI services, collaboration and communication among participating agencies are key. Underlying this collaboration is a strong theoretical and philosophical base and a passion for and commitment to making a difference in the lives of young children and their families.

IDENTIFICATION AND CHILD FIND ACTIVITIES

As a first step in identifying eligible children and families and providing services, administrators must answer two fundamental questions: Who are the children in need of EI services in a specific community, and where do those families and their children spend their time? The Education of the Handicapped Act Amendments of 1986 (PL 99-457) offered guidance as to who the recipients of EI services should be but also allows for individual communities to define their populations. IDEA Part C eligibility categories have defined eligible infants and toddlers as

- Experiencing developmental delays as measured and verified by appropriate diagnostic instruments and procedures indicating that the child is functioning at least 25% below his or her chronological age in one or more of the following developmental areas:

  - Cognitive development

  - Physical development, including fine and gross motor and sensory development, including vision and hearing

  - Communication development

  - Social or emotional development

  - Adaptive development; or

- Manifesting atypical development or behavior, which is demonstrated by abnormal quality of performance and function in one or more of the above specific developmental areas, interferes with current development, and is likely to result in developmental delay (even when subsequent developmental assessments do not document a delay); or

- Having a diagnosed physical or mental condition that has a high probability of resulting in developmental delay. (Examples include, but are not limited to, children with sensory impairments, inborn errors of metabolism, microcephaly, fetal alcohol syndrome, epilepsy, Down syndrome and other chromosomal abnormalities.)

Clear definitions of the terms *developmental delay, at risk,* and *likely to result in delay* were not provided in the federal legislation. The outlining of service eligibility definitions was left to state and local program managers as a means of providing services to all populations deemed in need within individual communities. Although evaluation and assessment instruments are more plentiful and useful than in the past, most still fall short of providing service providers with all the information needed to determine all of a child's and family's unique strengths and needs. Skilled and competent child development specialists from a variety of professional fields—early childhood education and EI, speech-language pathology, occupational therapy, physical therapy, medicine, nursing, social work, and others—must formulate their collective clinical opinions into an integrated, comprehensive profile.

PL 99-457 also stipulated that the assessment process involve the selection of appropriate tools for assessing family resources, priorities, and concerns. Typically, identification of family resources, priorities, and concerns is completed by interview during the assessment process. Child and family assessment findings drive intervention planning. The multidisciplinary decision-making team scrutinizes the child's current status in independent developmental areas and takes into account family preferences and perceptions when designing each family's unique service delivery package. Several effective research-based models for child and family assessment are outlined in other chapters.

A process for assessment is useless if no children are referred for potential eligibility. A comprehensive public awareness plan ensures that families with infants and toddlers who may be developmentally delayed will be aware of services that are available, both public and private, through a variety of methods. Effective EI programs outline public awareness and Child Find activities yearly. A keen administrator keeps a watchful eye on changes in community dynamics, including birthrates and incidence and prevalence data related to epidemiology of disabilities in the community. Growth or decrease in general population, availability of housing and child care, and access to medical facilities also affect referral rates. Community programs and service organizations that have direct contact with families with children under the age of 3 must be identified and educated about EI services. Some of these referral sources are logical, such as the medical community, social services organizations, and organized community groups. Others may be less obvious based on community structure. These may include single and working parent support groups, family child care providers, and child care center staff. Awareness activities may include distribution of program brochures through mailings, presentations to community groups and medical offices, and participation in child care fairs.

FAMILY-CENTERED INTERVENTION, SUPPORTS, AND STRATEGIES

The unique aspect of EI is the family-centered nature of program design and implementation. Current systems models of the family unit continue to emphasize the impact of interactions between the child and caregivers on the child's development. Although the belief that the child's social world in the first 3 years of life lies within the context of interactions with caregivers is fairly consistent among experts, the definition of *caregiver* continues to change rapidly. EI services designed for antiquated family models will not be effective because family involvement, in determination of priorities, time frames, and even the professionals involved, profoundly affects service efficacy.

The Changing U.S. Family

Family structures and parenting practices vary greatly in contemporary society (Bukatko & Daehler, 2004). Two-parent families represented only 69% of U.S. families in 2000, compared with 85% in 1970 (U.S. Bureau of Census, 2001). Single-parent births and divorced parents account for more than one in five families in the United States. Nontraditional families headed by grandparents or gay or lesbian parents are also on the increase, and more than 70% of married female parents work out of the home (Bukatko & Daehler, 2004). All of these factors must be considered when designing service delivery options for parents of young children in need of intervention services. A family-centered program philosophy is flexible, responsive to the changing needs of the child and caregivers, and respectful of cultural and ethnic differences (Buysse, Wesley, & Skinner, 1999). Families, although more loosely defined than at any other time in history, still exist within communities, and programs need to serve the unique communities in which they reside. Schedules for service provision need to be flexible to accommodate parent work schedules, child care arrangements, and other family commitments and obligations. Families residing in urban, rural, or suburban communities will require different configurations for service delivery, scheduling, staffing, and service location.

Understanding the Family as a System

Because family involvement is a key focus of EI, service providers need a strong knowledge base for addressing the needs of infants and toddlers with disabilities and at-risk conditions and a variety of strategies to provide information and support to caregivers. An understanding of basic family system concepts is needed to address the needs of family members as well as children. To develop effective intervention strategies, service providers must look beyond the immediate needs of the child related to the delay or disability and explore the family as a dynamic, interrelated system of relationships. Begun (1996) summarized basic family system research helpful to EI professionals: Families operate as more than a sum of parts. Values, behaviors, and processes are developed by each family to sustain the system. Family members are interdependent; change in any part of the family system will affect the entire system. The behavior of one family member influences and is influenced by the behavior of other family members. These concepts help EI service providers to explore not only how caregiver behavior affects the child with a disability but also how the child's behavior affects the family system.

Families have several subsystems that are ever-changing and overlapping. Three common family subsystems have been defined by researchers: marital, parental, and sibling. Other subsystems can also exist, such as other generations and step or half relationships (Begun, 1996). Each subsystem has its place in the larger family system and may take priority depending on specific circumstances. Parenting a young child with or without special needs, for instance, often results in changes in the preexisting marital subsystem of traditional families. Sibling subsystems will develop as subsequent members join the family. Although these adjustments are common to all families, they may have greater impact on a family whose child has a developmental delay or disability.

Family systems do not exist in isolation; they are part of a larger social context. This larger system provides the family with support or stressors. McWilliam and Scott (2001) suggested that EI service providers examine the ecology of the family's place in this larger system to provide effective intervention. Knowledge about a family's ecology is gleaned through ongoing conversations with family members. As an initial step in developing an intervention plan, it sets the course for optimal family involvement in the child's program. Family members are informed that their self-defined resources, priorities, and concerns will guide the child's assessment and treatment.

An ecomap can facilitate the development of a collaborative and respectful parent–professional relationship and the design of an intervention program that considers the larger family context (McWilliam & Scott, 2001). The ecomap outlines the relationships that evolve around a child and family. It helps family members examine their own support system and identify any gaps where additional support is needed. The child and family members who live with the child are placed at the center of the ecomap. Extended family members, close friends, and consistent caregivers are recorded in the next layer. Relationships through work, church, or community groups form the next layer. The outermost layer outlines other professionals who provide services to the family on the child's behalf. During the interview process, a family member describes each of these relationships. The interviewer notes whether the relationships appear to be supportive or not.

Ecomaps benefit both families and professionals. Families have reported that the development of an ecomap as part of the IFSP development process was helpful in forming partnerships with professionals (McWilliam & Scott, 2001). Professionals gain valuable information about the family's context of support as well as stressors that may affect the effectiveness of the intervention for the child, and they may recommend different service delivery options as a result. Figure 5.1 shows an ecomap for one child, Joe, and his family.

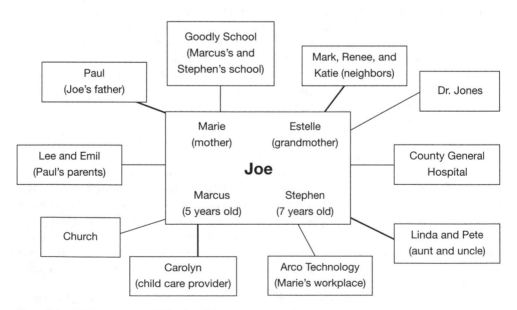

Figure 5.1. Family ecomap: Joe's family within a larger community context.

Family Support: Beyond Denial

The strong family involvement component of EI programs requires service providers to develop skills in providing emotional support for family members, sharing knowledge and resources, and teaching both child and adult learners. Supporting a family during the initial days, weeks, and months after the child's disability has been identified is both a challenging and rewarding task. The nature and severity of the child's disability, family resources, and family coping skills all affect the type of support needed. Service providers must develop trusting relationships with families, using ongoing open communication and collaboration as they partner in the intervention process.

In the past, EI professionals received training in the stages of grief that were typical of a family experiencing the effects of having a young child with a disability. These stages—denial and isolation, anger, bargaining, depression, and acceptance—were widely accepted and used by EI teams to determine family support strategies (Kubler-Ross, 1969; Rosen, 1955). Parents were expected to move through these stages during the EI period, and the interventionist's role was to support the family in moving toward acceptance. Parents whom professionals deemed difficult, demanding, or uninvolved were viewed as not accepting of their child's disability and were referred to as being in denial.

As parents have become more involved in EI policy, new theories have emerged about the way families handle their child's disability. In an article entitled "Rethinking Denial" (Gallager, Fialka, Rhodes, & Arceneaux, 2002), the authors explored the effects of parenting a child with a disability and suggested that professionals develop new attitudes to truly support families. The reframing of the concept of denial suggests that professionals no longer rely on stereotypical views of families during this time of crisis. Each family member accepts, processes, and communicates feelings and perceptions in unique ways and may frequently experience a change in feelings. Instead of progressing through linear stages, families describe a more circular framework of adjustment to parenting a child with special needs, with feelings that come and go at unexpected moments (Miller, 1994).

Family Support Strategies

New strategies for supporting families emphasize acknowledging and accepting different coping styles. Gallagher and colleagues (2002) suggested that EI professionals consider such strategies as the following:

- Supporting family members' hopes and dreams for their child

- Suspending judgment of family behavior

- Being patient and giving families time to adjust to unexpected events

- Using the period of adjustment as an opportunity to build trusting relationships with families

Families may require support beyond the skills of EI professionals and may be referred to other resources and support groups. Many families appreciate networking opportunities with other families who have children with similar needs. These family-to-family network systems may be set up through the EI program or by disability-specific support groups in the community.

COMMUNITY AND CULTURAL CONSIDERATIONS

It is important to recognize each family as a dynamic, unique, and valued system that has the most direct impact on the child's development. Professional development for all EI professionals in understanding how family systems develop and sustain is necessary for quality family-centered care. Essential to this learning is understanding and respecting cultural diversity. Rosin (1996) identified four elements of cultural and ethnic diversity that directly affect EI service delivery:

- Families participating in EI programs may come from different ethnic and cultural backgrounds than the service providers.

- Family structures have changed; there are now more single-parent families and more mothers who work outside the home.

- Increasing numbers of families live in poverty.

- Increasing numbers of parents are disabled.

Family-centered service delivery models acknowledge and respect differences and uniqueness. EI service providers seeking cultural competence exhibit the following qualities in their work with families (Rosin, 1996):

- They explore their own culture and upbringing and understand how their own values and beliefs affect their interactions with others.

- They explore the cultural makeup of the families they work with to avoid stereotypical assumptions.

- They research resources in the community that can provide formal and informal supports for the families they work with.

- They understand obstacles related to culture that may affect service delivery and develop strategies to overcome them.

Service providers will not make these discoveries and acquire cultural competence without ongoing professional development. A variety of options should be available for program staff to explore cultural considerations that affect the quality of service to families.

THE INDIVIDUALIZED FAMILY SERVICE PLAN PROCESS

The IFSP development process involves a collaborative exchange of information among family members, caregivers, and professionals and is flexible, interactive, and ongoing to ensure that the young child's continually changing needs are met (Howard County Maryland Infants and Toddlers Program [HCMITP], 2004). Part C of IDEA also emphasizes the importance of the early years in a child's social, emotional, cognitive, and physical growth. An effective IFSP process is guided by the following principles of recommended practice:

- Infants and toddlers are uniquely dependent on their families for their survival and nurturance. This dependence necessitates a family-focused services delivery model.

- Services are provided in a manner that is accepting and respectful of the diversity and uniqueness of families.

- Individual family strengths provide a foundation for planning effective intervention plans.

- Services include support and assistance to empower families as they care for their children.

- Families participate in all aspects of planning and delivery of services.

- Services are flexible, accessible, and responsive to family needs as they relate to the needs of the child.

- Services promote the integration of the child and family within the community.

- The complex needs of eligible infants and toddlers and their families require a coordinated, multiagency approach to planning and delivery of services in a timely manner (HCMITP, 2004).

A comprehensive yet concise statement of program beliefs and philosophy, such as the statements above, is essential to effective program administration. It provides administrators and service providers with vision as they work in the EI field.

Beginning the Process: Referral and Intake Activities

The IFSP process begins at the first contact with the child and family. Information gathered throughout the referral and assessment activities, as well as from a review of records from other agencies, is used by family members and service providers to design an individualized plan of services for the child and family. Figure 5.2 illustrates the IFSP process.

Referral information is gathered at a single point of entry, and a variety of intake activities are scheduled by the assigned service coordinator. As mentioned previously, an IFSP must be developed within 45 days of referral for eligible children. Intake activities may include written correspondence between the family and program, such as a welcome letter and a developmental questionnaire like the second edition of *Ages & Stages Questionnaires®* (Bricker et al., 1999). A sample welcome letter is shown in Figure 5.3. In some cases, such as with very young or premature infants, it may not be appropriate to send developmental questionnaires directly to families. Intake personnel may also offer to mail written information and let each family decide if this is the method of information gathering that the family prefers. Intake information may also be shared and gathered by phone or in person. Written materials may need to be available in other languages, and/or foreign language interpreters or bilingual service coordinators may need to be involved in gathering information from the family.

Initial contact between the family and service coordinator typically occurs by phone, when an intake session is scheduled. Intake sessions may occur in the family's home or the child care setting, at a center or medical facility, at a mutually

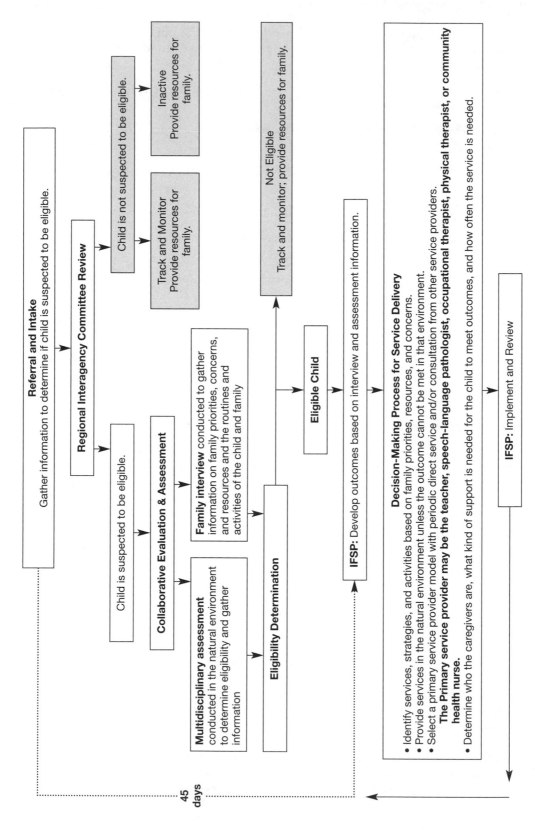

Referral and Intake
Gather information to determine if child is suspected to be eligible.

Regional Interagency Committee Review

Child is not suspected to be eligible.

Inactive
Provide resources for family.

Track and Monitor
Provide resources for family.

Child is suspected to be eligible.

Collaborative Evaluation & Assessment

Multidisciplinary assessment conducted in the natural environment to determine eligibility and gather information

Family interview conducted to gather information on family priorities, concerns, and resources and the routines and activities of the child and family

Eligibility Determination

Not Eligible
Track and monitor; provide resources for family.

Eligible Child

IFSP: Develop outcomes based on interview and assessment information.

Decision-Making Process for Service Delivery
• Identify services, strategies, and activities based on family priorities, resources, and concerns.
• Provide services in the natural environment unless the outcome cannot be met in that environment.
• Select a primary service provider model with periodic direct service and/or consultation from other service providers.
  The Primary service provider may be the teacher, speech-language pathologist, occupational therapist, physical therapist, or community health nurse.
• Determine who the caregivers are, what kind of support is needed for the child to meet outcomes, and how often the service is needed.

IFSP: Implement and Review

45 days

Figure 5.2. The individualized family service plan (IFSP) process. (Developed by Howard County Infants and Toddlers Program, Columbia, Maryland, September 2004.)

94

WELCOME TO THE _____
INFANTS AND TODDLERS PROGRAM!

Your referral information has been forwarded to a service coordinator with the _____ Center. The service coordinator will be in touch with you to schedule an intake visit. During that visit, the service coordinator will begin to gather information about the concerns your family has for your child.

Attached is the **Ages & Stages Questionnaire**® about activities children do. Please complete this questionnaire and give to the service coordinator during the intake visit. Your child may have already done some of the activities described, and there may be some your child has not begun doing yet. For each item, please check the box that tells whether your child is doing the activity regularly, sometimes, or not yet. If you need assistance in completing the questionnaire, please tell the service coordinator during your intake visit. The _____ Infants and Toddlers Program staff looks forward to working with you and your child.

Important points to remember for the **Ages & Stages Questionnaire**®:

- Be sure to try each activity with your child before checking a box.

- Try to make completing this questionnaire a game that is fun for you and your child.

- Make sure your child is rested, fed, and ready to play!

Sincerely,

Program Coordinator
888.555.1212
prog_coord@web.com

Program Administrator's Guide to Early Childhood Special Education: Leadership, Development, and Supervision by J.M. Taylor, J. McGowan, and T. Linder

Figure 5.3.   Sample welcome letter for families.

agreed upon community location, or by phone. The purpose of the intake session is to obtain parental permission for participation in the program, to begin to gather information about the family's concerns, and to provide the family with information about the program and other community resources, if appropriate. Releases are also obtained for exchanging of information between agencies and requesting necessary medical records pertaining to the child. Representatives from multiple agencies may participate in intake activities. It is important for service providers to be flexible in collecting information and to respect the family's decisions about location, scheduling, and participants in initial contact activities. Participation in EI programs is voluntary, and parents may withdraw at any time during the IFSP process. A checklist is often helpful to ensure that proper procedures are followed during intake sessions (see Figure 5.4). Checklists should be customized to meet local program requirements.

Children in the foster care system may require the assignment of a parent surrogate. Local and state programs often have procedures for parent surrogacy application. Service coordinators should be knowledgeable about this application process.

After intake activities have been completed, the service coordinator consults with interagency team members, which includes the parent and other professionals who may assist in determining next steps. Children who are not suspected to be eligible may be monitored periodically, or their case may be made inactive. Parents may re-refer the child at any time. Children who are suspected to be eligible for EI services continue with the IFSP development process and may require additional assessments to develop a service plan. Models for effective evaluation and assessment are found in other chapters of this book.

Individualized Family Service Plan Development and Natural Environments

Comprehensive evaluation under Part C requires the gathering of developmental information for determining eligibility and family assessment of resources, priorities, and concerns. This information forms the child's intervention plan. The IFSP process is defined by law as family centered; outcomes for intervention are to be determined by the family, and services are to be provided in the child's natural environment. Research has shown that children with disabilities often take longer to learn new skills and have more difficulty generalizing what they have learned to new situations than children without disabilities. They benefit from learning in everyday situations and settings where their skills are used and reinforced. These everyday settings and situations, referred to as *natural environments,* are where the child currently spends time or where the family would like for the child to spend time. Part C requires that, "to the maximum extent possible, early intervention services be delivered in natural environments." Natural environments for infants and toddlers with disabilities are homes, child care settings, and other places where typically developing children participate. EI services may only be delivered outside of these settings when justification is provided for why the outcome cannot be met within a natural environment.

Philosophical and Curricular Approaches to Service Delivery

Instruction in the natural environment is multifaceted. It involves the where, what, how, and who of service delivery. Although determination of service location is fairly clearly defined in Part C, the law gives little guidance about curriculum content for infants and toddlers—what to teach, how to teach, and who should teach.

The *DEC Recommended Practices in Early Intervention/Early Childhood Special Education* provides some guidance to program administrators, service providers, and families regarding curriculum content (Sandall, Hemmeter, Smith, & McLean, 2005). What and how to teach infants and toddlers with disabilities has shifted away from addressing specific skill deficits to the teaching of functional and meaningful skills. A "function, not services" approach to EI involves teaching the child the skills he or she will need to participate fully in everyday routines, interactions, and activities (Pilkington & Malinowski, 2002; Rapport, McWilliam, & Smith, 2004). Routine family activities are predictable, are repeated frequently, and are carried out by familiar

The service coordinator explains the purpose of the initial visit to the parent or caregiver during the initial phone contact; for example, "I would like to hear your concerns about your child."*

During the initial visit (in the home, office, or center or by phone), the service coordinator...

❏ Provides an overview of the purpose of the Infants and Toddlers Program—to coordinate service for infants and toddlers with developmental delays and their families

❏ Explains the process of intake, evaluation, and assessment and next steps to be taken

❏ Provides information to the family about the child's needs, the services provided in the jurisdiction, and the evaluation process used in determining whether a child is eligible for services

❏ Explains that participation is voluntary in the interagency program and ensures that the parents or guardians understand that information obtained by the program will be shared among the participating agencies but will not be released to a third party without their consent

❏ Informs parents or guardians that records will be maintained at a central program office and at the service coordinator's agency

❏ Informs parents or guardians of their right to review and obtain copies of any records obtained or completed by the Infants and Toddlers Program staff

❏ Identifies the kinds of records to be collected with the parent's or guardian's authorization, such as
  • Educational records
  • Speech therapy, occupational therapy, or physical therapy records
  • Medical records
  • Psychological records
  • Social history
  • Developmental history
  • Other pertinent agency records about the child

❏ Determines if a parent surrogate is needed and obtains the application; assists the caregiver in completing the application

❏ Obtains the parental signature on the consent form for evaluation and assessment and interagency release of information and records; indicates the specific records to be shared:
  • Explains to parents that they have the right to inspect and review all records relating to evaluation and assessments, eligibility determination, and development and implementation of the IFSP
  • Discusses parents' rights concerning individual complaints about services provided, or any other concerns involving records about their child or family

(continued)

Figure 5.4. Sample service coordinator checklist for intake visits. *, visits are conducted in the family's primary language.

Figure 5.4.   *(continued)*

❑   Provides parents with program brochures, including procedural safeguards

❑   Obtains intake information from parents and guardians using the program format

❑   Begins the evaluation and assessment process by
   • Discussing the family's resources, priorities, and concerns for the child and what type of assistance is needed
   • Reviewing developmental questionnaires completed by the family or completing the questionnaire with family members
   • Using a developmental protocol to gather additional information about the child
   • Beginning to gather information about the child's and family's daily routine using the routines-based family interview format

❑   Obtains permission from parents or guardians to request medical or other appropriate information about the child

❑   Provides the family with information about other community resources

❑   Refers the family to the appropriate agency(ies) to determine eligibility if the family is in immediate need of food, housing, medical care, and so forth

❑   Completes a written summary of the visit for the family, if requested

❑   Obtains the parent's permission if the parent requests that a copy of intake information be shared with the child's pediatrician or primary medical care provider

❑   Invites the parents or guardians to the multidisciplinary, interagency meeting where information about the child will be shared

After the initial visit, the service coordinator...

❑   Summarizes the initial visit information for the multidisciplinary, interagency meeting

❑   Reviews medical records to identify health concerns

❑   Shares information at the multidisciplinary, interagency meeting and makes plans for the next steps, including additional evaluation and assessments needed to determine eligibility, if appropriate

❑   Completes the Parent Choice Not to Participate letter if parents do not wish to pursue services or participate at this time

❑   Contacts the program coordinator to determine next steps to meet child and family needs when resources cannot be identified through the usual process

❑   Completes required documentation (paperwork), submits and files appropriately

❑   Ensures that the family knows the next steps in the process and whether additional information is needed

---

Program Administrator's Guide to Early Childhood Special Education: Leadership, Development, and Supervision by J.M. Taylor, J. McGowan, and T. Linder

caregivers. Incorporating intervention activities within these routines provides the child with multiple opportunities to practice skills in the situations and environments in which they will be used (Bricker & Cripe, 1992; Prizant & Bailey, 1992). Numerous EI professionals have developed procedures for gathering information about family routines. McWilliam and colleagues outlined a process for completion of a routines-based family interview. McWilliam's training manual, *Family-Centered Intervention Planning: A Routines-Based Approach* (1992), is an excellent resource for EI service providers. McWiliam's process is summarized in the following section.

The routines-based family interview is completed as part of the overall evaluation and assessment process. The interview may be completed by the service coordinator or any member of the intervention planning team, on a home visit or at a location of the family's choosing. The interview may also take place by phone or e-mail to accommodate family schedules. One team member may complete the interview, or another may join in as a recorder. The interview is not meant to be intrusive or time consuming. It may take place over several visits. The family should be told in advance of plans for the interview and arrangements made for a convenient time. Caregivers other than the parent may also be included in the interview.

The interviewer begins by asking the family members what their concerns and priorities are for the child. Next, the family provides specific information about the child's daily routines from awakening to bedtime. The family is asked three key questions about each routine:

- What does the child do during this routine?

- Who is the caregiver and what does the caregiver do during this routine?

- Is the caregiver satisfied with the way the routine is going?

Forms for completing the routines-based family interview may be found in Mc-William's training manual. Programs may also adapt forms for individual use. Figure 5.5 shows opening questions for the routines-based interview.

As the interview proceeds, the interviewer notes patterns for responses that indicate priority areas for the child and family. These are summarized, prioritized, and incorporated into outcomes on the IFSP. See Figure 5.6.

Development of Individualized Family Services Plan Outcomes

The IFSP is designed to enhance the family's capacity to meet the special needs of the infant or toddler with disabilities. IFSP outcomes are written in the words of the family and reflect skills, behaviors, or changes that the family would like to see for the child. Outcomes are typically broad yet observable behaviors. Professionals may guide family members in developing appropriate outcomes, but family members are the primary generators of outcomes. As outcomes are generated, it is often helpful for service providers to provide family members with information about developmental processes. For example, family members might want the child to walk as an outcome. It might be appropriate for team members to help the family identify the smaller steps toward that goal and break the outcome down into more achievable steps. Family members should understand that the intervention process is ongoing and that outcomes may be changed at any time.

Activities, strategies, criteria, and time lines are then developed for each outcome. Activities and strategies are the how of EI curriculum. Activities are short-term

Family _____ Child _____ Date _____

What are your family's main concerns?

What do you want _____ to work on?

What does _____ like?

Who does _____ spend time with during the day?

Are there other people that _____ spends time with?

Where else does _____ spend time (other than at home)?

Include weekends, special activities, other caregivers.

Routine	What do you do during this routine?	What does your child do during this routine?	How satisfied are you with this routine?

Include weekends, special activities, other caregivers.

Program Administrator's Guide to Early Childhood Special Education: Leadership, Development, and Supervision by J.M. Taylor, J. McGowan, and T. Linder
Copyright © 2009 Paul H. Brookes Publishing Co., Inc. All rights reserved.

Figure 5.5. Routines-based family interview opening questions. (From McWilliam, R.A. [1992]. *Family-guided intervention planning: A routines-based approach.* Tucson, AZ: Communication Skill Builders. Adapted by permission.)

skills that the child or family will participate in or learn in order to achieve the outcome. Activities fit in with routines in a natural way and are built around the child's and family's interests and abilities. Activities may also establish new routines that the family would like to add to the child's day. Strategies are the methods that will be used to achieve the skills that lead to the outcomes. Activities and strategies build on strengths and are selected in consideration of family resources, priorities, and concerns. Service providers observe successful strategies that family members already know and use and then build upon them (Cripe & Venn, 1997), assisting the family to expand and enhance these strategies.

Two approaches to routines-based intervention are currently in practice. They may be loosely defined as *embedded* and *naturally occurring*. Using an embedded approach, deficit areas are identified through assessment. Skills from these areas that the child needs to develop are selected. A routines-based interview is conducted to identify activities and interactions that occur during the child's and family's typical day. The family selects preferred routines that are enjoyable and flexible enough to incorporate intervention (Cripe & Venn, 1997). Each selected routine is broken down by parents or professionals into a predictable sequence, and target skills are embedded into these events. A matrix showing embedded skill by daily routine may be developed to identify the routine, targeted skill or skills, and teaching strategies (Cripe & Venn, 1997). The matrix may be used in the home and in other environments, such as the child care center, to ensure consistency.

Table 5.1 shows such a matrix for Joe. Assessment identified Joe's communication skills as an area of need. The intervention team determined that Joe needed to learn to communicate his wants and needs using single words and to follow simple directions during routines. The team outlined Joe's day and selected mealtime as a routine activity to target the use of specific single words, such as "juice" and "cracker," and to follow routine directions, such as "sit down" and "give me your cup." The skills selected were directly related to developmental progression and to the routine. Joe's intervention team will regularly review his skills, adding new targets and strategies as Joe progresses.

With a naturally occurring approach, the child's and family's routines set the course for skill selection. Through the routines-based family interview, the intervention team identifies the routines that the family would like to improve. The team then determines the skills that will help the child participate more successfully in the activity. As with the embedded approach, the family determines which routines are selected. Joe's family, for example, identified dinnertime as a routine in need of improvement. Joe displayed inappropriate behavior during the meal, such as crying and throwing things, and his parents were frustrated because they did not know what he wanted or how to respond to his tantrums. (Breakfast and lunch were not selected at this time as Joe's parents felt harried in the morning and often fed Joe in the car on the way to child care. He ate lunch at child care most days. His child care provider will be interviewed to see if she has concerns with this routine when Joe is in her care.) The team identified several skills that Joe could learn to improve the dinnertime routine, taking into account his developmental status. The team determined that Joe needed to learn to make choices, communicate his wants and needs, and follow instructions. He also needed to develop more independent self-feeding skills, such as drinking from a cup and spoon-feeding. A naturally occurring routine matrix was developed (see Table 5.2). This matrix is developed to put the plan in writing for

Family _____ Child _____ Date _____

Review of concerns. I heard you mention these concerns:

Which are the MOST important things you want to work on with _____?

Outcome 1

Outcome 2

Outcome 3

Outcome 4

Outcome 5

Outcome 6

Figure 5.6. Routines-based family interview summary.

Table 5.1.   Sample matrix for embedded skills by daily routine for Joe

Activity or routine	Skill or outcome	
	Joe will use single words to communicate his wants and needs.	Joe will follow simple directions for the routine.
Mealtimes (breakfast, lunch, snack, dinner)	Strategies for parent or caregiver: • Model single words (e.g., *juice, cracker, cookie, milk, apple*). • Use sign language for these items during modeling. • Prompt Joe to form appropriate sign when requesting item. • After gaining Joe's interest, playfully withhold food items until he indicates his request through sign, gesture, or verbalization (sabotage). • Reinforce all attempts with increased animation if Joe verbalizes. • Repeat back the appropriate pronunciation of the word if Joe verbalizes as you give him the food item. • If you cannot determine which item Joe wants, hold items in front of him and let him indicate his preference.	Strategies for parent or caregiver: • Simplify verbal directions to one- to three-word phrases (e.g., *sit down, come here, get cup, put in trash*). • Use gestures as appropriate. • After Joe responds appropriately to the direction, repeat it back to him with enthusiasm ("You sat down!"). • If Joe does not follow the direction, prompt him to be successful using the least amount of help needed (least to most prompt hierarchy). Always follow through, even if you need to use gentle hand-over-hand assistance.
Playtime	Select targeted words for play items that Joe prefers and use strategies outlined above.	Select targeted directions during play activities that Joe prefers and use strategies outlined above.

family members and other caregivers. The plan is reviewed frequently, and skills and strategies are modified based on family satisfaction and child progress.

Both of these approaches assume that intervention strategies will be carried out primarily by family members and caregivers. Professionals provide the family with coaching on techniques that may be successful. In Joe's case, both approaches provide the family with multiple opportunities each day to develop new skills. Repeated practice, for the child and caregiver, are necessary for learning to occur.

Criteria and time lines assist the family and service providers in determining when an outcome has been met or should be modified. A time line specifies when progress will be reviewed. Formal outcome review must occur at least every 6 months but may be done more frequently as needed. For Joe, criteria and time line may include statements such as the following:

• Criteria: Joe will use at least 10 single words to communicate wants and needs and follow directions during routines.

• Time line: In a 3-month period

Additional sample outcomes and guidelines for outcome development, which may be useful for professional development activities, are found in Table 5.3. The final step in developing the IFSP is determining who will be involved in working with the family on each outcome.

Table 5.2. Sample matrix for naturally occurring skills by daily routine for Joe

Routine	Skills needed for Joe to be more successful	Strategies for parent or caregiver
Dinnertime at home	Make choices so that he will not become so frustrated	Hold two food items in front of Joe just out of reach and let him indicate his preference using a verbalization, gesture, or sign.
Lunch and snack time at child care on weekdays, at home on weekends	Communicate what he wants	• Model single words (e.g., *juice, cracker, cookie, milk, apple*). • Use sign language for these items during modeling. • Prompt Joe to form appropriate sign when requesting item. • After gaining Joe's interest, playfully withhold food items until he indicates his request through sign, gesture, or verbalization (sabotage). • Reinforce all attempts with increased animation if Joe verbalizes. • Repeat back the appropriate pronunciation of the word if Joe verbalizes as you give him the food item.
	Follow instructions	• Simplify verbal directions to one- to three-word phrases (e.g., *sit down, come here, get cup, put in trash*). • Use gestures as appropriate. • After Joe responds appropriately to the direction, repeat it back to him with enthusiasm ("You sat down!"). • If Joe does not follow the direction, prompt him to be successful using the least amount of help needed (least to most prompt hierarchy). Always follow through even if you need to use gentle hand-over-hand assistance.
	Feed self more independently using a spoon and drinking from a cup	• Serve thickened foods that stick to the spoon (e.g., pudding, mashed potatoes) to promote success. • Use the small cup with a cut out and a small amount of preferred thickened liquid. Once Joe reaches for the cup, guide it to his mouth and provide gentle support to his upper lip and lower jaw.

Note. Additional matrices may be developed for other family-selected routines.

A Generalized Model for Service Delivery

The inception of specific guidelines for infants and toddlers has caused changes in philosophy about how service provision should occur and what skills should be taught. Much of the philosophical evolution stems from families themselves, through their involvement in local program and legislative development. EI services delivery models have always centered on the premise that infants and toddlers exist within a family and are dependent on their caregivers. These models have often focused on identifying developmental gaps and deficits and remediating those deficits through direct, hands-on instruction and therapy.

Service delivery models emphasize the need for a team approach in recognition that strengths and deficits in specific skill areas affect other developmental areas.

Table 5.3. Sample routines-based IFSP outcomes

Guidelines for outcome development	Sample outcome #1
Outcome: What I would like to see happen for my child/family The outcome specifies a broad yet observable target behavior determined by the family.	**Outcome: What I would like to see happen for my child/family** Danny will eat on his own so that mealtimes can go faster.
Strategies/Activities: *Activities* may be short-term objectives that the child and family will do to meet the outcome. They should fit in with routines and consider the child's interests and abilities. *Strategies* are the methods or courses of action to be used to achieve the objectives that lead to the outcome.	**Strategies/Activities:** **Activities** Danny will eat snacks or meals using a spoon or by finger feeding, as appropriate. **Strategies** • An adapted chair, spoon, and bowl will be used during mealtime when appropriate. • Preferred foods will be used initially to motivate Danny. • Newer or nonpreferred food will be introduced after some independence has been seen.
Criteria *Criteria* assist the family and service providers in determining when an outcome has been met or should be modified. Criteria are directly linked to activities/strategies and the outcome.	**Criteria** Danny will eat ¼ of his meal by spoon or finger feeding, as appropriate.
Timeline *Timeline* specifies when progress will be reviewed.	**Timeline** By January 2005
Person(s) involved *Person(s) involved* include the service provider, family members, and caregivers, as appropriate, who will implement the activities and strategies.	**Person(s) involved** Danny's parents Tina Talker, speech-language pathologist, 410-313-0000 Fanny Feeder, occupational therapist, may provide consultation as needed.

Sample Outcome #2	Sample Outcome #3
Outcome: What I would like to see happen for my child/family Danny will let his parents know what he wants to eat at meals and to play with or do at other times during the day so that he won't be so frustrated.	**Outcome: What I would like to see happen for my child/family** Danny will stick with things for longer periods of time so that his parents may have time to get other things done.
Strategies/Activities: **Activities** • Danny will make choices of foods, toys, and activities (outside, coloring, videos, and so forth). **Strategies** • Signs, pictures, and photos will be used to augment word approximations. • Choice boards will be designed for use throughout Danny's day.	**Strategies/Activities:** **Activities** • Danny will play with more toys in a variety of ways. • Danny will sit long enough to complete short activities. **Strategies** • Use a floor desk for Danny to play on. • Start with activities that Danny likes and that have a clear completion point, such as puzzles and shape sorters. • Use a timer to indicate to Danny when he can get up or move on to something else.

Sample Outcome #2 (continued)	*Sample Outcome #3* (continued)
Criteria	**Criteria**
Danny will use at least 15 signs, words, or pictures during his day to make choices of toys, activities, or foods.	Danny will sit long enough to complete four different short activities or play with four different toys throughout his day.
Timeline	**Timeline**
By January 2009	By January 2009
Person(s) involved	**Person(s) involved**
Danny's parents	Danny's parents
Tina Talker, speech-language pathologist, 410-313-0000	Tina Talker, speech-language pathologist, 410-313-0000
	Susie Special, EIS, may provide consultation as needed.

Sample Outcome #4	*Sample Outcome #5*
Outcome: What I would like to see happen for my child/family	**Outcome: What I would like to see happen for my child/family**
Danny will behave better when taken to other places.	Danny's parents would like to talk with other families who have children with delays so that they can share information.
Strategies/Activities:	**Strategies/Activities:**
Activities	**Activities:**
• Danny will come when called and stop when asked to stop.	• Mr. and Mrs. Jones will receive information about the Family Support and Resource Center.
• Danny will entertain himself appropriately for short periods of time outside of his home.	• Mr. and Mrs. Jones will receive information about local support groups and activities.
Strategies	
• Danny will be reinforced with preferred items (stamps, stickers, candy) and praise and hugs when he follows the direction given to him. This will first be practiced in his home and then out in the community.	
• Danny will use his choice board to select toys and activities brought on an outing. Toys/activities that he has been taught to use for longer periods of time at home will be placed in the box.	
Criteria	**Criteria:**
Danny will entertain himself appropriately with a variety of toys/activities for at least 30 minutes in a community setting.	Parental satisfaction will serve as criteria.
Timeline	**Timeline**
By January 2009	By next week, the service coordinator will give this information to Mr. and Mrs. Jones.
Person(s) involved	**Person(s) involved**
Danny's parents	Danny's parents
Tina Talker, speech-language pathologist, 410-313-0000	Tina Talker, speech-language pathologist and service coordinator, 410-313-0000
Susie Special, EIS, may provide consultation as needed.	Bea Friendly, Family Support and Resource Center parent coordinator, 410-555-0001

Developed by Howard County Infants and Toddlers Program, Columbia, MD, September 2004.

Thus, professionals from a variety of disciplines, including special education, speech-language pathology, occupational therapy, physical therapy, nursing, social work, and psychology, each representing their own area of expertise, come together to address common goals. Multidisciplinary and interdisciplinary models were popular in the past few decades. Under a multidisciplinary model, team members work independently of each other. They are aware of one another's activities and share ideas and resources, usually through informal communication, with or without family involvement.

With interdisciplinary teams, formal communication opportunities are planned. Typically, family members are involved. Professionals from individual disciplines work separately but come together at scheduled times to share information and modify activities (Rosin et al., 1996).

In these two models, professionals from the different disciplines define their own roles, and often the parent or caregiver is left to attempt to integrate the information provided from a variety of sources. Through feedback from family members and findings from child development research, a new, generalized approach to service delivery has evolved that emphasizes early development as an integrated and interactive process. The generalized model focuses on collaborative partnerships between families and professionals and among professionals themselves. It requires professionals to reexamine their traditional roles and practices and, when necessary, develop new skills that promote mutual respect and partnerships. It also provides families with access to services in as typical a fashion and environment as possible to promote participation of the child and family in the community.

The term *generalized* developed from negative responses to the transdisciplinary model, which was first introduced in the 1980s. Transdisciplinary teams use a systematic process to share roles and cross disciplines (Rosin et al., 1996). Communication, interaction, and cooperation are maximized as team members commit to learning from and teaching one another to implement coordinated services (Bruder & Bologna, 1993; Council for Exceptional Children, 1988; McGonigel & Garland, 1988; Rossetti, 1991; Tuchman, 1996; Woodruff & McGonigel, 1988). Family participation is essential in this model to ensure that the child's and family's changing needs are continually assessed and addressed.

Although EI service providers and families agree that an integrated approach is most effective, many were threatened by aspects of the transdisciplinary philosophy that were misinterpreted. Controversy continues to stem from misinterpretation of terms such as *role exchange* and *role release*. Role exchange is defined as team members' implementing methods and techniques taught to them by those in other disciplines, often working side by side during the learning process. In role release, team members practice the newly learned techniques under the supervision of "discipline experts" (Orelove, Sobsey, & Silberman, 2004; Woodruff & McGonigel, 1988). Appropriate training of all team members in theories, methods, and procedures from a variety of disciplines is key. Transdisciplinary models do *not* promote role replacement (McGonigel, Woodruff, & Roszmann-Millican, 1994). Speech-language pathologists do not provide physical therapy, nor do special educators provide occupational therapy. Colleagues expand their skills under the guidance of other professionals. When one colleague determines that his or her ability to address a child's or family's need has been exhausted, a more highly skilled professional becomes more directly involved. This is a focus of current generalized models. The use of a generalized philosophy or model is not selected based on availability of specific disciplines, cost effectiveness, or administrative convenience. This model provides coordinated, whole-child intervention that eliminates duplication and fragmentation of services and recognizes the family's key role in an effective intervention process (McWilliam & Scott, 2001).

Generalized EI teams develop and thrive through administrative support and leadership. Preservice and continuous professional training opportunities that support this model promote discipline-specific expertise and additional competencies in the following areas:

- Team building, including collaborative problem solving and decision-making strategies

- Colleague-to-colleague consultation, including role expansion, role release, and commitment to teach and learn from one another

- Family support strategies, including coaching and empowerment techniques based on characteristics of adult learners, respect for diversity, and cultural considerations

- Information sharing related to specific disabilities, developmental areas, and intervention strategies

In addition, administrators must recognize the importance of scheduling adequate time for team communication and collaboration, including assessment, intervention program reviews, and colleague-to-colleague joint sessions with families. Flexibility in scheduling may also be necessary, as different teams and different team members may require more or less time for these activities based on experience and skill.

The Primary Service Provider

Many proponents of a generalized model advocate using a primary service provider (McWilliam, 1999). Family members and young children respond more favorably to regular interactions with a primary person than to multiple professionals from specific fields of expertise. Although selection of one primary interventionist may be perceived by some families as a reduction in services, families who receive this type of service delivery model from the beginning support its use (McWilliam & Scott, 2001). The intervention team, including the family, determines the primary service provider based on the family's priorities and the outcomes that have been developed for the child. Optimally, this selection of the primary provider begins during the initial stages of the assessment process. During first contact with a family, the service provider may explain the generalized program philosophy and the central role of the family on the intervention team. Initial family preferences and program options are explored. As the assessment process proceeds, an arena approach is used. Using this transdisciplinary assessment technique, only family members and one assessment facilitator interact with the child. Other members of the intervention team observe and record the child's behavior (McGonigel et al., 1994). Observations are brought together in a collaborative, integrated profile of the child's current skills performance across all developmental areas.

After outcomes have been developed, the intervention team selects the primary service provider. This provider may be from the profession most immediately relevant to the child's or family's need and will deliver the most frequent service. Other professionals provide consultation, training, and support to the primary service provider and the family as needed to achieve the outcomes. The model is flexible and interactive to meet the changing needs of the child and family. The primary service provider is not expected to perform services for which he or she has not been competently trained. The primary service provider may change as the child grows and develops new skills and new areas of need are identified.

In the example presented previously about Joe, the intervention team determined that the EI/special education teacher would be the primary service provider for Joe's family. She possessed the skills needed to coach the family on communication strategies and behavioral support. The speech-language pathologist would consult with the teacher regularly and be available for joint sessions as needed. If Joe's communication skills did not progress as expected, and more direct, specific expertise in communication development was needed, the speech-language pathologist might become the primary provider.

Implementation of a generalized service delivery model requires training for service providers and time for collaboration to ensure that the child's and family's needs are met (Hanson & Bruder, 2001). Many programs focus funding and caseload determination on direct child-contact hours only. Administrators need to recognize that time spent consulting with colleagues is as valuable to positive child and family outcomes as time spent in direct contact.

Home Visiting

Service delivery through home visiting is the cornerstone of family-centered intervention for infant and toddlers with disabilities. Current recommended practices in home visiting have changed the way home visits are conducted. McWilliam (1999) stated, "The child does not learn from home visits—the family does." During home visits, professionals provide family members with the skills and supports needed to carry out the intervention throughout the week. Teaching and supporting caregivers in a home environment requires service providers to be flexible and intuitive. Professionals enter the home with a plan in mind to address the child's outcomes and family's priorities, but it is the family that sets the course for each session. See Figure 5.7 for a sample lesson plan format for home visits.

Effective communication between family members and the home visitor is essential to successful programming. Basic steps in family-centered home visiting are outlined here:

1. Asking the family what has been happening since the last home visit. This allows the service provider to understand not only how intervention has been carried out but also other important events that may have occurred that affect the intervention.

2. Reviewing strategies and techniques discussed at the previous visit. This may involve review of family priorities and IFSP outcomes.

3. Modifying previous strategies or techniques. The home visitor may model new strategies and talk through the demonstration. Talking through the demonstration enables the caregiver to understand why a strategy is selected and how it relates to the child's outcomes.

4. Practicing new strategies with the caregiver, providing encouragement and specific feedback. Redemonstration is provided, if needed.

Lesson Plan for Home Visiting

Child _____ Date _____

Time of visit _____ Length of visit _____ Family member present _____

Activity and IFSP Outcome/Skill	Materials	Comments

Figure 5.7. Lesson plan format for home visiting. Activities are planned with caregivers to meet individualized family service plan (IFSP) outcomes and to incorporate the learning or treatment into the child's daily routine.

5. Examining routines to determine how and when the strategy will be used.

6. Summarizing the session to ensure mutual understanding between the family member and professional.

Respectful home visitors also observe proper etiquette for guests in family homes. Some families may consider home visiting as intrusive, judgmental, and stressful and may prefer that visits not take place in the home (Klass, 2008). If the family is willing to accept home visits, the home visitor should tell the family what to expect during the visits. For instance, is the family member expected to participate actively in the session? How will siblings and other family members be incorporated into the visit? How will the visit progress and how long will it last? Can the visit be conducted in the family's native language? Respectful home visitors will provide families with this information prior to implementation. They may also discuss the format for visits with the family and allow for mutual decision making in the session format. Some families may desire a more formal session, with written information; others may desire a more informal plan. The home visit format should be reviewed frequently to ensure family satisfaction. An open, trusting relationship between family members and home visitors is essential to successful home visiting and child progress.

Klass (2008) outlined strategies for home visiting with "difficult" families, those who think concretely and have difficulty generalizing and those who live in chaotic conditions. Her strategies for working with parents or caregivers who may have intellectual limitations include the following:

• Be concrete and directive.

• Incorporate repetition.

• Use simple explanations.

• Model appropriate parenting behavior.

• Provide repeated opportunities for practice.

• Provide reinforcement.

When families live in unstructured or chaotic environments or situations, service providers may find it helpful to

• Give choices about times for visits, structure of visits, and strategies.

• Be persistent about the importance of parent involvement.

• Stress caring and commitment to the child.

• Model active, pleasurable involvement with the child.

• Provide consistent support and guidance.

Another factor to consider when implementing a home-based service delivery model is flexible scheduling. For instance, it might be important for home visitors to be in the home during routines, which may occur before and/or beyond traditional workday hours. For working families, home visitors might need to see children in their child care settings. Contact with family members may also occur through regular phone contact, e-mail, videotaping, or written correspondence.

Home visitor safety is also an important consideration for administrators and service providers. When traveling in the community and entering homes, service providers should keep these safety considerations in mind:

- Make certain your car is in good working condition.

- Post a sign in your car that identifies your program.

- Call the office before and after a visit that might be unsafe.

- Make a visit with a colleague rather than alone.

- In dangerous neighborhoods, make home visits in the morning.

- Meet families at a community site, such as a library or community center.

- If the family has a phone, call the parents just before the home visit so they can watch for you.

- Carry a cell phone.

- If a situation does not feel right, do not leave your car.

- When you leave the home, have your car keys in hand.

- Always be respectful and professional.

- Be organized with your materials and home visit plan.

- Leave a written schedule of your home visits with your program administrator.

After the home visit is completed, each service provider documents the visit in the child's record. Documentation procedures may vary according to local jurisdiction standards but should include the following:

- Date, time, and duration of the home visit

- Person present for the home visit

- A summary of the child's responses

- A summary of the family member's responses

- A summary of next steps

It is important to document factual, objective information only. Subjective and judgmental statements regarding the child, family members, or the home environment should not be included.

Working with families and children in the natural environment provides for optimal carryover and generalization. It permits the parent–professional relationship to develop to a more informal and personal level. With thoughtful planning, flexible implementation, and frequent monitoring, home visiting can be a highly successful service delivery model.

Individualized Family Service Plan Review

Children's rapid maturation rate during the first few years of life requires that the IFSP be a fluid document. Changes may be made at any time at the request of the family or service coordinator. Part C services end when the child no longer meets eligibility criteria or on the child's 3rd birthday. As the child approaches age 3, outcomes are developed to transition the child from Part C EI services to other programs and services for which the child may be eligible, such as Part B special education or other community programs. Families and professionals work together to ensure a smooth transition for the child and family.

RESOURCES FOR PROGRAM PLANNING AND IMPLEMENTATION

A variety of resources are available to teams as they design routines-based intervention plans. Most consist of activities and strategies for embedding skills into typical family routines. Popular resources, some of which contain reproducible handouts that can be shared with family members and caregivers, include the following:

- *Best Beginnings* (Hussey-Gardner, 1999)
- *The Carolina Curriculum for Infants and Toddlers with Special Needs* (Johnson-Martin, Attermeier, & Hacker, 2004)
- *HELP. . . at Home* (Park, 1989)
- *Helping Babies Learn: Developmental Profiles and Activities for Infants and Toddlers* (Furuno, 1993)

Several texts and videos are available that support routine and activity-based strategies. They provide guidance to program administrators as well as service providers and include forms and formats for developing intervention plans. Selected resources include

- *An Activity-Based Approach to Early Intervention* (Pretti-Frontczak & Bricker, 2004)
- *Family-Guided Activity-Based Intervention for Infants and Toddlers* (video) (Bricker, 1995)
- *Family-Centered Intervention Planning: A Routines-Based Approach* (McWilliam, 1992)
- *Rethinking Pull-Out Services in Early Intervention: A Professional Resource* (McWilliam, 1996)

CONCLUSIONS

EI programs provide services to infants and toddlers with delays or disabilities and offer support for their families. Guidance in program planning and implementation is found in Part C of IDEA; through publications, preservice and in-service training; and through colleague-to-colleague networking. The most valuable lessons professionals can learn, however, come from the day-to-day interactions with infants and toddlers and their caregivers. The IFSP development process emphasizes that family members are the first and most important teachers the child will ever have. Providing families with the information and support they need to help their child grow in everyday situations and routines will result in positive outcomes for all.

REFERENCES

Begun, A.L. (1996). Family systems and family-centered care. In P. Rosin, A.D. Whitehead, L.I. Tuchman, G.S. Jesien, A.L. Begun, & L. Irwin, *Partnerships in family-centered care* (pp. 37–63). Baltimore: Paul H. Brookes Publishing Co.

Bricker, D. (1995). *Family-guided activity-based intervention for infants and toddlers* [video]. Baltimore: Paul H. Brookes Publishing Co.

Bricker, D., & Cripe, J. (1992). *An activity-based approach to early intervention.* Baltimore: Paul H. Brookes Publishing Co.

Bricker, D., & Squires, J. (with Mounts, L., Potter, L., Nickel, R., Twombly, E., & Farrell, J.). (1999). *Ages & Stages Questionnaires® (ASQ): A parent-completed, child-monitoring system* (2nd ed.). Baltimore: Paul H. Brookes Publishing Co.

Bruder, M.B., & Bologna, T. (1993). Collaboration and service coordination for effective early intervention. In W. Brown, S.K. Thurman, & L.F. Pearl (Eds.), *Family-centered early intervention with infants and toddlers: Innovative cross-disciplinary approaches* (pp. 103–127). Baltimore: Paul H. Brookes Publishing Co.

Bukatko, D., & Daehler, M.W. (2004). *Child development: A thematic approach.* Boston: Houghton Mifflin.

Buysse, V., Wesley, P., & Skinner, D. (1999). Community development approach for early intervention. *Topics in early childhood special education, 19*(4), 236–243.

Council for Exceptional Children. (1988). *Early intervention for infants and toddlers: A team effort.* Reston, VA: Author. (ERIC Digest No. 461)

Cripe, J.W., & Venn, M.L. (1997). Family-guided routines for early intervention services. *Young Exceptional Children, 1*(1), 18–26.

Education of the Handicapped Act Amendments of 1986, PL 99-457, 20 U.S.C. §§ 1400 *et seq.*

Furuno, S. (Ed.). (1993). *Helping babies learn: Developmental profiles and activities for infants and toddlers.* San Antonio, TX: Communication Skills Builders.

Gallagher, P.A., Fialka, J., Rhodes, C., & Arceneaux, C. (2002). Working with families: Rethinking denial. *Young Exceptional Children, 5*(2), 11–17.

Hanson, M.J., & Bruder, M.B. (2001). Early intervention: Promises to keep. *Infants and Young Children, 13*(3), 47–58.

Howard County Maryland Infants and Toddlers Program. (2004, September). *Guidelines and resource handbook.* Columbia, MD: Author.

Hussey-Gardner, B. (1999). *Best beginnings: Helping parents make a difference.* Palo Alto, CA: VORT Corporation.

Individuals with Disabilities Education Improvement Act (IDEA) of 2004, PL 108-446, 20 U.S.C. §§ 1400 *et seq.*

Johnson-Martin, N.M., Attermeier, S.M., & Hacker, B.J. (2004). *The Carolina Curriculum for Infants and Toddlers with Special Needs* (3rd ed). Baltimore: Paul H. Brookes Publishing Co.

Klass, C.S. (2008). *Home visiting: Promoting healthy parent and child development* (3rd ed.). Baltimore: Paul H. Brookes Publishing Co.

Kubler-Ross, E. (1969). *On death and dying.* New York: McMillan.

McGonigel, M., & Garland, C. (1988). The individualized family service plan and the early intervention team: Team and family issues and recommended practices. *Infants and Young Children, 1*(1), 10–21.

McGonigel, M.J., Woodruff, G., & Roszmann-Millican, M. (1994). The transdisciplinary team: A model for family-centered early intervention. In L.J. Johnson, R.J. Gallagher, & M.J. LaMontague (Eds.), *Meeting early intervention challenges: Issues birth to three* (pp. 95–130). Baltimore: Paul H. Brookes Publishing Co.

McWilliam, R.A. (1992). *Family-centered intervention planning: A routines-based approach.* San Antonio, TX: Communication Skill Builders.

McWilliam, R.A. (1996). *Rethinking pull-out services in early intervention: A professional resource.* Baltimore: Paul H. Brookes Publishing Co.

McWilliam, R.A. (1999). It's only natural...to have early intervention in the environments where it's needed. In S. Sandall & M. Ostrosky (Eds.), *Natural environments and inclusion* (Young Exceptional Children Monograph Series No. 2). Denver, CO: Council for Exceptional Children, The Division for Early Childhood.

McWilliam, R.A., & Scott, S. (2001). A support approach to early intervention: A three-part framework. *Infants and Young Children, 13*(4), 55–65.

Miller, N.B. (1994). *Nobody's perfect: Living and growing with children who have special needs.* Baltimore: Paul H. Brookes Publishing Co.

Orelove, F.P., Sobsey, D., & Silberman, R.K. (2004). *Educating children with multiple disabilities: A collaborative approach* (4th ed.). Baltimore: Paul H. Brookes Publishing Co.

Park, S. (1989). *HELP...at home.* Palo Alto, CA: VORT Corporation.

Pilkington, K.O., & Malinowski, M. (2002). The natural environment II: Uncovering deeper responsibilities within relationship-based services. *Infants and Young Children, 15*(2), 78–84.

Pretti-Frontczak, K., & Bricker, D. (2004). *An activity-based approach to early intervention* (3rd ed.). Baltimore: Paul H. Brookes Publishing Co.

Prizant, B., & Bailey, D. (1992). Facilitating the acquisition and use of communication skills. In D.B. Bailey & M. Wolery (Eds.), *Teaching infants and preschoolers with disabilities* (2nd ed., pp. 299–362). New York: Charles E. Merrill.

Rapport, M.J.K., McWilliam, R.A., & Smith, B.J. (2004). Practices across disciplines in early intervention: The research base. *Infants and Young Children, 17*(1), 32–44.

Rosen, L. (1955). Selected aspects in the development of the mother's understanding of her mentally retarded child. *American Journal of Mental Deficiency, 59,* 522–528.

Rosin, P. (1996). The diverse American family. In P. Rosin, A.D. Whitehead, L.I. Tuchman, G.S. Jesien, A.L. Begun, & L. Irwin (Eds.), *Partnerships in family-centered care* (pp. 3–28). Baltimore: Paul H. Brookes Publishing Co.

Rosin, P., Whitehead, A.D., Tuchman, L.I., Jesien, G.S., Begun, A.L., & Irwin, L. (1996). *Partnerships in family-centered care.* Baltimore: Paul H. Brookes Publishing Co.

Rossetti, L.M. (1991). Models for infant-toddler assessment. In L.M. Rossetti (Ed.), *Infant-toddler assessment* (pp. 55–86). San Diego: College-Hill Press.

Sandall, S., Hemmeter, M.L., Smith, B., & McLean, M. (2005). *DEC recommended practices in early intervention/early childhood special education* (2nd ed.). Longmont, CO: Sopris West.

Tuchman, L.I. (1996). The team and models of teaming. In P. Rosin, A.D. Whitehead, L.I. Tuchman, G.S. Jesien, A.L. Begun, & L. Irwin (Eds.), *Partnerships in family-centered care* (pp. 119–143). Baltimore: Paul H. Brookes Publishing Co.

U.S. Census Bureau. (2001). *Statistical Abstract of the United States: 2001.* Retrieved July 18, 2008, from http://www.census.gov/prod/2001pubs0statab/sec01.pdf

Woodruff, G., & McGonigel, M. (1988). Early intervention team approaches: The transdisciplinary model. In J.B. Jordan, J.J. Gallagher, P.L. Hutinger, & M.B. Karnes (Eds.), *Early childhood special education: Birth to three* (pp. 163–181). Reston, VA: Council for Exceptional Children.

Program Planning for Preschoolers

Amy Aloi

A child miseducated is a child lost.
John F. Kennedy

What If?   As Jimmy's parents, child care teachers, and the local Child Find team sat in an individualized education program (IEP) meeting discussing his current placement, it was apparent that Jimmy was becoming a child lost. A referral to a special education team was initiated by the child care center that Jimmy attends due to concerns about Jimmy's language skills, aggressive behavior toward other children, and social skills. At age 5, Jimmy does not sit for circle time, throws frequent tantrums, and often refuses to do what the teachers ask. He has been asked to leave three other child care centers in the past year. His parents are worried that he will not be ready for kindergarten next year.

As part of the evaluation process, members of the Child Find team observed Jimmy in his classroom environment. It is a large, open space divided into learning areas, with 10–12 children and 2 adults in each area. On the day of the observation, while the children in Jimmy's area were having circle time, an adjacent group was engaged in free play. There were many distractions (e.g., telephones, intercoms, children's voices) and a lot of visual stimulation. Jimmy sat on the outskirts of the circle and was observed lying down, rolling around the floor, and kicking at other children. He also began pulling items off a nearby shelf when the teacher was not looking. He did not appear to be paying attention to what was going on during circle time.

When it was time for free play, Jimmy played with cars in the proximity of two other boys. At one point, Jimmy crashed his car into another child's. The child told him to stop and then told the teacher what had happened. Jimmy was reprimanded and asked to move away from the other boys because he "couldn't get along." He spent the rest of free time playing alone.

Clearly, many things are wrong about Jimmy's situation. Unfortunately, it is not uncommon; many other young children find themselves in similar circumstances. In a society in which many parents work outside the home, child care centers provide an invaluable service to families who need safe, stimulating environments for their children. However, there are ways to make child care centers and preschools more appropriate for children like Jimmy.

CHAPTER OVERVIEW

This chapter will discuss federal regulations related to services for preschoolers with and without disabilities, various community settings available, and some of the most well-known curricula and instructional approaches. Details about the importance of adapting curricular materials for children with disabilities, environmental considerations when setting up a preschool classroom, and the value of providing a literacy-rich environment will also be examined.

CHAPTER OBJECTIVES

After reviewing this chapter, the reader will

- Know legislative requirements pertaining to program planning for preschoolers

- Be familiar with the type of community settings and programs available for preschool-age children

- Understand some of the more well-known curriculum models used: Montessori, High/Scope, Reggio Emilia, theme-based models, and *The Creative Curriculum*

- Understand how to adapt materials for children with special needs

- Know ways to incorporate early literacy into the preschool classroom

LEGISLATIVE REQUIREMENTS

According to *The State of Preschool: 2004 State Preschool Yearbook* (as cited in "Survey," n.d.), 38 states currently fund one or more state prekindergarten initiatives. That leaves 12 states with no state-funded prekindergarten programs. Only two states, Georgia and Oklahoma, offer state-funded preschools that are open to all families. Recommendations from the National Institute for Early Childhood Education Research include increasing funding to improve access to and enhance the quality of prekindergarten programs, as well as having the federal government match state government spending on programs meeting certain standards (National Association for the Education of Young Children, 2004).

For children with disabilities, federal funds are available through Part B of the Individuals with Disabilities Education Act Amendments (IDEA) of 1997 (PL 105-17; §§ 611 and 619) beginning at a child's 3rd birthday and continuing through age 18 or older at the discretion of the state. The 1997 reauthorization of IDEA specified that intervention programs be provided in the child's most "natural environment" possible. For many preschoolers, this means regular community preschools or child care settings; in other words, the least restrictive environment (LRE). All possible opportunities should be pursued to place children with disabilities in inclusive settings with their peers who are typically developing. *Inclusion* refers to serving children with disabilities in the same settings designed for children without disabilities, that is, in the school and classroom they would attend if they did not have disabilities. Some public school systems are finding this difficult because there may not be an existing preschool program for children who are typically developing in which to place a child with a disability. These school systems must then pursue community programs that will enroll children with disabilities. In school systems that do have existing preschool programs for children who are typically developing, administrators face the task of ensuring that adequate space is available for including additional children, hiring new staff to accommodate them, and establishing new policies.

COMMUNITY SETTINGS

Preschool programs are offered by a variety of agencies in numerous settings. Head Start, for example, is a federally funded program but can be offered through a public school system, a social services department, or a private organization. Some programs are run by nonprofit organizations, such as churches and United Way agencies. Others are provided by employers or are privately owned or franchise chains. The quality of these programs varies significantly, although most must conform to minimum state and local licensing requirements.

Including children with disabilities in these community programs presents a number of challenges for all involved. First, simply being physically present in a class of preschoolers who are typically developing does not mean that a child is being fully included. To be fully included and to participate in the program to the fullest extent possible, a child with a disability may require specialized supports and curriculum modifications. Supports may include services from such additional staff members as speech-language pathologists, occupational therapists, or physical therapists. Additional supports can be costly and present budget concerns.

A second challenge when including preschoolers with disabilities in typical settings is the lack of training that most child care providers have received. Children with disabilities may need adults' help with facilitating social interactions with peers, or they may need behavioral supports. It is critical that staff members be trained to deal with the unique challenges of the children with whom they will be working.

Third, a center's policies may need to be changed or reworded to avoid placing limits on the participation of a child with a disability. For example, if there is a policy that children are not allowed to bring food from home, this could prevent a child with a severe food allergy from participating in snack time. In such a case, the child should be allowed to bring food from home so that he or she can enjoy snack time with the rest of the children. Perhaps having the child sit at the end of the table or away from foods that cause an allergic reaction would be a necessary modification, but it would enable him or her to participate in the regular routines of the class.

In addition to inclusion in community programs, children with disabilities may receive special education services in several other settings:

- A self-contained special education preschool, often seen in public school systems, is one way to educate preschoolers with disabilities. The class composition in such preschools is made up exclusively of children with special needs. These children receive direct instruction from a special educator; however, there may be little opportunity for interaction with peers who are typically developing.

- A special education preschool that includes both children with and without disabilities—for example, Head Start—offers the chance for peers to act as role models for children with special needs and appears to benefit both groups of children. For children with disabilities, the positive effects of peer models are seen in increased social interactions and more constructive behaviors. "Researchers have found that the behavior of children with disabilities appears to be positively affected by participation in activities and classrooms with typically developing children" (Guralnick, Connor, Hammond, Gottman, & Kinnish, 1996). For children who are typically developing, participating in an inclusive setting increases their knowledge about and positively influences their attitude toward individuals with disabilities.

- A combination of a half-day special education program and a traditional community preschool enables children with disabilities to benefit from individualized instruction and the positive influences of peers who are typically developing. In this type of model, as well as in a full-time community program, collaboration is the key to success. Special education staff members provide consultation to the preschool staff on how to modify the environment to best meet children's needs; they also monitor children's progress.

No single setting is better in meeting the needs of all children. A child's unique needs, disability, strengths, and weaknesses, as well as the availability of programs, are all factors in the child's educational placement. Regardless of the setting, a high-quality early childhood program should adhere to developmentally appropriate practices (DAP), as described by the National Association for the Education of Young Children (Bredekamp, 1987). DAP is not a curriculum model; rather, it is a set of guidelines to help practitioners and policy makers distinguish between appropriate and inappropriate teaching techniques to use with young children.

WELL-KNOWN CURRICULUM MODELS

Curriculum is

An organized framework that delineates the content children are to learn, the processes through which children achieve the identified curricular goals, what teachers do to help children achieve these goals and the context in which teaching and learning occur. (Bredekamp, Knuth, Kunesh, & Shulman, 1992, p. 4)

In essence, curriculum is *what* you teach. The term *curriculum model* refers to a structure that combines theory with practice, or *how* you teach. Developmentally appropriate curricula for preschoolers should focus on the whole child rather than on only one aspect of learning. They should be fluid, not fixed. In other words, they need to be adaptable to the changing child. Developmentally appropriate curricula emphasize development in all areas and integrate learning into all parts of the day.

Many curricula are in use today, with varying degrees of success. There are many curricula in a box, or kits designed to be all that is needed to run a successful preschool program. Kits come complete with materials, manuals, and scripts and can be extremely costly. Unfortunately, these kits may not provide the best materials, strategies, or assessment tools. A high-quality preschool program requires a curriculum model based on research that shows it to be effective. The following curriculum models, all of which have been validated through research, are some of the most well known in use today. The following descriptions of these programs include their benefits and drawbacks, especially in relation to the inclusion of children with disabilities (see Table 6.1).

Montessori

The Montessori model is based on the work of Italian pediatrician and psychologist Maria Montessori (Chattin-McNichols, 1991). Established in 1907, this model was originally designed for children living in poverty. It encourages independence and is very child directed. The teachers, or guides, in a Montessori program take their lead

Table 6.1. Benefits and drawbacks of select curriculum models

Curriculum model	Benefits	Drawbacks
Montessori	Belief in sensory learning Highly organized environment Materials carefully sequenced and ordered	Not widely used with children with disabilities Materials designed to be used in only one way and designed to prevent errors Not all Montessori schools have adequately trained teachers Not much opportunity for pretend play Majority of time spent in independent activities
High/Scope	Encourages creative exploration Emphasizes active learning Emphasizes socialization Establishes consistent routine, including plan-do-review sequence	Teachers may be unsure of their roles May not be enough teacher-directed activities for some learners Less structured environment
Reggio Emilia	Advocates that children learn by doing Based on child interest Encourages cooperation and collaboration among children and adults Places importance on relationships Encourages long-term projects	Complex approach Less exposure to it in the United States May be difficult for teachers to trust child to make decisions about what to investigate
Theme based	Integrates all areas of learning Helps children connect learning with things in the environment	Preplanned activities or lessons on topics selected by teacher may overlook child's interests
The Creative Curriculum	Advocates that children learn by doing Views environment as playing important role in learning Can integrate all areas of learning Includes assessment tool	Can be costly Must be followed correctly and embraced by all adults

from the children. Each child decides if he or she wants to do an activity or if it is something the child does not feel quite ready for. The curriculum focuses on five areas:

- Practical life: Self-help skills and independence

- Sensory awareness: The use of all five senses to learn

- Language arts: Letters, language, and writing

- Mathematics and geometry: Learning about numbers through manipulatives

- Culture: Geography, animals, and history

Montessori classrooms are made up of mixed-age groups so that older children can act as instructors for the younger ones. The environment is carefully prepared and ordered, and the materials are self-correcting, meaning that they can only be used in one way and are therefore designed to prevent errors and promote mastery through repetition. Teachers are carefully trained in the Montessori philosophy and methodology. True Montessori schools must be accredited through Association Montessori Internationale or the American Montessori Society (Chattin-McNichols, 1991).

High/Scope

High/Scope (Hohmann & Weikart, 2002) is an approach to teaching that supports children's active involvement with people, materials, and events. It is based on the belief that young children need to be actively involved in learning. Children are encouraged to make their own choices about materials and activities, with the adults playing a supportive role. The High/Scope approach emerged as a result of work by David Weikart on The Perry Preschool Project in the 1960s. The Perry Preschool Project, initiated in 1962, was a longitudinal study that demonstrated that early education could prevent future school failure.

The High/Scope Curriculum is built around 58 key developmental indicators (formerly key experiences) in five curriculum content areas:

- Approaches to learning

- Language, literacy, and communication

- Social and emotional development

- Physical development, health, and well-being

- Arts and sciences (math, science and technology, social studies, arts)

Another central element of the High/Scope approach is the plan–do–review process, which is included in the structure of the daily routine. Children are encouraged to plan what they are going to do during work time, how and where they are going to do it, and with which materials they are going to interact. They carry out their plan, then review with the class what they actually did.

Reggio Emilia

The Reggio Emilia approach, developed in Northern Italy, is based on the theory that children learn by doing and learn best when they are interested in the topic (Edwards et al., 1993). The Reggio Emilia curriculum is emergent, or one that builds on children's interests. It is a unique approach in many ways: First, teachers and children work together to plan and carry out long-term projects that may also include parent and even community involvement. Second, the classroom environment is considered an important and essential component of the learning process and is often designed to be homelike and beautiful. Third, the teacher's role is that of a learner alongside the child. Teachers purposely allow children to make mistakes and to start projects with no real purpose, with the intention of helping children learn from their mistakes. Teachers use documentation, similar to portfolios, as a tool in the learning process.

Theme-Based Models

A theme-based approach focuses on topics found in events, culture, and the shared environment. Typical preschool themes are holidays, seasons, weather, transportation, and the letters of the alphabet, such as The Letter People program (Abrams & Company, Waterbury, CT). In this program, each week a new letter is introduced and becomes the theme or topic for that week.

Themes provide a way to integrate the curriculum as well as unify topics so that they make sense to children. Thematic units can be planned around children's special interests and expanded to include a variety of learning activities. For example, if a group of children are attracted to the television show *Bob The Builder,* teachers might plan a construction theme. A workbench could be set up with child-friendly tools in the dramatic play area, wood pieces and sandpaper could be added to the block area, and golf tees and toy hammers could be used with playdough or clay. Planning with other team members allows for input from therapists, teachers, and other staff who see the children on a regular basis. Many areas of a child's development can be addressed through team planning and integrated into daily routines.

Toni Linder has taken the theme-based approach one step further in her curriculum called *Read, Play, and Learn!®* (Linder, 1999). This transdisciplinary play-based approach is literature based, with play center activities related to storybook modules. Each module features a different, high-quality children's story along with themed activities. Activities are divided into sensorimotor, functional, and symbolic levels to provide for children's differing needs. The curriculum includes 16 different modules, each containing a storybook; planning sheets; a list of vocabulary words; a materials list; a description of how to include the theme in every area or center in the classroom; suggestions for parent involvement; and an additional list of resources, books, and activities.

The Creative Curriculum

The Creative Curriculum (Dodge, Colker, & Heroman, 2002) is widely used by Head Start, child care, preschool, prekindergarten, and kindergarten programs. It claims to be one of the few curriculum and assessment systems that is inclusive of all children. *The Creative Curriculum* is based on research on how children learn. It provides thorough guidance for teachers, rather than a rigid script, and helps teachers understand how to work with children of varying abilities. *The Creative Curriculum* also includes a parent component and provides guides and resources to help staff build relationships with families. The 10 indoor interest areas recommended in the curriculum are

- Blocks
- Dramatic play
- Toys and games
- Art
- Library
- Discovery
- Sand and water
- Music and movement
- Cooking
- Computers

COMPONENTS OF A HIGH-QUALITY CURRICULUM

What do high-quality curriculum models have in common? Regardless of the model chosen for a preschool program, it must contain the following components.

Age Appropriateness

Teachers who are knowledgeable in the developmental sequence of children who are typically developing are usually able to plan appropriate activities that are meaningful and that promote learning. The fact that children learn best through play and in an environment that allows them time and opportunity to explore materials is an important consideration for all preschoolers, however, regardless of ability.

Individual Appropriateness

Although there are predictable patterns of development in young children, many variations exist as well. This is especially true for children with disabilities. Therefore, it is important for teachers to get to know each child as an individual. This can be accomplished using multiple sources of information, including parent reports, observations, curriculum-based assessments, screenings, and work samples.

Active Learning

Children need to be active rather than passive learners. In other words, they learn best when they are actively involved with materials. Children will understand more about seashells if they are allowed to explore them in the sand table, sort and count them in the math center, make collages with them in the art area, and look at them through magnifying glasses in the science center than if they merely hear the teacher read a story about them. Active learning also means that children learn about the things they are interested in, not what adults think they should be interested in or what the curriculum dictates.

Integrated Activities

Learning should take place during all aspects of the day, as well as within the daily routine. For example, snack time can be a time to work on language skills, math skills ("How many goldfish crackers do you want?" "Who has more?"), nutrition, following directions, socialization, self-help skills, and socialization.

Balance Between Teacher-Directed and Child-Directed Activities

The curriculum needs to include both teacher-led instruction and child-initiated activities. Children can express their interest in something they want to learn about; however, it takes a skilled teacher to establish existing skills and determine the next step. "The curriculum must include bridges that take the child from the known to the unknown. Many of these bridges are teacher planned experiences and activities that increase the child's skills or put previous knowledge into a new context" (Peck, Odom, & Bricker, 1993).

A High Value on Children's Play

Play is the way in which children learn. It is child initiated; adults observe the play and act as facilitators. Play must have a central role in any curriculum, allowing children opportunities to explore, experiment, and manipulate their environment. "Play is not something children do until they are ready to learn, play is what children do that readies them to learn" (Miller, 1996). Play can also be used to assess children's skills and abilities and can become the foundation for a preschool program. Linder's (2008) Transdisciplinary Play-Based Assessment enables observers to determine a child's behavior, learning style, and interests by watching the child play and interact with others. Because this assessment occurs under the most natural circumstance for the child—play—the child stays motivated and the observer is able to gather an accurate picture of the child across all domains.

An Environment Conducive to Learning

The classroom environment includes both the physical and instructional environments. The physical environment refers to the layout, size, and location of the classroom; the placement of furniture; and the equipment available. These can all have an influence on a child's learning. Careful planning of the physical environment helps reduce negative behaviors. For instance, by making sure that there are no wide-open spaces, the teacher reduces the likelihood that children will run through the room. Providing visual boundaries and cues helps children be less impulsive and more apt to follow rules and routines (see Photo 1 [door stop sign] and Photo 2 [footprints]).

The instructional environment includes the daily routine, schedule of activities, materials available, and the manner in which directions are given and transitions are handled. Organization and consistency are the keys to a successful instructional environment. A predictable, reliable schedule helps children feel comfortable and secure, making it more likely that they will follow the classroom rules and routines. The following are some tips to consider when arranging a preschool classroom.

The Physical Environment

For an optimal physical environment, keep these ideas in mind:

- Separate areas for quiet and noisy play. Quiet areas may include a reading corner, computer station, puzzles, and writing/ABCs. Noisy areas may include blocks, dramatic play, sensory exploration, and art.

- Centers or areas should be well defined with carpeting, furniture, or tape on the floor to create a visual boundary.

- Play areas can be closed to children's use by covering shelves with a blanket or piece of material.

- Restrict the number of children in the areas by setting up a system in which a designated amount of spots are established for children's pictures or names (names can be affixed using a material such as Velcro); once those spots are taken, the area is full (see Photo 3 [choice board]). A child may also have a personal choice board tailored to his or her own unique needs (see Photo 4 [personal choice board]).

- Try to keep visual distractions to a minimum around the large-group area or circle. Provide designated spots for children to sit, using carpet squares, tape on the floor, or even chairs (see Photo 5 [symbols]).

Photo 1. Door stop sign.

Photo 2. Footprints.

Photo 3. Choice board.

Photo 4. Personal choice board.

Photo 5. Symbols.

The Instructional Environment

- Have a consistent, predictable routine (see Figure 6.1).

- Post the schedule at children's eye level, using pictures to represent each time of the day.

- Give warnings before transitions occur (e.g., "In 3 minutes, the cleanup song will come on").

- Alternate active and quiet activities.

- Use props or manipulatives whenever possible during large-group times.

- Rotate toys to prevent boredom. Keep them in a closet when they are not being used, or trade with fellow teachers to provide variety.

- Ask an instructional assistant to monitor disruptive behaviors during large-group times.

- Post classroom rules, using picture symbols, and refer to them often.

- Be concrete and specific when communicating with children. Use gestures, modeling, and visuals; specifically engage their attention before demonstrating or explaining; break directions down into small, sequential steps.

- Use a timer or visual cues to indicate to a child when it is his turn. A bell can be the signal to share a toy, or a picture can be used to help a child remember to wait or ask for a turn.

(continued)

(continued)

- Provide social supports for children. Use peer buddies, practice specific skills through natural activities with one peer, and use social stories pertaining to specific situations. By taking photos of children engaged in appropriate behaviors, you can make stories based on what you want the child to do.

- Provide many opportunities for children to make choices, such as picking a daily job (see Photo 6 [classroom helpers]) or choosing a song (see Photo 7 [song choices]).

- Use some type of review strategy that helps children share their day in the classroom with their parents, such as recall books that are filled out and taken home daily (see Photo 8 [recall book]).

Curriculum Modifications for Jimmy

In Jimmy's case, the special education personnel and the child care center staff began a collaborative relationship to help him succeed in his environment. First, members of the team, which included Jimmy's parents, an early childhood special educator, a speech-language pathologist, and Jimmy's current preschool teacher, met to review assessments administered as part of the evaluation process. Although Jimmy's cognitive skills were age appropriate, he was having trouble in some other areas. Behavior and attention were a concern, as well as social skills. An IEP was written with input from each team member. Second, some environmental modifications were made:

- Carpet squares were used to designate each child's, including Jimmy's, own space during circle time.

- To indicate that playtime was over, the toy shelves were covered with cloth and a sign that said *Closed* was put over them.

- The teacher made sure to seat Jimmy in the front at circle time to minimize distractions.

- Screens and shelves were placed around the circle-time area to muffle sound and block some visual distractions.

Third, a visiting, or itinerant, early childhood special education teacher began providing services through regular visits to the child care center. During these visits, the itinerant teacher observed and participated with the children in the program. She worked with the staff to best enhance Jimmy's participation in the environment and made suggestions about the environment and ways to embed IEP goals in the typical routine. This model of collaboration among early childhood educators, early childhood special educators, and related service providers (speech-language pathologists, occupational therapists, physical therapists, vision or behavioral specialists) is becoming more and more prevalent as the inclusion of young children with disabilities in community settings becomes more widespread (Wolery, 1993).

Another result of the itinerant teacher's collaboration with Jimmy's preschool staff was the awareness of the need for social intervention. Jimmy clearly wanted to interact with his peers, but he did not know how. It also became apparent from many observations that other children had begun to reject Jimmy as a playmate. As a result, Jimmy was becoming increasingly aggressive and acting inappropriately toward his

Preschool Lesson Plan

Date: _____

Table time 8:25–8:50	Objective: Objective:
Opening 8:50–9:10	Opening routine: Story:
Small groups 8:25–8:50	Objective: Objective:
Worktime 9:30–10:15	
Recall 10:15–10:20	
Snack/oral motor 10:20–10:40	
Gross motor 10:40–10:55	
Dismissal 10:55–11:00	

Figure 6.1. Sample preschool lesson plan.

Photo 6. Helpers.

Photo 7. Song choices.

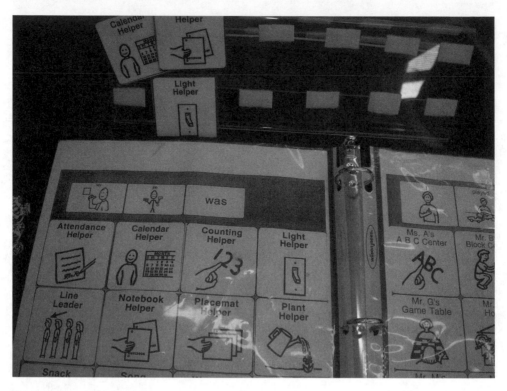

Photo 8.   Recall book.

peers. Research has shown that children with disabilities are at a relatively higher risk for peer rejection than children who are typically developing (Odom, Zercher, Li, Marquart, & Sandall, 1998). To implement some social intervention, the child care staff had to rethink their roles during children's free play time. Instead of using this time for cleaning up, doing paperwork, or making phone calls, staff members began providing suggestions for play, helping children delineate roles, and verbally cuing Jimmy to interact with the other children. Visual reminders for staff were posted throughout the room to help them decide which of Jimmy's goals to work on (see Photo 9 [goal posters]). Jimmy's family was encouraged to invite a friend from school over for play dates to encourage socialization in a one-to-one setting.

ADAPTATION OF MATERIALS

Regardless of the setting or model used, some adaptations may be necessary for the child with special needs. In addition to environmental and instructional modifications, modifications to materials and activities may be required for the child's specific needs. Developing adaptations and accommodations is an ongoing process that involves assessing the child's abilities and environment on a regular basis. A child's IEP goals and objectives can be embedded in many different ways. For example, the learning objectives within an activity might be individualized. If children are working with colored blocks and are being encouraged to sort them by color, one child may be working on an IEP goal of matching colors; another might be working on an

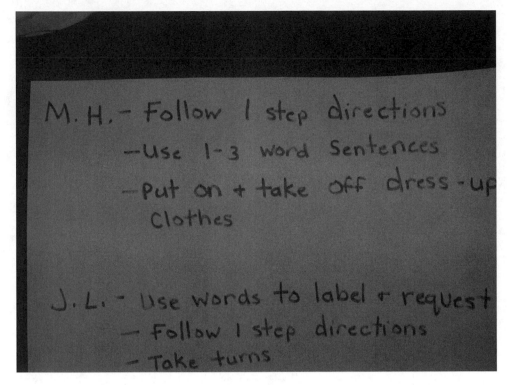

M. H. - Follow 1 step directions
 - Use 1-3 word Sentences
 - Put on + take off dress-up
   Clothes

J. L. - Use words to label + request
 - Follow 1 step directions
 - Take turns

Photo 9. Goal posters.

IEP goal of grasping and releasing. It may also be necessary to modify instructional materials for some children. A child with motor delays can participate in art activities using adapted scissors, crayons attached to hand splints with Velcro, or oversized, chunky paintbrushes. When planning activities, it is important for the teacher to note how lessons will be individualized for each child, including objectives and any adapted materials or modifications that may need to be put in place (see Figure 6.2).

The arrangement of the environment can also provide opportunities for staff members to work on a child's IEP goals. Skills lists can be posted in each area of the classroom with the child's initials and some objectives on which to focus in that particular area during various times of the day. These posters serve as reminders and also help make all staff members accountable for attending to a child's objectives (see Photo 10). In addition to skills posters, IEP boxes can be put together for individual children. These can simply be shoeboxes, labeled with the child's name, that contain materials needed to work on specific objectives. For example, a child with the goal of stringing beads can have a box containing strings and beads. The box should also contain data sheets so that staff members working with that child can record progress (see Figure 6.3). These boxes are not intended to take the place of naturalistic learning. Bead stringing, for instance, can be targeted in different ways and may include the entire class. Rather, these boxes provide a simple way for all staff members to work with a child with special needs on the appropriate goals and allow them to collect data. Box activities can also be used as fillers when there is extra time in the schedule. Peers can play along with the students, modeling the correct use of the materials.

Theme: Grocery Store	Book: Feast for 10	
Week of:	**Monday**	**Tuesday**
Arrival: Children hang up coats and back packs then find their names at table.	S.J. Recognize name in print A.L.: Remove coat independently B.D.: Follow routine directions	
Table work: Children all sit at table for a fine motor activity.	Objective: Puzzles C.R. and J.T.: Requesting; S.J. and L.T.: Assemble 6-piece puzzle	Objective:
Movement: Children gather at circle for a movement activity.	Objective: "Sammy" by Hap Palmer A.L. and C.R.: Imitate motor actions; B.D.: Participate in group activities	Objective:
Opening: Children sit on carpet squares and participate in opening	Calendar; Weather; Helpers; Song choice L.T.: Attend to activity for 5 min B.D.: Make a choice between 2 (jobs) using pictures	
Literature/story:	Feast for 10 by Caldwell	
Small groups: Teacher, assistance, & therapists may work with small groups of children on IEP goals.	1. Objective: Follow list to find items in grocery store. (AL, CR, and JT) Matching objects to pictures 2. Objective: Classify pictures of food, toys, and clothes. B.D. Identifying objects in pictures; J.T.: Naming objects 3. Objective: Cutting coupons. S.J. and B.T.: Use adapted scissors; L.T. and B.D. Work on snipping	1. Objective: 2. Objective: 3. Objective:
Worktime: Children plan where they will work. Teacher and Teacher Assistant help carry out their plans and work on individual IEP goals.	Dramatic Play area is set up as a grocery store Miss K works with children facilitating play in the grocery store Miss B works in the writing area to help children write "lists" Miss S works with children in playdoh to "bake" cookies to sell in the grocery store	
Snack/oral motor:	Pick up Cheerios with tip of tongue Juice, water	
Gross motor: Outdoor play or indoor gross motor activity	Relay Race: Putting things IN and taking things OUT of a bag	

134

Theme:		Book:		Week of:
Monday	Tuesday	Wednesday	Thursday	Friday
Objective:	Objective:	Objective:	Objective:	Objective:
Objective:	Objective:	Objective:	Objective:	Objective:
1. Objective:	1. Objective:	1. Objective:	1. Objective:	1. Objective:
2. Objective:	2. Objective:	2. Objective:	2. Objective:	2. Objective:
3. Objective:	3. Objective:	3. Objective:	3. Objective:	3. Objective:

Program Administrator's Guide to Early Childhood Special Education: Leadership, Development, and Supervision
by J.M. Taylor, J. McGowan, and T. Linder

Figure 6.2. Sample lesson plan forms.

Photo 10. Skills posters.

LITERACY INSTRUCTION

All children, regardless of their ability, can benefit from early literacy instruction (Morrow, 2001). This instruction should be meaningful to children and taught in such a way that it relates to all aspects of a child's environment. This is one reason that thematic instruction is an effective way to help very young children learn literacy skills. Themes create a framework, or a purpose, and naturally allow for the integration of other areas of the curriculum. Providing a literacy-rich environment is one of the single most important strategies a teacher can use to help develop early literacy skills. Here are some things to consider for creating such an environment:

- Label objects and materials with words and pictures or symbols (see Photo 11 [shelf labels]).

- Display children's names in a variety of places: on name tags, cubbies, placemats, and a word wall (see Photo 12 [word wall names]).

- Let children see you write; talk about the letters and words as you write them.

- Provide lots of materials and opportunities for reading and writing. Pointers are a great way for children to practice left-to-right progression when reading around the room (see Photo 13 [pointers]).

(continued)

(continued)

- Provide a Question of the Day relating to your theme for children to answer (see Photo 14 [question of the day]).

- Make class books with the children's names and pictures; they will become favorites in the reading corner.

- Make the reading corner comfortable, with large pillows, beanbag chairs, and child-size furniture.

- Read *daily* to your class, and also try to read one-to-one with a few children every day.

- Build time into your daily schedule for children to look at books independently, perhaps as they finish snack or while they are waiting for the next activity to begin.

A literacy-rich environment, along with meaningful activities such as finger-plays, poems, songs, wordplay, book discussions, and extension activities, may not be enough for some children. For these children, some direct or explicit teaching of literacy skills may be necessary. Therapists, such as speech-language pathologists, can be an invaluable resource in this regard. Their work with children on language-based activities and phonemic awareness can help provide needed practice for some children who may have difficulty acquiring these skills.

The term *phonemic awareness* refers to the knowledge that words are made up of sounds and that these sounds have names (letters). Early phonemic awareness is developed by singing songs, saying nursery rhymes, and reading stories and poems. These kinds of activities can become even more meaningful and concrete if songs, rhymes, and stories are paired with gesturing, signs, props, or extension activities.

The following are just a few examples of phonemic awareness activities that can be incorporated into the daily routine.

- Center a lot of classroom activities around the children's names. Nothing is more meaningful to children than their own names.

- Take attendance by using children's printed names on a kite along with a song: "If your name rhymes with _____, find your kite."

- Print children's names on hearts: "Find your heart and clap your name."

- Clap out syllables in children's names or other words.

- Sing songs for everything! Use familiar tunes, but make up your own words.

- Make a class book in which each child has a page with his or her name and photograph, along with pictures of objects that start with the same sound as the child's name. For example, Casey's page might have pictures of a cat, a car, and candy.

- Sing "Bingo," using a prop to show each time you take away one of the letters.

- Pair children's names with a personal symbol or their own photo until each child learns to read his or her name.

- Display environmental print, such as fast-food logos, cereal boxes, store names—whatever children recognize.

Name: _____

IEP Objectives:

1. _____
2. _____
3. _____
4. _____
5. _____

Progress/Comments:

Date:	Date:
Date:	Date:
Date:	Date:
Date:	Date:
Date:	Date:

Figure 6.3. Sample IEP box data form.

Photo 11.   Shelf labels.

Photo 12.   Word wall names.

Photo 13. Pointers.

Photo 14. Question of the day.

CHECKLISTS FOR NEW TEACHERS

Being a new teacher can be overwhelming at times, especially when one is working with preschoolers with special needs. Preparation and organization of paperwork and materials can go a long way in making the school year run more smoothly. The following are some checklists to help with staying organized.

Checklists For New Teachers

How Do I Organize Materials?

❑ Use old copy paper boxes and label by theme.

❑ Use plastic storage tubs.

❑ Label closet or cabinet shelves and store similar materials together: puzzles, games, fine motor activities, math materials, literacy materials.

❑ Use binders, file boxes, or hanging shoe bags to store pictures used for communication systems.

❑ Have a folder for each theme.

❑ Keep folders on storybooks and book extension activities.

Where Do I Start?

1. Study your children's IEPs. Become familiar with the types of disabilities they have.

2. Look around your room and see what materials you already have. Involve other staff members in setting up and arranging the space. Keep the following in mind:

    ❑ Separate areas for noisy and quiet play.

    ❑ Locate the circle-time area near a chalkboard or bulletin board.

    ❑ Locate the sand and water area on tiled floors, if possible.

    ❑ Clearly define play areas with furniture, partitions, and so forth.

    ❑ Label shelves with words and pictures of the materials that belong there.

    ❑ Cover bulletin boards with cloth (it lasts longer than paper). Use bulletin boards to display children's work.

3. Plan as a team with assistants, teachers, and therapists. Designate a day and time for planning, and do not let anything interfere with this time (see Figure 6.4).

4. Decide on a daily schedule and make sure it is practical (see Figure 6.1).

5. Contact each family prior to the start of school and make home visits, if possible.

(continued)

Checklists for New Teachers *(continued)*

---

6. Plan an open house for families. Give out information packets that include policies and procedures, a letter introducing staff members who will be working with the children, the daily schedule, a supply list, and so forth.

7. Plan ahead for the first week or two. If other staff members prepare the materials children will be using, give them plenty of time to do this.

8. For the first couple of weeks, teach children about the learning areas and classroom rules.

What Types of Activities Should I Do?

Use the materials you already have; do not worry about making elaborate new lessons in the beginning. Notice what children are interested in and use their interests to help plan activities. Make sure activities are appropriate for all children, and modify when necessary. Plan activities that are

❑ Goal related

❑ Theme related, including storybook themes

❑ Curriculum based

❑ Simple

How Do I Keep Track of All of the Paperwork?

❑ File paperwork immediately after each meeting.

❑ Make up a cheat sheet including each child's name and pertinent information (e.g., child's full name, parents' names, address, birthdate) and give a copy to staff who are involved with specific children.

❑ Save children's work to document their progress. Portfolios may be organized in many ways. One way is to keep a hanging file folder for each student, with separate files labeled by subject, such as Math, Literacy, Art, and Fine Motor. Collect and file work samples, photos, or documentation related to each subject.

❑ Keep folders for professional resources (e.g., articles on specific disabilities, articles on teaching literacy).

How Do I Organize Data Collection?

Record data on IEP goals often and embed the goals in the daily routine as much as possible (see Figure 6.2). All staff can record data. There are many different ways to organize data collection; find the one that works best for your team. Be sure that everyone understands the system. Here are some examples of data collection systems used in preschool classrooms:

❑ Keep a clipboard for each child with their data sheets on it. Hang the clipboards around the room for easy access.

(continued)

Program Administrator's Guide to Early Childhood Special Education: Leadership, Development, and Supervision by J.M. Taylor, J. McGowan, and T. Linder

Checklists for New Teachers *(continued)*

❑ Make a pocket folder for each child. On one side of the folder, clip blank data sheets; on the other side, clip data sheets that have already been completed. Move the sheets from one side to the other as data are recorded.

❑ Use white address labels to record anecdotal observations or language samples. They can be peeled off and stuck onto data sheets at a later time. Remember to record the child's name and the date on the labels.

❑ Keep a binder for each child containing a copy of his or her IEP, a pocket folder to hold work samples, blank paper for notes and to record telephone calls to parents, data sheets, and any other pertinent documents or curriculum-related materials.

❑ Use a form showing a grid that lists all of the children's names and weekly activities or objectives (see Figure 6.5).

How Can I Involve Parents?

❑ Contact parents prior to the start of school.

❑ Invite parents to come in and observe; let them know you have an open-door policy.

❑ Ask them to volunteer in the classroom. Make a schedule of volunteers and have meaningful things for them to do!

❑ Give parents specific things to do at home: cutting things out, sewing, saving items for use in the classroom.

❑ Keep parents informed through recall books, communication notebooks, weekly or monthly newsletters, telephone calls, and conferences.

❑ Ask parents for their input and opinions; after all, they know their child best.

CONCLUSIONS

A high-quality preschool program does not necessarily have to prescribe to a certain curriculum or philosophy. There are many effective preschool programs. A quality program operates on a continuous cycle of individualization through assessment, planning, and implementation. The curriculum can be individualized in many ways: through the learning environment, which includes not only room arrangement but also materials; the daily routine, which should be predictable and provide ample opportunities for making choices; and activities modified for varying ability levels. Remember that a child should not be made to fit a curriculum; the curriculum should be made to fit each child. In doing so, you will ensure that no child will fall through the cracks.

Unit Theme: _____ Date: _____
Book:
Dramatic Play:
Songs:
Art activities:
Snacks/oral motor:
Fine motor:
Gross motor
Speech/language activities:

Figure 6.4. Sample team planning sheet.

Name:	Objective:	Objective:	Objective:	Objective:	Objective:	Objective:	Objective:	Objective:	Objective:	Objective:

Program Administrator's Guide to Early Childhood Special Education: Leadership, Development, and Supervision
by J.M. Taylor, J. McGowan, and T. Linder

Figure 6.5. Sample grid to list all children's names and weekly activities or objectives.

REFERENCES

Bredekamp, S. (Ed.). (1987). *Developmentally appropriate practice in early childhood programs serving children from birth through age 8* (Rev. ed.) Washington, D.C.: National Association for the Education of Young Children.

Bredekamp, S., Knuth, R.A., Kunesh, L.G., & Shulman, D.D. (1992). *What does research say about early childhood education?* Retrieved April 9, 2006, from http://www.ncrel.org

Chattin-McNichols, J. (1991). *The Montessori controversy.* New York: Delmar Publishers.

Dodge, D.T., Colker, L., & Heroman, C. (2002). *The creative curriculum for preschool.* Bethesda, MD: Teaching Strategies.

Edwards, C., Gandini, L., & Forman, G. (1993). *The hundred languages of children: The Reggio Emilia approach to early childhood education.* New Jersey: Ablex.

Guralnick, M.J., Connor, R.T., Hammond, M.A., Gottman, J.M., & Kinnish, K. (1996). Immediate effects of mainstreamed settings on the social interactions and social integration of preschool children. *American Journal of Mental Retardation, 100,* 359–377.

Individuals with Disabilities Education Act Amendments (IDEA) of 1997, PL 105-17, 20 U.S.C. §§ 1400 *et seq.*

Hohmann, M., & Weikart, D.P. (2002). *Educating young children: Active learning practices for preschool and child care programs* (2nd ed.). Ypsilanti, MI: The High/Scope Press.

Linder, T.W. (1999). *Read, Play, and Learn!®: Storybook activities for young children.* Baltimore: Paul H. Brookes Publishing Co.

Linder, T. (2008). *Transdisciplinary Play-Based Assessment (TPBA2), second edition.* Baltimore: Paul H. Brookes Publishing Co.

Miller, R. (1996). *The developmentally appropriate inclusive classroom in early education.* Albany: Delmar.

Morrow, L.M. (2001). *Literacy development in the early years: Helping children read and write.* Boston: Allyn & Bacon.

National Association for the Education of Young Children. (2004). Final draft:Accreditation performance criteria. Retrieved October 6, 2005, from http://www.naeyc.org/accreditation/naeyc_accred/draft_standards/crit/completecriteria.html

Odom, S.L., Zercher, C., Li, S., Marquart, J., & Sandall, S. (1998, April). *Social relationships of preschool children with disabilities.* Paper presented at the Annual Conference of the American Educational Research Association, San Diego.

Peck, C.A., Odom, S.L., & Bricker, D.D. (1993). *Integrating young children with disabilities into community programs.* Baltimore: Paul H. Brookes Publishing Co.

Survey: Quality state preschool programs are rare. (n.d.). Retrieved April 10, 2006, from http://www.nea.org/earlychildhood/preschoolyearbook04more.html

Wolery, M. (1993). Early childhood special education. In A.E Blackhearst & W.H Berdine (Eds.), *An introduction to special education.* New York: HarperCollins College Publishers.

Administrative Issues for Integrating Technology into Early Childhood Settings

John Castellani and Linda A. Tsantis

The distance from the new-born baby to the five-year-old
is a chasm; the distance from the five-year-old to me is one step.
Leo Tolstoy

What If?   As the director of a program for young children with and without disabilities, you want to make sure your teachers and students have the latest technologies to support instruction and child development. The program recently received a gift of $10,000 from a donor who asked that the money be used for technology. You have appointed a committee of parents and staff to make recommendations for the use of this important gift. What kinds of issues do you want this committee to consider? For example, how much of the gift should be used for training? for hardware? for software? Could any of the money be used to upgrade administrative technology?

CHAPTER OVERVIEW

Early childhood administrators have one of the most important jobs in society. They ensure that programs and services are in place to prepare children for life. This requires using data, intuition, and professional experience to make appropriate decisions about how these programs and services are supported and delivered. Each year, early childhood administrators are faced with difficult choices about competing educational improvement options related to how technology can be used to support children's growth, especially for those students who require technology to perform everyday tasks. Administrative and instructional decisions are dependent on the best estimate of the effectiveness of the selected options for technology. The purpose of this chapter is to provide administrators with the information they need to make the best added value decisions that are justified through data-driven decision making.

CHAPTER OBJECTIVES

After reviewing this chapter, the reader will

- Know the definition of assistive technology

- Understand how students use technology to learn

- Understand technology research

- Understand how technology can be used to support instruction

- Understand how technology can be used to support administration

DEFINITION OF ASSISTIVE TECHNOLOGY

Assistive technology (AT) and other tools necessary for building developmental and achievement skills are an important part of the early childhood planning process. "Assistive technology device means an item, piece of equipment, or product system, whether acquired commercially off the shelf, modified, or customized, that is used to increase, maintain, or improve the functional capabilities of a student with a disability." (IDEA 2004). Consideration of AT options should include a discussion to ensure that AT is usable across home and school environments; planning for independence is critical. In early childhood settings prior to preschool, different supports are needed for young children in their home environments. Although public schools are required to provide AT supports for students who need them (see Table 7.1), the most frequent purchaser of AT for young children is the parent or caregiver (Wilcox, Bacon, & Campbell, 2004). One responsibility for individualized education program (IEP) team members, therefore, is to make sure that parents know how to locate and request the services, supports, and funding they need to begin using AT. In addition, teams need to coordinate with all care providers or adult service agencies an individual may encounter after leaving high school to ensure that AT moves transparently and efficiently with the student.

Because AT services are the important link to supporting AT implementation in home, community, and play settings, it is important to understand the definition of AT service. *Assistive technology service* refers to a service that directly assists a student with a disability in the selection, acquisition, or use of an AT device. AT services in-

Table 7.1.   Provision of assistive technology

(a) Each public agency shall ensure that assistive technology devices or assistive technology services, or both, as those terms are defined in IDEA 2004, are made available to a student with a disability if required as a part of the student's—

   (1) Special education;

   (2) Related services; or

   (3) Supplementary aids and services

(b) On a case-by-case basis, the use of school-purchased assistive technology devices in a student's home or in other settings is required if the student's IEP team determines that the student needs access to those devices in order to receive FAPE.

Key: FAPE, free appropriate public education; IEP, individualized education program.

Table 7.2. Assistive technology service

Assistive technology service includes
The evaluation of the needs of [a child with a disability], including a functional evaluation of the child in the child's customary environment
Purchasing, leasing, or otherwise providing for the acquisition of assistive technology devices by such child
Selecting, designing, fitting, customizing, adapting, applying, maintaining, repairing, or replacing of assistive technology devices
Coordinating and using other therapies, interventions, or services with assistive technology devices, such as those associated with existing education and rehabilitation plans and programs
Training or technical assistance for such child, or, where appropriate, the family of such child
Training or technical assistance for professionals (including individuals providing education and rehabilitation services), employers, or other individuals who provide services to, employ, or are otherwise substantially involved in the major life functions of such child

Source: IDEA, 2004; Title IA 602;2.

clude repair and maintenance, training in new AT skills, coordination of AT with other services, and ongoing evaluation of the need for and use of AT. Table 7.2 shows further types of AT services.

TECHNOLOGY AND THE NEW SCIENCE OF LEARNING

Children, regardless of disability, are being influenced by the prevalence of screen technologies. For both children in general and special education, advances in the new science of learning have created a greater understanding of the relationship between a child's developing mind and active learning through technology (Huffaker & Calvert, 2003). This concept has been put forth by the National Academy of Science and the National Research Council, both recognizing that technology has become an integral component of the way people live and learn and that exposure to technology begins from birth. However, it is important to understand where and when technology should be used to support child development and as a needed device or service.

RESEARCH ON THE USE OF TECHNOLOGY

Recent studies in child development report that children are able to learn more and learn earlier than ever anticipated (Kuhl, 2002). A Zero to Six study by the Kaiser Family Foundation (Rideout, Vandewater, & Wartella, 2003, p. 5) found that nearly "half (48%) of all children six and under have used a computer and by the time they are in the four- to six-year-old range, seven out of ten (70%) have used a computer." In the same study, results from parent surveys indicated that they were "most enthusiastic about the educational potential of computers," with 72% of the parents reporting that the computer helps children's learning (p. 8). Computer use in early learning is supported by research that determined "we no longer need to ask whether the use of technology is 'developmentally appropriate'"—it has become an expected ingredient to be included in the early childhood learning experience (Clements & Sarama, 2002, p. 17). The question for early childhood administrators is "What role do I play in supporting the integration of technology into early childhood settings?" The answer to this question depends on where and when the technology is used by young children and on understanding how to justify its costs and benefits. This chapter provides several examples of how technology can support children and presents a model for justifying its costs and benefits.

USING TECHNOLOGY TO SUPPORT INSTRUCTION

The first step for integrating technology into early childhood education is to accept the benefits that technology can have for children's development. In 1996, the National Association for the Education of Young Children (NAEYC) published a position statement on the use of technology in early childhood (NAEYC, 1996). It concluded that

- Early childhood professionals must apply the principles of developmentally appropriate practice and appropriate curriculum and assessment when choosing technology for use in their classrooms or programs.

- Used appropriately, technology can improve children's thinking ability and help them develop good relationships with peers.

- Technology should be integrated into daily learning activities.

- Teachers should work for equity in access to technology for all children and their families.

- Technology has a powerful influence over children's learning—it must not teach them to stereotype or use violence to solve their problems.

- Early childhood educators should work together with parents to promote appropriate uses of technology.

The second step for integrating technology is to be aware of the research on technology integration in early childhood settings. Support for using computers in early childhood instruction has been strengthened by studies of 3- and 4-year-old children in preschool settings. Findings revealed that the greatest impact on learning was the "range of lively group interactions" that computer use engendered among children, including language development, prosocial behavior, performance, collaboration, and play behaviors (Brooker & Siraj-Blatchford, 2002, p. 262).

Young children who experience the integrated use of technology in their learning environment show greater development in memory and visual perceptual skills, word identification, picture–word identification, and passage comprehension compared with peers who have not used computers (Sivin-Kachala & Bialo, 1994). Children who participate in a computer learning environment often provide assisted performance that results in mutually supportive collaboration in their problem-solving and play activities (Brooker & Siraj-Blatchford, 2002; Van Oers, 1999).

As a catalyst for assisted performance, the computer reinforces the importance of providing computer access to all young children and of supporting teachers to move from using technology for isolated learning activities to using interactive applications, in which students work in groups and collaborate. Assistive technology can do more than augment, extend, and amplify the learning experience for children at risk and for children with disabilities; it can allow them to be more fully included in mainstream education. Assistive technology allows the presentation and application of instructional content to be adjusted to compensate for specific disabilities (Westford Public Schools, 2004).

Education leaders must advocate for the most appropriate technology to be made available to all children and for assistive technologies to be provided for children with special needs. Adaptive and assistive technologies have the potential to radically transform education and dramatically affect the lives of children with special needs. According to the National Research Council, features of electronic learning technologies provide the flexibility needed to create customized learning environments—technology environments in which students can learn by doing, receive feedback, continually refine their understanding, and build new knowledge (Bransford, Brown, & Cocklings, 1999). In the case of children with special needs and/or who require technology for everyday tasks, educators are required by law to consider how assistive technology could support them (Castellani et al., 2005).

Other research also proposes that integration of computers into early childhood activities offers more effective and dynamic individualized learning environments (Clements & Sarama, 2002; Davis & Shade, 1994; Tsantis, Bewick, & Thouvenelle, 2003). Technology for children with special needs is also documented in the early childhood literature. O'Connor and Schery (1986) compared the use of traditional language intervention with the use of computer-aided language instruction. Results indicated that students made a great amount of developmental progress in a short period of time. In addition, the use of a microcomputer facilitated language growth in toddlers with multiple disabilities.

In two similar studies (Spiegel-McGill et al., 1989; Yoshikawa, 1995), researchers compared the abilities of computer and toy play activities to affect children's communicative interactions with their typical peers. Yoshikawa's study included five preschool children (two of which had social and language delays) and established that "dyadic computer activities may provide handicapped preschoolers with motivating contexts for practice, expansion, and refinement of social and language skills" (p. 202). Fazio and Reith (1986) found that when provided with the choice of a computer for free time, higher functioning children chose it 84% of the time, whereas lower functioning children chose the computer 70% of the time. Fazio and Reith also noted that after choosing to use the computer, the lower functioning children would stay with it for the full designated 10 minutes.

AT is not limited to computer use. Butler (1984) introduced several children ($1\frac{1}{2}$ to approximately 3 years old) to motorized wheelchairs to determine the effectiveness of the wheelchairs in encouraging mobility. Children learned the skills to operate the wheelchairs when the skills were taught together in a sequence, such as moving forward, starting and stopping, and circling. Children were able to learn and demonstrate these skills within a 1- to 5-day period. Parents of participants added that the powered mobility devices had positively influenced their children's emotional, social, and intellectual behaviors.

TECHNOLOGY AND ADMINISTRATIVE SUPPORT

The Quality Indicators for Assistive Technology project (QIAT Consortium, 2005) includes indicators for AT consideration, implementation, and transition as well as administrative support of AT. Other sets of indicators relate to financial, budgetary, and professional development and training issues. The main indicators for AT are included in Table 7.3.

Although each indicator is important, justifying the time, energy, expense, and value of supporting technology is key to the successful communication, evaluation,

Table 7.3. Quality indicators for assistive technology administrative support

1. The education agency has written procedural guidelines that ensure equitable access to assistive technology devices and services for students with disabilities, if required by FAPE.
2. The education agency has clearly defined and broadly disseminated policies and procedures for providing effective assistive technology devices and services.
3. The education agency has written descriptions of job requirements, which include knowledge, skills, and responsibilities for staff members who provide assistive technology services.
4. The education agency employs a range of personnel with competencies needed to provide quality assistive technology services within their areas of primary responsibility.
5. The education agency includes assistive technology in the technology planning and budgeting process.
6. The education agency provides continuous learning opportunities about assistive technology devices, strategies, and resources for staff, family, and students.
7. The education agency uses a systemic procedure to evaluate the components of assistive technology services to ensure accountability for student progress.

Source: QIAT, 2005.

Key: FAPE, free appropriate public education.

and implementation of AT decisions. Early childhood administrators need an appropriate set of measures that takes into account the impact of instructional and assistive technologies on the social, emotional, developmental, and instructional outcomes that are embedded in learning experiences. Although there are many ways to estimate, confirm, and predict the costs of technology, there is no formula that balances the benefits of assistive technology with its costs. It is this important balance that will evolve as *justification costs*. This will be better understood after examining existing measurement models.

In 2005, Gormley surveyed 44 of 50 state IDEA Part C coordinators on funding and other issues in assistive technology. He found that "Medicaid is the most frequently used state-funding source for payment of services and to purchase devices, although other sources such as Part C as the payor of last resort and DME/Medicaid Title XIX for devices are also used" (p. 5). They also found that the majority of state coordinators reported funding high-tech communication devices most frequently, as well as switch interfaces, switches, adapted chairs, off-the-shelf toys, and computers. A survey of parents, on the other hand, revealed that the most common technologies used were low tech. These were items such as Velcro (52%), plastic links (58%), oversized crayons (59.5%), attention-getting devices (46.4%), and bathtub inserts (38.2%). Items in the home funded by parents were more often low tech, whereas state-funded items were more often high tech.

Case Study: Luke

Luke is a bright, friendly 3-year-old boy who attends a preschool program three mornings each week. He has spina bifida and skillfully uses a power wheelchair to move around his preschool environment. Luke has diminished upper body strength; however, he is able to use his hands to participate in most tasks in the classroom. His endurance is poor and he tires easily with any exertion. He has an inquisitive mind and likes to participate in all activities. Luke has a one-to-one aide who accompanies him to school each day, but the IEP team has been questioning whether or not he is as independent as he could be with certain tasks. Luke makes it very clear that he wants to do as much as he can by himself.

Luke has responsibilities both at home and at school. These duties are

• Turning off the lights when exiting a room

• Passing out napkins during snack time and at dinner

• Feeding his fish at home as well as in the classroom

Luke is unable to reach the light switches and, due to limited space, has difficulty navigating his chair around the dinner table as well as the snack table at school. Also, he is unable to reach the fish tanks at home and at school from his wheelchair.

Luke's IEP states that he will participate in all home and classroom activities independently with accommodations provided. The IEP team discussed the activities he was having difficulty doing and decided that there were no changes needed in the IEP; rather, some simple environmental adaptations could make it possible for Luke to independently take care of his daily needs.

Once the adults focused on changing the environment rather than on changing Luke or the way he participated, the adaptations were easily made. The occupational therapist worked with Luke's parents and aide to make the necessary adaptations to his bedroom and other areas of the home. She purchased a new light switch and asked Luke's parents to drill a small hole through the end of the switch and install it in place of the old wall switch. Using a small ring, she then attached a 12-inch dowel with a screw eye to the switch. Luke could easily reach the dowel that hung down from the light switch and move it down to turn the lights off when he left the room.

At school, the classroom aide suggested rearranging the classroom to make a wider aisle around the snack table. This would allow Luke to navigate his wheelchair when it was his turn to distribute the napkins. After making this accommodation, the teacher and aide realized that it also helped make things easier for *them* by providing more room in which to maneuver the snack cart.

The IEP team members decided that cutting off the legs of the table on which the classroom fish tank was placed would make it easier for all the children to feed the fish and enjoy watching them swim in the tank. The maintenance staff sawed and sanded the legs of the table that week.

It looked like the implementation of Luke's new classroom and home accommodations would be easy for this team, and in fact it *was* mostly easy. Luke proudly turned off the lights every time the class left the room when it was his turn for that job. When it came time for him to feed the fish, although he could now reach the tank, he needed to learn how much food to give the fish. Also, although Luke could now maneuver around the tables at school and home to place the napkins for his classmates and to help his mother and father set the table, he was unable to stretch his arm to the table from his wheelchair to put these items in the right spot. The team talked about this difficulty and decided to give Luke a little time to problem solve before they intervened. They had noticed that sometimes Luke needed a little extra time to figure out, on his own, how to do tasks that involved motor skills.

The team agreed to check quarterly to determine if any new barriers to Luke's participation arose. They also decided to invite his parents and the three teachers who could potentially teach Luke in a community preschool placement to visit the classroom to ensure that they got a good start on planning for his participation.

IMPLEMENTING ASSISTIVE TECHNOLOGY

Educators and their stakeholders have questioned the cost of technology in relation to student achievement and whether other methods can support a child's developmental needs more cost effectively (Hawkes & Cambre, 2000). The real issue is not whether technology should be used but whether one type of technology is more cost beneficial than another. Anyone involved in purchasing and supporting communication and computer systems knows that costs for these systems can be very high. There are costs associated with the installation of computers that can house instructional software and with high assistive technology devices, costs to purchase a system (or software), training costs, and costs for individuals to maintain the appropriate level of access for the user. Although these costs can be prohibitive, if administrators or other persons responsible for any high-tech system can assess the costs relative to student achievement or the effects that having access to high technologies has on child development and learning, then the cost is justifiable. As mentioned previously regarding assistive technologies, there is a continuum of low- to high-tech devices available. Generally, low-tech strategies require very minimal resources. High-tech strategies generally require both higher actual costs and higher personnel costs (see Figure 7.1).

Administrators need to understand the selection, acquisition, and use of assistive technology and to be able to come up with a justifiable cost based on the impact that technology will have on students' functional and academic achievement and overall growth. This is called the justifiable cost of learning (JCL).

To develop a JCL, skilled administrators need to consider what data are available to prove or demonstrate trends that the technology is having an impact on student learning. This requires that there is an appropriate level of data for the justification. Both the challenges and benefits are often greater for young children than for older children and youth because growth is often seen more rapidly in younger children.

Technology is seen as cost effective if it

- Gives students the opportunity to engage in early learning experiences that would be impossible without the technology

- Allows young children the opportunity to explore their world

- Promotes active engagement in learning and enables students to enjoy what they are doing

- Promotes a measurable increase in the range of activities in which a student can participate

- Promotes understanding, collaboration, and tolerance among children of diverse backgrounds

- Improves child performance

- Is usable across all the environments a child will encounter

- Promotes better knowledge of and facility with the range of low to high technologies

- Is used to reduce other resources that would be needed if the technology were not present (adapted from Hawkes & Cambre, 2000)

In developing a JCL, it is helpful to prioritize each of the above items based on the individual child, the IEP team, and other stakeholder and system issues. The first step in doing this is to identify what type of environment you are operating in. The

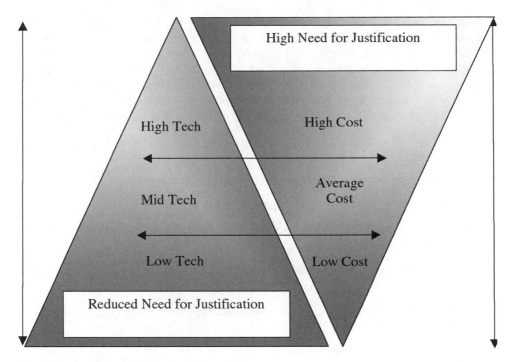

Figure 7.1. Justifiable cost of learning (JCL) continuum.

level of resources available will certainly affect the weight you assign to the above items, but there are other considerations. You may be operating in an environment that is rich in resources but lacking in the understanding of the importance of tolerance and collaboration among diverse learners. Or, you may be in a system with a lack of resources but a deep understanding of the importance of tolerance and collaboration. In either system, identifying what you need to justify technology costs will be critical to how you collect your data and the metrics used to determine the successful use of a device or technology.

The first step in developing or using any metric is to identify *what* needs to be measured and *how* to measure it. A research paper, *Assessing Costs and Benefits of Early Childhood Intervention Programs* (Karoly, Kilburn, Bigelow, Caulkins, & Cannon, 2001), offered decision makers metrics and guidelines to help analyze the costs and benefits of early childhood intervention programs.

Cost–benefit analysis (or benefit–cost analysis) entails comparing a program's benefits to a stakeholder with its costs to that stakeholder. Such a comparison requires putting benefits in comparable terms, and the terms conventionally chosen are dollars. Benefits that cannot be expressed in dollar terms cannot be compared in this manner and are included only in associated qualitative discussion. Cost–benefit analysis can help in deciding whether a program is of value to the stakeholder. Often, cost–benefit analysis is conducted from the perspective of society at large.

Since the implementation of No Child Left Behind (2001), there is increased pressure to provide documented accountability through established metric models. One widely used model is *return on investment* (ROI). This analysis model is typically used to provide information for informed decision making and/or informed choices between options by using one of two formulas. Using the ROI model in the context of evaluating the impact of technology in early childhood intervention programs, however, would require at least two perspectives to be considered: 1) that of the producer, or the learning service provider (school) and 2) that of the consumer, or the learner (individually and collectively) (Barker, 2001). Developing metrics to examine the use of assistive technology in early childhood environments could be adapted from an ROI model of cost analysis in education that includes the following:

- Testing the economic feasibility of integrating assistive technology into mainstream instruction

- Projecting future levels of assistive technology costs

- Estimating the cost of alternative instructional materials or innovations

- Comparing alternative ways of achieving the same objective and selecting the most efficient or economical

- Comparing the profitability of alternative projects (no technology intervention or inclusion)

- Improving the efficiency of resource utilization (shared technology) (Woodhall, 1987, pp. 393–399)

Although these measures are useful and appropriate in many situations, they do not adequately demonstrate the complex dimensions of the actual and perceived value and the specific benefits of instructional and assistive technologies. A more appropriate measurement would weigh the extent to which the total learning experience is enhanced by the technology—that is, the impact of the technology on the individual and on the group. A comprehensive measurement that acknowledges the importance of values and perceptions could provide data to create justification cost.

There are traditional means that can measure quality, such as identifying specific inputs and making comparisons. Value, on the other hand, is assessed through the perceptions of stakeholders. One way to conceptualize this is in the context of what has been described as *value on investment*, or VOI (Norris, 2003). According to the VOI model, value is determined by the weight given to stakeholders' support and expectations. To use this model, school leaders need to help stakeholders determine their criteria for quality and value.

Total cost of ownership (TCO) is a calculation designed to help assess both the direct and indirect costs and benefits associated with the purchase of any information technology. Research from the Gartner Group shows that the lack of readily available user assistance and support is a primary barrier to the successful adoption of new technology and technology-enabled methods. The concept of TCOs has been applied to schools, with extensive examination from both the Coalition for School Networking (CoSN) and Jamie McKenzie, author and editor of the journal *Digital Learning Spaces*. CoSN (2008) has proposed a TCO checklist to assist in a more comprehensive evaluation of technology ownership, including such items as professional development, support, connectivity, software, replacement costs, and retrofitting.

CoSN (2008), with support from the U.S. Department of Education and in conjunction with the North Central Regional Technology in Education Consortium and Gartner Group, produced a set of online tools that included a TCO framework for use by schools. The TCO framework allowed administrators to identify the total technology cost per student. A significant body of work surrounding TCO in the education environment has been undertaken by the Northwest Educational Technology Consortium (NETC), which offers an established, comprehensive web site and a PDF document (NETC, 2003) that summarizes the financial as well as philosophical arguments on these issues and included both hard cost and soft cost considerations (discussed later in this section).

According to McKenzie (2003), although the TCO model usually covers those costs associated with the computer itself, technical support, and depreciation, there are other factors that should also be investigated to gain a more accurate picture of the TCO in schools. McKenzie's representation would offer a "true cost of ownership" analysis to raise awareness about the costs and responsibilities for providing technology so that better judgments can be made. Some of these costs would be *opportunity costs*, defined by NETC (n.d.) as the costs in dollars and stress that occur as a result of forfeiting new choices because of old choices (for example, switching computer systems and no longer being compatible with software upgrades from the previous system).

In the special education arena, opportunity costs needs to be redefined as *responsibility costs* that are based on mandated, or hard, requirements and also on intangibles, or soft justifications, which serve to clarify the value of AT. Some costs are clearly aligned with hard, well-defined expenses incurred in meeting the AT needs and requirements identified in a student's IEP and protected under the Americans with Disabilities Act (ADA) of 1990. Other costs are aligned with soft, ethical and moral responsibilities to do what is right for students with disabilities and for the teachers who service them. Hard requirements combined with soft justifications can validate the decision to purchase and support assistive technology. The Justification of Assistive Technology Ownership (JATO) chart shown in Table 7.4 delineates the hard and soft variables that should be considered in compiling the expenses of AT.

Table 7.4.   Justification of assistive technology ownership (JATO)

Requirements	Justifications
Hardware	Level of inclusion
Software	Degree of success
Formal training	Range of improvement
Support	Increase in independence
License	Attitudinal set
Warranty	Perceptual change
Upgrade	Parental affiliation
Service	Peer acceptance
Lease	
Time	
Monitoring	
Evaluation	
Legal	
Vendor management	
Peripheral devices	
Downtime	
Number of users	

CONCLUSIONS

The job of an early childhood administrator is a vital one: ensuring quality educational experiences for children. An important part of this job is to consider and support technology to meet children's individual needs and to ensure that it fits into their daily routines. There are five ways you can address these issues right now:

- Create district operating guidelines that include AT.

- Review your agency's procedural manuals to ensure that AT is adequately addressed.

- Identify opportunities for staff members to plan for implementation of AT services.

- Analyze your budget to identify the places where AT is or can be included.

- Check with your state education agency to find out if an AT project (a federally or state-funded AT technical resource project or identified state AT specialist working with young children) exists in your state (Bowser & Reed, 2004).

There is support for ensuring quality technology consideration and implementation across the country, and as society continues to adapt to changing technology, children should be introduced to it as early as possible in the most considerate way to ensure developmental and educational progress. To accomplish this task, early childhood administrators need to consider the support of the overall instructional and developmental program to be able to justify what is needed for schools, staff, and children. Successful management of resources will yield young children who are able to progress through life at an appropriate pace. Ensuring opportunities for the use of technology are important for systems, communities, and individuals to thrive in a highly technical society.

REFERENCES

Americans with Disabilities Act (ADA) of 1990, PL 101-336, 42 U.S.C. §§ 12101 *et seq.*

Barker, K. (2001). *Return on training investment.* Amsterdam: Elsevier.

Bowser, G., & Reed, P. (2004). *A school administrator's desktop guide to assistive technology.* Arlington, VA: Technology and Media Division of the Council for Exceptional Children.

Bransford, J.D., Brown, A.L., & Cocklings, R.R. (Eds.). (1999). *How people learn: Brain, mind, experience, and school.* Washington, DC: National Academies Press, Committee on Developments in the Science of Learning; Commission on Behavioral and Social Sciences and Education.

Brooker, L., & Siraj-Blatchford, J. (2002). "Click on miaow!": How children of three and four years experience the nursery computer. *Contemporary Issues in Early Childhood, 3*(2), 251–273.

Butler, C. (1984). Motorized wheelchair driving by disabled children. *Archives of Physical Medicine and Rehabilitation, 65*(2), 95–97.

Castellani, J.D., Reed, P., & Zabala, J. (2005). *Has assistive technology been considered?: Policies, guidelines, and strategies for including technology on individualized education plans.* Columbia, MD: Center for Technology in Education, The Johns Hopkins University.

Clements, D.H., & Sarama, J. (2002). The role of technology in early childhood learning. *Teaching Children Mathematics, 8*, 340–343. References from the on-line version retrieved on September 7, 2005, from http://my.nctm.org/eresources/view_media.asp?article_id=1897

Coalition for School Networking (CoSN). (2008). *Digital learning spaces 2010.* Retrieved July 28, 2008, from http://www.cosn.org/resources/emerging_technologies/learningspaces.cfm

Davis, B.C., & Shade, D.D. (1994). *Integrate, don't isolate! Computers in the early childhood curriculum*. (ERIC Digest No. EDO-PS-94-17.) Retrieved September 7, 2005, from http://ceep.crc.uiuc.edu/eecearchive/digests/1994/shade94.html

Fazio, B., & Reith, H. (1986). Characteristics of preschool handicapped children's microcomputer use during free-choice periods. *Journal of the Division for Early Childhood, 10*, 201–219.

Gormley, W.T. (2005). The effects of universal pre-K on cognitive development. *Developmental Psychology, 41*(6), 872.

Hawkes, M., & Cambre, M. (2000, August). The cost factor: When is interactive distance technology justifiable? *T.H.E. Journal, 28*(1), 26–28, 30, 32. (ERIC Digest No. EJ618386.)

Huffaker, D.A., & Calvert, S.L. (2003). The new science of learning: Active learning, metacognition, and transfer of knowledge in E-Learning applications. *Journal of Educational Computing Research, 29*(3), 325–334.

Individuals with Disabilities Education Improvement Act (IDEA) of 2004, PL 108-446, 20 U.S.C. §§ 1400 *et seq.*

Karoly, L.A., Kilburn, M.R., Bigelow, J.H., Caulkins, J.P., & Cannon, J.S. (2001). *Assessing costs and benefits of early childhood intervention programs: Overview and application to the Starting Early Starting Smart Program*. Santa Monica, CA: RAND Corporation.

Kuhl, P.K. (2002, June). *Born to learn: Language, reading, and the brain of the child*. Paper presented at the Early Learning Summit for the Northwest Region, Boise, ID.

McKenzie, J. (2003, March). The true cost of ownership. *The Educational Technology Journal, 12*(7). Retrieved July 18, 2008, from http://www.fno.org/mar03/truecost.html

National Association for the Education of Young Children. (NAEYC). (1996). *Technology in early childhood settings*. Retrieved July 28, 2008, from http://www.naeyc.org/about/positions/PSTECH98.asp

No Child Left Behind Act of 2001, PL 107-110,115 Stat. 1425, 20 U.S.C. §§ 6301 *et seq.*

Norris, D.M. (2003, September 2). Value on investment in higher education. *ECAR Research Bulletin, 18*.

Northwest Educational Technology Consortium (NETC). (2003). *Open source software means more choices*. Retrieved July 18, 2008, from http://www.netc.org/openoptions/images/pdf/nect.circuit.pdf

Northwest Educational Technology Consortium (NETC). *Total cost of ownership*. Retrieved July 18, 2008, from http://www.netc.org/openoptions/pros_cons/tco.html

Quality Indicators for Assistive Technology (QIAT) Consortium. (2005, Revised). *Quality indicators for assistive technology services with QIAT Self-Evaluation Matrices*. Retrieved July 28, 2008, from http://natri.uky.edu/assoc_projects/qiat/qualityindicators.html

O'Connor, L.C., & Schery, T.K. (1986). The effectiveness of school-based computer language intervention with severely handicapped children. *Language, Speech, and Hearing Services in Schools, 23*, 43–47.

Rideout, V.J., Vandewater, E.A., & Wartella, E.A. (2003). *Zero to six: Electronic media in the lives of infants, toddlers and preschoolers*. Menlo, CA: Henry J. Kaiser Family Foundation.

Sivin-Kachala, J., & Bialo, E. (1994). *Report on the effectiveness of technology in schools, 1990–1994*. Washington, DC: Software Publishers Association.

Spiegel-McGill, P., Zippiroli, S., & Mistrett, S. (1989). Microcomputers as social facilitators in integrated preschools. *Journal of Early Intervention, 13*(3), 249–260.

Tsantis, L.A., Bewick, C.J., & Thouvenelle, S. (2003, November). Examining some common myths about computer use in the early years. In *Beyond the journal: Young children on the web*. Washington, DC: National Association for the Education of Young Children. Retrieved September 7, 2005, from http://www.journal.naeyc.org/btj/200311/CommonTechnoMyths.pdf

Van Oers, B. (1999). Teaching opportunities in play. In M. Hedegaard & J. Lompscher (Eds.), *Learning activity and development*. Aarhus, Denmark: Aarhus University Press.

Westford Public Schools. (2004). *Technology and student achievement*. Retrieved on September 22, 2005, from http://westford.mec.edu/tech/achievement.html

Wilcox, M., Bacon, C., & Campbell, P. (2004). National survey of parents and providers using AT in early intervention. University of Arizona Tots-n-Tech Research Institute. *Research Brief, 1*(3). Retrieved July 30, 2008, from http://asu.edu/clas/tnt/presentations/ResBriefParProviSurv9-16-04.pdf

Woodhall, M. (1987). *Lending for learning: Designing a student loan programme for developing countries.* London: Commonwealth Secretariat Publications.

Yoshikawa, H. (1995, Winter). Long-term effects of early childhood programs on social outcomes. *The Future of Children, 5*(3), 51–75. Retrieved July 28, 2008, from http://www.futureofchildren .org/usr_doc/vol5no3ART3.pdf

Transitions and Service Coordination in Early Childhood and Early Childhood Special Education

Brenda T. Hussey-Gardner and Haidee Kaye Bernstein

*All that we do to partner with families and involve them
in their child's education, health, and early development . . .
are the best buffer for the challenges children face as they grow and
are a primary component of planning effective transition services. . . .*
(Early Head Start National Resource Center, 2004, p. 16)

What If?   Shanique Washington was born 12 weeks early and weighed 1,000 grams. She had a number of health problems at birth and has been in the neonatal intensive care unit (NICU) for 3 months. She is finally going home in 1 week. Her mother, Shawna, is very concerned about caring for her at home. During Shanique's hospitalization, her mother has had the support of a cadre of health care professionals. The nurse practitioner who has coordinated Shanique's care has referred Shawna to the local early intervention (EI) program. Shawna is not sure what they will do to help her and is more concerned with Shanique's health care needs than with her rate of development. How should the local EI service providers proceed in this situation?

CHAPTER OVERVIEW

This chapter offers a description of the types of transitions experienced by children with disabilities from birth through 5 years of age and their families. This chapter describes the basic issues related to these transitions and offers suggestions for planning and effecting smooth transitions. Important information regarding the legisla-

Figure 8.1. Visiting the playground of a new school.

tion that drives these transitions is presented. The remainder of the chapter focuses on three types of vertical transitions that children with special needs frequently experience.

   After reviewing this chapter, the reader will

• Know a definition of transition

• Understand the differences between vertical and horizontal transitions and examples of each

• Know the legislation regarding transition

• Understand effective strategies for transition

• Understand the importance of coordination between key personnel and a child's family

WHAT ARE TRANSITIONS?

All children experience transitions; however, children with disabilities and their families experience more frequent and more intense transitions than do children without disabilities (Hains, Rosenkoetter, & Fowler, 1991). Transitions between settings and types of services can be stressful for families and difficult for children, and these times are crucial points for service providers to make individualized decisions to meet families' and children's needs. Service coordination and careful planning by personnel from multiple agencies can minimize concerns and optimize intervention opportunities.

Bruder offered this definition of transition:

> A successful transition is a series of well-planned steps that result in the place-ment of the child and family into another setting. Within the field of early child-hood intervention, transition is defined as the process of moving from one pro-gram to another, or from one service to another. (2004, p. 10)

Wolery (1989) suggested that the transition process should ensure service continuity, reduce family disruptions, prepare children for their program placements, and meet legal requirements. The care with which the transition is planned and who is in-volved in the process will determine the success and ease of the transition.

HORIZONTAL AND VERTICAL TRANSITIONS

Most young children experience transitions in their early life. These transitions are often categorized into two types: horizontal and vertical (Rosenkoetter, Whaley, Hains, & Pierce, 2001). *Horizontal transitions* involve the child and family in multiple, simultaneous activities under different providers and in different locations outside the home. For example, a 3-year-old may have breakfast at home, go to an early childhood special education (ECSE) program in the morning, and go to an after-care center in the afternoon before returning home at the end of the day. The framers of the Individuals with Disabilities Education Improvement Act (IDEA) of 2004 (PL 108-446) recognized the need for smooth horizontal transitions during a child's day or week. One example cited in IDEA 2004 is collaboration among Early Head Start programs, early education programs, child care programs, and services under Part C (§ 637[10]). This collaboration promotes, for example, a child's access to a Part C ser-vice (e.g., occupational therapy) while participating in Early Head Start.

Another type of horizontal transition is one that is experienced by children and families when service providers change within a program. These transitions between service providers may occur for a variety of reasons. Individual providers may take maternity or paternity leave, relocate or change jobs, or retire. On a system level, pro-viders may change as the result of new interagency agreements and contractual changes.

Vertical transitions involve a child and family's participation in one service sys-tem after another, sequentially, across time (Rosenkoetter et al., 2001). Most young children experience such vertical transitions as hospital to home, home to child care, home or child care to preschool, and home/child care/preschool to kindergarten. Children with special developmental needs and their families experience additional transitions related to necessary EI services. Vertical transitions for young children with special needs may include movement from the NICU to EI services, from EI ser-vices to preschool special education programs, and from preschool special education programs to kindergarten (Hanson, 1999). Figure 8.2 shows a continuum of transi-tions from birth to 5 years of age; children may enter or exit intervention services at any point along this continuum.

There are numerous possibilities for entrance into services. If a state considers prematurity as an eligibility category for EI services, infants born prematurely may enter the EI system under Part C of IDEA while they are still in the NICU. In a state where infants who are at risk or who have a high probability of a disability are not served under Part C, infants may enter the system at 1 year of age in the event that developmental delays are identified. In some states young children may transition

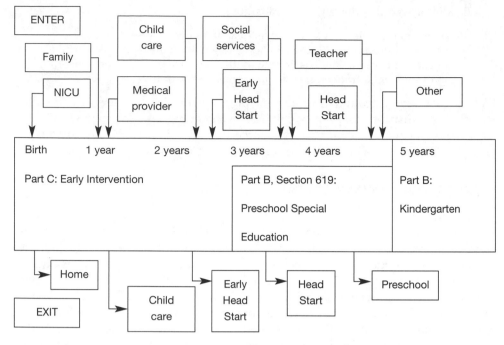

Figure 8.2.   Transitions for young children with special needs, ages birth through 5 years.

from EI into preschool special education; in others, they may be referred to preschool special education for the first time after their 3rd birthday.

Although the focus of this chapter is on the transitions into and between programs for young children with special needs, it is important to note that children may transition out of these programs and into community programs at any given point. This may occur as a result of parental request or because the children are no longer eligible to receive services. For instance, a child may be referred to Part C at 6 months of age due to a motor delay and then transition to community services at 18 months of age because he or she is no longer demonstrating delayed development.

LEGISLATION RELATED TO TRANSITION

In many ways, legislation drives the transition process. IDEA sets the parameters for federally supported intervention services for infants, toddlers, and children with disabilities. For families of children from birth through 5 years of age, IDEA also facilitates links between medical, social, health, mental health, and other needed services.

IDEA was originally passed in 1975 with the enactment of the Education for all Handicapped Children Act (EHA; PL 94-142), which provided services for all eligible students with disabilities from ages 5–21 (21 being the age at which a state generally stops providing public education to individuals). The Education of the Handicapped Act Amendments of 1986 (PL 99-457) extended free, appropriate services to children ages 3–5 and established a discretionary program for infants and toddlers (originally called Part H and now called Part C). All states opted to provide a system of services and, as the law required, began to establish "statewide, comprehensive, coordinated, multidisciplinary, interagency systems of services to children ages birth to 3 with disabilities or developmental delay" (§ 631[b][1] of Part C). States were also given the option to serve children from birth to 3 years of age who were at risk and to define the at-risk population that would be served. The first law actually called IDEA was the Individuals with Disabilities Education Act (IDEA) of 1990 (PL 101-476). Subsequent reauthorizations of IDEA strengthened the legislation; the most recent reauthorization, PL 108-446, was passed and signed into law in 2004.

Transition requirements are an important part of IDEA. The newest legislation adds a second optional eligibility category for infants and toddlers with disabilities. It gives states the option to allow parents to choose to have their children with disabilities who are ages 3–5 served through either the Part C EI program or the Part B, Section 619 preschool program. States can choose whether they want to adopt this part of the definition into their state law. If they do so, the program (Part C or Part B) in which an eligible child is served is the parent's choice. According to Part C, states may define infants or toddlers with a disability as

> Children with disabilities who are eligible for services under section 619 and who previously received services under this part until such children enter, or are eligible to enter, kindergarten or elementary school, as appropriate, provided that any programs under this part serving such children include
>
> (I) an educational component that promotes school readiness and incorporates pre-literacy, language, and numeracy skills; and
>
> (II) a written notification to parents of their rights and responsibilities in determining whether their children will continue to receive services under this part or participate in preschool programs under section 619. (Part C § 632[5][B][ii])

Families of 3- and 4-year-olds who are deciding whether their children will continue to receive services under Part C or participate in preschool programs under Section 619 must receive annual written notification of their rights and responsibilities (Part C § 635[c][2][A][i]).

IDEA requires several other transition planning activities. Part C requires that state plans include interagency agreements with the state education agency for Part B and have policies related to Child Find, flexible funding, and staff development. Part B requires that state plans include interagency agreements with the lead agency for Part C and Head Start and that they have policies related to Child Find, the use of individualized family service plans (IFSPs), and services beginning at age 3.

Another important piece of legislation that plays a significant role in the lives of many children is that regarding Head Start. One of the requirements of this program is that 10% of the program slots be reserved for children with disabilities. Head Start regulations lay out steps for facilitating a smooth transition between it and other programs. Head Start requires its grantees to develop procedures for screening and referral, transitioning from Part C to Part B, and preparing parents and teachers for transition (Administration for Children and Families, 2005). In addition, the program requires the development of interagency agreements as appropriate to support coordination of services and transition. Head Start Performance Standards related to transition must also be implemented.

The No Child Left Behind Act of 2001 (NCLB; PL 107-110) is yet another piece of legislation that emphasizes transition activities. This act is based on the premise that what a child learns before entering school (i.e., kindergarten) is vital to his or her success and that the first 5 years of a child's life are a time of immense physical, emotional, social, and cognitive growth. This legislation emphasizes coordination between Head Start, Early Reading First, and other early childhood programs and public schools. In particular, the law emphasizes transferring records among programs (with parental consent), establishing channels of communication, organizing meetings to discuss children's needs, transition-related training for personnel, and linking educational services.

An outgrowth of NCLB is the Good Start, Grow Smart: Early Childhood Initiative that addresses three major areas: strengthening Head Start; partnering with states to improve early childhood education; and providing information to teachers, caregivers, and parents. To close the gap between recommended practices and current practices in early childhood education, the U.S. Department of Education has established public awareness campaigns aimed at parents, early childhood educators, child care providers, and other interested groups (The White House, 2005).

THE FIRST VERTICAL TRANSITION: NICU TO PART C EARLY INTERVENTION

Premature births are responsible for 50% of neonatal disabilities (March of Dimes Birth Defects Foundation, 2008). Preterm birth is defined as a delivery occurring before the 37th week of pregnancy. In 2005, 525,000 infants were born prematurely; this number represents 12.7% of pregnancies in the United States (March of Dimes Birth Defects Foundation, 2008). In 2002–2004, the preterm birth rate was highest for black infants (17.8%), followed by Native Americans (13.4%), Hispanics (11.8%), whites (11.3%), and Asians (10.4%) (March of Dimes Birth Defects Foundation, 2008). The survival rate for infants born prematurely has increased dramatically since the late 1990s (Hack & Fanaroff, 1999; Hack et al., 2000), with the mortality rate decreasing by half since the mid-1990s (Linden, Paroli, & Doran, 2000). Despite this reduction in mortality, morbidity in prematurity remains high. Therefore, some states now consider prematurity as a high-risk category for Part C eligibility. For instance, infants born weighing less than 1,500 grams are automatically eligible for EI services in Hawaii; infants born weighing less than 1,200 grams are eligible in Maryland, and infants born weighing less than 1,000 grams are eligible in Illinois. States with EI eligibility criteria that include infants born prematurely play an important role in the NICU-to-home transition.

This section focuses on the NICU-to-home transition as it relates to EI. States that do not have such eligibility criteria in place need to ensure that parents are aware of the EI program and eligibility criteria so that they can gain access if needed at a later time due to developmental delay or atypical development. According to a new requirement in Part C on public awareness, states must include

> A public awareness program focusing on early identification of infants and toddlers with disabilities, including the preparation and dissemination by the lead agency...to all primary referral sources, especially hospitals and physicians, of information to be given to parents, especially to inform parents with premature infants...on the availability of early intervention services. (Part C § 635[a][6][10])

Distribution of EI program pamphlets as part of the NICU parent discharge packet is one way to accomplish this task.

Rationale for Collaboration Between
Early Interventionists and NICU Personnel

Many states have eligibility criteria that include infants born prematurely (see Chapter 8 appendix). However, many parents are not aware of EI resources in their community (Blitz, Wachtel, Blackmon, & Berenson-Howard, 1997). A coordinated effort of identification, evaluation, and service delivery among families, NICU staff, and EI providers can ensure appropriate infant referral and expedient delivery of EI services (Hussey-Gardner, McNinch, Anastasi, & Miller, 2002).

Exactly when and how discussions about Part C EI services begin varies greatly from state to state based on the requirements of each state's EI program and collaborative policies. In Colorado, for instance, all infants born weighing less than 1,200 grams are eligible for participation in the EI system. Across the state, interim individualized family service plans (IFSPs) are developed with families while infants are still in the NICU (see Figure 8.3). This collaboration resulted from the efforts of the Colorado Consortium of Intensive Care Nurseries, a network of 28 NICUs from across the state (Merrill, 2004). Variability may also exist within a state as a result of local EI and individual NICU policies.

In Tennessee, statewide policy calls for district EI offices to work with NICUs and NICU follow-up clinics to develop individual policies for implementing EI services during an infant's hospitalization and after discharge from the hospital (Tennessee Early Intervention System, 2001). Variability may exist even within a local EI program due to unique opportunities offered by different NICUs. In Maryland, the Baltimore City Infants and Toddlers Program receives referrals from numerous NICUs in the city but collaborates with the University of Maryland Hospital for Children to

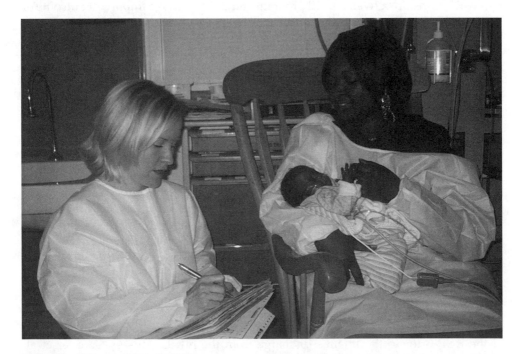

Figure 8.3.   Writing an IFSP in the NICU.

develop IFSPs prior to discharge from the NICU (Hussey-Gardner et al., 2002). Despite the variability, recommended practice suggests that discussions regarding EI services begin once the infant is medically stable and known to be potentially eligible for EI services.

In addition to infants born prematurely, infants identified as affected by illegal substance abuse or experiencing withdrawal symptoms resulting from prenatal drug exposure are to be screened by a Part C provider or designated primary referral source to determine if a referral for an EI evaluation is warranted (Part C § 637[a][6][B]). Finally, infants may also be referred from the NICU to EI services if they have a genetic or chromosomal disorder (e.g., Down syndrome).

Strategies for Fostering the Transition from NICU to EI

Hussey-Gardner, Baugh, and Miller (2001) described three levels of transition collaboration between NICUs and EI programs: 1) referral, 2) eligibility evaluation facilitation, and 3) IFSP development. They offered strategies for fostering the transition process at each of these levels.

Referral   To foster referrals, an EI liaison should be identified. This person must have a clear understanding of the state's EI eligibility requirements and system of service provision and should be familiar with the medical and developmental needs of infants born prematurely. A first step is for the EI liaison to tour the NICU(s) in the area. As part of the tour, the EI liaison will learn more about the infants the EI program will serve and will have the opportunity to identify key NICU personnel (e.g., medical director, nurse manager, social worker, developmental specialist, therapist). Following the tour, the EI liaison should arrange a meeting of key NICU and EI personnel to describe the EI program and to provide a rationale for developing a strong relationship between the EI program and the NICU. An important outcome of this meeting is to identify one person from the NICU to serve as a liaison to the EI program. One role of the NICU liaison can be to make referrals to the EI system. Ongoing roles of the EI liaison may include giving a presentation on the EI program to NICU staff, providing EI pamphlets for distribution to families, and supplying referral forms. The EI liaison should contact the NICU liaison several times a year to offer more pamphlets and to thank the NICU liaison for referrals. Yearly EI presentations are recommended for NICUs with high staff turnover.

Eligibility Evaluation Facilitation   In addition to making referrals, EI and NICU personnel can combine their efforts to foster the eligibility evaluation process. The EI liaison and NICU liaison can discuss NICU staff responsibilities to determine if appropriate evaluations are already being conducted. If so, a procedure can be established for providing this information to the EI system when referrals are made. If not, the EI and NICU liaisons can work together to identify missing pieces and to develop a plan for completing necessary components of the evaluation process. This may involve giving EI staff access to the NICU or identifying NICU staff who can take on the additional responsibilities. Funding sources may need to be identified to provide compensation for new components.

IFSP Development   At the highest level of transition collaboration—IFSP development—EI and NICU personnel can work together to facilitate the development of the IFSP prior to the infant's discharge from the NICU. Hussey-Gardner et al. (2002) stated that on-site service coordination is fundamental to the development of an IFSP prior to discharge. They noted several issues to consider when implementing on-site service coordination. First, because some families do not visit their infants regularly, it may be more difficult for the service coordinator to meet with the family to describe the program and obtain parental permission for participation. This process becomes even more difficult if the family does not have a telephone. One way to address this concern is to place information about EI services at the infant's bedside (see Figure 8.4 for a sample letter). This allows parents to gain information during nontraditional hours, when the service coordinator may not be present.

Second, in addition to contacting families in the NICU, the service coordinator can make telephone calls, mail letters, and conduct home visits prior to the infant's discharge from the NICU. Third, there is a narrow window for conducting eligibility

Maryland's PRIDE

January 3, 2005

Dear Mommy,

I'm really looking forward to the day I get to go home with you. I can't wait to learn how to play with rattles, sit, walk, and talk. I may learn these things on my own or I may need a little help.

There's a great program called Maryland's PRIDE that can help us with my development. Maryland's PRIDE stands for Maryland's Premature Infant Developmental Enrichment. Maryland's PRIDE is a special part of the Baltimore Infants and Toddlers Program that works with families in the NICU and NICU Follow-Up Clinic.

This is a free program. To begin, I will receive an evaluation by developmental specialists who will help you determine my needs. Based on these results, I may receive physical therapy, occupational therapy, special instruction, and/or toy lending.

I will always receive a service coordinator who will help us get the services I need. Melanie Smith will be our service coordinator. Melanie will be very important to us. As my needs change over time and as our family's routines change, Melanie will help us get services that work best for our family.

Even though participation in the program is voluntary, I think that Maryland's PRIDE can really help me. We can start the program now while I am in the NICU or we can wait until I am home from the hospital. The choice is yours.

Melanie would love to meet you! Please call her soon. You can call her office any time at 410-555-####. You can also page her between 8:00 a.m. and 9:00 p.m. at 410-555-####. If you'd like, you can ask the nurse to let you use the phone in the NICU to call Melanie right now.

Love,

Kaneisha

Figure 8.4. Sample letter from a neonatal intensive care (NICU) unit to be given to parents to inform them of an early intervention program. (From Maryland's PRemature Infant Development & Enrichment (PRIDE) program, Baltimore: University of Maryland.)

evaluations and developing the IFSP. If the evaluations are conducted too soon, the results may not accurately reflect the infant's EI needs at discharge. Therefore, it is desirable to conduct the eligibility evaluations 1–2 weeks prior to the infant's discharge. The 2 weeks preceding a discharge are busy for the infant and family. This necessitates that the service coordinator and staff conducting evaluations have flexible schedules that allow them to be available when the infant and family are available.

Regardless of the level of transition collaboration, Hussey-Gardner and her colleagues (2002) stressed that hospital staff education is essential for success. For the best possible collaboration and the smoothest transition between the NICU and the EI program, NICU staff should embrace EI, know eligibility criteria, and be aware of how the state EI program operates.

Merrill (2004) also offered several steps for building a medical and EI transitional coalition. The first step is for the early interventionist to educate him- or herself. This involves learning state guidelines for the eligibility of infants born prematurely and touring area NICUs. The second step is to identify key medical and EI players. The next step is to bring these key players together for a 1-day information-sharing meeting. The goal of this meeting is to build an effective team to develop written procedures that bring the discharge plan and the IFSP together. The final step is to assess methods and efficiency. Merrill noted that, in the beginning, the coalition may need to meet every month or every other month until the written protocol is developed. After that, she states that quarterly or semiannual meetings are desirable to address any issues that arise.

One Model of Collaboration: Maryland's Premature Infant Developmental Enrichment

Maryland's Premature Infant Developmental Enrichment (PRIDE) is a collaborative endeavor between the University of Maryland Hospital for Children and the Baltimore City Infants and Toddlers Program (BITP; Hussey-Gardner et al., 2002). Maryland's PRIDE began as a State of Maryland Demonstration Model Grant in 1994 and has evolved into a solid and ongoing contractual relationship between the hospital and the BITP. Maryland's PRIDE evolved to meet four primary needs: 1) to refer infants for services as early as possible, 2) to avoid duplicate evaluations, 3) to provide on-site service coordination, and 4) to expedite the process of accessing EI services. Prior to the initiation of Maryland's PRIDE, infants were not referred from the NICU, but infants eligible for EI services were referred from the NICU follow-up program. Following referral, the BITP assigned a service coordinator to each family, contacted the family, scheduled and conducted a multidisciplinary eligibility evaluation, and developed the IFSP within 45 days of referral. Services began within 30 days of the parent's signature on the plan. As part of Maryland's PRIDE, infants are now referred from the NICU as well as the NICU follow-up program.

The NICU at the University of Maryland Hospital for Children is a tertiary care facility that has a 40-bed capacity and is one of Maryland's major referral centers capable of delivering care to newborns. There are approximately 650 admissions to the NICU each year. Upon admission into the NICU, the developmental specialist tracks all infants to determine if they are potentially eligible to participate in Maryland's PRIDE. Two methods facilitate tracking: reviewing medical records and attending the NICU multidisciplinary rounds. The purpose of the multidisciplinary rounds is to conduct comprehensive discharge planning that encompasses medical and social issues relevant to the infant and entire family. Developmental specialists, neonatologists, nursing representatives, social workers, rehabilitative services representatives (e.g., physical, occupational, or speech therapist), and medical case managers attend these multidisciplinary rounds. Once an infant is identified as medically stable and potentially eligible for the BITP, the developmental specialist posts Maryland's PRIDE information at the infant's bedside for the family, makes a referral to the BITP, and informs the service coordinator.

The service coordinator then makes contact with the family to introduce the program. If the family desires to participate (approximately 95% of families choose to do so), an eligibility evaluation is conducted. The eligibility evaluation process begins with a thorough review of the infant's medical record to obtain results of previously administered developmental assessments. Such assessments may include, but are not limited to, the newborn hearing screen, retinopathy of prematurity exam, physical therapy assessment, and a feeding evaluation. These results are supplemented with an evaluation conducted by the developmental specialist. The evaluation frequently includes a modified NICU Network Neurobehavioral Scale (NNNS™) (Lester & Tronick, 2004) and the Best Beginnings Developmental Screen (Hussey-Gardner, 2005). During administration, the developmental specialist also observes the infant to determine the infant's approach, coping, and stress signals. In addition, he or she observes what strategies are useful in facilitating an alert state in the infant and what fosters calming when the infant is upset. The family is encouraged to observe the exam; interested family members can also be active participants in the evaluation process, eliciting responses from their infant under the guidance of the developmental specialist. Results and recommendations are discussed with the infant's family and multidisciplinary team (e.g., primary nurse, neonatologist, therapist, social worker). A detailed report summarizing the findings is placed in the infant's NICU, NICU follow-up, and EI charts.

The service coordinator and developmental specialist meet with the family to develop the IFSP at a time and location convenient for the family. This meeting may occur while the infant is in the NICU, or it may occur in the home or community following discharge. The plan includes evaluation results; family-identified infant strengths, needs, and priorities; outcomes; strategies and activities to meet these outcomes; location, frequency, intensity, and provider(s) of EI services; and linkages (non–EI services the infant will receive, such as primary health care, nursing care, NICU follow-up, Early Head Start). The service coordinator continues to work with the family following discharge by conducting home visits to provide ongoing developmental monitoring and anticipatory guidance, accompanying the family at NICU follow-up appointments, and coordinating services until the child turns 3 years of age and transitions to Part B and/or community resources.

THE SECOND VERTICAL TRANSITION: EI PROGRAMS TO ECSE PROGRAMS

Entering preschool is often a major change for children and their families. It involves new routines, settings, and people. For families with children with disabilities, the transition from Part C to Part B can be particularly stressful. Family involvement is mandatory in Part C, and parents are expected to make decisions for their children and encouraged to advocate for their children's needs. In fact, one of the goals of Part

Figure 8.5.   Talking about turning 3.

C is to teach families to be good advocates for their children. When a child enters a Part B program (for most children, this occurs at age 3), the school assumes the primary educational responsibility, and its values and priorities for the child's education may or may not match the family's (Johnson, 2001). Hanson et al. (2000) found that families were offered the services available in the district regardless of the appropriateness of the services in meeting the child's needs. Other types of services that were potentially relevant but not readily available were not discussed. Working through these differences may be difficult but is important.

Easing a child's adjustment to a new setting is important for several reasons. First, it reduces the amount of time that a child is distressed, and second, it minimizes classroom disruptions. A child who is having a temper tantrum, is crying, or is withdrawn needs more one-to-one attention. If a child with special needs is having trouble adjusting and is in a community setting designed for children who are typically developing, the teacher might conclude that the child needs a more restrictive placement or is not ready for school (Donegan, Fink, Fowler, & Wischnowski, 1994).

Hanson et al. (2000) found that key strategies and supports during the transition process include exchanging information between families and professionals, providing families with opportunities to visit preschool settings, providing support to families from a key person or guide (either a professional or another parent), ensuring the continuity of services, and maintaining a continued focus on the child's needs and concerns. Families and service providers should prepare the child for the transition to preschool by 1) discussing the setting in a positive tone, 2) encouraging the child to ask questions or relate fears, 3) visiting the program and providing exposure to some group experiences, 4) teaching the child specific skills and routines that are used in preschool settings, and 5) sharing information about the child between programs and establishing privacy rules. Care must be taken to ensure families' right to privacy (Donegan et al., 1994).

The Role of Transition Agreements and Policies

IDEA requires states to have a state-level transition agreement for children's movement from Part C to Part B. Beyond that requirement, states and counties have established a variety of agreements and policies across agencies. These linkages are key elements in the transition process. More linkages can translate to a greater array of services offered to a family.

In 1996, The National Early Childhood Technical Assistance Center (NECTAC) convened a work group to develop a list of situations considered instrumental in developing effective transition policies and practices for all early childhood transition levels. The members of this work group had previously provided technical assistance on transition in almost every state. Specifically, the work group found that conflicts in transition were most likely to occur when

- Services are limited

- Budgets are cut or caseloads are enlarged with no accompanying increases in support

- Transitions occur midyear and existing services are full

- Transitions are due to occur in late spring or the summer months

- Transition planners represent different professional, agency, or family cultures and are insensitive to the families' needs

- One agency believes it owns the transition to the exclusion of input from other agencies and/or the families

- Transition planners have no previous relationship or only negative relationships

- Transition planners have different expectations, especially for the nature of family involvement, appropriate assessment qualities, or the characteristics of services

- Key individuals fail to realize the importance for families of smooth transition during early childhood

- Strategies for resolving conflicts are not employed (Rosenkoetter et al., 2001)

NECTAC found that when these 10 items were addressed, early childhood transitions steadily improved. But when only some of the elements were addressed, local or state leaders typically struggled with transition problems and families reported challenges in transitioning between programs or services (Rosenkoetter et al., 2001).

When Should School Personnel and Families Begin the Transition Process?

The transition process should begin early. According to IDEA, states must describe how the lead agency will,

> In the case of a child who may be eligible for such preschool services, with the approval of the family, convene a conference among the lead agency, the

family and the local educational agency not less than 90 days (and at the discretion of all such parties, not more than 9 months) before the child is eligible for the preschool services, to discuss any services the child might receive. (§ 637[9][A][ii][II])

IDEA also states that for children who may not eligible for preschool services, reasonable efforts must be made to convene a conference among the lead agency, the family, and other service providers to discuss appropriate services (§ 637[9][A][III]).

Donegan et al. (1994) recommend starting the transition process 6 to 9 months before the transition. This allows enough time to prepare the child, family, and EI staff as well as to find the least restrictive and most appropriate setting for the child.

Discussions regarding transitioning out of Part C begin when a child turns 2 years of age. This gives the family and service coordinator a full year to prepare for the transition that will ultimately occur when the child turns 3. This year is needed not only to find the best placement for the child at 3 but also to prepare the family for the changes that will occur. This is particularly important if the service coordinator has been extensively involved in arranging linkage services for the child and family. The following scenario illustrates this point.

Case Study: Michael

Michael is a 24-month-old infant born prematurely with extensive medical complications. His mother is single, 19 years old, and without a support system. Susan became the family's service coordinator prior to Michael's discharge from the NICU. Following discharge, Michael's IFSP included weekly home-based physical therapy and Early Head Start. Over the first 2 years of Michael's life, Susan arranged all of Michael's medical appointments and arranged for transportation. The family did not have a telephone or a car, and Michael's mother had great difficulty arranging and keeping appointments. Susan would drive to the family's house to discuss and arrange the needed appointments, then drive to the family's home to inform Michael's mother of the appointments. Despite Susan's efforts, Michael missed half of all the appointments, necessitating additional appointments, transportation, and referral arrangements. When Michael was 18 months old, Family Preservation (a federally funded program dedicated to preserving families at risk of having their children placed in foster care) became involved to further assist Michael's family. At 21 months of age, Michael was diagnosed with cerebral palsy. Susan facilitated the acquisition of needed equipment.

During the first home visit following Michael's 2nd birthday, Susan told his mother that over the next year, they would make plans for Michael's preschool placement at age 3, after which Susan would no longer be the family's service coordinator. When Michael was 30 months old, he was diagnosed with intellectual disabilities. Susan helped his mother through this diagnosis and arranged for her to tour a preschool that could meet Michael's educational needs. His mother loved the site. When Michael was 33 months old, Susan accompanied him and his mother to a doctor's appointment. During this time the mother realized that Susan would no longer be a part of her life once Michael transitioned into the preschool program, and the mother would not have Susan to make appointments, arrange transportation, and ensure referrals. Following this appointment, Susan and Michael's mother began to plan for additional ways for the mother to get the assistance she would need after Michael turned 3.

THE THIRD VERTICAL TRANSITION:
ECSE PROGRAMS TO KINDERGARTEN OR PART B

Each year in the United States, approximately 4 million children make the transition from home or an early educational setting to kindergarten (Pacheo, Tullis, Everest, Baker, & Sutherland, 2004). In a survey of kindergarten teachers, the National Center for Early Development and Learning (1998) found that 48% of children entering kindergarten have moderate to serious problems in skills such as following directions, working independently, communicating, working within a group, and performing preacademic and academic tasks. Many of these children enter school from home, making kindergarten their first entry to a school environment. Others will enter from Head Start, preschool, or ECSE programs. This transition is often stressful for both the child and parent. As the child prepares to enter this new environment and adjust to new friends, teachers, and routines, the parent must make new connections with school personnel to ensure a smooth continuum of services.

Figure 8.6.   All smiles about kindergarten.

When Should the Transition Process to Kindergarten Begin?

IDEA does not set a specific timeline for transition to kindergarten. One reason for this is that the 619 preschool section of IDEA covers children ages 3–5, and most children start kindergarten while they are 5 years of age. However, the practical question of when transition planning to kindergarten should begin remains. The short answer is that it varies. Some families need a longer transition planning time than others, depending on the child's needs, the parents' concerns, and whether the child is continuing in the system or is newly diagnosed.

In Boston, a year-long citywide effort was undertaken to prepare children for kindergarten. Starting in September 2000 and continuing every month until children entered kindergarten the following year, parents received registration information, calls from school volunteers, and written information on activities to do at home to improve their children's learning skills. Kindergarten registration began in January, and placements were made in March. This gave parents time to prepare their children for kindergarten (Vaishnav, 2000).

Although ideal, such a lengthy transition period is often not feasible. In a survey of more than 3,500 kindergarten teachers, Rimm-Kaufman, Pianta, and Cox (2000) found that the majority of teachers implement some sort of transition practices, but after school starts. Teachers reported sending a letter to parents after the beginning of school, holding an open house after school starts, and sending home a brochure after school starts. The least common practices used included calling families before or after school starts and visiting children's homes or preschool programs. Unfortunately, low-intensity practices do little to involve families and build connections prior to the child's entrance to school (National Center for Early Development and Learning, 2002).

What Strategies Are Most Effective?

Several overarching principles promote successful transitions. They include placement decisions that meet individual needs; uninterrupted services; nonconfrontational and effective models of advocacy that families can emulate throughout their children's lives; avoidance of duplication in assessment and goal planning; and reduced stress for children, families, and service providers (Shotts, Rosenkoetter, Streufert, & Rosenkoetter, 1994). The next question is how to achieve these basic principles.

Most important, school personnel and families need to develop a strong partnership. When families and school personnel work toward the same goals, successful outcomes for children are more likely. Partnerships can be achieved through several avenues. First, school personnel should maintain consistent, effective communication using all modes of communication, including telephone calls, e-mail, letters, and meetings. Second, parents and school personnel should establish roles and expectations for child-related goals together. This is achieved through effective communication and is a vital part of the process. Third, when possible, parents and school personnel should consider a variety of program options (Johnson, 2001).

Pianta, Cox, Taylor, and Early (1999) suggested that schools need to base their strategies on three interrelated principles. First, school personnel reach out to families and preschools to establish and engage in two-way communication. Second, school personnel establish links with families before the first day of school. Third, school personnel reach out at a variety of intensities depending on the individual needs of the child and family; this would include low-intensity efforts such as flyers as well as high-intensity activities such as personal contacts or home visits.

The Florida Partnership for Parent Involvement (1999) advocates for the basic components of the transition model, stating that successful transition programs are child centered and should meet the individual needs of the child and family. Transition programs should promote child functioning and minimize family disruption. In addition, parents should be involved as teachers, learners, decision makers, and advocates. Furthermore, staff involvement from the sending and receiving programs is critical to successful programming. Finally, interagency or program collaboration is essential, and administrators must support all of these efforts. How these efforts are carried out can vary as long as all of the components are retained.

WHY COORDINATION BETWEEN FAMILIES AND KEY PERSONNEL IS VITAL ACROSS ALL AGES

The Head Start Information and Publication Center, under the auspices of the Administration for Children and Families (2003), listed the benefits for children, parents, and teachers of taking the time to establish effective transitions. These benefits easily transfer to transitions from EI to preschool and from preschool to kindergarten. Possible benefits to children include continuity with earlier experiences, increased motivation and openness to new experiences, enhanced self-confidence, improved relations with others, and a greater sense of trust. For parents, benefits may include increased confidence in their children's ability to achieve in the new setting, improved self-confidence in their own ability to communicate with staff and to effectively influence the system, a sense of pride and commitment in their ongoing involvement in the development of their children, and a greater knowledge and appreciation of early programs and staff. For professionals, the benefits may include increased knowledge of the children and an enhanced ability to meet individual needs, increased parental and community support, more resources and a larger network of professional support; increased awareness of programs in the community, and a renewed sense of professionalism and pride in their efforts to reach out to young children and their families.

CONCLUSIONS

Family and staff involvement increases when effective transition strategies are actively put into place at all levels. Figure 8.7 provides a flowchart and checklist of transition steps for children newly entering the system and transitioning from one service to another. The level of involvement a family has in a child's educational experiences is based on the professional's view of that involvement in these steps; furthermore, the professional's level of involvement is strongly influenced by his or her supervisor's attitude (Bohan-Baker & Little, 2002). This chain effect emphasizes the importance of forming teams to facilitate transition activities. When parents, professionals, and supervisors form these teams, families are more likely to become active partners in their child's transitions. Training programs and in-service training modules should actively promote family involvement from birth through elementary school. Table 8.1 lists web sites that offer important transition information for parents, professionals, and supervisors.

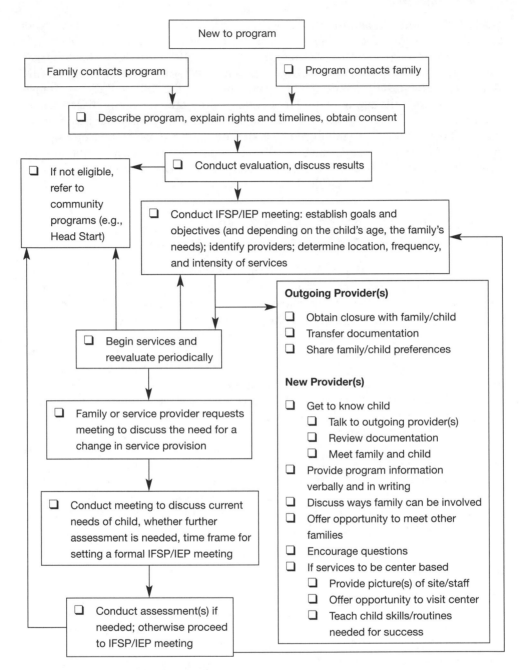

Figure 8.7. Transition flowchart and checklist.

Table 8.1. A selection of web sites offering transition information

Web site	Description
www.cec.sped.org	The Council for Exceptional Children is the largest international professional organization dedicated to improving educational outcomes for individuals with special needs.
www.ed.gov	Official web site of the U.S. Department of Education. It includes information on federal legislation, initiatives, and contacts.
www.fpg.unc.edu	One of the oldest multidisciplinary web sites dedicated to enhancing knowledge about families and children
www.headstartinfo.org	Provides important information on Head Start, including updates, partnerships, and collaboration, on-line publications, and locating a Head Start program. Also includes a link to the on-line publication "Easing the Transition from Preschool to Kindergarten: A Guide for Early Childhood Teachers and Administrators" (www.headstartinfo.org/recruitment/trans_hs.htm)
www.ihdi.uky.edu/nectc/	Provides information on the National Early Childhood Transition Center. Also includes a searchable database of transition research, policy, and practice; information on personnel development related to transition; transition stories; transition resources from other organizations; and information on IDEA reauthorization
www.naeyc.org	The National Association for the Education of Young Children is dedicated to improving the well-being of all young children, with particular focus on the quality of educational and developmental services. Site provides information on the association and early childhood issues. Also includes a link to important information about kindergarten readiness, transition, appropriate practices, resources, and a kindergarten database of state profiles (www.naeyc.org/ece/critical/kindergarten.asp)
www.nectac.org	The National Early Childhood Technical Assistance Center at the University of North Carolina at Chapel Hill web site has a current list of Part C and Section 619 contacts as well as legislative and procedural safeguards.
www.nichcy.org	A central resource of information on disabilities among infants, toddlers, and youth; IDEA; No Child Left Behind; and research on effective practices

REFERENCES

Administration for Children and Families. (2003). *Easing the transition from preschool to kindergarten: A guide for early childhood teachers and administrators.* Alexandria, VA: The Head Start Bureau: Head Start Information and Publication Center.

Administration for Children and Families. (2005). *Compilation of the Head Start Act.* Retrieved January 27, 2005, from www.acf.hhs.gov/programs/hsb/budget/headstartact.htm

Blitz, R.K., Wachtel, R.C., Blackmon, L., & Berenson-Howard, J. (1997). Neurodevelopmental outcome of extremely low birth weight infants in Maryland. *Maryland Medical Journal, 46*(1), 18–24.

Bohan-Baker, M., & Little, P. (2002, April). *The transition to kindergarten: A review of current research and promising practices to involve families.* Cambridge, MA: Harvard Family Research Project.

Bruder, M.B. (2004). *Early intervention for children with disabilities.* Retrieved December 4, 2004, from www.bridges4kids.org

Donegan, M., Fink, D.B., Fowler, S., & Wischnowski, M.W. (1994). *Entering a new preschool: How service providers and families can ease the transition of children turning three who have special needs.* Champaign, IL: University of Illinois at Urbana–Champaign, FACTS/LRE.

Early Head Start National Resource Center. (2004). *Transition strategies: Continuity and care in the lives of infants and toddlers.* Retrieved October 9, 2004, from www.ehsnrc.org/pdfiles/MPS transitions.pdf

Education for All Handicapped Children Act of 1975, PL 94-142, 20 U.S.C. §§ 1400 *et seq.*

Education of the Handicapped Act Amendments of 1986, PL 99-457, 20 U.S.C. §§ 1400 *et seq.*

Florida Partnership for Parent Involvement. (1999). *Transition provider tip sheets, #3: Developing a successful transition program.* Tampa: University of South Florida.

Hack, M., & Fanaroff, A.A. (1999). Outcomes of children of extremely low birthweight and gestational age in the 1990s. *Early Human Development, 53*(3), 193–218.

Hack, M., Wilson-Costello, D., Friedman, H., Taylor, G., Schluchter, M., & Fanaroff, A.A. (2000). Neurodevelopment and predictors of outcomes of children with birth weights less than 1000g: 1992–1995. *Archives of Pediatrics and Adolescent Medicine, 154*(7), 725–731.

Hains, A., Rosenkoetter, S., & Fowler, S. (1991). Transition planning with families in early intervention programs. *Infants & Young Children, 3*(4), 38–47.

Hanson, M. (1999). *Early transitions for children and families: Transitions from infant/toddler services to preschool education.* (ERIC EC Digest No. E581)x

Hanson, M.J., Beckman, P.J., Horn, E., Marquart, J., Sandall, S.R., Greig, D. et al. (2000). Entering preschool: Family and professional experiences in this transition process. *Journal of Early Intervention, 23*(4), 279–293.

Hussey-Gardner, B. (2005). *Best beginnings developmental screen.* Baltimore: University of Maryland.

Hussey-Gardner, B., Baugh, C., & Miller, M. (2001, December). *Maryland's premature infant developmental enrichment program.* Paper presented at the Maryland State Early Intervention Conference, Baltimore.

Hussey-Gardner, B., McNinch, A., Anastasi, J., & Miller, M. (2002, April). Early intervention best practice: Collaboration among an NICU, an early intervention program, and an NICU follow-up program. *Neonatal Network, 21*(3), 15–22.

Individuals with Disabilities Education Act (IDEA) of 1990, PL 101-476, 20 U.S.C. §§ 1400 *et seq.*

Individuals with Disabilities Education Improvement Act (IDEA) of 2004, PL 108-446, 20 U.S.C. §§ 1400 *et seq.*

Johnson, C. (2001). *Supporting families in transition between early intervention and school age programs.* Denver: Colorado Families for Hands and Voices. Retrieved January 26, 2005, from www.handsandvoices.org

Lester, B.M., & Tronick, E.Z. (2004). *NICU Network Neurobehavioral Scale (NNNS™): manual.* Baltimore: Paul H. Brookes Publishing Co.

Linden, D., Paroli, E., & Doran, M. (2000). *Preemies: The essential guide for parents of premature babies.* New York: Pocket Books.

March of Dimes Birth Defects Foundation. (2008). *Peristats.* Retrieved March 7, 2008, from http://www.marchofdimes. com/peristats.com/peristats/prematurity

Merrill, D. (2004, May). *Six simple steps to building a medical and early intervention transitional coalition.* Retrieved January 25, 2005, from www.pediatricservices.com/prof/prof-2.htm

National Center for Early Development and Learning. (1998, July). Kindergarten transitions. *NCEDL Spotlight #1.* Chapel Hill: University of North Carolina at Chapel Hill.

National Center for Early Development and Learning. (2002). Transition to kindergarten. *Early Childhood Research and Policy Briefs, 2*(2). Chapel Hill, NC: FPG Publications Office.

No Child Left Behind Act of 2001, PL 107-110, 115 Stat. 1425, 20 U.S.C. §§ 6301 *et seq.*

Pacheo, P., Tullis, E., Everest, M., Baker, H., & Sutherland, C. (2004). *Kindergarten transition study.* Camarillo, CA: California State University Channel Islands, Center for Excellence in Early Childhood Development.

Pianta, R.C., Cox, M.J., Taylor, L., & Early, D. (1999). Kindergarten teachers' practices related to the transition to school: Results of a national survey. *The Elementary School Journal, 100*(1), 71–86.

Rimm-Kaufman, S.E., Pianta, R.C., & Cox, M.J. (2000). Teachers' judgments of problems in the transition to kindergarten. *Early Childhood Research Quarterly, 15*(2), 147–166.

Rosenkoetter, S., Whaley, K., Hains, A., & Pierce, L. (2001, Spring). The evolution of transition policy for young children with special needs and their families: Past, present, and future. *Topics in Early Childhood Special Education, 21*(1), 3–15.

Shotts, C.K., Rosenkoetter, S.E., Streufert, C.A, & Rosenkoetter, L.I. (1994). Transition policy and issues: A view from the states. *Topics in Early Childhood Special Education, 14*(3), 395–411.

Tennessee Early Intervention System. (2001, January). *Premature infants: Guidelines for early intervention services.* Nashville: Tennessee Department of Education.

Vaishnav, A. (2000, August 29). Program aims to ease move to kindergarten. *The Boston Globe*, B1–B2.

The White House. (2005). *Good start, grow smart: The Bush administration's early childhood initiative.* Retrieved January 11, 2005, from http://www.whitehouse.gov

Wolery, M. (1989). Transitions in early childhood special educations: Issues and procedures. *Focus on Exceptional Children, 22*(2), 1–16.

Chapter 8 Appendix

Eligibility of Infants Born Prematurely

State	Automatic eligibility	Definition
Alabama	No	Early intervention (EI) staff are linked with the state perinatal system and the high-risk clinics around the state to facilitate referrals and talk to families.
Alaska	No	Any infant who has spent time in an neonatal intensive care unit (NICU) is referred and tracked.
American Samoa	Yes	Preterm birth at < 33 weeks' gestation
Arizona	No	
Arkansas	No	Because there are so many conditions associated with prematurity that can precipitate developmental delays, prematurity is considered a valid reason to refer a child to the program.
California	Yes	Infants are eligible when an interdisciplinary team determines that two or more of the following factors exist: preterm birth at < 32 weeks' gestation and/or birth weight < 1,500 grams; assisted ventilation for 48 hours during the first 28 days of life; small for gestational age (SGA); asphyxia associated with a 5-minute Apgar score of 0–5; severe and persistent metabolic abnormality; neonatal seizures; central nervous system (CNS) infection; biomedical insult; multiple congenital anomalies or genetic disorders; prenatal exposure to known teratogens; prenatal substance exposure; clinically significant failure to thrive, persistent hypotonia or hypertonia.
Colorado	Yes	Birth weight < 1,200 grams. In addition, the following SGA diagnoses are also considered "established" conditions and automatically qualify a child: Infant ≤ 6 months and evidence shows the child was born at the corresponding gestational age and weight: 33 weeks' gestation and birth weight ≤ 1,325 grams, 34 weeks' gestational age and birth weight ≤ 1,500 grams, 35 weeks' gestational age and birth weight ≤ 1,700 grams, 36 weeks' gestational age and birth weight ≤ 1,875 grams, between 37 and 40 weeks' gestational age and birth weight < 2,000 grams.
Connecticut	Yes	Infants born < 1,000 grams or born ≤ 28 weeks' gestation.
Delaware	Yes	Piloting a revised definition of birth weight ≤ 1,000 grams for any gestational age. Other babies who are small for birth dates as determined by a neonatologist to be at high risk of developmental delay. Children with birth weights between 1,000 and 1,250 grams will continue to have developmental evaluations as needed, but unless they are identified with developmental delays, they will not become eligible under Part C.
Department of Defense	Yes	Birth weight ≤ 1,000 grams, or other medical complications that place the child at significant risk as indicated by clinical judgment with written supporting evidence.

State	Automatic eligibility	Definition
District of Columbia	No	
Florida	No	
Georgia	No	However, several conditions that are the consequences of being born very prematurely are on the list of conditions for automatic eligibility (e.g., intraventricular hemorrhage).
Guam	Yes	An infant needs to meet one of the following criteria: 1) birth weight < 1,500 grams, prematurity < 30 weeks' gestational age, birth weight < 1,750 grams and < 37 weeks' gestational age, oxygen therapy > 7 days, Apgar scores < 6 at 5 minutes, persistent atypical patterns of neurological behavior, severe respiratory distress with or without mechanical ventilation > 24 hours, intraventricular hemorrhage (IVH), hyperbilirubinemia > 20 MAS requiring ventilation >24 hours, postmaturity > 42 weeks' gestational age; 2) having at least three of the following conditions with the presence of two circumstances regarding family situation/history: Medical condition PLUS two or more conditions: prematurity at 33–34 weeks' gestational age, symptomatic hypocalcemia < 7.5 mg unresolved after 2 days, meconium aspiration requiring antibiotics, hypoglycemia < 40 mg, birth weight of 1,750–2,500 grams without complications; 3) the above medical condition plus presence of two or more conditions: History of developmental disability (DD), evidence of emotional problems, teenage parents age 16 or younger, poor utilization of accessible medical care services, limited education, poor support system, poor history of parenting by own family, inadequate housing, inadequate economic resources, extended separation of parent and infant (due to medical factors), family history of deafness or blindness, maternal maturity > 40 years at birth with presence of one or more of the following: two previous abortions, stillbirth, hypertension, heart disease, toxemia, diabetes, cancer, sickle cell disease, major surgery during pregnancy, first child, multiple births.
Hawaii	Yes	Birth weight ≤ 1,500 grams or gestational age < 32 weeks.
Idaho	Yes	Birth weight < 1,500 grams, prematurity at ≤ 32 weeks' gestational age, intracranial hemorrhage (level 3 or 4 bleed) or infarct, intrauterine growth retardation (IUGR) as diagnosed by physician (≤ 10th percentile), SGA as diagnosed by physician (≤ 10th percentile), bronchial pulmonary dysplasia (BPD), feeding abnormalities/difficulties, or CNS instability as demonstrated by significant disorganized states of arousal and confirmed by a medical/therapeutic professional. Infants are also eligible if they are born at ≤ 36 weeks' gestational age plus one or more of the following significant environmental risk factors: parent–infant attachment risk factors (e.g., decreased responsiveness or reciprocity of infant, parental depression/withdrawal) as diagnosed by medical or mental health professional or clearly documented in medical history; parent with significant chronic, physical, or mental health problem or with a DD where supportive or therapeutic services could facilitate parenting; multiproblem or severely stressful life situation (e.g., parent perception of severe financial problems, drug/alcohol problems in family, incarceration, homeless); no prenatal care; maternal age ≤ 15 years; and foster placement of child.
Illinois	Yes	Birth weight < 1,000 grams.
Indiana	Yes	Infants born prematurely with a birth weight ≤ 1,500 grams and/or a chromosomal abnormality or genetic disorder; neurological disorder; congenital disorder; sensory impairment including

(continued)

State	Automatic eligibility	Definition
Indiana *(cont.)*		vision and hearing; severe toxic exposure, including prenatal exposure; or a neurological abnormality in the newborn period.
Iowa	Yes	A child determined to be premature by a qualified health professional using informed clinical opinion is eligible.
Kansas	Maybe	Infants born prematurely may be eligible due to established risk or based on informed clinical opinion. The NICU refers premature infants to Part C if the child has a diagnosed mental or physical condition that has a high probability of resulting in DD. This could include a combination of risk factors that when taken together makes DD highly probable, including but not limited to a combination of prematurity < 30 weeks, VLBW < 1,500 grams, small or large for gestational age, length of stay in the NICU > 45 days, apnea, or prolonged ventilation.
		When discharging premature infants, the NICU notifies Part C if the child is at risk of developmental delay because of biological or environmental reasons, including but not limited to low birth weight 1,500–2,500 grams, > 30 weeks' gestation, asphyxia, or respiratory distress. Part C may choose to monitor/provide tracking for these children.
Kentucky	No	
Louisiana	No	Birth weight < 1,500 grams and/or < 32 weeks gestation. In addition, infants with one of the following criteria are eligible: IVH Grade III or IV, posthemorrhagic hydrocephalus, periventricular leukomalacia (PVL), or other significant intracranial disorders.
Maine	Maybe	Prematurity or complications at birth may indicate risk of developmental delay and may qualify a child for services. Children should be referred to determine eligibility.
Maryland	Yes	Infants, including those born prematurely, with one of the following: birth weight < 1,200 grams, IVH grade III or IV, chromosomal disorder (e.g., trisomy 21), symptomatic congenital infection, significant effects of maternal drug abuse (e.g., fetal alcohol syndrome, infants affected by intrauterine drug exposure), severe congenital malformations (e.g., congenital hydrocephalus), inborn errors of metabolism (in which no treatment is available or inadequate treatment), neurodegenerative disorders (e.g., adrenoleukodystrophy, Tay-Sachs disease), epilepsy (in which seizures are frequent or difficult to control, or underlying condition is associated with frequent cognitive impairments), severe encephalopathy, blind or significantly visually impaired, deaf or significantly hard of hearing, AIDS, lead poisoning (≤ 20 μg/dL), or other diagnosed conditions with high probability of DD (e.g., BPD, surgical NEC).
Massachusetts	No	Children are eligible if they meet at least four of the following criteria: If < 18 months old, birth weight < 1,200 grams, premature birth at < 32 weeks' gestational age, NICU stay of ≥ 5 days, or Apgar score of < 5 at 5 minutes. Children < 3 years are also eligible if the total number of days as an inpatient in a hospital or extended care facility > 25 days in a 6-month period (this does not apply to the birth admission of a premature child); diagnosis at birth of IUGR or SGA; weight for age/height < 5th percentile or > 95th percentile; chronic feeding difficulties (i.e., conditions must exist over an extended period of time: severe colic, stressful or extremely conflicted feedings, refusal or inability to eat, or failure to progress in feeding skills); insecure attachment/interactional difficulties (child appears to have inadequate or disturbed social relationships, depression, or indiscriminate aggressive behavior and the family perceives this as an issue); blood level ≤ 15 μg/dL; suspected CNS abnormality related to

State	Automatic eligibility	Definition
Massachusetts *(cont.)*		infection, trauma, metabolic issues, asphyxia, in utero drug exposure, or abnormal muscle tone; multiple trauma/loss that has an impact on the care and/or development of the child; maternal age < 17 years or female has three or more children at < 20 years; maternal education ≤ 10 years; parental chronic illness or disability affecting caregiving ability; lack of family social supports, adequate food, clothing, or shelter; opened or confirmed protective service investigation; substance abuse; domestic violence.
Michigan	No	Infants with intracranial hemorrhage and BPD do qualify.
Minnesota	No	Infants with IVH Grades III or IV and BPD do qualify. Infants with certain prenatal/perinatal conditions also qualify, these include prenatal toxic exposures such as fetal alcohol syndrome, prenatal infections such as cytomegalovirus, infants born weighing ≤ 1,500 grams, Grades III and IV intracranial hemorrhage (e.g., PVH-IVH, stroke), congenital diaphragmatic hernia. Teams can always use informed clinical opinion regarding other issues related to prematurity.
Mississippi	No	Teams are encouraged to give strong consideration for the use of informed clinical opinion to rule more preemies eligible. Mississippi is in the process of drafting guidelines for teams to consider when evaluating preemies.
Missouri	Maybe	Infants with a birth weight < 1,500 grams and one or more of the following conditions qualify: Apgar < 6 at 5 minutes, IVH Grades II/III/IV, ventilator dependence ≤ 72 hours, and asphyxia.
Montana	No	
Nebraska	No	Infants born prematurely are referred for tracking.
Nevada	Yes	Extreme prematurity, until child is 1 year corrected age (<1,000 grams or <27 weeks' gestation). A child who is premature with a difficult NICU history could be made eligible via a wide variety of conditions (e.g., BPD, ROP); decisions are made on case-by-case basis.
New Hampshire	No	
New Jersey	No	
New Mexico	Yes	Birth weight < 2,500 grams or preterm birth at < 35 weeks' gestational age.
New York	Yes	Birth weight < 1,000 grams
North Carolina	Maybe	A child is eligible if there are at least three concerns with the child or family that could result in a delay or disability. Examples of such concerns include birth weight < 1,500 grams, preterm birth at < 32 weeks' gestation, respiratory distress with positive airway pressure for > 30 days or mechanical ventilation for > 6 hours, apneic episodes with bradycardia occurring for > 30 days, intercranial hemorrhage, hyperbilirubinemia, hypoglycemia; prenatal substance exposure; maternal age < 15 years; family or social support issues.
North Dakota	Yes	A child is eligible if two of the following conditions are present: birth weight < 1,500 grams; preterm birth at < 32 weeks' gestational age; IVH; ventilator dependent for ≥ 72 hours; asphyxia; had ECMO, RDS, IUGR, or PVL.
Northern Mariana Islands	Yes	Birth weight < 1,500 grams.

(continued)

State	Automatic eligibility	Definition
Ohio	Yes	Birth weight < 1,500 grams. Children with a birth weight 1,500–2,500 grams are also eligible if one of the following is present: birth trauma, IVH Grade III or IV, intrauterine hypoxia, birth asphyxia, RDS, BPD, infections specific to the perinatal period, other fetal cerebral vascular accidents or strokes and neonatal hemorrhage, hemolytic disease of the fetus or newborn, kernicterus, NEC, short gut syndrome, hematological or bleeding disorders, or persistent pulmonary hypertension of the newborn.
Okalahoma	No	
Oregon	No	
Pennsylvania	No	Infants born prematurely and transitioning from the NICU are eligible for tracking.
Rhode Island	Yes	Birth weight < 1,500 grams
South Carolina	Yes	Criteria include, but are not limited to, birth weight (1,200 grams or ≤ 28 weeks' gestational age (until age 2 years), IVH grade IV, ROP stage 4 and 5 retrolental fibroplasia, seizures with congenital brain malformation, specific metabolic and chromosomal abnormalities or specific visual and hearing abnormalities.
South Dakota	No	
Tennessee	Yes	Preterm birth at < 30 weeks' gestational age. Infants born at a gestational age of 30–36 weeks also qualify if they meet one or more of the following criteria: IUGR (< 10th percentile), hypoxic-ischemic encephalopathy (HIE), seizure activity in neonatal period, meningitis in neonatal period, IVH Grade III/IV, abnormal CT/US findings including ischemia and significant thrombosis, hydrocephalus, major malformations, disorders of myelination, microcephaly at < 10th percentile for gestational age or metabolic derangement (e.g., inborn error of metabolism, prolonged hypoglycemia > 8 hours, bilirubin reaching exchange level). Infants born at a gestational age of 30–36 weeks who meet at least two of the following criteria are also eligible: Apgar score of < 3 at 5 minutes; prolonged ventilation for apnea or hypoventilation for > 48 hours; prolonged hypoxemia for > 24 hours, hypotonia for > 48 hours, prolonged hypotension for > 8 hours. Infants who have been determined eligible for EI services because they meet the criteria for prematurity will receive a reevaluation to determine continued eligibility by age 2 years.
Texas	No	
Utah	Maybe	NICU graduate with one of the following conditions qualify: tube feedings required either full or partial to maintain adequate nutrition; inability to take 100% of nutrition by mouth; difficulty pacing and/or coordinating suck–swallow–breathe, especially if 38–40 weeks or older; long, difficult time to learn to eat; unusually high or low tone; significant tremors when at rest; fluctuating tone, such as low tone when resting and high tone when overstimulated; inconsolability not attributable to typical premature irritability, GER, or other medical conditions; neurologically based significant irritability; inability to come to a quiet-alert state, persisting throughout hospitalization; severe sleep disorder, unable to maintain deep sleep for ≥ 2 hours
Vermont	Yes	Infants are eligible by severe complications at birth if they have two or more of the following conditions: birth weight < 1,500 grams, preterm birth at < 32 weeks' gestational age, Apgar scores < 6 at 5 minutes, IVH Grade III or IV, IUGR, RDS, asphyxia, PVL, BPD. Infants who have one of the conditions listed above may be referred for information and periodic screening if desired by the family.

State	Automatic eligibility	Definition
Virginia	No	
Washington	No	
West Virginia	No	Low birth weight, when present with 3 of 20 other risk factors, would meet the at-risk eligibility criteria.
Wisconsin	Yes	Birth weight < 1,000 grams or preterm birth at ≤ 26 weeks' gestational age. Eligible diagnoses also include chromosomal anomalies, cerebral palsy, metabolic disorders, degenerative or progressive neurological disorders, abnormal movement patterns (ataxias), CNS trauma (shaken baby syndrome), prenatal infections (e.g., toxoplasmosis, rubella, CMV), visual impairment/blind, fetal alcohol syndrome, hearing impairment/deaf, brain hemorrhage (IVH grade III/IV), autism or pervasive developmental disorders, anomalies of the brain (microcephaly) or spinal cord (meningomyelocele), other genetic high-probability diagnoses (e.g., Prader-Willi, deLange, Williams syndromes). Other concerns associated with poor developmental or behavioral outcomes are evaluated for eligibility.
Wyoming	No	

Professional Development and Mentoring

Cynthia A. Johnson

*Education—continuing education, continually honing and expanding
the mind—is vital mental renewal. Sometimes that involves the external
discipline of the classroom or systematized study programs; more often it does
not. Proactive people can figure out many, many ways to educate themselves.*
Stephen R. Covey (1989, p. 295)

What If?   Tanya hurried to gather her materials to plan the next unit for her preschool special education class with her team members. As a first-year teacher, she felt that the opportunity to plan with other professionals was essential. Her school district had introduced a new literacy program for preschoolers this year. Although experienced teachers, her colleagues were also just learning to implement the program. There was another districtwide in-service planned next week to follow up on strategies for implementing the new literacy program. Tanya made a mental note to check with the teacher who was assigned to be her mentor to see if they could meet for coffee after the in-service. She also wanted to schedule a time for her mentor to observe her teaching a literacy lesson and provide some feedback for her. Tanya felt fortunate that she worked in a school system with comprehensive staff development that included a mentoring program for first-year staff.

CHAPTER OVERVIEW

Carefully planned and implemented, ongoing professional development is an integral part of an early childhood special education (ECSE) program and provides numerous benefits (Linder, 1983). Lifelong learning is essential to administrators, practitioners, and families who use knowledge of current research findings and contemporary practice standards to provide family-centered interventions and advocacy services. Current standards for high-quality professional development and an array of professional development options are delineated in this chapter, along with suggestions for planning and implementing a systematic professional development program.

After reviewing this chapter, the reader will

- Be aware of the importance of ongoing professional development

- Be familiar with an array of professional development options for families, administrators, and practitioners and with strategies for selecting an appropriate model

- Know how to survey families, administrators, and practitioners for professional development needs

- Understand the process of designing a comprehensive professional development program for families, administrators, and practitioners that is consistent with current recommended practice

- Have a strategy for evaluating professional development activities in order to plan improvements

- Understand the basic process of setting up a mentoring and/or coaching system for novice practitioners

- Know a minimum of three strategies for effective mentoring and/or coaching of novice teachers

THE ROLE OF PROFESSIONAL DEVELOPMENT

Effective professional development for all educators focuses on strengthening instruction for children by enhancing the awareness, knowledge, and skills of personnel (Malone, Straka, & Logan, 2000). High-quality professional development comprises a planned set of actions and support systems designed and implemented to accomplish these goals (Killion, 2002). For experienced staff members, professional development presents an opportunity to expand or improve current skills through updates or new information. Novice staff members benefit from professional development that facilitates their application of knowledge to their instructional skills. ECSE administrators use carefully planned professional development to improve program consistency and maintain a common philosophical orientation (Linder, 1983). Professional development is also used to facilitate the process of change in knowledge, attitudes, and skills of practitioners and families to improve outcomes for children and families. Professional development is a critical component of each state's early intervention (EI) and special education plans and is required by federal regulation. This component is known as the *comprehensive system of personnel development.*

One example of a state's efforts to guarantee professional development in each local jurisdiction is the Maryland State Department of Education's publication of the Maryland Teacher Professional Development Standards (2004). These standards were developed with the input of nearly 1,000 educators through a series of 72 focus groups that took place around the state. The intent of the standards was to guide efforts to strengthen teaching in the state's classrooms. The standards offer encouragement to local programs and school systems to work with institutions of higher education and other stakeholders to ensure that professional development is of high quality and easily accessible to all teachers. The standards also emphasize the role of teachers in constructing professional development programs. The nine standards that characterize high-quality professional development programs are

1. Content knowledge and quality teaching: High-quality professional development deepens a teacher's content knowledge as well as the skills necessary to learn and use the best instructional strategies and assess student progress.

2. Research based: Effective professional development helps teachers apply research to decision making.

3. Collaboration: Effective professional development assists teachers in collaborating to improve instruction.

4. Diverse learning needs: Professional development activities ensure that teachers have the knowledge, skills, and dispositions to meet their students' varied learning needs.

5. Student learning environments: Professional development includes activities that help teachers create safe, secure, and supportive learning environments.

6. Family involvement: Professional development provides teachers with skills and knowledge to involve families and community members as partners in the educational process.

7. Data driven: Professional development is based on rigorous analysis of data.

8. Evaluation: Professional development is evaluated on its effectiveness in improving teaching and student learning.

9. Design and teacher learning: Professional development includes ongoing opportunities for practice, reflection, and feedback.

The National Staff Development Council has also published standards for professional development (2001). These standards are organized into three categories: context standards, process standards, and content standards. Under the context standards, staff development organizes professionals into learning communities, requires skillful program and district leaders who guide continuous instructional improvement, and ensures that resources that support adult learning and collaboration are in place.

According to the process standards, staff development uses disaggregated (i.e., school-specific) student achievement data to determine staff learning priorities and guide efforts toward continuous improvement. Multiple sources of information can support educators when they are applying research to clinical situations (e.g., classroom, community-based services). Staff development uses learning strategies appropriate to the intended goal, applies knowledge about human learning and change to instruction, and provides educators with the knowledge and skills to collaborate with families, other professionals, and paraprofessionals.

The content standards focus on staff development that prepares educators to understand and appreciate all students, create safe and orderly learning environments, and hold high expectations for student academic achievement. Well-planned professional development also deepens educators' content knowledge and application of research-based instructional strategies and provides them with knowledge and skills to involve families and other stakeholders.

The National Staff Development Council (2001) standards serve as a guide for designing high-quality professional development for all ECSE programs. The comprehensive nature of the standards challenges administrators to consider a wide array of options for providing professional development and to use a systematic approach to planning and implementing their professional development programs.

OPTIONS FOR PROVIDING PROFESSIONAL DEVELOPMENT

The Maryland Teacher Professional Development Standards (Maryland State Department of Education, 2004) specify that effective professional development for educators involves opportunities for learning with peers, strong leadership, adequate resources, and a clear consensus about expectations for teacher quality. Effective professional development is based on an array of options and a careful selection process that matches the intended outcomes of the professional development activity and participants' prior knowledge and experience with learning strategies and settings. The National Staff Development Council's (2001) standard for design and strategies supports this selection process. The rationale discussed for this standard states that many educators equate professional development with formal trainings, workshops, courses, and large-group presentations. In fact, professional development also takes place through many daily job-embedded activities, such as collaborative planning with colleagues, consultation with other professionals, colleague-to-colleague consultation, coaching, and review of child progress. Professional development occurs at the ECSE team level, the program level, and the district level through a variety of informal and formal strategies. The National Staff Development Council suggests that the most powerful forms of professional development often combine learning strategies to facilitate development of knowledge, skills, and attitudes that result in improved student learning. A variety of professional development strategies and suggestions for selection are presented here.

Learning Communities

A learning community, as defined by the National Staff Development Council (2001), consists of a team of educators who meet on a regular basis, preferably several times per week, for joint lesson planning and problem solving. In many ECSE programs, teams of professionals representing such various disciplines as ECSE, speech-language pathology, occupational therapy, physical therapy, and psychology meet regularly to plan and to assess programs and children's progress. When teams are committed to continuous improvement, they are also considered learning communities. The collective inquiry model, which incorporates group reflection, joint planning, and coordinated action, is essential to professional learning communities (DuFour & Eaker, 1998). Learning communities may be of various sizes and serve different purposes. Early childhood special educators may be members of several learning communities. Such learning communities as schoolwide faculties, school improvement teams, program-level teams, and regional or topic-specific networks in a specific area of interest may prove supportive of an individual teacher. Teams determine the areas in which additional learning would be beneficial and may plan such activities as reading pertinent journal articles, reviewing specific texts, attending workshops, inviting others with expertise in a specific area to assist them in acquiring necessary knowledge or skills, and planning classroom observations of one another with follow-up discussions.

The ECSE administrator's role is to ensure that practitioners are included in appropriate learning communities and to support the work of individual groups. Effective administrators who facilitate professional learning communities lead through shared visions and values and involve staff members in decision making (DuFour & Eaker, 1998).

Distance Education

Distance education, as defined by the *American Journal of Distance Education* (2008), is a teaching and learning relationship in which participants are geographically separated and communicate through technical media, such as audio and video teleconferences, audio and video recordings, personal computers, correspondence texts, and multimedia systems. An increasing number of distance learning opportunities use the Internet in a variety of ways to facilitate the exchange of information and skills. Distance education provides flexibility in location and time, which can be a great advantage for busy professionals.

Audio and Video Recordings Professional development in the form of audio and video recordings enables participants at various locations to experience the same information at times that are designated for a specific group or to review the information on an individual basis. This type of format does not provide opportunities for participants to interact with presenters or individuals at other locations. Professional development facilitators often supplement audio or video recordings with discussions or follow-up activities with participants at a given site. Administrators may select this format when they want information by a selected presenter or team of presenters to be delivered to participants at multiple locations and possibly on different dates and times. This format is especially useful in rural settings where, because of geographic considerations, it may be difficult to gather groups for seminars or other types of educational experiences led by an expert or veteran practitioner or researcher. The technical assistance requirements for this type of professional development activity are not extensive due to easy availability of audio and video equipment in many program locations.

Audio/Video Teleconferences and Web Seminars Professional development offered by audio or video teleconference or web seminar typically accommodates participants who require a convenient location. Several host locations may be established, and a group of participants gathers at these locations at a specified date and time for the teleconference or web seminar. The format of the teleconference often includes opportunities for interaction with the presenter and participants at other locations. The web seminar model uses a telephone connection for the audio and a computer with an Internet connection for viewing slides that accompany the presentation. Participants have the opportunity to ask questions of the speakers. The Council for Exceptional Children (CEC; n.d.) described the web seminar as being similar to participating in a radio talk show. Audio or video teleconferences and web seminars may be useful when members of the targeted audience are not in reasonable proximity to a central location for a large-group in-service, as may frequently occur in rural locations. The technical requirements for this model of distance education, however, are more extensive than would be required for audio and video recordings. When planning teleconferences or web seminars, therefore, administrators need to consider their district's capacity to provide the necessary technical support.

On-Line Courses On-line professional development opportunities are becoming increasingly available to educators. Several models for on-line learning are available that can be categorized as either self-paced modules without an instructor or interactive courses with an instructor. On-line self-paced modules are helpful for participants who need knowledge on a specific topic that may not be needed by others at the same time. An example would be an EI specialist who is hired mid-year and requires information about developing individualized family service plans (IFSPs). The administrator designing a professional development plan with this new staff member might select an available on-line module as a component of the plan to provide a knowledge base on the topic prior to other professional development activities to develop skills in this area. In addition to identifying appropriate modules, administrators will need to ensure that participants have access to computer equipment necessary for web access and use of the on-line modules. Administrators should also establish a time line for completion of the modules so that the timing of follow-up training is appropriate.

Interactive on-line courses are offered by many institutions of higher education as alternatives to traditional face-to-face, on-site courses. Typically, a specific time frame is designated for completion of the course. Participants have the flexibility to review the lecture materials and complete the assignments on days and times that fit their schedules. Rather than present the learner with a solitary experience, interactive on-line courses provide numerous opportunities for communication and engagement with the instructor and other class participants through messages posted to the site and real-time chats that occur at designated times or when participants happen to log on at the same time. Although some individuals may feel that their learning style may not make them good candidates for on-line learning, recent research indicates that participants can learn as well in an on-line delivery format as in an equivalent face-to-face course, regardless of learning style, provided that the course is developed in keeping with adult learning theory and sound instructional design (Aragon, Johnson, & Shaik, 2002). Interactive on-line courses have been found to be learner centered due to the high degree of student participation with the instructor as well as other learners (Lee & Gibson, 2003). Administrators may consider including an interactive on-line course in the professional development plan for specific individuals when these individuals need flexible professional development opportunities. Participants should ensure that they have access to computer equipment and software that meets the minimum technical requirements specified for course participation.

Large-Group Meetings

The traditional model of professional development—the large-group meeting—still has a place on the continuum of professional development delivery options. The large-group in-service model brings together practitioners (usually from a number of sites) with common professional development needs for specific learning activities. Information at an awareness level that is intended to be part of the shared knowledge of a group of practitioners, administrators, and/or family members may be effectively communicated in a large-group format (Malone et al., 2000). Seminars, lectures, traditional courses offered by institutions of higher education, and conferences offered by a variety of sponsors typically are presented in the large-group format. If the agenda also includes opportunities for interaction and application of the presented information, the usefulness of this model increases. Follow-up to large-group meetings is a critical component of the overall professional development plan. The notion that a one-time workshop format will result in implementation of new skills often prevails in spite of contradictory evidence (Malone et al., 2000). Subsequent large-group in-services that provide an opportunity for teams or individuals to share the results of their implementation of the learning from previous in-services have been effective in facilitating positive changes in attitudes in other participants and have motivated additional participants to implement new strategies. Follow-up activities using other professional development models are also helpful.

Small-Group Meetings

Conducting professional development activities in a small-group format permits the administrator to tailor the content and strategies to individuals with similar learning needs. Additional benefits of a small-group format include increased opportunities for active participation and discussion by all members of the group and improved flexibility in selection of location and time. A small-group format is often used effectively when designing follow-up to large-group meetings and to facilitate transfer of new information into practice or to review outcomes once new practices are implemented (Malone et al., 2000). A number of interactive learning activities may be planned for a small-group format, including book discussions, make-and-take sessions for developing materials, examination of recommended practices, materials show and tell, demonstrations, and role playing.

Consultation-Based Technical Assistance and Coaching

On-site consultation-based technical assistance by program specialists is a job-embedded strategy designed to facilitate skill development in specific areas of instruction or intervention. This model is often used as a follow-up to professional development activities designed to enhance knowledge. Technical assistance visits provide opportunities for participants to engage in problem solving about issues they have identified as they begin implementing new strategies. The technical assistance follow-up visits also enable administrators and professional development providers to assess the level of implementation of new information.

Coaching is an effective strategy for assisting practitioners and families of young children to build skills and competencies. The steps in the traditional coaching model include the following (Showers, Joyce, & Bennett, 1987):

1. The coach provides an explanation of the theory behind the strategy or skill and relates it to previous learning. Written information and guidelines may also be provided.

2. The coach demonstrates the new strategy or skill.

3. The learner practices the skill in front of the coach.

4. The coach provides prompt and specific feedback. Opportunities for more practice are provided.

5. The coach and learner develop a plan for additional practice. This action plan includes a commitment to try the new skill or strategy during specific activities, with follow-up from the coach during the first 2 weeks after the initial coaching session. Additional practice follows with scheduled feedback from the coach.

   The coaching model can also be used successfully with family members and caregivers to help them develop specific skills for facilitating achievement of child or family outcomes or goals. Coaching is also a highly effective strategy for colleague-to-colleague consultation and mentoring. The relationship between the coach and the learner typically develops over time and needs to be based on trust and respect. Therefore, administrators and facilitators designing professional development plans that include coaching should schedule multiple opportunities for coaching over a period of time.

Observations at Model Sites

ECSE practitioners benefit from observing colleagues who possess competencies in identified skill areas. Professional development facilitators and administrators are frequently able to identify or develop model sites that may serve three major functions (Malone et al., 2000). The first is to provide a venue for other professionals to observe exemplary practices. Observation and follow-up reflection and discussion help professionals identify ways to alter their current practices or implement new strategies. Second, model sites may serve as controlled settings for professionals to receive hands-on experience and coaching to develop targeted skills prior to using the skills in their own settings. A third function of a model site is to provide a venue for developing instructional materials, such as videotapes, that may be used during professional development activities.

CONSIDERATIONS FOR PLANNING HIGH-QUALITY PROFESSIONAL DEVELOPMENT ACTIVITIES

High-quality professional development programs take into account characteristics of the adult learner, brain-compatible learning, and the features of professional development found in high-achieving schools. These elements lead to the following four considerations for developing successful program activities.

Meet Participants' Needs

Adult learners are often not tolerant of professional development activities that do not meet their needs. When the content of professional development does not match their needs, adults may disengage from the activities. The professional development planning team has an obligation to differentiate the instruction based on participants' knowledge and skills. This may be accomplished using a variety of strategies. Grouping participants based on their current performance levels is one strategy. When groupings are more heterogeneous, providing a leadership role for the participants with a higher level of knowledge or skills is often effective. This strategy can also have a positive influence on the attitudes of participants who are reluctant to embrace the new concepts or skills but who respect the opinions and expertise of their colleagues. Providing tiered instruction to a heterogeneous group is an additional strategy for differentiation.

Involve Participants in Professional Development Decisions

Adult learners desire to be active participants in planning new learning so that it meets their immediate learning goals. Individuals may develop personal professional development plans; such plans may also be the responsibility of a learning community (Garmston & Wellman, 1999). Planning in a learning community requires that participants develop a level of trust that permits them to share what they know as well as what they do not know with one another. When educational practitioners routinely collaborate to focus on improving student performance, their professional development needs and plans will center on strategies to achieve this goal.

Sousa (2003) reported the outcome of a study conducted by the Georgia Council for School Performance in 1998, which examined the relationship between staff development and school culture. One difference between higher and lower achieving schools was that practitioners in higher achieving schools collaborated more on decisions about professional development than did practitioners in lower achieving schools.

Create a Positive Learning Climate

The literature on brain-compatible instructional strategies shows that the emotional atmosphere of the learning environment has a significant influence on a participant's ability to learn and remember (Sousa, 2003). Adult learners expect to be treated with respect, acknowledgement of their experiences, and acceptance of the contributions they make to the professional development activities. Adult learners may also be anxious about their learning abilities; a positive, low-stress atmosphere lessens these anxieties. Professional development activities should incorporate a supportive rather than critical approach to individual and group growth (Linder, 1983). A facilitator style that incorporates humor and an attitude of mutual respect and learning contributes to a positive climate (Sousa, 2003). Effective professional development planners also ensure that the physical environment is comfortable for participants so that such environmental factors as a room that is too cool, a seating arrangement that is too cramped, or hunger or thirst do not inhibit their attention and participation.

Ideally, all participants in professional development activities attend because they have a desire to do so and not because they are required to. The climate in a required activity with reluctant participants will be much different than that in an optional activity or a required activity in which the participants clearly see the relevance of the information to their needs.

Use Instructional Strategies that Promote Positive Outcomes

Adult learners expect that professional development activities will be well organized and pragmatic. Strategies used during professional development in high-achieving schools include the following (Sousa, 2003, pp. 269–270):

- The format includes an ongoing series of professional development activities.

- The rationale and principles behind the new skills are explained.

- New skills are demonstrated live or on videotape.

- Sufficient guided practice is provided in the training.

- Peer coaching/observation is part of the training.

- Peer study groups are part of the training.

- Sufficient follow-up and support for implementing new skills are provided.

- The change process is studied and used to guide innovations in the school.

This information supports the practice of including a variety of professional development activities, as described previously in this chapter, to achieve the intended professional development goals. Novelty is a brain-compatible instructional strategy that enhances participants' interest and engagement. The use of music, humor, technology, and guest speakers during professional development activities may be unexpected and therefore add an element of novelty (Sousa, 2003).

Discussing new learning is also a brain-compatible strategy that matches an adult learner's desire to be an active participant in the learning process (Sousa, 2003). Talking facilitates memory storage of new information and incorporates a sensory experience that contributes to learning. In addition, talking about new information assists learners in making connections to past experiences. Future application of the new information can also be facilitated by structured opportunities to discuss case studies and engage in problem-solving activities.

Studies of brain function indicate that movement is also linked to new learning (Middleton & Strick, 1998). Activities that incorporate movement contribute an element of novelty, promote socialization with others, and provide a multisensory component.

DESIGNING A COMPREHENSIVE PROFESSIONAL DEVELOPMENT PLAN

One of Covey's (1989) seven habits of highly effective people is to "begin with the end in mind." This habit truly serves as a guiding principle for the ECSE administrator when planning professional development and is in accordance with the principle of including practitioners in developing programs that address their own learning needs. This can be accomplished by facilitating individualized professional development plans (IPDP) for individual practitioners. The goals for an IPDP are developed collaboratively by the individual staff member and the administrator. The goals may address areas in need of improvement as identified by either participant; they may also address areas of professional interest for the staff member. A wide array of professional development activities needs to be considered when designing an IPDP, and the staff member's preferences should be taken into consideration. Program leaders can use the aggregated data from all IPDPs developed by professionals in the program or system to identify professional development needs for the whole group or specific subgroups. For example, if most professionals have identified a need to learn more about new federal laws and regulations pertaining to young children with disabilities and their families, specific in-service sessions and small-group follow up can be scheduled to address this issue.

IPDPs intended to facilitate programwide change or improvement may require the input of a diverse group of stakeholders, such as families, practitioners, paraprofessionals, administrators, and community-based representatives. This professional development team has the following tasks:

- Identifying professional development goals that support the program's and system's goals

- Based on the local program's or system's goals, conducting a needs assessment

- Developing a longitudinal plan that includes professional development content, process, and activities

- Identifying available resources for professional development

- Designing an appropriate evaluation system for professional development activities

Identifying Goals

The first step in determining the goals of any professional development program is to identify the gap between current practices and the standards that have been set for performance by local, state, or federal organizations. Review of a variety of data sources is necessary to determine a program's current status in the identified outcome areas and determine if a professional development goal is needed. These data sources may include 1) information on student achievement; 2) data on compliance with local, state, or federal laws, regulations, or guidelines in such areas as development of individualized education programs (IEPs) and IFSPs; 3) qualifications of practitioners; and 4) current implementation of specific instructional practices.

Figure 9.1 provides an example of a review conducted by a local school district of the achievement of beginning kindergarten students with and without disabilities in the area of literacy skills. The data indicated that 36% of the kindergarteners with disabilities were judged to be proficient in the language and literacy indicators identified by the state, compared with 60% of the kindergarteners without disabilities. This gap in achievement indicated the need for a programwide goal in this area. Understanding that young children with disabilities have different learning rates and styles than their peers who are typically developing, the professional development team set a goal that in 1 year, 46% of beginning kindergartners with disabilities would be judged to be proficient in the language and literacy indicators. To achieve this goal, the planning team identified a need for improvement in the literacy instruction provided in the preschool special education program for 4-year-old students. Observations conducted by early childhood special educators and input from the planning team established that literacy instruction at this level was not consistent throughout the district, although teachers had a set of curriculum objectives to guide their instruction. The planning team decided that using a research-based, balanced literacy program would improve instruction. The program administrator and planning team reviewed a number of preschool literacy programs and selected one that

Standard/goal	Data sources	Current performance	Goal of professional development program
By 2007, 60% of all kindergarten students score in the proficient range in the language and literacy area of the Work Sampling System (WSS).	Kindergarten WSS data for children with individualized education programs (IEPs) and children without IEPs.	36% of kindergarten students with IEPs scored in the proficient range in the language and literacy area on the WSS. 60% of kindergarten students without disabilities scored in the proficient range.	In one year, 46% of the kindergarten students will score in the proficient range in the language and literacy area on the WSS.

Figure 9.1.   Sample of a plan for identifying goals of professional development.

they felt was a good match for their system. An ongoing professional development program was identified as an important component of the implementation of the new literacy program.

Conducting a Needs Assessment

Once goals for professional development have been identified, the status of practitioners' competencies to achieve the goals must be assessed. This assessment may involve direct observation by an administrator or a program coordinator, examination of results of student testing pertaining to the goals, or self-assessment instruments.

Needs assessment surveys have been developed in an array of formats. Common elements include a list of competency areas aligned with a rating scale for each knowledge or skill statement. Practitioners are asked to rate their current competency level for each area (see Figure 9.2).

In such formats as the one shown in Figure 9.2, participants are also asked to rate their interest in participating in professional development activities addressing specific competency areas. Research on adult learners reveals that adults are motivated to learn when they perceive a need to know the information presented; therefore, it is useful to survey interest as well as competency levels. If learners report low competency and high interest in specific area, this is easily identified as a focus for the professional development content. However, if an area in which learners report low competency is also rated as low interest, the professional development team would be wise to consider including preparation activities that highlight the importance of the skill prior to conducting activities to build knowledge or skills in that area.

Gathering information on the attitudes of practitioners is an important component of the planning phase and enables the professional development planning team to more clearly identify the goals as well as the content and processes that will be most effective. Feedback provided via written needs assessments may not provide administrators and planning teams with sufficient information on attitudes. Administrators might consider conducting focus groups to accurately evaluate the attitudes of a representative group of practitioners (Killion, 2002).

Developing a Plan

Armed with specific goals and information about the needs of the intended participants, the professional development planning team next develops a longitudinal plan for professional development that addresses content, process, and activities. Members of the team apply their knowledge of the content and process standards for high-quality professional development, previously outlined in this chapter, and their knowledge about the roles of professional development delivery models to select those models that will best help participants develop new knowledge, transfer the knowledge to applied settings, and develop attitudes that will result in achievement of program or system goals.

A sample professional development plan for the first year of implementation of the new preschool balanced literacy program previously described is presented in Figure 9.3. The overall goal of this plan was for 46% of the beginning kindergartners with disabilities to be judged proficient in the area of language and literacy on the statewide assessment in one year. The planning team decided that improvement of literacy instruction for 4-year-old students with disabilities would advance the literacy skills of the beginning kindergarteners. A new, balanced literacy program was

Needs Assessment for Service Providers

Your input in determining topics for professional development activities for service providers for infants and toddlers and their families is very important to us.

Circle appropriate number: 3 = High   2 = Some   1 = Low

Topic	Current competency			Interest in additional learning			Comments
Area: Communication and Interpersonal Skills (with families, teams, community providers)							
Knowledge and Skills:							
Establishing respect and rapport	3	2	1	3	2	1	
Providing empathetic listening and support	3	2	1	3	2	1	
Achieving streams of interaction: Balancing and initiating	3	2	1	3	2	1	
Offering suggestions, questioning, and problem-solving	3	2	1	3	2	1	
Consulting with team members	3	2	1	3	2	1	
Consulting with community providers	3	2	1	3	2	1	
Area: Getting the Job Done							
Processes and Procedures:							
Referral/intake process	3	2	1	3	2	1	
Assessment and Evaluation Process:							
Arena assessment in natural environments	3	2	1	3	2	1	
Assessment of family resources, priorities and concerns	3	2	1	3	2	1	
Routines-based family interview	3	2	1	3	2	1	
IFSP Process:							
Developing IFSP outcomes, strategies, and activities	3	2	1	3	2	1	
Flexible primary service providers model	3	2	1	3	2	1	
Documenting progress	3	2	1	3	2	1	
Transition Process:							
Exploring community options	3	2	1	3	2	1	
Determining eligibility for special education	3	2	1	3	2	1	
Knowledge and Skills:							
Understanding and incorporating program goals	3	2	1	3	2	1	
Maintaining efficient organization	3	2	1	3	2	1	
Awareness of legal and ethical issues	3	2	1	3	2	1	

(continued)

Program Administrator's Guide to Early Childhood Special Education: Leadership, Development, and Supervision by J.M. Taylor, J. McGowan, and T. Linder
Copyright © 2009 Paul H. Brookes Publishing Co., Inc. All rights reserved.

Figure 9.2.   Sample needs assessment form for an infants and toddlers program. (From Howard County Infants and Toddlers Program, Ellicott City, MD; adapted by permission.)

Figure 9.2. *(continued)*

Topic	Current competency			Interest in additional learning			Comments
Area: Support and Service Coordination							
Policies and Procedures:							
Meetings and timelines	3	2	1	3	2	1	
IFSP/Program reviews	3	2	1	3	2	1	
Knowledge and Skills:							
Promoting informal supports	3	2	1	3	2	1	
Networking with community agencies, institutions, and organizations	3	2	1	3	2	1	
Promoting active parent involvement	3	2	1	3	2	1	
Area: Cultural Sensitivity							
Knowledge and Skills:							
Culturally diverse backgrounds	3	2	1	3	2	1	
Social class differences	3	2	1	3	2	1	

The following section addresses current trends and topics in early intervention. Staff development in this area promotes new learning and keeps service providers in touch with the latest research in our field. Please add additional areas, as needed.

Topic	Current competency			Interest in additional learning			Comments
Current Trends and Topics in Early Intervention							
Technology and the NICU (prematurity, health issues)	3	2	1	3	2	1	
Infant mental health (attachment disorders, interventions)	3	2	1	3	2	1	
Brain development	3	2	1	3	2	1	
Technology application and intervention with infants and toddlers	3	2	1	3	2	1	
Foreign adoption	3	2	1	3	2	1	
Other:	3	2	1	3	2	1	

Indicate your position or title:

___ Early Intervention Specialist   ___ Instructional Assistant   ___ SLP ___ OT

___ PT   ___ School Psych. ___ Community Health Nurse ___ Social Worker ___ Other:

Additional comments:

Program Administrator's Guide to Early Childhood Special Education: Leadership, Development, and Supervision by J.M. Taylor, J. McGowan, and T. Linder

Objectives	Purpose of activity	Delivery option	Date, time, location	People involved	Evaluation method
Present professional development series goal Present the vision for use of a consistent, research-based literacy program for 4-year-old preschoolers Provide an overview of the new balanced literacy program and plan for implementation	Knowledge Attitudes	Large group	August 30 8:30 AM–3:30 PM Professional Development Center	ECSE Admin, resource staff, consultants	Pre-post test Participant evaluation form
Discuss implementation of new program Discuss questions and identify areas of need	Knowledge Attitudes Skills	Small group	Scheduled with each team during September	ECSE resource staff	Participant evaluation form
Provide materials and lesson plan ideas for the upcoming literacy program unit Share what is working for individual teams Answer questions about the literacy program	Knowledge Attitudes Skills	Large group	October 21 12:30–3:30 PM Professional Development Center	ECSE Admin, resource staff, consultants, volunteers from teams	Participant evaluation form
Provide information about the new literacy program for families	Knowledge	Large group	October 29 7:00–9:00 PM Location: TBD	ECSE Admin, volunteers	Participant evaluation form
Provide coaching and feedback for classroom staff	Skills	Consultation-based technical assistance and coaching	Nov.–Dec. Scheduled with individual teachers	ECSE Admin, resource staff, consultants	Coaching feedback form

(continued)

Figure 9.3. Sample professional development plan.

Figure 9.3. *(continued)*

Objectives	Purpose of activity	Delivery option	Date, time, location	People involved	Evaluation method
Provide suggestions for extension activities and "make and take" Share best practices via video	Skills	Large group	January 25 12:30–3:30 PM Professional Development Center	ECSE Admin, resource staff, volunteers from teams	Participant evaluation form
Present a self-assessment tool Provide additional suggestions for implementation	Skills	Small group	Feb.–March Scheduled with individual teams	Resource staff	Self-assessment tool
Observe best practices Discuss implementation questions	Skills	Observation at model sites	April Scheduled with individual teachers	Resource staff, ECSE Admin, identified teachers	Observation checklist and feedback
Review progress during year Identify next steps	Knowledge Attitudes Skills	Large group	May 10 12:30–3:30 PM Professional Development Center	ECSE Admin, resource staff, consultants	Participant evaluation form

identified, and the planning team designed a professional development series to support the first year of implementation. The objectives for each of the activities planned during the year are listed in Figure 9.3. The choice of professional development delivery option for each activity is linked to the activity's purpose.

Identification of Resources

The planning team is responsible for reviewing the resources required for the professional development plan, including personnel, materials, time, and compensation. Identification of experts within the group of practitioners who will participate in the professional development is often efficient and effective (Linder, 1983). At times, administrators find it necessary to contract with professionals outside of the school district or agency when local expertise has not yet been developed. Establishing a partnership with an institution of higher education is another strategy for involving professionals with expertise in specific areas targeted for professional development.

Implementation of new initiatives (e.g., those shown in Figure 9.3) often involves the use of materials not currently available to practitioners. It is essential to identify funds to purchase the required materials so that participants do not experience frustration when they see new strategies demonstrated but are unable to implement them because the materials have not been procured.

In addition to procuring funds for materials, program leaders must set aside sufficient time for professional development activities. This may be difficult because time is often at a premium in many ECSE programs. Savvy administrators make the best use of the opportunities already available within the school or district calendar. Many school districts, recognizing the need for ongoing professional development, have designated teacher workdays each year as professional development days. Other administrators schedule professional development activities during summer breaks or after school. They may incorporate the use of job-embedded professional development activities as well as delivery models such as distance learning that accommodate the need for flexibility in location and time. It is important for the planning team to consider whether participation in the professional development activities is intended to include all practitioners or if it is voluntary; activities should be scheduled accordingly. Compensation for participants is an important consideration if the activities take place after work hours.

Evaluating the Effectiveness of Professional Development

Professional development programs are evaluated for a variety of purposes. The specific purpose for evaluation guides the design of the evaluation procedure and tools. Three overall reasons for evaluation are suggested by Patton (1997). The first is to facilitate improvements in the professional development program. Administrators and professional development planning teams seek information about the strengths and weaknesses of the program's processes and activities to make adjustments and to maintain an appropriate pace of program development and implementation (Malone et al., 2000). Evaluations designed to facilitate program improvements may be conducted after each professional development activity and analyzed by the planning team when setting up subsequent activities. A sample professional development activity evaluation form is shown in Figure 9.4. Participants can use the form to rate their satisfaction with components of the activity, make suggestions for future activities, and rate achievement of the learning objectives established for a specific

Early Childhood Special Education Program
Preschool Literacy
Professional Development Series Feedback Form

Date of Activity: _____

Your feedback is very important to us! Please complete the following items and provide any comments that you feel may be helpful in planning future sessions.

	Strongly disagree				Strongly agree
SATISFACTION					
The information was presented effectively.	1	2	3	4	5
The content was appropriate.	1	2	3	4	5
The learning environment was appropriate and comfortable.	1	2	3	4	5
LEARNING					
I am familiar with the goals of the preschool literacy professional development series.	1	2	3	4	5
I am familiar with our program's vision for use of a research-based literacy program.	1	2	3	4	5
I am familiar with the components of the new balanced literacy program for 4-year-old preschoolers.	1	2	3	4	5
I have the knowledge I need to begin implementation of the new literacy program.	1	2	3	4	5

I have the following suggestions for future professional development activities:

As a result of today's professional development activity, I plan to:

Please rate the effectiveness of this session:

Very effective		Somewhat effective		Not effective
5	4	3	2	1

Thanks for coming to the session and participating in the learning activities.

Figure 9.4. Sample professional development series feedback form.

session. The statements in the learning objectives section of the feedback form need to be modified for each professional development activity. The form can also help participants link their new knowledge to implementation by having them state what they plan to do as a result of the professional development activity.

The second purpose of professional development evaluation is to identify effective components of professional development strategies. This information also may be gathered via questions on event-based feedback forms. For example, the professional development event for the new literacy curriculum included videotaped demonstrations of a literacy lesson in a large-group setting. This videotape offered a model for implementing the new curriculum. The evaluation form for this professional development activity might include a question about the effectiveness of viewing the videotape. If the results of the evaluation suggest that participants judged the videotaped demonstrations to be an effective component of the professional development activity, this format could be included in future sessions.

The third and most important reason for evaluating professional development is to assist administrators and professional development planning teams in forming judgments about the overall effectiveness of the ECSE program and making decisions about adjustments. Evaluation conducted for this purpose is based on tangible results and enables the planning team to determine if the goals specified for professional development have been achieved. A number of tools can be used for this type of summative evaluation. For example, changes in practitioner knowledge can be evaluated by pre–posttest measures. Changes in participants' skills can be measured by direct observation and observer or self-assessment checklists. Changes in attitudes can be measured by participant questionnaires, self-rating scales, observations, or interviews (Malone et al., 2000). Student achievement data, too, offers important information about the effectiveness of professional development. Many measures of student achievement are conducted on an annual basis or in the fall and spring. In general, results-oriented evaluation of professional development should be completed on an annual basis, at a minimum.

Analysis of evaluation data is used by the professional development planning team to revise and update the professional development plan. The planning team also determines the most appropriate format for disseminating the results of professional development evaluations. The final phase of evaluating professional development activities is determination of the appropriateness of the evaluation strategies. Improvement of the professional development process should be ongoing (Killion, 2002).

MENTORING PROGRAMS FOR NOVICE PRACTITIONERS

Professionals in their early years of employment have unique needs that may extend beyond the parameters of traditional professional development programs. Appropriate support for novice teachers can have a profound impact on helping them remain in their field (Whitaker, 2000). Retention of high-quality special educators has been identified as a priority by many programs and school systems.

Meeting the Needs of Novice Practitioners

The CEC (2003) supports the use of mentoring programs for novice practitioners as a strategy for increasing retention and assisting with the transition from preservice education to teaching. Whitaker (2000) found positive effects of a mentoring program on teacher retention. In addition, mentoring was significantly correlated with new special education teachers' job satisfaction and development of self-confidence, motivation, and self-image as competent educators.

Although of critical importance during the first and second years in a profession, mentoring is useful for experienced staff as well. A less formal mentoring relationship is established whenever one professional seeks to learn from another professional who has expertise in a specific area or skill.

Benefits for Mentors

Although the benefits of mentoring for novice practitioners are more easily identified, it is important to note that veteran teachers benefit from their role as mentors. Huling and Resta (as cited in Sousa, 2003) described the following ways mentoring contributes to the professional development of experienced teachers:

- Improvement of skills through assisting the protégé

- Increase in reflective practices

- Renewal and strengthening of commitment to education

- Enhancement of self-esteem and satisfaction from helping a colleague and contributing to the future of education

In addition to these benefits, mentors appreciate formal recognition for their role and the opportunity to form collegial relationships with other mentors and beginning practitioners, as well as tangible benefits such as stipends, university or professional credit, and access to materials for their classroom (White & Mason, 2003).

Purpose and Guidelines for a Mentoring Program

The CEC (1998) suggested five purposes for mentorship programs:

1. To facilitate application of knowledge and skills

2. To convey advanced knowledge and skills

3. To assist timely acculturation to the school climate

4. To reduce stress and enhance job satisfaction

5. To support professional induction

The CEC also established principles and guidelines for a mentoring program (White & Mason, 2003). The guidelines are based on three principles:

1. An array of supports, including mentoring, should be available to all beginning teachers.

2. Effective mentoring relationships that provide meaningful supports to teachers are dependent upon several key components.

3. School districts have an obligation to ensure that their mentoring programs include those key components for effectiveness.

The guidelines established by the CEC for a mentoring program include the following six items (White & Mason, 2003):

1. The objectives, purposes, and options of the mentoring program are clear and have been agreed upon by all stakeholders: beginning teachers, experienced mentors, and representatives from district and building level administrators.

2. Information concerning roles, expectations, policies, provisions, and desired outcomes of the mentoring program is ready available and shared with beginning teachers, mentors, and administrators.

3. The mentoring program is planned and adequately funded.

4. All first-year teachers are expected to participate in the mentoring program.

5. Mentoring for special education staff may be coordinated with other, more general, mentoring programs within the school district but must specifically address those issues unique to special education.

6. The mentoring program is designed to provide assistance and support only and is not related to any formal evaluations, certification requirements, or reemployment issues.

Roles and Responsibilities

A mentoring program has a number of key stakeholders: the beginning teacher, the mentor teacher, the building administrator, and the mentoring program coordinator. Each of these individuals has specific roles and responsibilities. The following section presents a summary of these roles and responsibilities, as described by White and Mason (2003).

The Beginning Teacher It is essential that beginning teachers enter into the mentorship as willing participants with a commitment to attend all mentoring program sessions, complete activities relevant to mentoring, and form partnerships with their assigned mentors. This partnership is best established when beginning teachers request assistance proactively, remain open and responsive to feedback, and use reflective skills to enhance their teaching. Scheduled activities ideally include observing experienced teachers, including the mentor teacher, and reviewing these observations with the mentor teacher. The use of self-assessments is helpful to facilitate the reflection on teaching strategies that is a critical component of development for beginning teachers. Continuous improvement of the mentoring program depends on feedback from all participants, especially beginning teachers. Therefore, participation in evaluating the mentoring program is a key responsibility for this group of stakeholders.

The Mentor Teacher Mentor teachers guide, assist, and support beginning special education teachers during the first year of teaching. A willingness to serve as a mentor teacher and enter into a professional and confidential relationship with a beginning teacher based on respect and trust is essential to the success of the mentor program for both parties. The mentor teacher provides support and guidance in a variety of areas. The following categories of support were suggested by Odell and Ferraro (1992):

- Instructional: teaching strategies

- System: policies and procedures of the school district or program

- Resource: materials and equipment for instruction

- Emotional: active listening and support

- Managerial: time management and completion of paperwork requirements

- Parental: strategies for working collaboratively with families

- Disciplinary: strategies and procedures for promoting positive behavior in the instructional setting

Being observed by the beginning teacher provides the mentor teacher with opportunities to model appropriate instructional techniques, classroom management skills, and professional behavior. Observing the beginning teacher and holding post-observation conferences allow the mentor teacher to provide feedback on targeted aspects of instruction. Evaluating the mentorship program itself is also an important responsibility of mentor teachers. High-quality mentoring programs provide opportunities for mentors to get together periodically to share experiences and refine their knowledge about mentoring practices (Sousa, 2003).

The Building Administrator   As part of the mentoring team, building administrators provide support and encouragement for the mentoring program and the specific mentor–beginning teacher dyad. The building administrators' responsibilities also include assisting with such logistical arrangements as providing release time for beginning teachers and mentors to complete observations, conference with each other, and attend planned training sessions. Limiting the extracurricular responsibilities of those involved in mentoring is also effective in providing them as much time as possible to complete mentoring activities. Building administrators serve an important role in the selection of qualified mentors by identifying special educators who possess the instructional expertise as well as the interpersonal skills to be successful mentors. Building administrators also have a responsibility to contribute to continued improvement of the mentorship program by formally evaluating the program.

Mentoring Program Coordinator   The mentoring program coordinator organizes and facilitates the implementation of the mentoring program. The coordinator's responsibilities include the following:

- Providing information to administrators and securing their support for the mentoring program

- Establishing guidelines for release time and compensation of participants for time spent outside of work hours

- Identifying potential mentors and securing their commitment to participate in the program

- Planning orientation for mentors and regular meeting of new teachers and mentors

- Guiding the development and use of appropriate resource materials

- Facilitating continuous improvement of the mentorship program through evaluation by all participants

- Collaborating with administrators to identify and meet additional support needs of beginning teachers, when warranted

Setting up a Mentoring Program

Once the mentoring program coordinator establishes support for a mentoring program, the next essential activities are selecting mentors, matching mentors with beginning teachers, and establishing a schedule for orientation and ongoing training for beginning teachers and mentors.

Mentor Selection and Establishment of Mentoring Dyads Candidates who may be mentor teachers are best identified by building administrators or other personnel who are familiar with the instructional and interpersonal skills of the teachers. Successful mentor teachers typically have a minimum of 3–5 years of successful special education teaching experience in their current district (White & Mason, 2003). An essential consideration when matching mentor teachers with beginning teachers is the experience of the mentor teacher with the population assigned to the beginning teacher. For example, an experienced preschool special educator who has never taught kindergarten would not have the experience necessary to provide the full range of support to a beginning special education teacher assigned to a kindergarten classroom. This same preschool special educator, however, might be an excellent match for a beginning preschool teacher. Consideration should also be given to the locations of the mentor teacher and the beginning teacher. Although frequent contact between the two may be facilitated if they are assigned to the same building, successful mentoring relationships have been established with mentor teachers and beginning teachers working in separate facilities. When a sufficient number of mentor teachers are not available in the same building to meet the needs of the beginning teachers, the mentoring program coordinator may consider assigning more than one beginning teacher to a mentor teacher. This should be done with caution, however, as the demands on the mentor teacher typically make it most reasonable for the mentor to support only one beginning teacher during any given year.

Orientation and Training Mentor teacher training is an important component of the mentoring program. Although master teachers possess expertise in their field, they may need additional professional development to acquire the skills necessary to successfully support a beginning teacher. Ideally, orientation and initial training for mentor teachers occurs before the school year begins, with additional training sessions scheduled during the year. If there is not sufficient time prior to the beginning of the school year for extensive training, an initial meeting of mentors and beginning teachers is held at the start of the school year and ongoing training is scheduled during the year. Mentor teacher training topics may include the following (White & Mason, 2003):

- Adult education principles

- Effective adult communication skills

- Consultation strategies, including how to give constructive feedback and social support

- Classroom observation skills

- Advising and coaching skills

- Problem-solving skills

Ongoing Training for Mentors and New Teachers Planned opportunities for mentors and new teachers to meet as a group and discuss specific topics represent a useful component of many mentoring programs. The mentoring program coordinator typically schedules and plans these sessions with input from the participants. Topics may be selected based on upcoming activities and responsibilities within the program. For example, a session on effective interaction strategies with families and completing report cards may be planned prior to the end of the first marking period and the first parent conferences scheduled in the fall. A session addressing procedures for determining eligibility for extended school-year services may be planned in January or February, prior to IEP meetings. Each session should provide the mentors and beginning teachers with an opportunity for one-to-one discussion and problem solving in addition to the presentation of information. The mentor and new-teacher dyads can also plan appropriate follow-up activities to take place prior to the next formal meeting.

Strategies for Effective Mentoring

Each mentoring relationship will require a different set of strategies. The Mentor Academy, for California's new teachers (New Teacher Academy, 2008), suggests six qualities of a high-performance mentor. The first is that the mentor commits to the roles and responsibilities of mentoring. A key strategy for meeting the demands and fulfilling the responsibilities of the mentoring role is to establish regular contact with the beginning teacher. Although the demands of each individual's job and personal responsibilities make it challenging to arrange these contacts, it is essential that this time be scheduled and protected. Mentors and beginning teachers who work in the same building may already have frequent opportunities to interact and may be part of a shared learning community. It is important to supplement these opportunities with contacts that provide a chance for personal connection and the type of social support that might not occur during the course of carrying out daily responsibilities. Some mentor and beginning teacher dyads have created these opportunities by scheduling informal monthly meetings after work and communicating by e-mail or phone on a weekly or more frequent basis. Mentors and beginning teachers who do not work in the same building will find it necessary to schedule more frequent meetings. Whitaker (2000) found that more unstructured and informal contacts were the most frequent and most effective mentoring activities in a survey of first-year teachers who participated in a required mentoring program.

The second quality of the high-performance mentor, as suggested by The Mentor Academy, is accepting the beginning teacher as a developing person and professional. This can be communicated by establishing a collaborative relationship in which each person contributes equally to the development of the mentoring plan, including identifying the areas to be targeted, the activities that will be completed, the logistics of scheduling the activities, and evaluation of the mentoring relationship. A written action plan is helpful in recording decisions on these issues. A sample mentoring program action plan is shown in Figure 9.5. It specifies the improvement goals and activities planned collaboratively by the mentor and protégé for a 3-month period. Open communication is an essential component of collaboration and is also a strategy for establishing the mutual trust necessary for a successful mentoring relationship. Effective, open communication encompasses active listening as well as articulating thoughts in a clear, nonjudgmental, and constructive manner.

Protégé <u>Tanya</u>   **Mentor** <u>Beth</u>   **Date** <u>August 30th</u>

Month	Improvement goals	Activities
September	Managerial: Set up the classroom effectively Instructional: Implement the new literacy program Emotional: Establish a working relationship with paraprofessionals	Beth will visit Tanya's classroom and make suggestions for classroom set-up. Tanya will e-mail Beth questions about the literacy program. Beth will offer some tips about establishing a relationship with paraprofessionals.
October	System: Develop first IEP Parental: Prepare for parent conferences Emotional: Continue working on relationships with team members	Tanya and Beth will review a draft of the IEP together. Beth will make suggestions for ways to prepare for conferences. Tanya and Beth will communicate via phone or e-mail, as needed, to discuss specific challenges.
November	Instructional: Implement the new literacy program Managerial: Complete report cards Emotional: Provide support, as needed	Tanya will observe in Beth's class-rooom and Beth will observe Tanya and provide feedback. Beth will share with Tanya how she completes report cards and provide samples. Beth and Tanya will continue to communicate via phone or e-mail.

Figure 9.5. Sample mentoring program action plan. (From Howard County Public School System and Johns Hopkins University Mentoring Program 2002; adapted by permission.)

The Mentor Academy's third quality of the high-performance mentor is reflection on interpersonal communication and decisions. A successful mentor relationship provides a safe environment for the mentor and beginning teacher to openly share their reflections about their behaviors and style of communicating and interacting with colleagues and families. When beginning teachers encounter interpersonal difficulties, they may share their feelings and seek assistance from the mentor in handling the situation. Active listening is a strategy that mentors use effectively to convey understanding of the situation. Emotional and personal support for the beginning teacher has been cited as the most effective type of support, based on feedback from beginning teachers (Whitaker, 2000).

The fourth quality of the high-performance mentor is serving as an instructional coach. Coaching is a key strategy in assisting adult learners to acquire new skills or improve current ones. As described previously in this chapter, coaching involves establishing a safe, respectful relationship between the coach and the learner. This mirrors the effective mentoring relationship and makes coaching a very natural strategy for mentoring.

The fifth and sixth qualities of the high-performance mentor suggested by the Mentor Academy are modeling a commitment to personal and professional growth and communicating hope and optimism for the future. As members of a common learning community in the mentoring program, mentors can convey their commitment to continuous personal and professional growth through their participation in professional development opportunities. Mentors have a unique opportunity and responsibility to shape the way in which beginning teachers view their profession. It is understandable that mentors and beginning teachers will discuss frustrations and dissatisfaction at times; however, the successful mentor focuses on proactive discussions and problem-solving strategies to reframe concerns discussed with the beginning teacher.

Evaluating the Mentoring Program

High-quality mentoring programs include periodic evaluations of the program by all stakeholders. Data from these evaluations are used to plan future mentoring program activities and identify the types of activities that have the greatest impact on child and family outcomes, as identified by participants. A sample evaluation form is included in Figure 9.6. This form may be used by both mentors and beginning teachers. The form elicits information about the types of activities in which the mentor and protégé have engaged, the frequency of the activities, and the importance of the activities to positive child and family outcomes. In addition, mentors and protégés are asked to describe the benefits gained through their participation in the mentoring program, identify the components that were most helpful, and suggest any changes to the program. An overall satisfaction rating is included. Mentoring program coordinators may also find it helpful to conduct informal interviews with mentors and new teachers to determine their level of satisfaction with various aspects of the mentoring program and elicit their suggestions for program improvement.

Administrators gather data to assist in determining if the mentoring program achieved the goals established for a specific time frame. Data on the retention of new teachers can be gathered yearly and can be used longitudinally to determine if participation in a mentoring program resulted in higher rates of retention over a period of time. To target areas of support for future mentoring program activities, information can also be gathered from administrators regarding their level of satisfaction with novice practitioners.

CONCLUSIONS

Professional development is an essential component of a high-quality ECSE program. This chapter outlined a process for planning, implementing, and evaluating a professional development program that highlights the administrator's leadership and the commitment of a team of practitioners who use a coordinated and systematic approach in alignment with established standards for high-quality programs. A variety of options for the design and delivery of professional development that matches specific goals and participants' needs were discussed, and a mentoring program to meet the unique needs of beginning practitioners was described.

The following points about professional development are provided for ECSE administrators to consider when reflecting on their current practices:

- What role does professional development play in my ECSE program?

- Is the current plan for professional development focused on the needs of individual practitioners, or does it also incorporate the needs of the program as a whole?

- Is professional development included as a component of programwide improvements or changes?

Evaluation Form for Mentoring Program Activities

Name (optional): _____ Check one: Mentor _____ Protégé _____ Date: _____

Please indicate whether you have participated in the following activities through your involvement with the mentoring program, the frequency of participation in the activity, and the level of importance of each activity to positive child/family outcomes.

Activity	Interaction mode(s)				Frequency	Importance to positive Child/family outcomes (please circle)
	Phone	In person	E-mail	Other		Not Very — Very
1. Loan of professional books, journals, or other written materials						1 2 3 4 5
2. Loan of instructional materials						1 2 3 4 5
3. Loan of evaluation/assessment materials						1 2 3 4 5
4. Advice re: instructional practices						1 2 3 4 5
5. Advice re: evaluation/assessment practices						1 2 3 4 5
6. Advice re: collaboration with families						1 2 3 4 5
7. Advice re: collaboration with colleagues						1 2 3 4 5
8. Observation and feedback (note if mentor or protégé observed)						1 2 3 4 5
9. Suggestions for professional development activities						1 2 3 4 5
10. Assistance with disciplinary concerns						1 2 3 4 5

(continued)

Program Administrator's Guide to Early Childhood Special Education: Leadership, Development, and Supervision
by J.M. Taylor, J. McGowan, and T. Linder

Figure 9.6. Sample evaluation form: Mentoring. (From Howard County Public School System and Johns Hopkins University Mentoring Program 2005; adapted by permission.)

Figure 9.6. *(continued)*

Activity	Interaction mode(s)				Frequency	Importance to positive Child/family outcomes (please circle)				
	Phone	In person	E-mail	Other		Not Very				Very
11. Referral to another person, agency, or organization for information						1	2	3	4	5
12. Review of IEP/IFSP; assistance with other systems issues						1	2	3	4	5
13. Other (please describe)						1	2	3	4	5
14. Other (please describe)						1	2	3	4	5

Please describe the benefits you gained through participation in the mentoring program.

What components of the mentoring program were most helpful?

What changes would you suggest to the mentoring program?

Please rate your overall satisfaction with the mentoring program:

Very Dissatisfied	Somewhat Dissatisfied	Neutral	Somewhat Satisfied	Very Satisfied
1	2	3	4	5

Additional comments:

Program Administrator's Guide to Early Childhood Special Education: Leadership, Development, and Supervision
by J.M. Taylor, J. McGowan, and T. Linder
Copyright © 2009 Paul H. Brookes Publishing Co., Inc. All rights reserved.

- Are stakeholders in the professional development plan included in the planning of the professional development program?

- Are the goals for a professional development plan based on review of available data and related to student achievement or outcomes for children and families?

- Does the professional development plan include a series of activities and a variety of options matched with the goals of improving knowledge, attitudes, and skills?

- Are strategies used that are consistent with characteristics of the adult learner, brain-compatible learning, and recommended practices for high-quality professional development?

- Are evaluation methods in place to assist the planning team in determining areas in need of improvement in the professional development program and to determine achievement of the professional development goals?

- Is there a need for a mentoring program for novice practitioners?

REFERENCES

American Journal of Distance Education. (2008). Definition of *distance education.* Retrieved on November 1, 2008, from http://www.ajde.com

Aragon, S.R., Johnson, S.D., & Shaik, N. (2002). The influences of learning style preferences on student success in online versus face-to-face environments. *The American Journal of Distance Education, 16*(4). Retrieved January 7, 2005, from http:www.ajde.com/Abstracts/abs16_4b.htm

Council for Exceptional Children. (n.d.). *Web seminars: Frequently asked questions.* Retrieved January 14, 2005, from http://www.cec.sped.org/Content/NavigationMenu/Professional Development/ProfessionalTraining/WebSeminars/FAQs/Web_Seminars__Frequently_Asked_ Questions.htm

Council for Exceptional Children. (2003). *What every special educator must know: Ethics, standards, and guidelines for special educators* (5th ed.). Arlington, VA: Council for Exceptional Children.

Covey, S.R. (1989). *The seven habits of highly effective people.* New York: Fireside.

DuFour, R., & Eaker, R. (1998). *Professional learning communities at work.* Bloomington, IN: National Education Service.

Garmston, R.J., & Wellman, B. (1999). *The adaptive school: A sourcebook for developing collaborative groups.* Norwood, MA: Christopher Gordon.

Killion, J. (2002). *Assessing impact: Evaluating staff development.* Oxford, OH: National Staff Development Council.

Lee, J., & Gibson, C.C. (2003). Developing self-direction in an online course through computer-mediated interactions. *The American Journal of Distance Education, 17*(3). Retrieved January 7, 2005, from http:www.ajde.com/Abstracts/ abs17_3c.htm

Linder, T.W. (1983). *Early childhood special education: Program development and administration.* Baltimore: Paul H. Brookes Publishing Co.

Malone, D.M., Straka, E., & Logan, K.R. (2000). Professional development in early intervention: Creating effective inservice training opportunities. *Infants & Young Children, 12*(4), 53–62.

Maryland State Department of Education. (2004). *Standards set for professional development for teachers.* Retrieved December 30, 2004, from http://www.marylandpublicschools.org/MSDE/divisions/ instruction/prof_standards.htm

Middleton, F.A., & Strick, P.L. (1998). Cerebellar output: Motor and cognitive channels. *Trends in Cognitive Sciences, 2,* 348–354.

National Staff Development Council. (2001). *NSDC's standards for staff development.* Retrieved December 30, 2004, from http://www.nsdc.org/standards/index.cfm

New Teacher Academy. (2008). Mentor academy. Retrieved on November 1, 2008, from http:// newteachercenter.org/ti_mentor_academy_series.php

Odell, S.J., & Ferraro, D.P. (1992). Teaching mentoring and teacher retention. *Journal of Teacher Education, 43*(3), 200–204.

Patton, M.Q. (1997). *Utilization-Focused Evaluation: The new century text* (3rd ed.). Thousand Oaks, CA: Sage Publications.

Showers, B., Joyce, B., & Bennett, B. (1987). Synthesis of research on staff development: A framework for future study and a state-of-the-art analysis. *Educational Leadership, 45*(3), 111–120.

Sousa, D.A. (2003). *The leadership brain.* Thousand Oaks, CA: Corwin Press.

Whitaker, S.D. (2000). Mentoring beginning special education teachers and the relationship to attrition. *Exceptional Children, 66*(4), 546–566.

White, M., & Mason, C. (2003). *Mentoring induction principles and guidelines.* Retrieved November 1, 2008, from the Council for Exceptional Children web site: http://www.cec.sped.org/content/NavigationMenu/ProfessionalDevelopment/ProfessionalStandards/mip_g_manual_11pt.pdf

Supervision of Professionals, Paraprofessionals, and Volunteers

Frank J. Masci and James R. McGowan

Information is the currency of democracy.
Ralph Nader

What If?   You have been the director of a program for young children with and without disabilities for approximately 1 year. So far, the program has run pretty smoothly, and you are beginning to feel comfortable as a leader. One of your best teachers has been displaying some unusual behaviors recently. She has been coming to work late on most days, and twice her instructional assistant has had difficulty finding her. You have counseled this teacher on the importance of timeliness and keeping colleagues posted as to her whereabouts, but today she came in late again. What do you do?

CHAPTER OVERVIEW

In this chapter we examine the elements of effective supervision of education professionals, paraprofessionals, and parent or community volunteers. After presenting a very brief history of supervision in schools, we turn our attention to the importance of standards and a discussion of crucial supervisory activities. Then, we present practical suggestions for implementing a supervisory plan. We touch briefly on the legal issues surrounding supervision (a more detailed treatment of legal issues is found in Chapter 14) and look at the relationship among supervision, professional development, and mentoring. Finally, we consider implications for future research and clinical/educational practice and offer conclusions. In most cases, we describe supervisory activity and practice in terms of the classroom, although we realize that the early childhood special education (ECSE) administrator often operates outside the school and classroom. It is our hope that the processes we describe are sufficiently universal that they may be used with minimum modification in a variety of other settings.

After reviewing this chapter, the reader will

- Understand the importance of supervision of professionals, paraprofessionals, and volunteers

- Know the history of school supervision

- Understand the effectiveness of clinical supervision

- Know how the Council for Exceptional Children (CEC) and Interstate School Leaders Licensure Consortium (ISLLC) standards addressing supervision guide and inform supervisors

- Understand crucial activities for supervision, including observation, written documentation of observations, and analysis of observation data

- Understand how to recruit and train volunteers

- Understand legal issues relating to nonperforming staff

- Understand the importance of reflecting on the supervision process

WHAT IS SUPERVISION?

One of the most important responsibilities of the ECSE administrator is supervising staff and volunteers. Few activities undertaken by the administrator provide as much information about the effectiveness of instruction and the success of students as does the process of supervision described by Glickman (as cited in Firth & Pajak, 1998). For our purposes, we define *supervision* as a process that includes the collection, analysis, and sharing of data, obtained chiefly through direct observation for purposes of improving staff performance and child outcomes. This type of systematic, planned supervisory activity is most often called *clinical supervision* (Cogan, 1973). Although often linked with evaluation of staff members' performance, especially when the supervisor is also an administrator, supervision by itself is generally perceived as a supportive, collegial process.

BRIEF HISTORY OF SUPERVISION AND SUPERVISORY RESEARCH

As Pajak (2000) pointed out, the initial concept of school supervision appeared in the literature as early as 1875, in *Chapters on School Supervision* by Payne. During the next 75 years, the dominant focus of writings on supervision was on inspection and improving efficiency, although a number of authors helped to separate supervision from administration. The focus on inspection and improving efficiency paralleled the leadership theory known as *Principles of Scientific Management*. As described by Burton (as cited in Barr, Burton, & Brueckner, 1947), supervision was concerned with the following:

1. The improvement of the teaching act (classroom visits, individual and group conferences, directed teaching)
2. The improvement of teachers in service (e.g., teachers' meetings, professional readings, bibliographies and reviews, bulletins, intervisitation, self-analysis and criticism)
3. The selection and organization of subject-matter (e.g., setting up objectives, studies of subject-matter and learning activities, experimental testing of

4. Testing and measuring (e.g., use of standardized and local tests for classification, diagnosis, guidance)

5. The rating of teachers (the development and use of rating cards, of checklists, stimulation of self-rating) (Barr, Burton, & Brueckner, 1947, p. 5)

Clearly, the focus was on teaching and its related parts. Barr et al. (1947) also included many checklists, further underscoring the scientific, inspection-oriented approach to supervision. Chapter 8 in Barr, for example, was dedicated to "Studying the Teacher Factors in Pupil Growth." Section 7 (pp. 347–353) of that chapter included many useful checklists that clearly defined the practice of teaching and the respective supervisory role, which consisted chiefly of inspecting, informing, and inspecting again. Little responsibility was placed on the supervisor for providing assistance and/or staff development; teachers were on their own for that. In practice, this model of supervision persisted into the 1960s and 1970s and may even exist in isolated instances today. This somewhat lock-step approach to supervision was also reflected in beliefs about educational practice: It was not uncommon for supervisors to expect that all teachers in the district would be teaching the same subject on the same day. Supervision in these decades was something done *to* the teacher, according to Anderson and Snyder (as cited in Firth & Pajak, 1998).

In subsequent decades several different strands or, as Pajak (2000) called them, *families* of clinical supervision developed. The chart shown in Table 10.1 succinctly describes the growth and divergence of clinical supervisory models up to the mid-1990s.

Table 10.1.   Four families of clinical supervision

Family	Approximate years of emergence	Major principles
Original clinical models Goldhammer Mosher & Purpel Cogan	1960s to early 1970s	Collegiality and mutual discovery of meaning
Humanistic/artistic models Blumberg Eisner	Mid-1970s to early 1980s	Positive and productive interpersonal relations with holistic understanding of classroom events
Technical/didactic models Acheson & Gall Hunter Joyce & Showers	Early to mid-1980s	Effective teaching strategies, technique, and organizational expectations
Developmental/reflective models Glickman Costa & Garmston Schon Zeichner & Liston Garman Smyth & Retallick Bowers & Flinders Waite	Mid-1980s to mid-1990s	Teacher cognitive development, introspection, and discovery of context-specific principles of practice

From Pajak, E. (2000). *Approaches to clinical supervision: Alternatives for improving instruction* (2nd ed., p. 7). Norwood, MA: Christopher-Gordon; reprinted by permission.

Blumberg (1980) heralded the growing humanistic movement in supervision that emphasized the creation of "productive working environments" (p. 2). Blumberg described a survey used by a colleague, Reeves, in which students were asked to assume the role of a teacher who is about to be observed: "You are a teacher. You have just received notice that you will be observed by your supervisor. What is your reaction?" (p. 2). Students gave the following responses:

1. I'd tell the children to be on their good behavior.
2. I'd put up displays of student work.
3. I'd make sure my lesson plan book is up to date and my desk was neat.
4. I'd be very anxious, but after he arrived I'd probably teach a regular lesson.
5. I'd give her what she wants—individualized instruction. (as cited in Blumberg, p. 3)

These statements reflect Blumberg's major theses that all was not well with supervision and that those facing supervision saw the situation as somewhat unpleasant. A casual inspection of chapter titles in Blumberg (1980) indicates a departure from traditional thinking about supervision toward a view that was more supportive of teachers' morale, environment, and motivation. He seems to have captured a shift in the focus of supervision that had clearly begun in the work of Cogan (1973), who in the mid-1950s introduced the practice of clinical supervision. This was further expanded by one of Cogan's students, Goldhammer (1969), who indicated a concern for "what schools can be like" (p. 1). Goldhammer announced a new vision for the action and work of supervisors, which included a counseling approach for supervisors in working with teachers that was highly collaborative. This was truly a departure from the inspection methodologies of the early and mid-20th century. It would be remiss, even in this abbreviated historical presentation, to ignore the work of Wiles and Lovell (1975), who articulated the importance of the human dimension. Sergiovanni (1977) and Sergiovanni and Starratt (1979) also presented research findings supporting the more humanistic approach to supervision and emphasizing the importance of the student in these efforts.

Supervision is not simply the completion of checklists on teacher performance; rather, it involves working to understand teacher behavior and the conditions under which teachers operate. Once these variables are identified, steps toward improving child outcomes can be undertaken. Our belief is that the primary purpose for which education exists is for children to learn and succeed. Those engaged in research and theory development related to educational supervision in the mid- and late 20th century clearly pointed toward a collaborative, supportive environment in which teachers can grow and thrive (Cogan, 1973; Glickman, 2002; Pajak, 2000).

Most recently, technological advances have been largely responsible for two major trends affecting supervision: the need to mold our students into a knowledgeable, technology-capable work force and the need to be considerate of affective, social justice, and multicultural issues. Although there are some points of agreement between the theorists who espouse these differing viewpoints (Pajak, 2000), the special education administrator must understand the ramifications of these issues as they relate to effective supervision at the program and district levels. Perhaps the greatest value of this brief historical survey is to demonstrate that methods and theories change over time and that, increasingly, the human dimension of education is taking on more importance.

RESEARCH ON THE EFFECTIVENESS OF CLINICAL SUPERVISION

Several studies have supported the effectiveness of the clinical supervision of veteran teachers. Blumberg and Amidon's 1965 study (as cited in Acheson & Gall, 1992) found that teachers rated those supervisors highest who used indirect supervisory methods (see "Matching Styles" in this chapter for a description of nondirective methodology). Shinn's 1976 study (as cited in Acheson & Gall) found that teachers expressed support for all types of clinical supervision, including indirect methods. In 1975, Martin (as cited in Acheson & Gall) found that teachers reacted more favorably to evaluation by supervisors who had been trained in systematic observation techniques than to those who had not.

A smaller group of researchers have studied the effectiveness of the supervision of novice teachers. Huling-Austin, Putman, and Galvez-Hjornebik (as cited in Firth & Pajak, 1998) found that new teachers reported that a supportive teacher was most important to their success. This notion was further supported by Goldsberry's finding (as cited in Firth & Pajak) that mentor teachers are an important part of the new teacher induction process.

STANDARDS

As demonstrated in Chapter 2, there is considerable overlap between the administrative standards of the CEC (CEC, 2003) and the standards of the ISLLC (Council of Chief State School Officers, 1996). In this section, we will focus on the CEC and ISLLC standards that specifically address supervision and how these standards guide and inform special education administrators in their role as supervisors. The relationships between the two sets of standards described in this section are drawn from Table 2.4 (see Chapter 2), "Comparison of CEC Beginning Administrator Standards and ISLLC Standards."

There appear to exist three main areas of congruence between CEC administrator and ISLLC standards related to supervision: 1) instruction, 2) management/ administration, and 3) ethical practice. Above all, supervision must have as its goal the improvement of outcomes for all learners. ISLLC's focus on instruction is expressed in Standard 2: "Advocating, nurturing, and sustaining a school culture and instructional program conducive to student learning and staff professional growth." The related CEC standard is Standard 2: Development and Characteristics of Learners. Both standards stress the importance of effective instruction and the concern for the learning of all children.

Good administrative and management practices support and nurture effective instruction and student achievement. In the supervisory context, such practices demand that the administrator be informed by research, carefully orchestrate and organize the supervisory process, and provide constructive support to those working directly with children or with program development at the district level. ISLLC Standard 3: "Ensuring management of the organization, operations, and resources for a safe, efficient, and effective learning environment" and the CEC Standards on Foundations (1), Instructional Planning (7), and Collaboration (10) are concerned with developing sound practices that assist and challenge children.

Finally, both CEC and ISLLC, in Standards 9 and 5, respectively, underscore the critical need for the ethical behavior of leaders. Because school system administrators at all levels and in all disciplines often possess considerable evaluative power, it is imperative that they exercise this power honestly and with integrity.

CRUCIAL ACTIVITIES FOR SUPERVISION

Most educators would probably equate supervision with classroom or workplace monitoring and observation, a process widely known as *clinical supervision*. Goldhammer, Anderson, and Krajewski (as cited in Glickman, Gordon, & Ross-Gordon, 2001, p. 316) listed nine characteristics of clinical supervision, which are shown in Table 10.2. Glickman et al. (2001) condensed those characteristics into five steps:

1. Preconference with teacher
2. Observation of classroom
3. Analyzing and interpreting observation and determining conference approach
4. Postconference with teacher
5. Critique of previous four steps (Glickman et al., 2001, p. 316)

Glickman (1981) noted that supervisors need to recognize both their own supervisory orientation and the different stages of teacher development and adjust their supervision accordingly. Pajak (2003) added a further dimension by arguing that supervisors must identify the teaching styles of those whom they supervise and take these styles into account in the supervisory process.

SUPERVISION OF PROFESSIONAL STAFF

The ECSE administrator, functioning in the role of supervisor, typically works with a range of professionals providing services to children and families. The largest and most formalized group receiving monitoring, observation, and evaluation is usually made up of teachers; therefore, we will confine our discussion to this group, although many of the principles mentioned here could also be applied to the supervision of paraprofessionals (which will be discussed later in this chapter).

Glickman (2002) listed four ways supervisors can provide classroom assistance. The traditional approach, clinical supervision, has been touched on in previous sec-

Table 10.2.   Nine characteristics of clinical supervision

It is a technology for improving instruction.

It is a deliberate intervention into the instructional process.

It is goal oriented, combining the school's needs with the personal growth needs of those who work within the school.

It assumes a professional working relationship between teacher(s) and supervisor(s).

It requires a high degree of mutual trust, as reflected in understanding, support, and commitment to growth.

It is systematic, although it requires a flexible and continuously changing methodology.

It creates a productive (i.e., healthy) tension for bridging the gap between the real and the ideal.

It assumes that the supervisor knows a great deal about the analysis of instruction and learning and also about productive human interaction.

It requires both preservice training (for supervisors), especially in observation techniques, and continuous in-service reflection on effective approaches.

From Glickman, C.D., Gordon, S.P., & Ross-Gordon, J.M. (2001). *SuperVision and instructional leadership: A developmental approach* (5th ed., p. 316). Boston: Allyn & Bacon; adapted by permission.

tions and is presented in more detail here. Three other types of supervision, which involve other staff in addition to the supervisor, include peer coaching, critical friends, and study groups (see Glickman, 2002, pp. 9–23, for descriptions of these additional structures). This section considers the practical aspects of supervising teachers following the more widely used principles of clinical supervision.

Announced and Unannounced Visits

The first overall decision that must be made by the administrator is whether to conduct announced or unannounced observations of teachers in their classrooms. If the administrator follows the steps presented by Glickman et al. (2001), which include holding a preconference, the issue of announcement is moot. However, there are occasions when the administrator may wish to observe the teacher without prior notification. The two most common reasons for conducting unannounced observations are teacher nervousness (some people prefer unannounced observations because an announced observation creates for them an uncomfortable level of anticipation) and suspecting that a teacher behaves differently when he or she knows about the observation in advance. The administrator should weigh the factors favoring announced versus unannounced observations.

Developing an Organizational Structure for Observing and Conferring

Planning for observations and conferences requires considerable organization, but the extra time involved should prove worthwhile and efficient in the long term. Teachers tend to appreciate the efforts of an administrator who models planning and organization because teachers are held to these expectations; there is also a better chance of behavior change if a teacher respects the administrator and the supervisory process. Carefully spacing observations will help the administrator avoid the problem of trying to squeeze multiple observations into the few remaining days before any sort of evaluation deadline.

A number of documents are necessary for the organization of supervisory observations. First is a list of all professional staff for whom the administrator is responsible for supervising, complete with the required number of observations and conferences dictated by the program's or district's policy. The list should also include each staff member's number of years of experience and evaluation status. In most programs or districts, staff members who have been less successful, beginning staff, and staff new to the district may require more frequent observations than high-performing, experienced teachers. This list is usually provided by the program director or the district central office.

Other necessary documents are a general calendar for the academic year and the program's or district's calendar. The former should have ample space for entering observation and conference information (e.g., many calendar formats are available for the computer); the latter should contain districtwide holidays, professional or inservice days, and evaluation system deadlines. The supervisor first transfers all program or district information to the general calendar and then adds any pertinent local information (e.g., special school events that would prevent observation, such as assemblies, field trips, or testing programs). Next, dates for preobservation conferences, observations, and postobservation conferences for each staff member are assigned. These dates should be spaced out over the academic year and kept within the program's or district's evaluation framework.

Finally, about a week prior to the planned observation, the supervisor completes and sends to the staff member a brief observation notice form that lists the dates of the pre- and postobservation conferences and observation. The form should also provide space for the staff member to indicate (as appropriate) the topic of the lesson, objectives, and planned assessments. It is useful to include space for the staff member to request input from the observer on a specific aspect of the class. Many teachers, for example, value the supervisor's impressions of classroom dynamics or of the behavior of individual students. Using such tools as the ones in several of the books in the reference list may prove useful in structuring the observations and accompanying conferences.

Holding the Preobservation Conference

Admittedly, given the time constraints of a program leader, holding a preconference for each observation may seem impractical. If the supervisor's goal is to improve instruction and child outcomes, however, it makes sense to be as prepared as possible for the observation and to signal the importance of the observation by meeting about it beforehand. A face-to-face preobservation conference encourages dialogue between supervisors and staff members. The staff member can ask questions, provide a more detailed description of the lesson or activity, and confirm the viability of the strategies planned. The supervisor might make suggestions that could improve the instruction and/or validate the staff member's plans for the lesson or activity.

What to Observe and What Data to Collect

During the first observation of the year, it is appropriate to gather general data on the teacher's lesson using one or more observation techniques described in the next section. If the initial observation reveals areas of a staff member's performance that need to be addressed, the administrator can focus more on these areas in future observations. Many accomplished and secure staff members will request this more specific focus for subsequent observations; they recognize that although their overall performance is exemplary, they can always grow in selected areas with support.

Documenting the Observation

Many effective observation instruments and methods have been developed through extensive research and are discussed at length in the references listed at the end of this chapter. For the beginning administrator, one method that continues to be used extensively is the verbatim note-taking, or script tape, method. Goldhammer (1980), in addition to suggesting the possibility of video- and audiotaping as sources of data for the observation, provided a concise account of verbatim note-taking, which he called "hand recording" (p. 78). (Interestingly, Goldhammer predicted that in the future supervisors would be able to bring machines into the classroom; of course now, more than 25 years later, this machine can easily be identified as the laptop computer.)

Whether the administrator elects to take notes by hand or on the computer, the verbatim note-taking (from this point on called *script taping*) process described by Goldhammer and other authors is still relevant today. On the computer or on the first of several sheets of paper, the administrator records the date of the observation and the time the observation begins. It is also helpful to include a brief introductory paragraph about what is initially going on in the classroom. This may include the type of activity or subject being observed and the number of children involved. Next, the administrator develops a code for indicating who is speaking during the lesson or activity (e.g., "T" for Teacher, "C" for child). Then, he or she begins recording everything that is said in the classroom for about 30 minutes. Script taping is difficult and requires considerable practice, but it is a surprisingly rich source of data.

Realistically, some of the teacher–child dialogue will be missed (missed data should be indicated by a dash). It is also important to periodically record the time elapsed, as the issue of attention span is critical, especially with younger children. During most observations, dialogue will cease at some point and the children will become engaged in an activity. When this occurs, simply note the time the activity begins and ends and describe what is happening. The goal of the script tape method is to provide a reasonably accurate written account of what the administrator has observed, one that captures the staff member's and children's words as accurately as possible.

Acheson and Gall (1992) provided an extensive treatment of a variety of observational techniques, including selective verbatim techniques involving the use of seating charts, wide-lens techniques (e.g., anecdotal records, script taping, audio and visual recordings, journal writing), and checklists. Their chapter on checklists described one of the most well-known supervisory systems, the Flanders Interaction Analysis System (pp. 164–170). For samples of evaluation forms appropriate for the ECSE setting, please refer to the Appendix.

Analyzing the Observation Data

Once the script taping is completed, the administrator examines the entire script tape. Although many administrators leave the classroom or site to analyze the data in their office later, we suggest that the administrator remain in the classroom or at the site and work on the analysis there. This may seem like a minor point, but given the disruptions common in the life of the special education administrator, remaining in the classroom provides a degree of protection from disruption. Few people will interrupt an administrator during an observation.

During the analysis phase the administrator reads carefully through the notes, looking for patterns of teacher behavior, timing/pacing of instruction, and/or children's time on task. Examples of common findings are the predominance of teacher talk, insufficient time given for children to respond to the teacher's questions, or activities inappropriate to the attention span of young children. The administrator should choose no more than three or four areas of concern to discuss in the post-observation conference, as well as several examples of exemplary practice, if at all possible.

Matching Styles

During the analysis phase the administrator should also be conscious of Pajak's (2003) admonition to take into consideration the teacher's predominant style of teaching, particularly if it differs from the administrator's. For example, the administrator may favor a more constructivist approach in the classroom, whereas the teacher observed may use a more direct teaching style. The administrator should accept the teacher's style and offer suggestions that allow for improvement while maintaining the integrity of that style.

Similarly, Glickman cited the need for administrators to become aware of their own supervisory orientation. He described three such orientations:

> In the *directive orientation*, the supervisor emphasizes the behaviors of presenting, directing, demonstrating, standardizing, and reinforcing in developing an assignment for the teacher. In the *collaborative orientation*, the behaviors of presenting, clarifying, listening, problem-solving, and negotiating are used to develop a contract between teacher and supervisor. In the *non-directive orientation*, the behaviors of listening, encouraging, clarifying, presenting, and problem-solving are used to create a teacher self-plan. (1981, p. 36)

Glickman (1981) further contended that teachers have differing levels of development based on their degree of commitment and their capacity for abstract thinking. Figure 10.1 presents his model of four teacher categories. One of the administrator's tasks, according to Glickman (1981), is to match supervisory orientation to the category of development (depicted in Figure 10.1) demonstrated by the teacher being observed. In general, he suggested that the directive orientation be used with teacher dropouts, the collaborative orientation with unfocused workers and analytical observers, and the non-directive orientation with professionals. We encourage the ECSE administrator to consult both Glickman (1981) and Pajak (2003) for a more complete treatment of these concepts.

Holding the Postobservation Conference

Although much has been written about the postobservation conference, our experience has shown that there are several critical elements. To provide the most meaningful feedback, the administrator should hold the conference within a day or two of the observation. At the beginning of the conference, the administrator should wel-

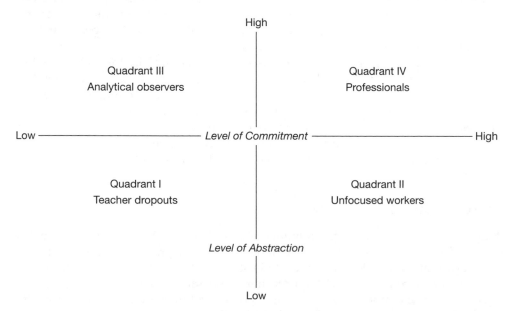

Figure 10.1.   Paradigm of teacher categories. (From Glickman, C.D. [1981]. *Developmental supervision: Alternative practices for helping teachers improve instruction* [p. 48]. Alexandria, VA: Association for Supervision and Curriculum Development; reprinted by permission.)

come the staff member and make sure he or she is as comfortable as possible. This may be especially difficult if the staff member senses that there will be negative aspects to the conference. Assuring the staff member that you are committed to providing mentoring and support or that you see this as an opportunity to work together and problem-solve can help reduce anxiety and the potential for confrontation.

The bulk of the conference should involve the use of data from the script tape or other data collection sources. The staff member should be encouraged to participate in the data analysis. This can be facilitated by giving the staff member a copy of the script tape prior to the conference. As mentioned previously, it is usually most productive to focus on no more than three or four problematic findings. Few people can remember and be expected to act on a long list of criticisms. The goal here should be to highlight the most critical areas needing correction. Because most people respond better to a situation that holds out hope for improvement and continued employment, the administrator should also try to include commendations.

The administrator should close the conference with a written plan of action. This is especially important if there were essentially negative findings. A plan of action might include setting a date for another observation within the week, having the teacher submit lesson plans for a specified period of time or submit a log of calls to parents of children who were off task, or having the teacher commit to professional development activities.

Issues of Diversity

Because one of the most important goals of supervision is to ensure the success of all children, it is imperative that the administrator be especially sensitive to how staff members treat each child. In special education in particular, where, for example, overrepresentation of African American males has become a national concern, this cannot be overstated. Similarly, strategies that address the elimination of the achievement gap that persists between children of majority families and children of minority families continue to be debated throughout the country. The administrator must be vigilant in observing, pointing out, and requiring correction of any staff practices that might contribute to the lessened success or discouragement of any child. Certainly, in the unlikely event that the administrator observes an example of racism, belittling, or inappropriate punishment of a child, the correction and subsequent disciplining of the staff member must occur as soon as it is possible to meet privately with the staff member. The incident must also be documented in writing (see Legal and Documentation Issues Related to Nonperforming Staff).

Union/Association Considerations

In some programs or school districts, part or all of the process of teacher supervision and evaluation is influenced by teachers' unions or association contracts and negotiated agreements. Deadlines, documentation procedures, and forms used for evaluation and sometimes even for observation of staff are subjects of discussion among teacher organizations, administrator organizations, individual program advisory groups, and the school districts' leadership. School districts usually incorporate the results of this process of supervision and evaluation into their supervision and evaluation documents. The ECSE administrator should become thoroughly familiar with and adhere strictly to the terms covered in these documents. For independent, nonprofit programs, the union issues may not be a current consideration, but program boards of directors and leaders should be prepared in case such matters arise.

What If There Are Problems?

Fortunately, the vast majority of staff members perform at better-than-acceptable levels. The administrator should expect, however, to encounter occasional problems. Often the problems are short term: A staff member experiences an off day or tries a strategy that is unsuccessful. Generally, if the supervisor feels this is not typical behavior, the problem can be addressed and a follow-up observation should reveal improvement. The staff member may also be new to teaching and simply lack some important instructional strategies and management skills. The beginning administrator is encouraged to read Gordon (1991), an excellent resource for working with beginning teachers, and Nolan and Hoover (2008). The needs of new staff tend to be quite different from those with more experience and may require more extensive resources. These include but certainly are not limited to the assignment of a mentor, creation of a supervisory team, and more frequent meetings with the administrator and/or this team.

If, however, the administrator encounters a staff member whose behavior is frequently or consistently problematic, who is resistant or hostile to constructive criticism, or who ignores repeated requests for change, systematic action must be taken. The first step in the process of documentation is to create a file for the staff member to hold all written material pertinent to that staff member's functioning. This written material might consist of copies of all observations, including supplementary materials, such as lesson plans, handouts, and worksheets; copies of all correspondence, such as memoranda or e-mails between the administrator and the staff member that communicate information, offer support, or require specific action by the staff member; and evidence of the staff member's participation in training required by the administrator. All of these documents must be signed by both the administrator and staff member to prevent the latter from claiming that he or she has never seen them.

So that the potential for real behavior change exists, it is essential to provide appropriate resources and support for the staff member. Other educators, such as staff development teachers, department chairs, or district-level specialists, should be asked to assist. Possible supports and resources for all teachers, especially those who are experiencing difficulty, include but are not limited to peer support; mentoring; attendance at relevant conferences; review of appropriate journal articles, books, or other professional literature; self-management of a specific problem; and targeted in-service activities or speakers. There is also a wealth of on-line resources that provide advice and curriculum materials for teachers. The administrator should also increase the number of observations of the staff member and consider multiple-day observations, thereby establishing a clearer pattern of instruction and interaction. These additional observations must be kept to a reasonable number to avoid both overly stressing the staff member and inviting charges of harassment.

If the staff member's performance remains problematic even after additional support and observation, the administrator should create, well in advance of the district's evaluation deadline for teachers who will be recommended for disciplinary action, a chronological list summarizing all of the supports and resources provided and the dates of all written communications and observations. Should the teacher contest any disciplinary action, this list, with its supporting data, will assist the administrator in defending the action taken, which according to the policies and procedures of the school district could include freezing of salary, deferral or denial of tenure, or dismissal. As unpleasant and as time consuming as this process is, it is nonetheless necessary so that each child is assured of the best possible education. Keeping this goal in mind can go a long way toward mitigating the stress for an administrator who is involved in documenting poor staff performance.

SUPERVISION OF PARAPROFESSIONALS

In educational settings, effective paraprofessionals are essential to the smooth functioning of classrooms and intervention activities. The nature of their jobs, however, often dictates a different form of supervision by the special education administrator. For those paraprofessionals with classroom responsibilities, such as instructional assistants, observation similar to that for teachers is certainly possible and advisable. For those support staff who operate outside the classroom, such as office workers, and sometimes outside the school or community setting, such as bus drivers and aides, data may still be collected primarily through observation, with the modifications noted in this section.

Union/Association Considerations

Unions or associations representing paraprofessional staff often have specific evaluation requirements; the special education administrator would be wise to become familiar with these. Within the parameters of both the employee's contract and the school district's policies and procedures, the administrator must decide on a course of action that will produce the data necessary for a fair and accurate evaluation.

Creating a Plan or Schedule for Observing

Because job requirements differ widely among the various types of paraprofessional positions, we will attempt to provide suggestions for each group of support staff. The common denominator in the process, as with professional staff, is the gathering of data through direct observation whenever possible.

Classroom Assistants   Staff who assist the classroom teacher are known by various titles: teacher assistants, teacher aides, paraprofessionals, paraeducators, or special education instructional assistants. Ideally, their job is to provide additional help to the teacher and children; often they are assigned clerical duties that, if overused, can compromise their effectiveness in the classroom. The fact that classroom assistants are expected to work primarily in a supportive role in the classroom allows the ECSE administrator to observe them much as he or she would a teacher. It is important to remember, however, that the assistant is under the direction of the teacher, and although a certain degree of initiative is desirable, it is the teacher's ultimate responsibility to guide the activities of the assistant.

Because the roles of teacher and assistant are so entwined, the special education administrator should consider involving both in the supervisory plan for the assistant. Certainly, the teacher must provide the administrator with expectations for the assistant as well as a list of specific responsibilities. Based on this information, the administrator may then develop a strategy for observation. Regularly scheduled visits to the classroom should include the collection of data but may need to be modified if the amount of dialogue encountered between assistant and child is minimal or difficult to collect without becoming intrusive. If the assistant is working with an individual child or a small group of children, the administrator may decide to use a timed recording strategy. Using a notepad, the administrator simply notes the time in 2- to 5-minute intervals down the margin of the page and then describes what is going on within that time frame. Any dialogue that ensues is also captured so that after about 30 minutes the administrator has a reasonably comprehensive picture of the assistant's activities and performance. As with the script tape used in teacher observation, the administrator then analyzes the data (and may also share the data beforehand with the assistant) and confers with the assistant as soon as possible after the conference. If the observation includes negative elements, the administrator must also develop a plan of improvement that highlights the areas requiring change and establish deadlines for meeting these requirements.

Administrative Office Staff   Administrators with responsibility for supervising office staff often rely on what might best be described as drive-by observation to gather informal performance data. Although data collected in this way can prove useful, the administrator should attempt to add additional components, such as formal observation, evaluation of work samples, and efficiency analysis.

In the formal observation process, the administrator finds a nearby area in the office and conducts a timed observation, such as that described previously for the classroom assistant. During this procedure, the administrator should attend to the staff member's phone skills (e.g., Is he or she courteous and helpful? Is the information given accurate?); interpersonal skills with co-workers, visitors, and professional staff; and ability to multitask, as most office staff are situated in work areas accessible to everyone, including the general public. Once the data are collected, the administrator follows the same procedures described previously: analyzing the data, conferring with the staff member, and if necessary developing a plan for improvement.

Data may also be obtained though evaluation of the staff member's documented work. As office workers submit typed work (e.g., memoranda, correspondence, reports, e-mails) to the administrator many times during the year, the administrator has a large amount of data to work from. Perusal of these various written documents should provide the administrator with a sense of the accuracy of the documents (i.e., Are they correct and complete?); the technical aspects of the documents (i.e., Are they formatted in a way that makes them readable? Are spelling, grammar, syntax, and punctuation flawless?); and whether they have been submitted on time. If the administrator finds errors or a pattern of missing deadlines, it is imperative that the issues be addressed directly with the staff member as soon as possible and that a plan of improvement be developed.

Both direct observation of the staff member by the administrator and analysis of work samples can be used to determine the staff member's efficiency. Even though much of the work of the early leadership researchers has fallen into disfavor, the notion that a job can be subjected to analysis and an efficient approach to that job be developed as a result of that analysis is still relevant today. Sometimes a simple discussion of what the staff member encounters in a typical day can also reveal a plan of action. Such tasks as determining what documents to file and when to file them, requesting due dates for projects, and prioritizing work according to both importance and due date are areas the administrator should discuss with the staff member and develop a plan to address them.

Other Support Staff   Administrators may also be responsible for supervising bus drivers and aides, building service/custodial staff, maintenance, and cafeteria staff. Again, direct observation of these staff members is not only possible but advisable. It may require riding a bus, being present in the cafeteria or kitchen (highly likely on a daily basis anyway), periodically checking on workers engaged in maintenance projects, or walking around the building (something every administrator should do several times a day) to check on the facilities' cleanliness. If the administrator adopts the practice of always carrying a notepad and pencil, data gathering is facilitated.

Indirect data collection is also possible: input from parents, staff, other visitors, and the children about bus service, the physical condition of the building, the quality of the cafeteria food, or the results of a maintenance project can become part of an employee's evaluation if it is written down and shared in a timely manner with the employee.

What If There Are Problems?

A common element of all supervisory and evaluative processes is the collection of written data that are shared with and signed by the employee as soon as possible after they are collected. This process of documentation is crucial because it establishes a written record that will allow the administrator to defend actions toward an employee. As with professional staff, the first step the administrator must take if a problem is identified through data collection is to provide the employee with support and resources. Sometimes this becomes the responsibility of the administrator, but often others may be enlisted to help. For example, an office worker having difficulty prioritizing tasks may be paired with another who is skilled in this area. Also, many school districts offer training courses that may prove helpful in enhancing an employee's skills.

If additional resources and support fail to resolve the problem, the written record—because it captures what was observed and how the administrator interpreted it—becomes invaluable because it also clearly establishes the action required for correction of the problem(s) and the time frame for remedy. Should an employee's performance deteriorate even after assistance, or should the employee challenge the administrator, the written record will provide the administrator with the data necessary to defend any administrative actions, as the documentation will offer a chronology of performance and a time line for improvement.

Although a detailed account of how the administrator deals with repeated challenges from an ineffective employee is beyond the scope of this chapter, most school systems have developed detailed procedures for the administrator to follow in this situation. Most, if not all, rely on the keeping of the type of written documentation described in previous sections of this chapter.

RECRUITMENT, SUPERVISION, AND RECOGNITION OF VOLUNTEERS

Supervision of such volunteers as parents, older adults, employees of businesses in partnership with the school, or community members is quite different than supervising paid staff members. As the term implies, volunteers are donating their time and can withhold their services if they wish. Because pay and formal evaluations are not involved, other methods and incentives must be found to attract and retain those who wish to help and who support positive outcomes in schools and the community. This is especially important in this era of budget cutting and downsizing; a good volunteer force can provide much-needed assistance to overworked staff. The suggestions included in this section are directed primarily to programs in schools, although the general procedures could be adapted to a variety of early childhood settings.

Recruitment and Training

Probably the best way to recruit volunteers is to establish strong lines of communication with relevant community individuals and organizations. Parent newsletters, invitations to special events, and a good public relations network that keeps local news sources informed all provide parents and the community at large with information about the program and its children. Many times people who read about the school call to offer their services; they should be welcomed and encouraged to volunteer. Of course, all individuals who work or volunteer in a program serving children must undergo appropriate background checks and not present a health danger to children, staff, or others associated with the program.

The appointment of a volunteer coordinator, preferably from the ranks of potential volunteers, presents a more active approach to recruiting volunteers. When people offer to volunteer, they can be directed to the volunteer coordinator, freeing the administrator for other duties. The volunteer coordinator, working closely with the administrator, can also provide initial education for potential volunteers and assist in their placement. This leaves the administrator with the following responsibilities: discussing the specific volunteer needs of the school with the volunteer coordinator, providing a place for training, and arranging for background checks through the program or district. This last task is critical: No one should be allowed to work directly with young children unless he or she has undergone a thorough local and national criminal background clearance process.

Once the volunteer coordinator compiles a list of cleared volunteers, the training process can begin. As part of initial training sessions, volunteers need a general orientation to the program, basic principles of human growth and development, and a brief period of classroom observation. If possible, those school staff who will have volunteers working with them should be present for at least a portion of the training. Because it is conceivable that new volunteers will come in throughout the school year, it may also be necessary to hold periodic training sessions for them; it is not advisable to allow untrained volunteers to work in the classroom. Most people will appreciate the school's insistence on training because it signals that the school is serious about ensuring that children receive the best possible level of assistance.

Supervising Volunteers

The procedures described for staff supervision also apply, with modification, to the supervision of volunteers. Perhaps the greatest modifications involve intensity, formality, and frequency of observation. A preobservation conference or preobservation form is usually not practical. Informal observation notes, rather than systematic procedures such as script taping, are more appropriate when observing volunteer efforts, and because the volunteer usually works no more than one or two days per week, the administrator will not have the opportunity for frequent or consecutive observations. Finally, though a brief postobservation conference should be held, it should serve to recognize and thank the effective volunteer. Criticism or negative comments about the staff member with whom the volunteer works must be treated diplomatically and kept in strict confidence. The supervisor must avoid using negative comments from a volunteer for purposes of a staff member's evaluation, as this could ultimately jeopardize the volunteer program. Perhaps the best approach to this situation is to establish and foster a school climate in which continuous improvement is valued and all people engaged in working with children have the opportunity to discuss constructively in an open, but structured, forum.

What If There Are Problems?

As with most staff, most volunteers work effectively and provide valuable services to children and teachers; however, very infrequently a volunteer may prove ineffective. The administrator often hears about a volunteer's unsuitability from the teacher working with the volunteer, from parents of children in the class, or through the volunteer's own negative comments. If any of these prove correct, the administrator has an obligation to confer with the volunteer and discuss concerns candidly but diplomatically in a timely fashion; the volunteer coordinator should also be made aware of these concerns. If no improvement occurs after this conference, then the administrator may need to end the volunteer's services.

Recognizing Volunteer Efforts

On an informal basis, the administrator should commend volunteers whenever possible. On a more formal basis, the administrator must work with the volunteer coordinator to make sure that volunteers are periodically recognized. Usually this takes the form of a reception for volunteers that includes refreshments, brief words of thanks from staff, and certificates of appreciation. If funds permit, a small token of appreciation, such as a coffee mug or T-shirt with the school logo, can be presented to each volunteer. Many schools hold such receptions toward the end of the school year and find that volunteers really appreciate the recognition.

LEGAL AND DOCUMENTATION ISSUES RELATED TO NONPERFORMING STAFF

In the administrator's role as supervisor of instruction, his or her goals should always provide avenues of professional development for teachers that are directly linked to child outcomes. As outlined previously in the chapter, we believe in supervision that is relationship oriented and humanistic in nature. At times, however, some staff fail to improve and actually become nonproductive. This has always been problematic but has been particularly addressed in No Child Left Behind (NCLB) Act of 2001 (PL 107-110).

As instructional leaders, administrators must deal with nonproducing staff and either help these staff members perform at a satisfactory level or take action to remove them. Assisting staff in making improvements has already been addressed. Here we outline a general plan for addressing nonperforming or unsatisfactory staff, based on our experience as school leaders and in the context of legal and documentation requirements.

The acronym NEAT was developed in workshops conducted by Noel Farmer and James McGowan during the fall of 2005 with several school districts. These workshops were based on their experiences as central office leaders who were directly responsible for dismissing teachers who, over time, failed to perform satisfactorily. The acronym was based on observations of hearing officers' expectations in dismissal proceedings and strategies employed by the school district and nonperforming staff members' attorneys. The letter *n* in NEAT stands for *notice.* Nonperforming staff must always know the specific deficiencies that are to be addressed. The instructional leader must always demonstrate a pattern of informing staff of what needs to be changed.

The *e* in NEAT stands for *explanation.* The nonperforming teacher must receive an in-depth account of alleged deficiencies and must be afforded an opportunity to explain the circumstances that constitute the unsatisfactory performance in question.

The *a* stands for *assistance.* It is the responsibility of the leader to develop, in collaboration with the staff member, a plan to address the unsatisfactory performance, including direct assistance. This may involve mentoring, observing the satisfactory performance of other staff, peer coaching, or attending classes designed to improve skills. The focus of this plan must be the improvement of the staff member's performance.

The *t* stands for *time.* Staff members who need to improve their instructional skills must be given sufficient time to do so. They must be allowed to identify, practice, and implement new processes and/or strategies, all of which takes time. It is inappropriate and unrealistic (not to mention unfair) to inform a nonperformer on one day of the deficiencies and expect to see changes the next day.

Following the procedures captured by the acronym NEAT will help ensure that legal requirements are met. We have outlined a process that is focused on improvement but also follows basic legal requirements for documentation of nonperforming staff. Any strategy or procedures developed should first be closely discussed with attorneys-at-law who are familiar with both the codified and the case law related to dismissing staff. (See also Chapter 14 for additional information about legal issues.)

LINKING SUPERVISION TO PROFESSIONAL DEVELOPMENT AND MENTORING

To create the healthiest possible educational environment for children, all staff members must receive continuous support and encouragement through both supervision and professional development. Simply put, professional development must become an integral part of the supervisory process (see Chapter 9 for detailed coverage of professional development). This may be difficult when professional development consists of a few in-service days designed to focus on issues critical to the school, scheduled periodically throughout the school year. Although these sessions can be helpful, the issues raised must be revisited on a regular and frequent basis, and staff must implement the practices suggested in their classrooms or at their worksites if change is to occur. Two further steps are also necessary: Implementation results must be shared with the rest of the school or work group, and the administration (or a designated committee) must monitor and track all progress. In these ways, supervision and professional development become complementary. Chiefly through careful documentation, patterns emerge that can help administrators, in concert with their staff, determine if practices are useful and consistent.

Mentoring, whether for beginning staff or those more experienced staff who are struggling, should also be an important component of the supervisory process. Although formal mentoring programs do exist in some school districts, most administrators will probably find it necessary to create, train, and nurture their own local cadre of mentors. Mentorship programs can be as simple as buddy systems, in which an experienced and competent staff member skilled in working with adults is paired with a novice at the beginning of the school year. Unless the administrator checks periodically on the progress of the mentor pairs, requires and collects a log of contacts, and/or provides for regular meetings designed to share successes and failures, this mentor approach will probably not survive beyond the first few crucial weeks of school. Some school districts have begun implementing more elaborate systems of mentorship that train educators to be mentors to new or struggling staff. (See Chapter 9 for more details on mentoring programs.)

IMPORTANCE OF REFLECTION

The importance of reflecting on the procedure, process, method, tone, and relationships relating to the supervision of all staff cannot be understated. It is critical that ECSE administrators periodically and systematically take the time to consider their actions and make adjustments to their practices as needed. This is not an easy thing to do. Time constraints are very real and pose the greatest threat to reflection. Nonetheless, if administrators are ever to improve their skills in staff supervision, it is critical that they take time following each postconference to review and critique the efficacy of the supervisory process they have employed. Self-reflection is an important process of professional development for program leaders. Administrators would also do well to encourage staff commitment and buy-in to the process of supervision. Providing ways for staff to offer feedback in a nonthreatening fashion (e.g., suggestion boxes, survey in which anonymity is maintained) offers program administrators another avenue for professional improvement. In this way, leaders gain valuable information while encouraging reflection among staff, and the entire process of supervision becomes an open dialogue in which the possibility of professional growth exists for all.

It is equally important that suggestions for change or retention of elements of the process be written down and kept in a clearly accessible growth log. Regular examination of this log will help ensure that what worked (or what did not) is remembered and applied in future supervisory activities.

IMPLICATIONS FOR FUTURE RESEARCH AND CLINICAL PRACTICE

Pajak (2000) compared the art and science of supervision as conceived by Eisner. In his most recent book, Pajak (2008) defined the relationship between the art and science of supervision when he stated the case for supervising teachers: "The challenge facing supervision is currently identified as helping teachers relinquish the mechanical applications of techniques in favor of developing a professional identity that builds on and incorporates personal values, beliefs, talents, interests, and abilities" (Pajak, 2008, p. 246). The case made by Pajak regarding teachers can be extended to supervisors and interpreted to say that supervisors must do more than go through the mechanical motions of supervising. They must become professionals who incorporate personal values, beliefs, talents, interests, and abilities into the process of supervision.

This is clearly an area requiring more research of a qualitative nature. Some districts, however, are encouraging or at least experimenting with more prescriptive or directive teaching strategies that may require more direct forms of supervision. There are several overall implications for research raised by this issue. First, the matching of teaching and supervisory styles, discussed previously, becomes all the more important. Second, the validity of the more humanistic approaches to supervision must be thoroughly examined. Finally, there will need to be studies undertaken to compare districts adopting more prescriptive approaches with those whose approaches rely more on individual teacher judgment.

Pajak (2000) also examined two emerging areas of supervision and teaching: the movement toward democratic learning communities and standards-based supervision. As both of these areas are drawing increased attention, research into their efficacy should be considered. Certainly, in the wake of increased state testing driven by NCLB, standards-based supervision will become more the norm. If clinical practice is to be expanded, both through attention to standards and through democratic learning communities—the latter characterized by shared mission, vision, and values; collective inquiry; collaboration; action research; and the use of continuous improvement that is results oriented (DuFour & Eaker, 1998)—the field needs a better understanding of the culture that developed around the tenets of a more directive, undemocratic supervisory approach.

CONCLUSIONS

It is clear that educational supervision has paralleled the process and techniques that were present in industrial management. It has moved from espousal of directive and controlling activities on the part of the supervisor to activities that more fully engage the supervisee in the assessment of his or her own performance and growth. For a more inclusive type of supervision to continue, it is necessary for educators to be fully aware of and prepared to use the volumes of research that have validated more humanistic approaches. It is equally important for educators not to succumb to what appear to be easy fixes (i.e., highly directive teaching strategies and early 20th-century supervisory practices that involve more telling than enabling).

Supervision, especially in the area of special education, should promote the learning and enhanced performance of staff who come in contact with children in the increasingly complex arena where research and the accompanying educational practices makes quantum leaps every year. We feel that the more humanistic approaches to supervision have the greater probability for the enhancement, engagement, and ownership for all parties involved in the critical task of educating young children with disabilities.

REFERENCES

Acheson, K.A., & Gall, M.D. (1992). *Techniques in the clinical supervision of teachers.* White Plains, NY: Longman.

Barr, A.S., Burton, W.H., & Brueckner, L.J. (1947). *Supervision* (2nd ed.). New York: Appleton-Century-Crofts.

Blumberg, A. (1980). *Supervisors and teachers: A private cold war.* Berkeley, CA: McCutchan Publishing.

Cogan, M.L. (1973). *Clinical supervision.* Boston: Houghton Mifflin.

Council of Chief State School Officers. (1996). *Interstate school leaders licensure consortium (ISLLC) standards for school leaders.* Washington, DC: Author.

Council for Exceptional Children. (2003). *CEC knowledge and skill base for all beginning special education administrators.* Arlington, VA: Author.

DuFour, R., & Eaker, R. (1998). *Professional learning communities at work: Best practices for enhancing student achievement.* Bloomington, IN: National Education Service.

Firth, G.R., & Pajak, E.F. (1998). *Handbook of research on school supervision.* New York: Macmillan.

Glickman, C.D. (1981). *Developmental supervision: Alternative practices for helping teachers improve instruction.* Alexandria, VA: Association for Supervision and Curriculum Development.

Glickman, C.D. (2002). *Leadership for learning: How to help teachers succeed.* Alexandria, VA: Association for Supervision and Curriculum Development.

Glickman, C.D., Gordon, S.P., & Ross-Gordon, J.M. (2001). *SuperVision and instructional leadership: A developmental approach* (5th ed.). Boston: Allyn & Bacon.

Goldhammer, R. (1969). *Clinical supervision: Special methods for the supervision of teachers.* New York: Holt, Rinehart, and Winston.

Goldhammer, R. (1980). *Clinical supervision: Special methods for supervision of teachers* (2nd ed.). New York: Holt, Reinhardt, & Winston.

Gordon, S.P. (1991). *How to help beginning teachers succeed.* Alexandria, VA: Association for Supervision and Curriculum Development.

No Child Left Behind Act of 2001, PL 107-110, 115 Stat. 1425, 20 U.S.C. §§ 6301 *et seq.*

Nolan, J.F., & Hoover, L.A. (2008). *Teacher supervision and evaluation: Theory into practice* (2nd ed.). New York: John Wiley & Sons.

Pajak, E. (2000). *Approaches to clinical supervision: Alternatives for improving instruction* (2nd ed.). Norwood, MA: Christopher-Gordon.

Pajak, E. (2003). *Honoring diverse teaching styles: A guide for supervisors.* Alexandria, VA: Association for Supervision and Curriculum Development.

Pajak, E. (2008). *Supervising instruction: Differentiating for teacher success.* Norwood, MA: Christopher-Gordon.

Sergiovanni, T.J. (1977). *Handbook for effective department leadership.* Boston: Allyn & Bacon.

Sergiovanni, T.J., & Starratt, R.J. (1979). *Supervision: Human perspectives.* New York: McGraw-Hill.

Wiles, K., & Lovell, J.T. (1975). *Supervision for better schools.* Englewood Cliffs, NJ: Prentice Hall.

Health Issues in Settings for Young Children

William Scott Taylor and Janeen McCracken Taylor

*It was once said that the moral test of a Government is how
that Government treats those in the dawn of life, the children; those
who are in the twilight of life, the elderly; and those in the shadow of life,
the sick, the needy, and the handicapped [i.e., individuals with disabilities].*
Hubert H. Humphrey, Senator, United States Congress

What If?   Carson attends a preschool program for 3- and 4-year-old children with and without disabilities. The school is located in New Mexico, where there is little rainfall and the humidity is very low. On the second day of school, Carson is sitting at a table when his nose starts to bleed profusely. Some students run or walk to his side to see what has happened. The teacher, Ms. Salzedo, is a few feet away. She is a first-year teacher and has taken the school's health and safety class, and she immediately reaches for the protective gloves in the coat of her pocket. What else should Ms. Salzedo do about Carson's nosebleed? Whom should she notify? What should she do to prevent other children from being exposed to Carson's blood?

CHAPTER OVERVIEW

The goal of this chapter is to provide an overview of current medical information as it applies to health issues in early childhood education settings. The information presented is derived primarily from the American Academy of Pediatrics publications and selected sources from the medical literature and will therefore have a decidedly medical bent.

   After reviewing this chapter, the reader will

- Understand the importance of health practices in early childhood education settings

- Be able to develop strategies for minimizing communicable diseases

- Understand the importance of local health care resources

- Understand the risk of communicable disease exposure to women of childbearing age

- Be able to develop policies, procedures, and practices related to health issues

CONTEMPORARY HEALTH ISSUES IN EARLY CHILDHOOD SETTINGS

Although the specific goals and strategies for early childhood special education (ECSE) may be the subject of earnest debate among educators and informal conversations among families of young children, there is consensus that the environment in which services occur must be both safe and healthy (American Academy of Pediatrics [AAP], American Public Health Association [APHA], Maternal and Child Health Bureau [MCHB], & Health Resources and Services Administration [HRSA], 2002). This protected world comprises children, adults (e.g., family members, staff, volunteers), and the building and its contents. All who enter this world have a vested interest in good health and safety practices. Not surprisingly, this concept has wide acceptance; for example, the AAP et al. indicated that

> Health involves more than just the absence of illness and injury. To stay healthy, children depend on adults to make healthy choices for them and to teach them to make such choices for themselves over the course of a lifetime. Child development addresses physical growth and development in many areas: gross and fine motor skills, language and emotional balance, cognitive capacity, and personal skills. Thus health and safety issues overlap with those considered part of early childhood education and mental health. Such overlap is inevitable and indeed, desirable. (2002, p. xv)

This statement primarily reflects the views of the health care community, but there are other organizations with their own valid organizational approaches, missions, perspectives, standards, recommendations, guidelines, and requirements. The National Association for the Education of Young Children, Head Start, the Child Welfare League of America, the U.S. Department of Defense, the National Fire Protection Association, and the Child Care Bureau are examples of such organizations. It is fair to say that all have the health and welfare of children and their families as their highest priority. Detailed information is available from all of these sources on the Internet or from organizational headquarters.

In the United States, data on the prevalence of disabilities among children are fragmentary, often difficult to access, sometimes inconsistent, not current, and erratically reported (Parrino & Thacker, 1994). Lack of definitive data does not, however, imply lack of concern for the health and safety of such children. For example, child care settings are potential sites for early detection of developmental disabilities and referral for appropriate intervention (Feldman, 2004). Others have noted that although children with disabilities are at risk for the same diseases and injuries as other children, their disabilities may increase that risk. For example, children with cleft palate have more frequent ear infections, and children with spina bifida have more frequent urinary tract infections (Blackman, 1997). More research is needed on these topics, but this does not diminish the necessity to apply the principles of child health to the fullest extent in early special education settings.

The largest body of information concerning problems associated with communicable diseases in group settings comes from research conducted in child care centers (Aronson & Shope, 2005). These facilities usually provide care and support for relatively large numbers of children and provide valuable information about the transmission characteristics of diseases. Research findings related to communicable diseases in child care centers can be applied to any setting involving groups of young children. Early childhood education classrooms, infant centers, preschool programs for children with disabilities, and kindergartens are all confronted with health issues.

Just as parents have a responsibility for evaluating school systems for older children, they have the same responsibility when seeking services for infants and children in ECSE settings. The National Resource Center for Health and Safety in Child Care (n.d.) encourages parents to ask such questions as these:

- Are there enough adult staff to meet children's needs?

- Do the children in the program seem happy?

- Is there an adequate quiet or rest area?

- Is there a clean diaper-changing area?

- Are toilets and sinks clean and easy to reach?

- Is the facility smoke free?

- Are play areas safe and enclosed properly?

- Are there adequate health and safety policies?

- Are licensure requirements met?

- What health care training is required for employees?

- Does a health care consultant participate in the development of policies?

Those responsible for planning, policies, curricula, and oversight of programs should be prepared to answer these and similar questions.

Risk Factors for Transmission of Communicable Diseases

Many factors may contribute to the transmission of infectious diseases in child care settings. Transmission is facilitated by children's naturally occurring behaviors (e.g., nose picking, mouthing of objects, drooling) their immature toileting skills, and their lack of knowledge about good health practices. In addition, caregivers may have insufficient training in infection control, and program policies on positive health practices may be inadequate. Other major factors contributing to the transmission of communicable diseases include limited space; poor air quality; inappropriate ratio of staff to children; and poorly designed or managed staff–child assignments, such as having staff who change diapers also be responsible for food preparation. Separating children in diapers from children not in diapers is also important but often not possible. Also, as much as parents are asked to keep their children home when they are ill, some parents may bring ill children to the center to avoid the cost or inconvenience of making other arrangements.

Diseases in Early Childhood

Concerns of administrators, teachers, care providers, staff, parents, and public health officials about infections can be grouped into four areas:

1. Infections that cause illness primarily in young children (e.g., *haemophilus influenzae* type b [Hib])

2. Infections that infect children and adults equally (e.g., viral diarrhea)

3. Infections that are generally mild in children but may cause serious illness in adults (e.g., hepatitis A)

4. Infections that cause little or no illness in children or adults but can result in serious illness or conditions in the unborn children of susceptible women (e.g., cytomegalovirus [CMV] disease, rubella, parvovirus B19, and toxoplasmosis)

Although all illness should be taken seriously, some illnesses are more problematic and require special attention. Table 11.1 lists infectious diseases in group settings. Diseases that can cause significant community health problems require notification of state and/or federal agencies. The Epidemiology Program Office of the Centers for Disease Control and Prevention (CDC) maintains a list of Nationally Notifiable Infectious Diseases, which is updated yearly and is available on the CDC web site (http://www.cdc.gov). Several of the diseases recorded in Table 11.1 are on this list. It is not important to acquire an extensive knowledge of all listed diseases, but it is important to know that such a list exists and which diseases are problematic in group settings for children.

Because of the contagious nature and/or severity of some illnesses, the AAP recommends using the criteria listed in Table 11.2 to exclude or dismiss children from child care settings. The AAP et al. (2002) publication *Caring for Our Children: National Health and Safety Performance Standards: Guidelines for Out-of-Home Child Care Programs* should be consulted for a complete description of the exclusion and readmission criteria.

The short-term exclusion of children with many mild infectious diseases is likely to have only a minor impact on the incidence of infection among other children; therefore, it is not recommended to exclude such children. When such a problem arises, parents should be asked to consult their health care provider and to inform the child's program director of the advice received. It is the responsibility of the program administrator to contact the health consultant or local health care department for information regarding isolation policies (Aronson & Shope, 2005).

It is important that staff understand their roles in the control of infectious disease. They must be aware of symptoms or unusual behaviors that might indicate illness, be aware of illnesses on the exclusion list, and know at what point an affected child is no longer considered infectious. Understanding the likelihood of recurrence and what special precautions to take are also important. Important information and recommendations can be obtained through association and close communication with families, health care providers, and public health officials (AAP et al., 2002).

Modes of Transmission

Many factors contribute to the transmission of infectious agents in early childhood education settings, the most important of which relate to young children's immune

Table 11.1. Infectious diseases in group settings

Disease	Mode of transmission	Causative agent
Upper respiratory infection[a]	Respiratory	V
Streptococcal sore throat[a]	Respiratory	B
Otitis media (i.e., ear infection)[a]	Respiratory	V or B
Haemophilus influenzae type b[a]	Respiratory	B
Meningitis	Respiratory	V or B
Tuberculosis	Respiratory	B
Hepatitis A[a]	Fecal-oral	V
Hepatitis B	Body fluid	V
Hepatitis C	Body fluid	V
Influenza	Respiratory	V
Shigella diarrhea[a]	Fecal-oral	B
Salmonella diarrhea[a]	Fecal-oral	B
E. coli diarrhea	Fecal-oral	B
Giardia diarrhea[a]	Fecal-oral	O
Rotavirus diarrhea	Fecal-oral	V
Viral gastroenteritis[a]	Fecal-oral	V
Impetigo	Direct	B
Ringworm	Direct	F
Scabies[a]	Direct	O
Herpes simplex	Direct	V
Methicillin-resistant *S. aureus* (MRSA)	Direct	B
Parvovirus B19	Multiple	V
Cytomegalovirus (CMV)[a]	Multiple	V
Chickenpox[a]	Multiple	V
Head lice[a]	Direct	O
Pinworms	Fecal-oral	O
Acquired immunodeficiency syndrome (AIDS)	Body fluid	V
Conjunctivitis (pink eye)[a]	Direct	V or B
Mumps	Respiratory	V
Croup	Respiratory	V
Whooping cough	Respiratory	B
Measles (rubeola)	Respiratory	V
German measles (rubella)	Respiratory	V
Roseola	Direct	V

*Key:*V, virus; B, bacteria; F, fungus; O, other.

[a]Frequent occurrence in group settings for children.

Sources: Taylor and Taylor (1989) and Wald (2004).

system vulnerability. Once infection is established, transmission easily occurs because of the close relationship with other children and adults in child care settings. Diseases can be transmitted through a number of avenues: respiratory, fecal-oral, direct contact, body fluids, and multiple routes.

Respiratory Route   The mode of transmission for some organisms is the airborne route. Agents that can be transmitted in this way include most respiratory viruses and some bacteria, as noted in Table 11.1. The organisms float and remain in the air and may settle on nonporous surfaces, where they can remain infective, often for hours. Infection can occur indirectly by inhalation of infected droplets, but more frequently individuals are infected by touching infected surfaces and then touching

Table 11.2. Exclusion/dismissal criteria

Such unexplained fever or signs or symptoms of illness as
• Lethargy
• Uncontrolled coughing
• Unexplained irritability or crying
• Difficult breathing or wheezing
Diarrhea
Blood in stools
Vomiting illness
Persistent abdominal pain
Mouth sores with drooling
Rash with fever or behavior change
Purulent (i.e., containing or discharging pus) conjunctivitis
Head lice
Scabies
Tuberculosis
Impetigo
Strep throat or other streptococcal infection
Chickenpox
Whooping cough
Mumps
Hepatitis A
Measles
German measles (rubella)
Some respiratory illnesses
Shingles (herpes zoster)
Oral herpes (herpes simplex)

Source: American Academy of Pediatrics, American Public Health Association, Maternal and Child Health Bureau, & Health Resources and Services Administration (2002)

their eyes, nose, or mouth. The warm, moist membranes in these areas allow the organism to thrive, multiply, and eventually cause infection. Finger to moist membrane spread is the most common mechanism for transmission of viral and bacterial illnesses. Children are commonly taught to cover their mouths with their hands when they cough or sneeze, but this actually increases the chance of spreading the infection because infected children tend to contaminate their hands and clothing with infected secretions from their noses, eyes, and throats. A better alternative is to direct sneezes or coughs into the crook of the arm. Washing hands after coughing or sneezing would also help prevent the spread of illness, but such a strategy is impractical much of the time (e.g., when playing outdoors).

Although the common cold is usually a mild illness with symptoms lasting 7–14 days, it is a leading cause of both doctor visits and school absenteeism. Colds are most prevalent among children, probably because of relative lack of resistance in this age group and frequent contact with other children who are infected. In general, young children experience 6–10 colds per year whereas adults experience 2–4 per year. Women seem to have more colds than men, possibly as a result of their more frequent exposure to infected children. Colds can be caused by a wide variety of viruses, such as rhinoviruses, parainfluenza virus, respiratory syncytial virus, adenoviruses, and enteroviruses. In most cases it is not important to identify the specific viral family because of the mildness and short duration of the illness and the extreme difficulty and expense of laboratory identification. Multiple infections often occur because of the large variety of types and subtypes of each virus and failure to develop immunity after exposure.

Viruses are frequently shed from infected sites like the eyes, nose, or throat even before symptoms develop. This is why these infections are so difficult to control in group settings of children; children may be infectious before showing any symptoms. The degree of illness may range from asymptomatic to runny nose, sore throat, earache, croup, bronchitis, pneumonia, or a combination of these problems.

The most common complication of viral respiratory infections is superimposed bacterial infection of the middle ear (i.e., otitis media). The peak age of incidence is 6–18 months, which is similar to that of viral upper respiratory infections. Most children will have had at least one episode of otitis media by their second birthday, but many will have had several by this time. As previously noted, it is not recommended that children with mild respiratory infections be excluded from care settings because this strategy has not been shown to achieve an overall reduction of infection. This does not mean that other means of preventing or limiting infection are of no value; for example, it still makes sense (and is vital) to wash hands frequently.

Contrary to popular opinion, being exposed to cold weather, getting chilled, and getting overheated have little or no effect on the development, severity, or duration of a cold. At the same time, it is true that changes in relative humidity may affect the survivability of viruses. Colder weather, with its generally lower humidity, may permit viruses to live longer, and it also makes nasal membranes more vulnerable to infection (National Institute of Allergy and Infectious Diseases, 2001).

Fecal-Oral Route   Some bacteria and viruses pass from mouth to stomach and along the intestinal tract until they find susceptible cells. Here they may cause local tissue injury, producing cramping and diarrhea. The fecal-oral route of disease transmission is fairly common among young children because they are novice hand washers and lack the maturity to use good hygiene. Diapered children with these infections will frequently pass the infection to others by contact with even microscopic amounts of infected stool. With frequent diaper changing, it is inevitable that hands, floors, diaper-changing tables, toys, countertops, toilets, and faucet handles will be contaminated by either the children or staff. Infection can be spread by the fecal-oral route if frequent and thorough hand washing is not performed, especially after diaper changing and before food preparation, as eating contaminated food can result in illness. Given the prevalence of diapering among children younger than 3 years of age, it is not surprising that contamination of the environment through this route is highest in settings with this age group. Illnesses that are spread through this route, however, are easier to control environmentally than those transmitted through the respiratory route.

Rotavirus infection is the most common cause of intestinal infection in infants and children and a leading cause of hospitalization in this age group. It is the most common organism found in child care settings. When looking at all diarrheal illness in child care settings, rotavirus has been found to be the offending agent in as many as 24% of cases (Wald, 2004).

Like respiratory viruses, infections spread by the fecal-oral route may be asymptomatic, especially in newborns and infants. Because large quantities of virus are shed in even small amounts of stool, the organisms are frequently prevalent on a variety of environmental surfaces during outbreaks. Many such outbreaks have been found in child care settings. The illness often looks like a respiratory infection at first because initial symptoms may be a runny nose or cough. As the illness progresses, varying combinations of fever, vomiting, and diarrhea appear and usually last 3–5 days. In some cases, dehydration may be so severe as to warrant hospitalization. Hepatitis A, viral gastroenteritis, and *Giardia* diarrhea are other examples of illnesses spread by this route.

Direct Contact Route   Several infections—encompassing bacterial, viral, fungal, and parasitic—can be spread by direct contact with contaminated material (objects called *fomites*), whether it is infected mucus, stool, surfaces, clothing, or skin. Some infections can be transmitted by indirect contact with contaminated objects, toys, or clothing. Transmission by direct contact in its narrowest context implies skin or head contact with organisms that produce skin diseases. Such contact may involve sharing combs or hairbrushes, clothing, or bedding. Examples of illness spread by this route are impetigo and head lice.

Body Fluid Contact Route   Very serious infections are usually spread by intimate contact with blood or other body fluids of an infected person. This kind of exposure is not ordinarily a common source of infection in child care settings, but it is often impossible to know who might be infected. This fact mandates the use of practices to prevent transmission of these diseases. Such practices are often called *universal precautions* (i.e., handling all body fluids in a safe manner) and are discussed further in another section of this chapter.

Hepatitis B virus (HBV) may cause infections that are completely asymptomatic, but at the other extreme they can be fatal. Infection is more likely to be asymptomatic in children than in adults. Because the most common modes of transmission of HBV in general are by contact with blood or through sexual activity, the prevalence is higher in adults than children. Young children usually acquire the infection from their mothers at the time of delivery. For this reason, it is important to know the presence of even asymptomatic infection in the mother. Testing for HBV status is routinely performed during pregnancy so that a newborn can be treated immediately after birth as necessary.

Transmission of HBV in child care settings is an uncommon event in the United States. Because the risk of transmission is low, exclusion of HBV-infected children from care settings is not recommended, nor is HBV screening necessary for entry into a program. All non-infected babies are now immunized against HBV, so the spread of this illness should continue to decrease. Human immunodeficiency virus (HIV), hepatitis C, and hepatitis D are other examples of illnesses spread by this route.

Multiple Route Contact   Cytomegalovirus (CMV) infection warrants special attention because although it does not usually cause significant illness in children or adults, it can have devastating effects on a developing fetus. In addition, it can be transmitted by more than one route. CMV infects 50%– 85% of adults in the United States by the age of 40 years and is the most frequent viral infection occurring in the womb (CDC, 2002). Once an individual is infected, the virus remains alive but usually stays dormant for the remainder of that person's life. Under ordinary circumstances the infection is not problematic. It is, however, of special concern in unborn babies, infected people who work with children, people with compromised immune systems (e.g., people with HIV), or those who are taking drugs to suppress the immune system.

The primary (i.e., first) infection may produce only mild symptoms, often described as a transitory mononucleosis-type illness. CMV may subsequently be shed in body fluids and thus can be found in urine, saliva, blood, tears, semen, and breast milk. After the primary infection, shedding of the virus is often recurrent and intermittent and is not usually accompanied by symptoms or manifestations of illness.

Transmission occurs from person to person in situations where there is close contact, but it may be preventable by careful hygienic practices when handling children and items such as diapers. Because asymptomatic infection in children is common, it is not necessary to screen children for the disease or to exclude known infected children from care settings. Investigators have demonstrated that peak infection rates occur between 1 and 3 years of age, when viral excretion may be documented in as many as 70% of children in care settings (Wald, 2004).

The incidence of primary CMV infection in pregnant women in the United States is 1%–3%. The risk of fetal infection appears to be exclusively related to mothers who experience primary infection during their pregnancy. Even in this situation, 2/3 of the infants will not become infected, and only 10% of the remaining 1/3 will have evidence of infection at birth. Of these, 5% may exhibit clinically significant hearing loss, visual impairment, developmental delays, and/or learning disabilities (CDC, 2002).

The recommendations for pregnant women with regard to CMV include

- Practicing good personal hygiene, especially hand washing, after contact with any child in a care setting; using rubber gloves may be beneficial (Dobbins et al., 1994)

- Evaluating a child for possible CMV infection when unexplained illness is experienced

- Although controversial, testing the blood for CMV antibody

- Reassuring mothers that breast feeding is not generally contraindicated in infected women

Recommendations for staff providing care to infants and children include the following:

- Female employees should be thoroughly educated about CMV and the importance of good hygienic practices.

- Routine laboratory testing for the CMV antibody is not currently recommended but can be performed to determine an individual's immune status with regard to CMV after consultation with one's health care provider.

- Susceptible women should not routinely be transferred from child care to other duties.

- Pregnant women should be informed of the risks of CMV, including possible effects on the unborn child; antibody testing in this group is not usually recommended but should be discussed with health care providers.

Although some of these recommendations may seem contradictory or worrisome, they are nevertheless grounded in extensive laboratory and clinical research

Table 11.3. Recommendations for prevention of congenital cytomegalovirus disease

| | Transmission | | |
Intervention	Child–child	Child–staff	Child–mother
Desirability of prevention	No	Yes	Yes
Possibility of prevention	No	Yes	Yes
Utility of testing	No	Prepregnancy	Prepregnancy
Avoidance of casual contact	No	No	No
Pregnant or planning pregnancy		Avoid contact with saliva/urine	Avoid contact with saliva/urine
		Hand washing (gloves?)	Hand washing (gloves?)
		Antibody testing?	Antibody testing?

From Dobbins, J.G., Adler, S.P., Pass, R.F., Bale, J.F., Jr., Grillner, L., & Stewart, J.A. (1994). The risks and benefits of cytomegalovirus transmission in child day care. *Pediatrics, 84*(8, Suppl. 2), 1016–1018; adapted by permission.

and advice from knowledgeable sources (CDC, 2002). Table 11.3 provides a summary of recommendations that may be useful.

Role of Immunization

The CDC's web site (http://www.cdc.gov/vaccines/recs/schedules/child-schedule .htm) provides the most up-to-date recommended immunization schedule. Currently, there are 13 diseases that are preventable by standard childhood immunizations. The timely, appropriate immunization of children should continue to drastically reduce these diseases in infancy and childhood. It is gratifying that studies have demonstrated that children who are involved in child care settings are more likely to have up-to-date immunizations than those who are not. Almost all states have laws requiring age-appropriate immunization for children attending licensed child day care programs. Information on immunization rates in unlicensed settings is sparse (Cochi, 1994).

The decline in incidence of Hib disease after the introduction of Hib vaccines and their use in routine infant vaccination demonstrated the effectiveness of vaccination as a prevention strategy. This example is especially interesting because it is known that children in group settings have a two- to five-fold higher risk for Hib disease than those in home care (Cochi, 1994).

Parents should be encouraged to review immunization schedules with their health care provider. Child care administrators should check such schedules at least annually, as changes in vaccines, timing, or number of injections may change from year to year.

These preventable illnesses can be minimized in child care settings by making sure that all children are vaccinated on schedule; providing educational materials to parents about the recommended schedule (e.g., brochures from the local health department, materials from AAP); and being aware of current local, state, and federal health agency policies. Immunization requirements for children in care settings may vary by state. Such requirements should be checked regularly and can be found online at http://www.immunize.org/laws. There may be medical reasons why a child has not received certain immunizations; in these situations a statement from a health professional should be provided and documented.

Certain immunizations are also recommended or required for care providers and teachers. Unless there are medical contraindications, care providers and teachers should have the following immunizations:

- Chickenpox (unless documented to have had the disease)

- Hepatitis B virus

- Influenza (annually)

- Measles, mumps, rubella (unless documented to have had these diseases)

- Poliomyelitis

- Tetanus and diphtheria (including a booster every 10 years)

In addition, staff members should be encouraged to receive immunizations for pneumococcal pneumonia if 65 or older and to consider hepatitis A virus vaccine or, in the event of a hepatitis A outbreak, gamma globulin (Aronson & Shope, 2005).

Role of Families in Children's Health

Families (as well as service providers) have a responsibility to help prevent the spread of communicable diseases. In some instances, however, their knowledge about hygienic practices, prevention, and treatment of communicable diseases may be marginal. One goal of out-of-home care of infants and young children is to identify parents who are in need of instruction in health issues and ensure that they get the information that will enable them to provide the appropriate care at a critical time in a child's growth and development. It is important to solicit parents' participation in health education efforts to maximize positive outcomes for their children. The following recommendations may be employed to achieve this goal:

- As part of the intake process, reviewing the child's health record with families, including current health assessment, can give them a better understanding of the health report and of immunization requirements. Such reviews should occur regularly on a scheduled basis or whenever any new information about the child's health status arises.

- Families should be encouraged to voice concerns about any health care practices whenever they arise.

- Families should be encouraged to discuss health care practices in center-based meetings, as appropriate.

- Families should be directed to primary care and preventive health services when necessary; these services may be provided by private or public health care professionals.

- Families should understand the necessity for and documentation of permission for medical treatment and emergency medical information for children with special needs; sample forms are available from the AAP (http://www.aap.org).

- Families should be encouraged to use the same hygienic practices in the home as in the child care setting (e.g., hand washing, diapering procedures). Parents should be given the opportunity to observe staff modeling healthy behavior.

- Families should understand that some of the diseases contracted in care settings may be a source of infection to themselves, siblings, and other family contacts.

These recommendations could be part of a comprehensive family education plan that would include the topics of safety, oral health promotion, healthy lifestyle choices, well-child care, child development, caregiver health, domestic violence, conflict management, child behavior, medical emergencies/first aid, child advocacy skills, and special needs (AAP et al., 2002).

Health Risks and Responsibilities for Staff

Adults in child care settings are at increased risk for both acquiring and spreading communicable diseases. This is not surprising in view of the frequency with which teachers and other caregivers come in contact with nasal secretions, oral secretions, urine, and stool (e.g., when changing diapers, when cleaning up after toileting accidents).

Risks to Staff   Adults who work in care programs have been found to have more symptomatic illnesses than those who do not work with children, especially in their first year or so of contact with children. The frequency of these infections seems to diminish thereafter as some immunity is acquired (Aronson & Shope, 2005). Because many illnesses can be transmitted in the early phase of disease, often days before symptoms are evident, caregivers must know what precautions to take to prevent infection.

A small survey of 89 participants in 20 states was conducted by the Child Care Employee Project in 1989. In addition to safety risks, the following occupational health risks to those employed in child care were identified:

- *Repeated exposure to illness*—All respondents reported exposure to colds, flu, and other common illnesses; 33% mentioned exposure to such serious illnesses as tuberculosis, hepatitis, and *Giardia*; 66% stated they had contracted illnesses at work.

- *Lack of supportive policies for staff health*—58% reported working when ill; 38% reported no regular breaks; 60% reported no isolation area or staff to supervise ill children; most centers had exclusion policies that were often disregarded.

- *Contact with pesticides to control flies, roaches, and mice*—44% of respondents reported this finding.

Although this study was reported some time ago, anecdotal reports suggest that these problems continue to exist in care settings.

Teaching children about safety and hygienic practices helps protect not only other children but also staff members. One way to do this is to model appropriate practices both at home and at the center. When a child observes the same healthy routines in both places, it serves as a powerful reinforcement of positive behaviors (Taras, 1994).

Staff Responsibilities   Due to high turnover rates in the child care field, many early childhood programs experience a constant stream of poorly paid, inexperienced, and poorly trained staff who are not well informed about preventive health practices (Calder, 1994). Untrained or poorly informed care providers represent a serious risk to children. In addition they may not seek medical attention when appropriate because of lack of health insurance. Although some care providers and teachers of young children have had the opportunity to participate in training dealing with educational health issues, the majority of providers do not have specific training in this area (Taras, 1994).

The following preventive measures must be ongoing and monitored for compliance:

- Regular health assessments of staff

- Exclusion of both ill children and staff until they are no longer sick

- Separate staff assignments for food preparation and diapering

- Hand washing for staff, children, family members, and volunteers

These measures can only be accomplished by adequate training. Unfortunately there are a number of barriers that must be overcome to provide such training. These include lack of access to affordable training, lack of time to perform necessary hygienic procedures, training that does not meet the needs of participants, and few career development opportunities (Kendrick, 1994).

Although AAP guidelines for health measures largely address the health of children, there are a number of standards related to practices promoting health and preventing illness in adult caregivers. For example, the standards include a recommendation for a pre-employment staff health appraisal to assess vaccination status and staff members' ability to perform typical duties, such as lifting, frequent hand washing, and moving quickly (Hawks, Ascheim, Giebink, Graville, & Solnit, 1994).

Full-time care providers and teachers should have a pre-employment health appraisal that includes a medical history, a physical examination, screening tests, and a statement of professional evaluation. This assessment should be repeated every 2 years. Documentation should include the following (AAP et al., 2002):

- Health history

- Physical and dental examination

- Vision and hearing screening

- Tuberculosis (TB) testing

- Up-to-date immunization or certified immune status

- Evaluation for possible hepatitis A or pneumococcal vaccine

- Assessment of risk of exposure to common childhood illnesses, including parvovirus B19, CMV, and chickenpox

- Assessment of any other job-related health concerns, including orthopedic, psychological, and neurological problems

In the event of certain illnesses or injuries, a licensed health professional's release to return to work should be provided. Examples of such instances are conditions that might impair job performance, prolonged illness, job-related injury, concern about or symptoms of a harmful communicable disease, and workers' compensation issues or liability risks for the program or school related to the health problem (Aronson & Shope, 2005). In addition, center administrators, caregivers, and teachers should visually and verbally assess colleagues and volunteers daily for obvious signs of ill health. Any symptoms or injuries should be reported immediately, especially those that might affect their health or the health and safety of children (AAP et al., 2002).

Health Consultants

It is recommended (AAP et al., 2002) that all early childhood settings have a health consultant. Some states have regulations that require a consultant; others do not. Health consultants can serve several roles in care settings for young children with or without special needs. Health care consultants may provide advice or a specific service. Pediatricians, family care specialists, pediatric nurse practitioners, family health nurse practitioners, pediatric nurses, and public health nurses are logical sources of these services. As consultants, health care professionals may provide medical evaluation of children for enrollment and medical evaluation of prospective employees, help sites interpret/comply with Occupational Safety and Health Administration requirements, develop health policy recommendations, provide health education programs, help manage outbreaks of diseases, and serve as a resource for community health services. Consultants in these roles can be especially helpful in situations involving children with special health care needs.

Funding sources for health consultants include grants, gifts, fund-raising activities, assistance from state health agencies, and volunteerism from the medical community. Finding a consultant with the appropriate training and experience can be challenging. Consultants might be found by querying local health care agencies, local health clinics, pediatric hospitals, the state chapter of the AAP, and the Healthy Child Care America program (http://www.healthychildcare.org).

Hygienic Practices

There are several practices that can help reduce the risk of illness transmission in early childhood settings. Discussed here are daily health checks, exclusion, hand washing, and universal precautions.

Daily Health Check   A staff member need not have a medical background to conduct a rapid, efficient health check of children. A health consultant should provide training when necessary. Some care settings use a simple daily symptom checklist to note significant behavior changes, skin rashes, fever, vomiting, diarrhea, and other symptoms children may exhibit. When such symptoms are observed, this information should be shared with parents. A decision may be made to dismiss a child for the day or to refer the affected child to a health care provider.

Exclusion   One of the measures suggested to reduce transmission of infectious diseases within the child care setting is exclusion of sick staff (Swanson et al., 1994). In addition to the exclusion list for sick children (see Table 11.2), the AAP provides such a list for staff. The lists are identical except for the addition of meningococcal infection and Hib infection in the staff exclusion list.

Hand Washing   Diarrhea occurs at a rate of 0.7 to 2.6 episodes per child and 0.8 to 3.0 outbreaks per center, per year in care settings (Matson, 1994). It is not surprising that care settings are likely to be the first exposure to diarrheal organisms. This observation is confirmed by studies showing that incidence of diarrhea among infants and toddlers attending care centers is 30%–50% higher than among children of similar age who are cared for at home or in child care homes. The problem is complicated by the fact that infection in some children may be asymptomatic but transmissible to others in whom serious illness may result.

The scope of the problem has been illustrated by a number of studies. For instance, Cody, Sottnek, and O'Leary (1994) observed that 16% of young children (2–3 years old) were infected with *G. lamblia,* an organism known to cause diarrheal disease in susceptible individuals. Organisms were frequently recovered from Formica and stainless steel surfaces. Laborde, Weigle, Weber, Sobsey, and Kotch (1994) demonstrated that fecal contamination is widespread in child care settings. The most important sources identified were hands, toys, sinks, and faucets. These and other studies have consistently demonstrated that hands are the most important vehicle of transmission. It is not surprising that staff working in infant settings had more frequent hand contamination than those working with toddlers. It is a common observation that centers with formal hand-washing procedures have a lower incidence of hand contamination by fecal organisms.

It is important to remember that hand washing is also an essential element in the prevention of respiratory infections and infections spread by direct contact. Although frequent hand washing in these settings might be intuitive, it should nevertheless be reinforced by policy and instruction for staff, parents, and when appropriate, children. Studies have consistently demonstrated that instruction in hand-washing techniques is effective in controlling infections in care settings. Public health community consensus is that hand washing is the single most effective measure in the prevention of communicable disease (AAP et al., 2002).

Staff and other adults should wash hands regularly by a defined schedule (see Table 11.4) using a defined technique (see Table 11.5). It is helpful to have reminders, simple instructions, or diagrams (see Taylor & Taylor, 1989) posted in all hand-washing areas. Having children wash their hands can also be expected to help in the control of infectious disease; therefore, caregivers should provide assistance

Table 11.4. Hand-washing schedule

When arriving for the day

When moving from one group of children to another

When moving from one area to another

Before and after
- Eating, handling food, or feeding a child
- Administering a medication

After
- Diapering or toileting
- Handling body fluids
- Wiping noses, mouths, or sores
- Handling uncooked food
- Handling pets or other animals
- Playing in sandboxes
- Cleaning
- Handling garbage

When leaving for the day

From Taylor, J.M., & Taylor, W.S. (1989). *Communicable disease and young children in group settings* (p. 56). Boston: College Hill; adapted by permission.

Table 11.5. Hand washing procedure

Check availability of a clean, disposable paper (or single-use cloth) towel.

Turn on warm water, no less than 60° F and no more than 120° F.

Leave water running.

Moisten hands with water and apply liquid soap.

Rub hands together vigorously until a soapy lather appears, and continue for at least 10 seconds; rub areas between fingers, jewelry, and back of hands, and wrist areas.

Rinse hands until they are free of soap and dirt.

Leave water running.

Dry hands with paper towel(s).

Turn off water faucets with paper towel.

Use the paper towel to open the door to the restroom.

Dispose of paper towel appropriately.

Use hand lotion if desired.

From American Academy of Pediatrics, American Public Health Association, Maternal and Child Health Bureau, and Health Resources and Services Administration. (2002). *Caring for our children: National health and safety performance standards. Guidelines for out-of-home child care programs* (2nd ed., p. 98). Elk Grove Village, IL: American Academy of Pediatrics.

with hand washing even for infants and toddlers. After such assistance staff members should wash their own hands.

There are several commercial products available to assist in the hand-washing education process. One such product is Glo Germ (http://www.glogerm.com/). The kit contains a bottle of oil or gel, a bottle of powder that simulates germs, and an ultraviolet (UV) lamp. The oil or gel and powder are rubbed on the hands, like hand lotion. After hand washing, turning the UV lamp on the hands spots the "germs" left behind. These "germs" glow brightly and are easily seen. This or similar products are extremely valuable tools for reinforcing the value of hand washing in preventing infectious disease. Training methods such as this have been shown to be effective in continuous improvement in staff hand washing (Soto, Guy, & Belanger, 1994).

Universal Precautions Universal precautions are based on the concept of performing a task as if all contact during a particular activity (e.g., snack, diaper changing) involved infection, even in the absence of signs or symptoms of illness. Universal precautions interrupt the chain of infection as spread by potential and known biohazards. Contamination can result from blood or other body fluids (e.g., mucous, urine). The CDC has written standards for universal precautions to be used in hospital settings. A modified version for use in child care settings has been outlined by the AAP (AAP et al., 2002) and includes the following:

- All surfaces that may come in contact with potentially infected body fluid must be disposable or of a material that can be sanitized.

- Staff should use techniques to minimize contact with potentially contaminated surfaces or material; often this can be accomplished by the use of gloves.

- If utility gloves are used, they should be cleaned after every use with soap and water, dipped in bleach solution, and hung to dry.

- Disposable gloves should be used only once.

- When gloves are worn, hand washing is still necessary on completion of the task.

- Bleach solution is not a good cleaning agent, but it is effective in killing organisms that cause communicable diseases. Two minutes of contact with a solution of 1/4 cup of household liquid bleach in 1 gallon of water prepared fresh is an effective method of sanitizing surfaces and spills.

Initially, spills should be wiped up with paper towels that are then discarded in a secure trash can. The area should be washed or mopped with soap or detergent, then rinsed. Disinfection with bleach solution and air drying is the final step in this process.

Other Health Care Measures   Consideration should be given to other common sense practices, such as the following:

- Providing a diaper-changing area that is separated from other activities

- Cleaning and disinfecting diapering areas after each use

- Keeping diapered children separate from nondiapered children when possible

- Keeping children with diarrhea at home

- Cleaning and sanitizing toys, utensils, and equipment frequently

- Making certain that sores on children and staff are always covered

- Requiring physician approval before a child with an undiagnosed rash can attend care settings (ARCH, n.d.)

The Building

Many buildings used for educational programs were not designed with the primary concern of preventing or limiting the spread of communicable diseases. ECSE sites vary widely, from home-based programs to group settings. The buildings that house these programs may be a public or private school, neighborhood center, church, library, or other community setting. Sometimes these buildings have been retrofitted to accommodate health requirements, often inadequately. Most directors do not have the benefit of designing program space or the funds to remake an existing space. It is important to have knowledge of space design principles and make as many thoughtful modifications as necessary to ensure maximum health benefits. Unfortunately, some degree of compromise is usually inevitable.

The AAP (AAP et al., 2002) provides information on requirements for the overall space, equipment, indoor and outdoor play areas, swimming facilities, water play areas, interior and exterior walkways, steps and stairs, facility maintenance, and transportation. Most of these requirements are related to accident prevention or prevention of exposure to environmental hazards. Standards specifically related to control of contagious disease include hand-washing sinks, sewage facilities, containment of garbage, containment of soiled diapers, waste containers, diaper containers, disposal of infectious or toxic wastes, standard first aid kits, sharing of personal articles, supplies for bathrooms and hand-washing sinks, general requirements for toilet and hand-washing areas, location of toilets, toilet learning/training equipment, and diaper-changing tables (AAP et al., 2002). Although these requirements are encyclopedic in their depth and breadth, knowledge of and implementation of as many standards as possible should be a primary goal of every program.

THE FUTURE

In 1994, Goodman and colleagues noted the following issues and future directions related to infectious disease.

- *Inadequate health surveillance*—Clinicians tend to underdiagnose and not associate episodes of infectious disease with risk management in group care settings. This is complicated by the fact that many infections with implications related to disease control are underreported to local and state health authorities.

- *Inappropriate use of antibiotics*—Medications may be overprescribed or erratically administered in attempts to control minor infections; such practice has led to the emergence of antibiotic-resistant organisms.

- *Asymptomatic carriers*—For some diseases, carriers play an important role in the transmission of the disease in both children and adults, and even the community as a whole. How to attack this problem in some illnesses is often uncertain.

- *Fear of HIV infection*—Anxiety, although somewhat lessened in recent years, continues to exist, even though transmission of HIV in child care settings is at least rare if not nonexistent.

- *Prevention of vaccine-preventable diseases*—Unfortunately, the resurgence of some childhood diseases sporadically occurs from time to time. This represents a failure to vaccinate all children on schedule, according to recommendations.

- *Occupational health and safety*—Some issues remain unresolved relating to risks and prevention efforts targeted toward primary maternal infection with CMV and parvovirus B19 in pregnant care workers.

- *Impact on the community*—Transmission of diseases like hepatitis A and respiratory infections to family members, care providers, and the community can result from infections in care settings.

- *Care of mildly ill children*—Exclusion policies, economic impact, and the risk of transmitting even mild illnesses to others all need examination.

Goodman and colleagues (1994) recommended the following future directions:

- *Stronger vaccination requirements*—There is a need to enhance laws, regulations, and other requirements for vaccination of children.

- *Development of new vaccines*—Continued research in to the development and distribution of new vaccines should continue.

- *Evaluation of prevention strategies*—The efficacy and cost benefits of strategies to prevent infection and injuries, including hand washing and facility design, need continual assessment.

- *Technical assistance in caring for children with HIV or other special health care needs*— As the number of affected children increases and becomes more clinically complex, care providers will require more assistance in managing such issues.

In 1996, the National Foundation for Infectious Diseases issued the following challenges and research opportunities:

- Identification of effective disease control measures

- Evaluation of the efficacy of current prevention recommendations

- Training of employees in infection control measures and techniques

- Evaluation of prevention and control strategies

- Identification of behavioral and educational opportunities to facilitate adherence to good infection control practice

It is disappointing to note that these concerns have apparently received little significant attention in recent times since there has been a paucity of new helpful policy and research since the 1990s, and "future directions" remain essentially unchanged. Certainly this situation exists not because of lack of concern but because of lack of funding. In the meantime, we must all practice what we preach and continue our advocacy for children and their families at every available opportunity.

CONCLUSIONS

Groups of small children are fertile grounds for communicable disease transmission, and the risk of contracting communicable diseases in children with disabilities in child care settings may be somewhat increased because of a specific disability. The routes of communicable disease transmission are respiratory, fecal-oral, direct, body fluid, and multiple routes. Many communicable diseases can be prevented by appropriate immunization, but hand washing is the single best measure in prevention of communicable diseases. Staff training in health and safety practices is also critical in limiting communicable disease transmission. In addition, every child care facility should have a health consultant arrangement. Ability to further limit transmission of communicable diseases in child care settings is somewhat limited by funding for research and policy development.

REFERENCES

American Academy of Pediatrics, American Public Health Association, Maternal and Child Health Bureau, & Health Resources and Services Administration. (2002). *Caring for our children: National health and safety performance standards. Guidelines for out-of-home child care programs* (2nd ed.). Elk Grove Village, IL: American Academy of Pediatrics.

ARCH National Resource Center for Respite and Crisis Care Services. (n.d.). *Protecting staff and children from the spread of disease: A guide for program directors and managers* (Factsheet 43). Retrieved April 20, 2005, from http://www.archrespite.org/archfs43.htm

Aronson, S.S., & Shope, T.R. (Eds.). (2005). *Managing infectious diseases in child care and schools.* Elk Grove Village, IL: American Academy of Pediatrics.

Blackman, J.A. (1997). *Medical aspects of developmental disabilities in children birth to three.* Rockville, MD: Aspen.

Calder, J.C. (1994). Occupational health and safety issues. *Pediatrics, 94*(6 Pt. 2), 1072–1074.

Centers for Disease Control and Prevention, National Center for Infectious Diseases. (2002). *Cytomegalovirus (CMV) infection.* Retrieved June 10, 2005, from http://www.cdc.gov/ncidod/diseases/cmv.htm

Cochi, S.L. (1994). Overview of policies affecting vaccine use in child day care. *Pediatrics, 94*(6 Pt. 2), 994–996.

Cody, M.M., Sottnek, H.M., & O'Leary, V.S. (1994). Recovery of *Giardia lamblia* cysts from chairs and tables in child day-care centers. *Pediatrics, 94*(6 Pt. 2), 1006–1008.

Dobbins, J.G., Adler, S.P., Pass, R.F., Bale, J.F., Jr., Grillner, L., & Stewart, J.A. (1994). The risks and benefits of cytomegalovirus transmission in child day care. *Pediatrics, 94*(6 Pt. 2), 1016–1018.

Feldman, M.A. (Ed.). (2004). *Early intervention: The essential readings.* Malden, MA: Blackwell.

Goodman, R.A., Sacks, J.J., Aronson, S.S., Addiss, D.G., Kendrick, A.S., & Osterholm, M. (1994). Child day-care health: Themes, issues, and future directions. *Pediatrics, 94*(6 Pt. 2), 1118–1120.

Hawks, D., Ascheim, J., Giebink, G.S., Graville, S., & Solnit, A.J. (1994). American Public Health Association/American Academy of Pediatrics national health and safety guidelines for child-care programs: Featured standards and implementation. *Pediatrics, 94*(6 Pt. 2), 1110–1112.

Kendrick, A.S. (1994). Training to ensure healthy child day-care programs. *Pediatrics, 94*(6 Pt. 2), 1108–1110.

Laborde, D.J., Weigle, K.A., Weber, D.J., Sobsey, M.D., & Kotch, J.B. (1994). The frequency, level, and distribution of fecal contamination in day-care center classrooms. *Pediatrics, 94*(6 Pt. 2), 1008–1011.

Matson, D.O. (1994). Viral gastroenteritis in day-care settings: Epidemiology and new developments. *Pediatrics, 94*(6 Pt. 2), 999–1001.

National Institute of Allergy and Infectious Diseases. (2001). *The common cold.* Retrieved June 10, 2005, from http://www.niaid.nih.gov/factsheets/cold.htm

National Resource Center for Health and Safety in Child Care. (n.d.). *A parent's guide to choosing safe and healthy child care.* Aurora, CO: University of Colorado Health Sciences Center at Fitzsimons.

Parrino, S.S., & Thacker, S.B. (1994). The challenge of day-care health among children with disabilities. *Pediatrics, 94*(6 Pt. 2), 1052–1054.

Soto, J.C., Guy, M., & Belanger, L. (1994). Hand washing and infection control in day-care centers. *Pediatrics, 94*(6 Pt. 2), 1030.

Swanson, G.S., Piotrkowski, C.S., Curbow, B.C., Graville, S., Kushnir, T., & Owen, B.D. (1994). Occupational health and safety issues in child-care work. *Pediatrics, 94*(6 Pt. 2), 1079–1080.

Taras, H.L. (1994). Health in child day care: The physician–child-care-provider relationship. *Pediatrics, 94*(6 Pt. 2), 1062–1063.

Taylor, J.M., & Taylor, W.S. (1989). *Communicable disease and young children in group settings.* Boston: College Hill.

Wald, E.R. (2004). Infections in day-care environments. In R.D. Feigin, J.D. Cherry, G.J. Demmler, & S.L. Kaplan (Eds.), *Textbook of pediatric infectious diseases* (2nd ed., pp. 3244–3259). Philadelphia: W.B. Saunders.

Chapter 11 Appendix

Immunization Schedule for Children, Birth to Six Years Old

Recommended Immunization Schedule for Persons Aged 0 Through 6 Years—United States • 2009

For those who fall behind or start late, see the catch-up schedule

Vaccine ▼ Age ►	Birth	1 month	2 months	4 months	6 months	12 months	15 months	18 months	19–23 months	2–3 years	4–6 years
Hepatitis B[1]	HepB	HepB		see footnote 1		HepB					
Rotavirus[2]			RV	RV	RV[2]						
Diphtheria, Tetanus, Pertussis[3]			DTaP	DTaP	DTaP	see footnote 3	DTaP				DTaP
Haemophilus influenzae type b[4]			Hib	Hib	Hib[4]	Hib					
Pneumococcal[5]			PCV	PCV	PCV	PCV				PPSV	
Inactivated Poliovirus			IPV	IPV	IPV						IPV
Influenza[6]					Influenza (Yearly)						
Measles, Mumps, Rubella[7]						MMR		see footnote 7			MMR
Varicella[8]						Varicella		see footnote 8			Varicella
Hepatitis A[9]						HepA (2 doses)				HepA Series	
Meningococcal[10]										MCV	

- Range of recommended ages
- Certain high-risk groups

This schedule indicates the recommended ages for routine administration of currently licensed vaccines, as of December 1, 2008, for children aged 0 through 6 years. Any dose not administered at the recommended age should be administered at a subsequent visit, when indicated and feasible. Licensed combination vaccines may be used whenever any component of the combination is indicated and other components are not contraindicated and if approved by the Food and Drug Administration for that dose of the series. Providers should consult the relevant Advisory Committee on Immunization Practices statement for detailed recommendations, including high-risk conditions: http://www.cdc.gov/vaccines/pubs/acip-list.htm. Clinically significant adverse events that follow immunization should be reported to the Vaccine Adverse Event Reporting System (VAERS). Guidance about how to obtain and complete a VAERS form is available at http://www.vaers.hhs.gov or by telephone, 800-822-7967.

1. Hepatitis B vaccine (HepB). *(Minimum age: birth)*

At birth:
- Administer monovalent HepB to all newborns before hospital discharge.
- If mother is hepatitis B surface antigen (HBsAg)-positive, administer HepB and 0.5 mL of hepatitis B immune globulin (HBIG) within 12 hours of birth.
- If mother's HBsAg status is unknown, administer HepB within 12 hours of birth. Determine mother's HBsAg status as soon as possible and, if HBsAg-positive, administer HBIG (no later than age 1 week).

After the birth dose:
- The HepB series should be completed with either monovalent HepB or a combination vaccine containing HepB. The second dose should be administered at age 1 or 2 months. The final dose should be administered no earlier than age 24 weeks.
- Infants born to HBsAg-positive mothers should be tested for HBsAg and antibody to HBsAg (anti-HBs) after completion of at least 3 doses of the HepB series, at age 9 through 18 months (generally at the next well-child visit).

4-month dose:
- Administration of 4 doses of HepB to infants is permissible when combination vaccines containing HepB are administered after the birth dose.

2. Rotavirus vaccine (RV). *(Minimum age: 6 weeks)*
- Administer the first dose at age 6 through 14 weeks (maximum age: 14 weeks 6 days). Vaccination should not be initiated for infants aged 15 weeks or older (i.e., 15 weeks 0 days or older).
- Administer the final dose in the series by age 8 months 0 days.
- If Rotarix® is administered at ages 2 and 4 months, a dose at 6 months is not indicated.

3. Diphtheria and tetanus toxoids and acellular pertussis vaccine (DTaP). *(Minimum age: 6 weeks)*
- The fourth dose may be administered as early as age 12 months, provided at least 6 months have elapsed since the third dose.
- Administer the final dose in the series at age 4 through 6 years.

4. Haemophilus influenzae type b conjugate vaccine (Hib). *(Minimum age: 6 weeks)*
- If PRP-OMP (PedvaxHIB® or Comvax® [HepB-Hib]) is administered at ages 2 and 4 months, a dose at age 6 months is not indicated.
- TriHiBit® (DTaP/Hib) should not be used for doses at ages 2, 4, or 6 months but can be used as the final dose in children aged 12 months or older.

5. Pneumococcal vaccine. *(Minimum age: 6 weeks for pneumococcal conjugate vaccine [PCV]; 2 years for pneumococcal polysaccharide vaccine [PPSV])*
- PCV is recommended for all children aged younger than 5 years. Administer 1 dose of PCV to all healthy children aged 24 through 59 months who are not completely vaccinated for their age.

- Administer PPSV to children aged 2 years or older with certain underlying medical conditions (see *MMWR* 2000;49[No. RR-9]), including a cochlear implant.

6. Influenza vaccine. *(Minimum age: 6 months for trivalent inactivated influenza vaccine [TIV]; 2 years for live, attenuated influenza vaccine [LAIV])*
- Administer annually to children aged 6 months through 18 years.
- For healthy nonpregnant persons (i.e., those who do not have underlying medical conditions that predispose them to influenza complications) aged 2 through 49 years, either LAIV or TIV may be used.
- Children receiving TIV should receive 0.25 mL if aged 6 through 35 months or 0.5 mL if aged 3 years or older.
- Administer 2 doses (separated by at least 4 weeks) to children aged younger than 9 years who are receiving influenza vaccine for the first time or who were vaccinated for the first time during the previous influenza season but only received 1 dose.

7. Measles, mumps, and rubella vaccine (MMR). *(Minimum age: 12 months)*
- Administer the second dose at age 4 through 6 years. However, the second dose may be administered before age 4, provided at least 28 days have elapsed since the first dose.

8. Varicella vaccine. *(Minimum age: 12 months)*
- Administer the second dose at age 4 through 6 years. However, the second dose may be administered before age 4, provided at least 3 months have elapsed since the first dose.
- For children aged 12 months through 12 years the minimum interval between doses is 3 months. However, if the second dose was administered at least 28 days after the first dose, it can be accepted as valid.

9. Hepatitis A vaccine (HepA). *(Minimum age: 12 months)*
- Administer to all children aged 1 year (i.e., aged 12 through 23 months). Administer 2 doses at least 6 months apart.
- Children not fully vaccinated by age 2 years can be vaccinated at subsequent visits.
- HepA also is recommended for children older than 1 year who live in areas where vaccination programs target older children or who are at increased risk of infection. See *MMWR* 2006;55[No. RR-7].

10. Meningococcal vaccine. *(Minimum age: 2 years for meningococcal conjugate vaccine [MCV] and for meningococcal polysaccharide vaccine [MPSV])*
- Administer MCV to children aged 2 through 10 years with terminal complement component deficiency, anatomic or functional asplenia, and certain other high-risk groups. See *MMWR* 2005;54[No. RR-7].
- Persons who received MPSV 3 or more years previously and who remain at increased risk for meningococcal disease should be revaccinated with MCV.

The Recommended Immunization Schedules for Persons Aged 0 Through 18 Years are approved by the Advisory Committee on Immunization Practices (www.cdc.gov/vaccines/recs/acip), the American Academy of Pediatrics (http://www.aap.org), and the American Academy of Family Physicians (http://www.aafp.org).

DEPARTMENT OF HEALTH AND HUMAN SERVICES • CENTERS FOR DISEASE CONTROL AND PREVENTION

CS109164

Budget and Finance in Early Childhood Programs

Kevin J. McCracken

Every time you spend money,
you're casting a vote for the kind of world you want.
Anna Lappe

What If?   Brenda Tijeras is the director of a child care center that serves 43 children with disabilities and 46 children with no known disabilities. She has been in this position for just 3 weeks, having spent the first 10 years of her career as a lead teacher in an inclusive early childhood special education (ECSE) classroom. Brenda has an appointment with the treasurer of the center's board of directors in a week. At this meeting, the two will go over the center's finances, including current budget issues, strategies for ensuring careful management of financial resources, and planning for future fiscal needs. Brenda is not quite sure how to prepare for this meeting.

OVERVIEW

Directors and managers of not-for-profit (NFP) programs often assume their leadership roles following years of effective direct service provision. Though they may have strong clinical skills and experience, these nascent managers often have little or no experience in management or administration. The transition from direct service provider to administrator can be difficult for many reasons, all of which may be exacerbated by a lack of financial training and background. This chapter offers information about financial matters in the world of NFP organizations. Although a comprehensive guide would entail a separate book, this chapter serves as an effective primer for those seeking a quick, broad understanding. Because it is assumed that the reader has very little knowledge of financial management, basic terms and concepts are defined.

After reviewing this chapter, the reader will

- Understand financial management principles, including accounting basics and financial statements

- Understand how to budget and manage budgets

FINANCIAL MANAGEMENT PRINCIPLES

It is helpful to first explore a comparison of NFP and for-profit (FP) entities. A common assumption is that the former intends not to make any profit. Nothing could be further from the truth. Many NFP agencies will never show a profit because they are mostly dependent on grant, United Way, or government funding. Many others can, and do, show a profit. The difference between the NFP and FP worlds has little to do with showing a profit. The difference lies primarily with what the entity does with any profits that it realizes. In the FP world, profits can flow to the owner(s) of the enterprise. Not every FP business makes a profit, but when a business does, those dollars flow right to the owner(s).

In the NFP world, any profits realized must go back into the organization. In fact, there are no owners of an NFP entity. The board of directors serves as guardian of the agency but has no ownership. Therefore, almost by default—if not by design—profits must go back into the organization and not into someone's pockets.

Of course, there are also differences in the way NFP and FP organizations pay taxes and report financial operations. NFP agencies are generally exempt from income and sales taxes because they operate for the public good rather than for a profit. They must still report financial information to the Internal Revenue Service, but the required forms and procedures differ from those for FP businesses.

Perhaps the most important difference between the two types of organizations has less to do with finances than with philosophy. FP businesses exist primarily for the purpose of increasing shareholder wealth. Many FP businesses also do much good in their communities, but almost none of them would claim that they exist to serve the common good. In contrast, NFP organizations *do* exist to serve the common good, and considerations about profitability are nearly always secondary (if considered at all).

Serving the common good has important implications for performance measurement. In the FP world, profitability is the primary measure of performance. Of course, there are also quality measures (e.g., Malcolm Baldrige National Quality Award, ISO 9000) and other financial measures (e.g., market share, revenue trends), but nothing is more important than profitability. Because it is concrete and because it directly affects shareholders' wealth, profitability will always be the primary indicator of performance.

In the NFP world, measuring performance is often difficult. If there is little or no expectation of profitability, then one must look for other, often less concrete, measures. Take, for example, a school. Standardized tests can measure student performance, but there are other factors (poverty, condition of the building, teacher salaries) that influence those outcomes, making conclusions difficult to draw. Determining how well managers and administrators perform with respect to the organizational mission is often a fundamental challenge in the NFP world.

Accounting Basics

In addition to leading an organization in fulfilling its mission, a task for which they are often well prepared, administrators must also manage the financial performance of the organization. In order to do this effectively, they must understand the information system that quantifies business activities: accounting.

Accounting includes processes, a lexicon, concepts, standards, and reports. It describes the financial operation of an entity and supports management decisions. Reports, or statements, become the method for disclosing business activities to external groups. A basic understanding of accounting is essential to effective financial management.

There are two basic types of accounting: financial and management. Financial accounting focuses on information for external users, such as donors, regulatory bodies, taxing authorities, creditors, and investors. Financial accounting reports are standardized and contain generally the same type of information, with the same format, across organizations. Indeed, financial accounting is governed by a private organization, the Financial Accounting Standards Board, which determines the standards for reporting. Managers within an organization rely heavily on these standardized reports when making business decisions, but the reports exist primarily to communicate information to external stakeholders.

Management accounting, on the other hand, focuses on the information needs of internal decision makers. Both types of systems incorporate the same types of processes and standards, and both use the same data. The fundamental difference is that financial accounting exists to help managers predict and control business operations. There is a lack of standardization in management accounting, which contributes to organizations' developing their own individualized reports. Not every organization relies on management accounting, but the lesson here is that it exists.

Managers need not be limited to reports intended for external reporting. Instead, they can create whatever accounting report meets their needs. As long as it is used only for internal purposes, they are not restricted by GAAP, verification requirements, or monthly (e.g., quarterly, annual) reporting cycles. This is not to say that management accounting reports are any less useful. As long as they contain accurate and relevant information, these reports may indeed be the most useful tools a manager can wield.

Another duality that exists in accounting relates to how transactions are recognized and recorded: cash-basis versus accrual-basis. Few businesses use cash-basis accounting, and it is mentioned here only for comparison purposes. This is the type of accounting that most people use to manage their personal finances. They record cash as it goes into and out of an account. No record is made of bills that are pending or income that is earned but not yet received. This method is adequate for personal finances and very small organizations. The vast majority of organizations, however, are too complex for a simple cash-basis system.

With accrual-basis accounting, every transaction is recorded, even if it does not involve receiving or disbursing cash. For example, payroll expenses are recorded daily even though an organization may disburse payroll only every 2 weeks. This method gives a more accurate measure of an organization's financial status because it accounts for every transaction as it occurs. It is more timely and accurate, and it allows managers to make better informed decisions.

An accounting system includes a hierarchy of recording systems. Each transaction is recorded in the general ledger—the master document that encompasses the entire organization. Within the general ledger exist accounts, such as payroll or office supplies. The larger and more complex the organization is, the greater the number of accounts within the general ledger. Each organization will have its own unique general ledger that, hopefully, meets its needs.

Despite the wide variability in accounts, there are some universal financial categories and accounts. These are best explained by what is known as the accounting equation. This equation represents the foundation of financial accounting and also describes the general categories of transactions. The equation is

$$\text{ASSETS} = \text{LIABILITIES} + \text{OWNER'S EQUITY}$$

Assets are any kind of economic resource that the organization expects will yield some benefit. This broad category is divided into two subcategories: current assets and long-term assets. Current assets are any resource that the organization can liquidate (turn into cash) within a short period of time (usually 12 months). Table 12.1 lists common examples of assets, both current and long term.

Liabilities are economic obligations that an organization incurs. These too are categorized as current or long term, using the same 12-month parameter. In service-oriented organizations, *salaries payable* is usually the largest liability. Other current liabilities include *accounts payable,* which represents any promise to pay for goods or services received. Included here are things such as utility payments, insurance payments, and money owed for operating supplies purchased on account.

Money that an organization owes to repay a loan is categorized in two different ways. The amount owed during the next 12 months is listed as a current liability under the account *notes payable.* The balance of the money owed is also listed under *notes payable* but is categorized as a long-term liability. Financial statements will have different sections for current and long-term liabilities.

In the FP world, the accounting equation also includes *owners' equity.* This represents the cumulative value of the company to the owner(s). It is the value of what an organization owns (assets) minus what it owes (liabilities). In the NFP world, however, there are no owners, so organizations instead refer to this as the *fund balance.* The concept is the same; it represents the difference between an organization's assets and liabilities. For the purposes of NFP accounting, one can substitute *fund balance* for *owners' equity.*

Table 12.1. Examples of assets

Current assets

Cash—money, certificates of deposit, and checks

Accounts receivable—money owed to the organization as the result of an informal agreement or implied promise (i.e., payment not yet received for services rendered)

Notes receivable—promissory notes

Inventory—merchandise intended for sale

Long-term assets

Land—property owned by an entity and used for the purpose of its operations

Building—office, warehouse, store, and so forth

Equipment, furniture, and fixtures—items used in the operation of the entity

Financial Statements

Accounting provides the processes and procedures for recording financial transactions. It also provides the mechanisms for reporting transactions. The reports, called *statements*, reflect the proper categorization and recording of all transactions. They allow managers to make informed decisions about the operation of the organization. Financial statements also allow people outside the organization to understand what is happening inside the organization. The three most common statements are the *balance sheet, income statement*, and *statement of cash flows*.

The balance sheet, also known as the *statement of financial position*, gives an account of an entity's assets, liabilities, and fund balance. It does this as of a specific date and is often likened to a financial snapshot of an organization. It simply describes what an organization owns and owes on a certain date. Following the accounting equation, an organization's assets will equal its liabilities plus the fund balance. Figure 12.1 shows a sample balance sheet. Balance sheets are usually produced monthly. When they are compared with previous balance sheets or those of similar organizations, one can draw conclusions about trends and make comparisons.

Evaluating the balance sheet in Figure 12.1, one can see that the accounting equation holds true. The total assets ($234,029) equal the value of the total liabilities ($144,031) plus the fund balance ($89,998). Indeed, the balance sheet intends to show a balance between those two amounts. It is a positive measure of fiscal health to show that the value for total assets is greater than the value for total liabilities. In addition, the ratio of current assets to current liabilities is almost 2:1 or 2.00 in the example. This financial ratio, known as the *current ratio*, is a quick measure of a firm's ability to pay its bills in the short term. Most successful businesses show a current ratio between 1.50 and 2.00 (Diamond, Stice, & Stice, 2000).

Another valuable financial metric that relates to the balance sheet is the *debt ratio*, which is the ratio of total liabilities to total assets. In this example, total liabilities divided by total assets is 62%. General guidelines suggest that a debt ratio below 0.60 is safe and above 0.80 is high risk. Most businesses operate between 0.60 and 0.80 (Horngreen, Harrison, & Bamber, 2002).

If the balance sheet is referred to as a snapshot, then the income statement can be described as a video. It incorporates the financial activities over a period of time and reveals the profitability during that period. It is a summary of revenues and expenses over a period of time. Also referred to as a *profit and loss statement*, it reports net income or net losses, otherwise known as the *bottom line*. Figure 12.2 provides an example of an income statement.

In this statement, one sees that XYZ Not-for-Profit provides a service for which it receives money. It adjusts the gross amount to account for discounts and estimates of uncollectible debt. This adjustment yields the *net service revenue* amount. The example depicts numerous types of expenses and offers a total. In this example, the organization has shown a profit for its primary operations. Subtracting *total expenses* from *net service revenue* shows a *net income* of $19,303. In addition, the organization has additional income that does not directly result from the provision of services. In many NFP agencies, there will be little or no service revenue. Instead, there may be grant or government funding and/or donations.

As reported by the income statement, net income is perhaps the best indicator of an organization's financial performance. In addition, this statement will yield more

ABC Not-for-Profit
Balance Sheet
7/31/2007

Assets
Current assets:

Cash	$8,752
Accounts receivable	2,868
Less: Reserve for bad debts	
Prepaid expenses	26,242
Total current assets	**$37,862**

Fixed assets:

Vehicles	10,917
Furniture and fixtures	1,403
Equipment	4,914
Buildings	68,913
Land	110,020
Total fixed assets	**$196,167**

Total assets	**$234,029**

Liabilities and capital
Current liabilities:

Accounts payable	$6,016
Payroll taxes payable	2,713
Accrued wages payable	8,752
Short-term notes payable	1,230
Short-term bank loan payable	850
Total current liabilities	**$19,561**

Long-term liabilities:

Long-term notes payable	8,950
Mortgage payable	115,520
Total long-term liabilities	**124,470**

Total liabilities	**$144,031**

Capital:

Fund balance	89,998
Total capital	**89,998**

Total liabilities and capital	**$234,029**

Figure 12.1.   Sample balance sheet.

XYZ Not-for-Profit
Income Statement
For the Year Ended June 30, 2007

Revenue:

Gross service revenue	$216,924
Less: Adjustments and allowances	$6,872
Net service revenue	**$210,052**

Expenses:

Bank charges	$420	
Contract labor	$8,799	
Delivery expenses	$750	
Depreciation	$24,589	
Dues and subscriptions	$580	
Insurance	$1,920	
Interest	$560	
Maintenance	$2,110	
Miscellaneous	$6,320	
Office expenses	$1,255	
Operating supplies	$1,560	
Payroll taxes	$27,644	
Postage	$76	
Professional fees	$250	
Property taxes	$3,485	
Rent	$6,960	
Repairs	$650	
Telephone	$1,380	
Travel	$1,520	
Utilities	$3,000	
Vehicle expenses	$4,776	
Wages	$92,147	
Total expenses		**$190,749**
Net Operating Income		**$19,303**

Other income:

Interest income	$2,540	
Grants	$1,200	
Donations	$1,896	
Total other income		**$5,636**
Net income (loss)		**$24,939**

Figure 12.2. Sample income statement.

information when compared with the previous year's statement. Trend information about declining revenues or stable expenses, for example, will emerge. Also, the astute manager will compare these figures with those of other similar agencies or with industry benchmarks to determine how his or her organization compares with others.

Notice that the statement lists *depreciation* as one of the expenses. Accounting rules allow businesses to allocate the cost of physical assets over the course of each asset's useful life. This is known as depreciation. It represents the wear and tear of each asset as it occurs during each economic period of its useful life.

For example, a company may purchase a new van worth $10,000. The company expects to drive the van 20,000 miles each year, and the van is expected to last 100,000 miles. At the end of 5 years, when the van has 100,000 miles of wear and tear, it will no longer have economic value to the company. It will have some residual salvage value but will no longer be useful or valuable to the operation of the business. Depreciation represents the decrease in value for a given reporting period. It would appear as an expense because expenses in general reduce the value of assets.

When the van is purchased, the company must record the acquisition of a $10,000 asset. With each passing year, the van becomes less valuable to the company. There are various methods to calculate depreciation, but using the straight-line method, the depreciation expense for the van would be $2,000 each year. The value of the van after the first year would be $8,000, and the accumulated depreciation for the same period would be $2,000. Together, the current value of the asset and the accumulated depreciation will equal the original value of the asset, in this case $10,000. Thus, depreciation becomes a way for a company to write off the cost of acquiring an asset over the estimated useful life.

The income statement is essential for determining profitability, but because it includes noncash expenses like depreciation, it has limited value in helping managers control the flow of cash into and out of an organization. Particularly in small agencies, managing cash flow is a top priority. A successful and profitable business can go bankrupt if it cannot pay its bills. Managers must always place the highest priority on cash management. The *statement of cash flows* is invaluable in this effort (see the sample in Figure 12.3).

This statement reports the cash transactions for a given period and details the increase or decrease in cash. It indicates where money came from and where it went. Every transaction included in the statement of cash flows comes from either the income statement or the balance sheet. It includes the adjustment of noncash transactions, such as depreciation or a write-off. An accountant or accounting software makes the adjustments. When a company shows a large noncash expense like depreciation or a write-off, the income statement may show a loss, but the statement of cash flows may show an increase in cash for the same reporting period.

BUDGETING AND BUDGET MANAGEMENT

In addition to understanding basic accounting processes and statements, a manager must develop facility with budgets and the budgeting process. A *budget* is a financial plan that links an agency's strategic plan, short-term goals, and long-term goals with available resources. It is a guide for allocating those resources to each unit or subunit, and it reveals whether or not an agency will meet its organizational goals. It is much more than numbers, commas, and decimals. It is a grand statement of an agency's values, mission, and managerial expertise.

123 Not-for-Profit
Statement of Cash Flows
For the Year Ended June 30, 2007

Cash flows from operating activities

Cash received from customers	$210,052
Cash paid for wages and other operating expenses	(137,195)
Cash paid for interest	(560)
Cash paid for taxes	(3,485)
Other	(24,501)
Net cash provided (used) by operating activities	**$44,311**

Cash flows from investing activities

Cash received from sale of capital assets (e.g., plant, equipment)	$0
Cash received from disposition of business segments	0
Cash received from collection of notes receivable	0
Cash paid for purchase of capital assets	(16,500)
Cash paid to acquire businesses	0
Other	0
Net cash provided (used) by investing activities	**($16,500)**

Cash flows from financing activities

Cash received from issuing stock	$0
Cash received from long-term borrowings	16,500
Cash paid to repurchase stock	0
Cash paid to retire long-term debt	0
Cash paid for dividends	0
Other	0
Net cash provided (used) in financing activities	**$16,500**

Increase (decrease) in cash during the period	**$44,311**
Cash balance at the beginning of the period	17,520
Cash balance at the end of the period	**$61,831**

Figure 12.3. Sample statement of cash flows.

Prepared with consideration and managed closely, a comprehensive budget enables an agency to serve as many people as resources will allow with maximum efficiency and effectiveness. Competent administrators embrace the budget and the budgeting process as an opportunity to further the social mission. Less competent administrators will view the budget as an unpleasant necessity with minimal relevance.

Budgets exist to satisfy multiple needs. They are the roadmaps that help administrators decide in which direction to take the agency. They also serve as the benchmark against which subsequent financial performance is measured. Often, grantors require information from an agency's budget as part of a grant proposal. Thus, the budget can become an important tool for securing additional funding. Information from the budget is also used in management accounting reports. Perhaps most practically, the budget is often submitted to an agency's board for approval in order to continue operations.

The creation of a budget is an important process in the operation of an agency. As such, it deserves thoughtful attention, accurate forecasting, and conservative estimates. It is also useful to involve any staff members in the budget process who have responsibility for any line item in the budget. Handled poorly, the development of a budget can be a divisive process that highlights the variance in authority and responsibility that exists in an organization. Employees can view it as an authoritarian tool wielded by unknowledgeable managers who fail to understand the real world of service provision. If developed in an inclusive manner, however, the budget can be a unifying tool that aligns everyone's individual goals with those of the agency.

Budget development is also more than an allocation of resources. It is an opportunity for managers to clarify values and to measure performance against the agency's mission. The budget development process can bring out managers' personality traits not usually seen at other times. Managers will often defend their territory with tenacity and ruthless abandon. Budgeting meetings can be contentious and unpleasant. As long as participants are respectful and honest, this process can actually strengthen an agency. Vigorous discussion of an agency's values, mission, and priorities is helpful and productive. It is worthwhile for each manager to review the mission prior to developing the budget. A clear and consistent understanding of the mission will help clarify the process.

Managers should evaluate each program represented in the budget to determine if it furthers the social mission. This is an evaluation based on alignment of values. In addition, managers should evaluate each program to determine the cost per each person or unit served. This is an evaluation based on efficient use of limited resources. Managers must ask if they can better allocate the committed resources to a more efficient or effective program. Both evaluations are critical to the success of an agency, and managers must apply them objectively.

Budget development begins about 3 months prior to the start of the fiscal year. The timing depends on the complexity of the budget, the timing of monthly and quarterly financial reports, and the timing of the board approval process. If started too early, there will not be enough information from the current fiscal year to accurately assess the agency's performance, thereby reducing the reliability of the new budget. If begun too late, the budget will reflect a lack of consideration of accurate forecasts, past performance, and critical evaluation of programs. In either case, the value of the budget to the agency will be limited.

When reviewing financial performance in the current year, managers ought to look for anomalies, such as a budget line item with a large variance from the budgeted amount. Understanding the possible reason(s) for the variance will help managers make more accurate projections and/or operational changes. Variance is usually explained by inaccurate projections of revenues or expenses, unforeseen changes in operations (e.g., a new grant award or program development), or external forces largely beyond the agency's control (e.g., a new state administration that changes funding mechanisms or makes drastic budget cuts).

The budget creation process is also an opportunity to evaluate potential funding sources in the coming fiscal year. This involves analyzing external forces, such as the general economic outlook, state and federal budget trends, governmental leadership, and community needs. The inclusion of new revenues can allow managers to create some lofty goals, but they must be based on sound and conservative estimates.

Otherwise, disaster may loom. Few things create problems for an NFP entity like stated dependence on yet-to-be realized revenue streams.

Once the budget is established, managers need to evaluate the agency's financial performance at least monthly. This is done by looking at statements of actual financial performance as compared with budgeted goals. Any unit that is underperforming or overspending needs swift evaluation and adjustment. There is a tendency among managers, especially when reviewing quarterly reports, to adopt a wait-and-see approach. Waiting for the next report to see if there is a trend that requires action is an easy way to avoid making difficult decisions. Usually, trends require a couple of months to reveal themselves. Any given month can contain unusual variance from budgeted resources for a number of reasons: seasonal variation of usage, unusual and one-time expenses, or even adverse weather. If an anomaly reveals itself in two consecutive months, it likely requires action. Early intervention often yields the greatest results. Making operational changes in months 10 or 11 of the fiscal year will have minimal effect on the final numbers simply because there will not be enough time to see the positive effects of those changes. The benefits of those changes may well appear in the following fiscal year, but that may not be enough to satisfy the board of directors. Managers must constantly monitor and guide the agency's financial performance, but months 2–9 of the fiscal year are the most critical.

CONCLUSIONS

Every financial decision made by a manager is also a strategic decision. Each action, though based on financial data, must align with the overall strategy and mission of the agency. For example, an information technology (IT) technician employed by a private school realized that her school could earn a small amount of revenue by returning used toner and ink-jet cartridges to a firm that reimburses NFP agencies for those items. She realized that by collecting those items from other local agencies, she could generate hundreds of dollars of additional revenue each year for the school. This is not a lot of money, but it would pay for several new printers—something few IT directors would turn down. After time, she was spending 2–3 hours each week visiting with other agencies' IT staff and collecting used cartridges. The principal soon realized that the salary expense for the time needed to collect the cartridges exceeded the additional revenue. That was not enough reason for her to intervene in the situation, however. It was the misalignment of the employee's actions with the mission of the school that led to the intervention. Her actions were well intended, but they did not further the mission of the agency.

Effective managers and administrators realize that every time they make a financial decision, it must align with the organization's mission and values. The direction an organization takes is the summation of all decisions made by managers and administrators. Astute managers know that every time they make a financial decision, they cast a vote for the kind of agency they want.

REFERENCES

Diamond, M.A., Stice, E.K., & Stice, J.D. (2000). *Financial accounting: Reporting and analysis.* Cincinnati, OH: South-Western College Publishing.

Horngreen, C.T., Harrison, W.T.. Jr., & Bamber, L.S. (2002). *Accounting* (5th ed.). Upper Saddle River, NJ: Prentice Hall.

Proposal Writing and Grant Management

Naomi Chowdhuri Tyler

Lack of money is no obstacle. Lack of an idea is an obstacle.
Ken Hakuta

What If? Dr. Elizabeth Skye is the director of Nuestros Niños, an early intervention (EI) and child care center in a large, urban neighborhood. Although the center is known for the quality services it provides, Dr. Skye constantly seeks opportunities to improve the program. For example, the professional literature continues to acknowledge the link between language ability, reading skills, and behavior, and she wants to provide a stronger classroom-based language program. She recognizes the importance of helping her teachers become proficient in understanding the results of various language evaluations and instituting subsequent classroom interventions guided by the test results. This would require that Nuestros Niños' teachers receive training on how to 1) interpret the results of the tests and 2) implement research-validated interventions. Dr. Skye would also like to provide parent training to support home environments that are rich with language stimulation and reading to strengthen children's literacy exposure and instruction. Dr. Skye knows that many of her parents from low-income backgrounds do not use the public library system due to transportation challenges. She also knows that the parents want their children to succeed and flourish academically but are unaware of the association between early literacy exposure and school success. This knowledge has spurred her interest in developing a large lending library at the center.

Amy Hernandez, the speech-language pathologist (SLP) who currently works with the programs at Nuestros Niños, has been trained in administering language evaluations and has conducted parent and teacher trainings. Amy is willing to increase her hours at Nuestros Niños to help provide training if there is additional funding to cover her extra time and the costs of the tests and instructional materials. Amy suggests to Dr. Skye that she can increase parent turnout if transportation vouchers, child care, and refreshments are provided, and even more if the parents receive some sort of financial incentive to attend.

Dr. Skye decides to search for additional sources of funding to help her cover the expenses of the programs she would like to start. As the quotation at the beginning of this chapter indicates, her financial constraints may be only a temporary setback, as she has good ideas and worthwhile projects that are deserving of outside funding.

CHAPTER OVERVIEW

This chapter describes how to translate an idea into something that can be funded. It also details how to prepare and submit a grant proposal and manage a grant.

CHAPTER OBJECTIVES

After reviewing this chapter, the reader will

• Recognize the factors that make an idea fundable

• Know a minimum of two sources for external funding

• Understand the proposal preparation and submission process

• Know the essential components of a successful application for external funding

• Know the general criteria by which proposals are reviewed

• Understand the components of successful grant management.

GETTING STARTED

There is no shortage of great ideas in this world; however, not all of them are appealing to potential funding sources. EI personnel must match their programmatic goals to the specifications provided by funding agencies. Fortunately, there are many agencies and organizations dedicated to improving the educational outcomes of infants, toddlers, and young children, so a wide range of funding options exists.

Developing a Good Idea into a Fundable Idea

There are two ways to develop an idea and find a funding source. One is to examine the needs of a program, develop an idea that would address those needs, expand that idea into a proposed program, and then search for funding. Another is to look at several funding sources, find out what types of programs they support, and see if there is anything that can be done within one's program that aligns with those interests. In both cases, the proposed program needs to be fundable, or worthy of financial support from a funding agency.

The most important consideration when determining if an idea is fundable is whether it fits within the funding agency's vision, goals, or program criteria. Consider two funding agencies: Agency A provides funding for in-service teacher training to increase linguistic and behavioral outcomes for children with developmental delays; Agency B provides funding for parent training on nutrition and food preparation to help reduce or prevent childhood obesity. Agency A would be a good match for the teacher-training component of Dr. Skye's proposed program; however, her parent-training component might not necessarily fit within the agency's funding parameters. She can look elsewhere to fund that portion, but Agency B would *not* be a good match because its primary goal is to combat childhood obesity, not increase young children's linguistic competence. On the other hand, there might be a third option (Agency C) that has a broader mission to support EI services for children to better prepare them for school. Dr. Skye could submit a proposal to Agency C, as both teacher and parent training could be justifiable components of a program to prepare children for school.

Funding Sources

The search for funding should encompass both public and private agencies. Private funding sources include foundations and corporations. Public funding typically comes from federal and state agencies. Federal grant applications are more detailed and explicit than most state and private funding sources; therefore, anyone who can write a winning federal grant proposal is most certainly prepared to write proposals for other funding sources! Many of the examples in this chapter are taken from federal funding sources in order to prepare you for the most rigorous of applications.

One of the largest private funding agencies is the United Way, which provides financial support to nonprofit agencies. Funding from the United Way is typically handled at the local city or county level through a competitive grant process, so the first step in the search for funds should be to contact the local agency. The United Way's web site (http://national.unitedway.org/) also provides information on other nonprofit organizations that might be funding possibilities.

The search for federal funding can begin on the government's grant web site (https://www.grants.gov). This site provides information about and access to over 1,000 grant programs that are funded through 26 different federal agencies. The web site contains a database of federal funding that can be searched by keywords (e.g., *early childhood, early reading*).

There are several additional ways to find funding sources. Early childhood organizations usually have a history of receiving funding from certain foundations or agencies, which means that they will probably receive announcements for future funding opportunities from those organizations. Directors can check to be sure that they are included on mailing lists for potential funding sources. Web site announcements, newspaper ads, word of mouth, and professional contacts can also provide information on potential funding sources and grant application releases.

Application Packages

Both public and private funding sources generally require some type of grant application for programs to receive funding. The application process varies greatly. An application can be as simple as a brief introductory letter, general overview, and budget sent unsolicited to an agency for consideration, or as complex as a grant competition in which proposals must contain agency-specified sections and compete with other proposals for a limited amount of funding. Most grant competitions provide some sort of grant application package—also referred to as Request for Proposals (RFP), Request for Applications (RFA), Call for Investments, or application kits—that explains the requirements of the proposal. These RFPs are usually available on-line or in paper format, upon request. The RFP is very important, as it explains every aspect of what a grant application should contain. General requirements, due dates, page limits, spacing allowances, evaluation criteria, and appendix requirements are just some of the details to be considered. All instructions should be followed explicitly; too many grant writers have had proposals rejected because they submitted too late, went over the specified page limit, or were outside the allowable margin and spacing specifications.

One of the first items to look at in an RFP is the overall priority for grants funded from the agency, referred to by such terms as Absolute Priority, Core Criteria, or General Requirement. In essence, this is a requirement of the particular grant competition that every proposal must meet to be considered for funding. For example, the following is a portion of the Center-Based Education Criteria from a United Way agency application (United Way of Metropolitan Nashville [UWMN], 2007, p. 4):

> Only centers who meet the following criteria will be considered for an investment:
> - year-round, full day programs in Davidson County with high average daily attendance
> - at least 75% of children served qualify for free and reduced meals, are English language learners or have a diagnosed disability or delay
> - assess children and set goals in all developmental domains
> - have qualified staff, preferably degreed teachers, or make accommodations to support the hiring and retention of degreed teachers in classrooms for 3–5-year-olds
> - demonstrate a history of low teacher turnover
> - are Three Star and/or NAEYC accredited

Some RFPs also contain suggested areas of focus, referred to by such terms as Invitational Priorities or Preferred Investment Criteria. Proposals that address these focus areas may or may not be given preference. The following is a portion of a federal Invitational Priority (United States Department of Education [USDOE]):

> The Secretary is especially interested, for applicants serving children with limited English proficiency, in receiving applications that include a specific plan for the development of English language acquisition for these children during and from the start of their preschool experience . . ." (2007, p. D14)

Finally, some funding agencies give additional points to projects that address specific areas of interest. Here is an example of a Competitive Preference Priority: "Up to ten (10) points to an application that employs randomized experimental designs in conducting evaluation of outreach activities" (Office of Special Education Programs [OSEP], 2003, p. C-22).

Competitive Preference points will not get a very poor proposal funded over a good one. If there are two or three good proposals being considered, however, Competitive Preference points could make the difference, so whenever possible the Competitive Preference Priority should be addressed.

PROPOSAL PREPARATION

A comprehensive proposal can provide the framework for an efficient and a productive project. This section addresses the proposal preparation process, including considerations for grant writers before they start the writing process, components of grant proposals, and submission guidelines.

Prewriting Considerations

An overeager grant writer might be tempted to hunker down with a large pot of coffee and begin the writing process. Yet, before anything is written, it is a good idea to lay out a writing timeline in order to be sure you can accomplish everything necessary before the due date. Additionally, there are several factors that a good grant writer takes into consideration before beginning to write.

Who Is the Audience?   Most agencies use review panels, composed of two or more individuals, to read and rate submitted proposals. Although the reviewers often are experts in the particular area for which the grant is written, this is not always the case. For example, to ensure appropriate representation of expertise in the review process, the staff of the U.S. Department of Education's OSEP make a concerted effort to include individuals with disabilities and parents of children with disabilities on their review panels. Local United Way agencies often use teams of trained community volunteers to review their proposals. Review panels for private foundations might comprise advisory board members. Of course, the best way to understand the review process and the gain a thorough understanding of how reviewers evaluate proposals is to serve on a review panel. Grant writers who have had the opportunity to be grant reviewers gain invaluable knowledge which strengthens any future grant proposals that they write. Here are some tips for writing to the diverse audience members who will be reviewing a proposal.

1. Assume that readers might not have specific knowledge of early childhood special education (ECSE) or any other area discussed in the proposal. Therefore, briefly explain any program or intervention that the proposed project will use. For example, rather than simply stating "The proposed project will use XYZ Reading Program," the reader should have enough information to understand why XYZ Reading Program was chosen. Summarize how the program works, offer research showing its effectiveness, and explain why it is a good match for the project.

2. Define field-specific terminology, and do not assume that technical jargon or abbreviations used in a proposal will be understood. It is helpful to have someone or several people outside of ECSE read through the proposal and make a list of anything not understood. Those sections can then be revised for clarity.

3. Consider the perspectives of different reviewers. For example, a reviewer who is the director of a child care center will want to ensure that compliance with federal and state requirements for child care centers is maintained; a parent might want to see family involvement in the project; a foundation's board member may be interested in the bang for the buck, or what types of outcomes the project will produce using the funds supplied.

Writing Style   Keep in mind that reviewers will be reading many proposals and could be working late into the night. Grant writers need to do everything possible to make the proposal easy to understand. Table 13.1 gives some examples of the points discussed below.

1. Write for clarity and simplicity. Long, convoluted sentences; complex phrases; and large, impressive-sounding terms are unnecessary in grant writing. Necessary points should be made as clearly and succinctly as possible.

2. Use the active rather than passive tense. A grant writer should tell the reviewers what an agency is going to do with the money, not what they are going to try to do or what they would like to try to do.

Table 13.1.   Proposal examples

Suggestion	Not so good	Better
Write clearly and simply.	Project READ will obtain and utilize the evaluation results from the Fall assessments to develop and implement reading programs that will be uniquely tailored to each child's individual needs.	Individualized reading programs for each child will be based on the Fall testing results.
Use an active tense.	The staff of Project READ plans to try and implement the reading program by the end of Sept.	The new reading program will be in place by the end of September.
Make things easy to find.	A table indicating the training levels of the current center staff can be found in Appendix B.	A table indicating the training levels of the current center staff can be found in Appendix B (blue), page B-5.
Put anything important in the narrative.	See Appendix B for personnel qualifications and the project's timeline.	The qualifications of the key personnel are as follows: Dr. Elizabeth Skye will be the project director. She has 10 years experience . . .

3. Make things easy to find. Reviewers get frustrated when the text refers to a table that they cannot find. To solve this problem, include the page number of the table in the text. A table located in Appendix B can be hard to find when the combined appendices measure an inch thick. Consider numbering appendixes (e.g., A-1, B-2) or even copying them on different colored paper (e.g., Appendix A is yellow, Appendix B is blue).

4. Put anything important in the proposal narrative. Reviewers do not have to read every appendix, only those required by the grant competition. Grant writers who try to save space by putting key tables and figures in appendices risk frustrating reviewers or having important information skipped.

Writing Team   There is value in recruiting a team of individuals who can help with the grant writing process. There are often multiple components to each proposal, so the ability to divide and conquer will aid in completing a proposal more quickly, which is especially important when due dates are rapidly approaching. A second benefit to having a team is that each member can also act as a reviewer, possibly pointing out problems in the proposal that one lone writer may not have identified. Having a person who can act as a copy editor also helps assure consistency and helps the proposal read more smoothly for the reviewers.

Proposal Components   Grant competitions often specify that proposals contain particular sections or components, such as an abstract or a budget. Grant competition managers are typically very specific about what should be included within those components and provide evaluation criteria, or standards by which each section is graded or scored. Each section is also given a maximum point value. Reviewers use the evaluation criteria to assess the quality of a proposal section and award points accordingly. A grant writer should carefully address each of the listed evaluation criteria for every section of a proposal.

To understand this better, it might be helpful to compare the proposal to an instruction manual or a recipe. When putting together a shelf or baking a cake, it is important to follow the instructions exactly as they are written. If the instructions say to follow steps A, B, and C or to use ingredients 1, 2, and 3, one should do A, B, and C and use 1, 2, and 3. Drilling extra holes or using different parts for the shelf, or leaving out ingredients for the cake, could result in an unsteady shelf or an ill-tasting cake. Similarly, adding or substituting components or failing to address certain evaluation criteria in a grant proposal will almost always prevent it from being funded.

Funding agencies have varying requirements for the number of sections that each proposal should include. Federal agencies tend to require longer proposals, and thus more sections, than state or private organizations. Funding agencies use many different names to refer to the required sections or pieces of a proposal. This chapter will include some of those different names; regardless of the name or section title, the primary goal is to focus on the information that should be included in that section.

Grant writers also need to determine how much space to dedicate to each section. This can be accomplished by comparing the points awarded to each section with the total page allotment. For example, Dr. Skye is writing to a grant competition with a 40-page limit and a total of 100 points possible. The RFP states that the Needs section is worth 20 points, or one fifth of the total points. Therefore, she should dedicate one fifth of her total space, or 8 pages, to this section. One common mistake of novice grant writers is to dedicate too little space to sections that are worth a large percentage of the points or too much space to sections worth not as much.

Abstract   The abstract is a brief summary (i.e., no more than one page) of the proposed project and is usually placed at the front of the proposal. The page limit specified in the application generally does not include the abstract. This one-page summary may be 1) sent to various funding agencies to see if what is proposed aligns with their grant program; 2) used to inform potential advisory board members of the purpose of a project; and 3) given to individuals from whom letters of support are requested. Grant competition managers may use the abstract to identify and select reviewers who have related backgrounds or experiences. The abstract is often the first thing that a reviewer will read, so it must make a positive impact. Some agencies require a transmittal letter instead of an abstract. This letter usually comes from a top official or director of the organization applying for funding and serves the same purpose as the abstract, so it should contain the same elements.

Abstract Checklist

An abstract should include

❑   The title of the project or program

❑   A one- to two-sentence overview of the project

❑   The goals and objectives for the project

❑   The intended outcomes for the project

Need for the Project   This section may be referred to by many different names (e.g., Significance, Relevance, Needs Assessment), but the main purpose of this section is to explain the importance of funding for this particular project. The evaluation criteria are key to structuring this section. Here is a sample Needs evaluation criterion from a state grant application (Tennessee Department of Education):

> Provide evidence that the community to be served . . . has a high percentage or large number of children and families that might be considered "most in need" of family literacy services. Indicate the number of families you expect to serve in your first, second, and third program years. (2005, p. D-1)

A grant writer could efficiently structure this section of the proposal by developing headings that correspond to the items listed in the evaluation criterion (e.g., Community Description; Family Literacy Services; Families to Be Served).

The Needs section of a proposal should contain data and information that build a compelling case, showing a documented need for the project. Data collected from many sources should be included to justify the significance of the proposed project as it pertains to national, state, local, and individual service agency needs. The data should reflect the most recent numbers available, preferably collected within the previous 1 or 2 years from such sources as National Association for the Education of Young Children (NAEYC), reports from the state education agency, data from other state agencies, data from EI agencies, local school district reports, reports from relevant committees, or task force meeting minutes. The Needs section can end with a description of how the proposed project will address the stated needs, usually in the form of project outcomes. The outcomes described in this section will be used to evaluate the grant's progress later, so they should be objective and measurable. Outcomes can include things such as the number of teachers trained, the number of children served, and academic or behavioral results. United Way applications often include an Outcomes form in the RFP, which must be filled out and submitted with the proposal.

For Dr. Skye's proposal, she collected data to show the following:

- An increased need for early language and reading services for children with developmental delays

- Language and literacy challenges faced by children in high-poverty, urban settings

- Demographics of her center's students, including parental income and educational levels, race/ethnicity, and primary languages

- A call for higher quality EI services from local school districts

- Time spent on language intervention in her center and how that could be increased

- Methods to improve language and early literacy instruction in the center

- Survey results of Nuestros Niños' parents showing the amount of time engaged in early literacy activities at home

- Letters of support from parents (included in an appendix) stating their willingness to implement language and literacy strategies at home with the proper training

Dr. Skye ended the Needs section with a summary of how her project would result in stronger language skills, reduced behavior problems, and increased reading skills for the children at Nuestros Niños, resulting in better long-term outcomes for students with and without disabilities. These outcomes would be due to the combined training efforts of 16 teachers and teaching assistants and 140 parents, who would serve 96 children per year.

Needs/Relevance/Significance Checklist

The Needs section should

❑   Make a compelling case for the funding being requested

❑   Use current, descriptive data to illustrate the specific needs faced by the applicant
      organization

❑   Summarize the project outcomes and how they will address the stated need

---

Quality of the Project Services   As with the Needs section, this section can be
identified by various names (e.g., Approach, Program Activities, Program Description, Activities and Services), all of which refer to the quality of the proposed program. The main purpose of this section is to assure the reviewer that the proposed
project will be of high quality and that the educational practices, techniques, or interventions used are research-validated methods proven to be successful with the target population. Each funding agency has a unique method for requesting descriptions of the quality of the proposed program. Again, the evaluation criteria guide
the text for this section and act as the points the reviewers should look for when reading the proposal. Consider the following sample evaluation criteria, taken from different RFPs.

1.   Application of up-to-date knowledge: Describe " . . . the extent to which profes-
     sional development to be provided by the proposed project reflects up-to-date
     knowledge from research and effective practice." (OSEP, 2004, p. C-1)

2.   Indicators of program quality: "The extent to which the training or professional
     development services to be provided by the proposed project are of sufficient
     quality, intensity, and duration to lead to improvements in practice among the re-
     cipients of those services." (USDOE, 2007, p. C-35)

3.   Demonstration of service integration: "Describe how the program connects and
     collaborates with other service providers so that the program is integrated with
     the broader service community and avoids duplication of service. (United Ways
     in Greater Kansas City [UWGKC], 2007, p. 4).

4.   Goals, objectives, and activities: "Describe, in detail, the program activities. How
     do you define success for the program participants and how does that connect
     with the program activities?" (UWGKC, 2007, p. 2)

The first criterion can be addressed with a brief literature review of relevant
areas to justify the methods or practices used in the proposed project. Reference articles or works older than 5 years should be avoided. Unless a seminal work in the
field is being cited, old references can give the reviewers the perception that the applicant organization is not keeping up with the latest knowledge in the field, which
then reflects poorly on its ability to provide high-quality services.

In addition to showing that the methods to be used reflect up-to-date practice,
the Quality of Project Services section should include proof that the applicant organization has a history of providing high-quality programs (see second criterion above).
One way to do this is by providing indicators of quality, such as the school's or
program's mission statement and educational philosophy, description of teacher–

student ratios, teacher retention rates, current use of validated practices, accreditations, and any recognition or awards received.

The third evaluation criteria above emphasizes the importance that many funding agencies place on service integration and coordination with other agencies. This type of collaboration has many benefits. First, coordination across centers has a financial advantage, as costs of teacher training and professional development can be shared. Secondly, the opportunity to work together encourages staff members to share ideas, philosophies and knowledge of other resources. The leveraging of joint resources allows for better reporting of goals and stronger outcomes when agencies can combine their data. Finally, the larger EI community benefits when centers and agencies can reach a broader base and address families' needs in more communities.

A thorough description of the proposed program is necessary to address the last criterion. The project's proposed goals, objectives, and activities should be listed with a description of all relevant services. A project's *goals* should be broad, *objectives* are more specific details within a goal, and the *activities* are implemented to achieve the project goals and objectives. Table 13.2 provides an example of how goals, objectives, and activities can be laid out for a proposal. The description of services must be very clear and include such details as the length of time for each training, the amount of time per day or week the teachers will use the proposed methods, and the techniques by which parents will be trained. When reviewers are not given enough clarification on these details, they may assume that the program has not been well planned and mark the proposal down accordingly.

Some funding agencies may require that the proposals address issues of sustainability. In other words: How will the program continue once the grant funding has ended? In some cases, this can be addressed in this section; in others, the Quality of the Management Plan (coming up!) is a good place to discuss sustainability. In either case, the proposal should describe the center's marketing or business plan, how future funding entities will be identified and resources solicited, and any potential partnerships that can be developed to cut costs.

Table 13.2. Portion of a table for goals, objectives, and activities

Goal 1: Improve language skills of children in the program.	
Objectives	Activities
1.1 Conduct teacher trainings.	a. Conduct training on understanding and interpreting language assessment results.
	b. Conduct training on language interventions.
	c. Conduct regular review and update sessions.
1.2 Gather data on students	a. Gather baseline data on students.
	b. Gather continuous language data on students.
	c. Analyze language assessment results.
1.3 Conduct parent trainings.	a. Conduct parent training on home-based language enhancement activities.
1.4 Implement interventions	a. Implement classroom interventions.
	b. Implement home-based interventions.
1.5 Evaluate language activities.	a. Survey teachers for input and suggestions.
	b. Meet with teachers to improve program.
	c. Survey parents for input and suggestions.
	d. Meet with parents to improve program.

Dr. Skye began her Quality of Program Services section with a literature review that focused on early language development, factors that can inhibit language development, and the impact of language skills on child behavior, social skills, and reading development. She included information on the importance of EI for reducing the severity of many disability-related characteristics and cited positive outcomes from studies in which early child care professionals had implemented interventions similar to those she plans to use. Next, she included her project's goals, objectives, and activities and outlined her proposed program. She continued by describing the specific details of the teacher and parent trainings and the language and reading interventions to be implemented. She described plans to coordinate teacher training sessions with another EI center, located at a local university, and explained the benefits of cost-sharing professional development expenses and of the access to the university's faculty for information on best practices. During their proposed joint training days, time would be set aside during a working lunch for informal group discussions on pre-set talking points that related to best practices in early literacy. To show that Nuestros Niños has a history of providing high-quality services, Dr. Skye included the program's mission statement and philosophy of learning, noted that the program was accredited through NAEYC (she included a copy of their accreditation letter in an appendix), information on the Center's curriculum, described their low teacher turnover rates, and stated that the program had received the Outstanding Early Intervention Program Award in 2007.

Quality of Project Services Checklist

The Quality of Project Services section should include

❑   A brief literature review, using recent articles, justifying the proposed methods or instructional techniques

❑   Indicators of the overall quality of the school or program seeking funding

❑   A thorough description of the project's services

❑   The goals and objectives for the proposed project

Quality of Project Personnel   The purpose of the Personnel section, also known by such names as Staff and Volunteer Capacity or Staff Qualifications, is to ensure that the personnel involved in the project have the necessary expertise to perform their proposed duties. Some agencies provide a form that must be filled out for every staff member. Other grant competitions provide evaluation criteria, such as "Describe the people (number and qualifications) and their role in delivering this program" (UWGKC, 2007, p. 3), and expect that the qualifications of key personnel will be described in a narrative format. The term *key personnel* refers to those people involved directly with the management and implementation of the proposed project. The project director, any coordinators, and external consultants should be included. It is not necessary to write about every teacher and staff person associated with the applicant program.

Generally, there should be a paragraph about each key person that briefly summarizes his or her expertise, role, and responsibilities for the proposed project. It is important that the job description and the qualifications of these individuals match. Reviewers might be skeptical about awarding funding for a complex project to a proposed project director with no experience in grant management. On the other hand, a reading coordinator who has a master's degree in reading and 12 years of experience coordinating similar programs for a local school district would be rated favorably. Personal awards or accomplishments unrelated to the project should be excluded. In other words, leave out the information on triathlon times or county fair ribbons! This paragraph should sound less like a book jacket biography (e.g., "Coordinator Montès lives in Baltimore with her husband and three children") and more like an application for a job (e.g., "Coordinator Montès has a master's degree in speech-language pathology, has 6 years of experience as an SLP, and has conducted over 30 teacher and parent trainings on early language enhancement strategies").

Once the qualifications of the grant's key personnel have been described, the overall qualifications and characteristics of the rest of the staff should be highlighted. Besides the obvious goal of staffing the project with the most qualified people possible, a good grant writer will want to emphasize the proposed staff's education, experience, and accomplishments. The growing awareness of the impact of culture and language on the learning process has prompted some funding agencies to include priorities or evaluation criteria regarding the diversity of program staff. Both of these areas can be addressed by including a table that summarizes particular competencies or trainings (e.g., the number of teachers with bachelor's degrees, master's degrees, training in certain areas) and the diversity of personnel (e.g., gender, race/ethnicity, dual-language abilities).

Grant applications that contain a Personnel section may also require an appendix of *abbreviated* vitae or résumés of the key personnel. It is a waste of resources (e.g., grant writer's time, a reviewer's time, trees) to include every single page of a vita or résumé. Instead, develop a standard format and include only the items from each résumé that are relevant to the project. A standard format might include the following headings: Name; role on proposed project; education; relevant experience.

Quality of Project Personnel Checklist

The Quality of Project Personnel section should contain

❏   A paragraph for each key person that describes his or her role on the project and qualifications

❏   A table summarizing important qualifications or characteristics of additional project staff

❏   An appendix containing abbreviated vitae or résumés for each key person.

Quality of the Management Plan   The Management Plan is a section common in USDOE grants. Other funding agencies may not have a separate section for project management; instead, they may include management evaluation criteria within the Project Services, Approach, or Evaluation section. The purpose of this section is to show reviewers and the funding agency that the project will be well managed and accomplish the goals and objectives within a specified time frame and the budget parameters. Here is a sample evaluation criterion that relates to project management: "The adequacy of the management plan to achieve the objectives of the proposed project on time and within budget, including clearly defined responsibilities, timelines, and milestones for accomplishing project tasks" (USDOE, 2007, p. C-36).

Aside from a brief description of how the project will be managed, the Management Plan section may include information on how the achievement of objectives will be monitored and what type of feedback system will be used to continuously improve the project. The use of formative and summative assessment procedures are often listed in evaluation criteria as a means to gather information for program improvement. Formative assessment involves the continuous use of various data collection measures throughout the course of a project; for summative assessment procedures, data are collected at the end of a specified time period (e.g., the end of a year, the end of a funding cycle). Both provide important information to a project director on quality indicators or progress toward outcomes. In addition to validated data collection measures used to acquire information on child or family progress towards specified outcomes, such informal measures as focus groups of parents or teachers may also be used to gain information on how they think a program is working or suggestions for improvement.

A lot of the information necessary for this section can be provided in the form of figures or tables. Figure 13.1 shows an example of a time line, tied to the project's goals and objectives, that indicates when key activities will be accomplished. A sample project monitoring table is shown in Table 13.3; it illustrates how the assessment of project activities can be tracked and lists the key personnel responsible for each activity.

Dr. Skye started her Management Section by giving an overview of the project director's role in the management of the proposed project. Her personnel loading chart (i.e., amount of time each person will commit to the project), time line, and project monitoring table showed that grant responsibilities were clearly delineated and that goals, objectives, and activities would be monitored for completion within a specified time frame. She also scheduled parent and teacher focus groups at regular

Goal 1: To improve language skills of students in the program.

Objective 1.1: Conduct teacher trainings												
	Year 1				Year 2				Year 3			
Activities	Q1	Q2	Q3	Q4	Q1	Q2	Q3	Q4	Q1	Q2	Q3	Q4
a. Conduct training on understanding and interpreting language assessment results												
b. Conduct training on language interventions												
c. Conduct regular review and update sessions												

Figure 13.1. Portion of a sample timeline.

Table 13.3. Portion of a sample project-monitoring table

	Person(s) responsible	Data source/ How assessed	Outcome	Timeline
Goal 1: Improve language skills of children in the program				
Objective 1.1 Conduct teacher trainings.	Skye Hernandez	Training evaluations, number trained	100% of NN staff trained	1st quarter
Objective 1.2 Gather data on students	Skye Hernandez NN staff	Language assessments, weekly probes, IFSP progress	average improvement by at least __ percentile on all assessments	1st quarter for initial assessments, ongoing for other activities

Key: NN, Nuestros Niños; IFSP, individualized family service plan.

intervals throughout the year to provide feedback to the project director and advisory board members as a means of improving the project.

Quality of the Management Plan Checklist

The Management Plan should contain a

❑   Summary of how the achievement of goals and objectives will be monitored

❑   Description of a feedback system to continuously improve the project

❑   Method of connecting goals and objectives to a time frame (i.e., a time line)

❑   Method of indicating how goals and outcomes will be monitored (i.e., project monitoring table)

Adequacy of Resources   The purpose of the Resources section (also referred to by such terms as Program Capacity, Organization Capacity, Commitment of Resources) is to assure the reviewers and funding agency that the applicant organization has the necessary means to accomplish the proposed program. The proposal should provide a clear explanation of the personnel, instructional materials, technology, physical space, and collaborative relationships available to ensure the program's success. Here is an excerpt of a Resource criterion from a state-level RFP (Hawaii Department of Education):

> Organization, capacity, and commitment of school resources. Describe the school's overall capacity to carry out the Reading First grant program. How will the school organize itself to support this initiative? . . . Describe other existing school resources (e.g., funds, time, personnel, other) that will be committed to this initiative. (2006, p. B-2)

The first issue to address in the Resources section is the capacity of the organization to sponsor the proposed program. This portion of the proposal should contain detailed information on the number of personnel allocated to the project and their respective time commitments. In some cases, this will be a reiteration of information in the Personnel section, but there should also be a justification of how this personnel allotment affects the capacity of the program. The availability of classroom space should be addressed for programs that are expanding, providing additional therapy services, holding training sessions, or including any other type of service that requires dedicated physical space, such as a lending library for parents. If the proposed program is similar to other projects that the applicant organization has engaged in recently, that should be mentioned. A history of successful projects contributes to the line of reasoning that the agency is poised and ready to implement another high-quality program.

The second area to address in the Resources section is the budget. Although the proposal will have a separate budget section, often with an accompanying budget narrative, the Resources section is the place in the proposal where the case is made for the effectiveness of the applicant agency's budgetary procedures, including but not limited to the reasonableness of the budget in comparison to the requested funds; the outcomes to be achieved with the proposed budget; the reasonableness of the budget in comparison to the number of children to be served; and the capacity of the applicant organization to distribute and monitor funds accordingly. Depending on the RFP, an applicant may need to provide summaries of its revenue and/or expenditures during a particular period of time as justification that it is fiscally responsible.

Dr. Skye addressed staffing strengths as the first component of Nuestros Niños' resources. She reiterated the number of staff involved in the project and the number of hours each would dedicate to the proposed program every week; she also included letters of support from them indicating their enthusiasm to begin the new program. She discussed how the program's low turnover rate was indicative of both a high-quality program and the staff's commitment to the center and community. Dr. Skye explained that the center had a large meeting room, separate from the classrooms, that would be used for staff and parent training sessions and would also house the family lending library. She described the listening and writing centers and the average number of children's books in each classroom that are currently used to enhance language and reading skills and how these materials would provide the base from which the proposed program would build. With regard to the adequacy of the budget, Dr. Skye reiterated the costs of the project with respect to the numbers of children and families served and teachers trained, even dividing the costs of the grant by the number of students to come up with a per-child dollar amount. She summarized the last 5 years of Nuestros Niños' funding history to reinforce the fact that the organization is able to manage funds.

Adequacy of Resources Checklist

The Adequacy of Resources section should include

❏   Organization resources available for the project, including personnel, time, instructional materials, and space

❏   Justification of the budget and the proposed project's cost effectiveness

❏   Information that shows the organization's ability to manage the funds appropriately

---

Quality of Project Evaluation   The purpose of the Evaluation section is to delineate methods that are in place to ascertain the project's progress towards goals and objectives and to determine the quality of the program. It is important to have a strong evaluation plan to determine whether the center is meeting its objectives. Not all grant competitions have a Project Evaluation section, but they may incorporate evaluative components within the Project Management or Project Services sections. Here are sample evaluation criteria for Project Evaluation:

- Describe the process to be used to determine whether progress is being made toward achieving the required component of the prekindergarten at-risk program.

- Describe procedures to be used to determine the success of the prekindergarten at-risk program.

- Describe procedures to be used to show measurable outcomes for family participation. (Illinois State Board of Education, 2005, pp. 16–17)

Criteria for project evaluation may require the use of formative and summative strategies that yield data the project director can use to improve the program quality, as addressed previously in the Project Management section. Other criteria may require the grantee to collect data on project outcomes and report them to their advisory board and/or include them in grant reports.

Some funding agencies require the services of an external project evaluator, someone not directly involved with the project who is hired to conduct an independent evaluation. One advantage to using an independent evaluator is that he or she is a neutral party, so the evaluation will be objective. Depending on the extent of the evaluation activities, however, a project evaluator can be costly, so expense estimates need to be generated so that costs can be included in the budget. The evaluator's credentials should be delineated in the personnel section to make the case that the individual is sufficiently qualified to conduct an assessment of the project's progress.

The RFP that Dr. Skye responded to required the use of an external evaluator. She contacted the director of another local EI program, Dr. Nakayla Dawkins, who has many years of experience with both local and state grants management. Dr. Dawkins agreed to be the project's external evaluator. In the Evaluation section, Dr. Skye explained the types of data that Dr. Dawkins would use to evaluate each project goal and objective, the number of times per year this evaluation would occur, what types of evaluation reports would be generated, and how the Nuestros Niños staff, parents, and advisory board members would use the evaluation data to improve the project.

Quality of Project Evaluation Checklist

The Project Evaluation section should provide

❑   An explanation of how the goals and objectives will be evaluated

❑   A description of the types of data to be collected

❑   A discussion of how the data will be used, and by whom, to improve the project's quality

---

Budget   The budget is a separate, very important section of the proposal. Although in many competitions it receives no points, a badly conceived or poorly explained budget will definitely result in a proposal's being rejected. Not all RFPs have specific evaluation criteria for this section; however, remember that evaluation criteria referring to the adequacy and effectiveness of the budget may be included in the Adequacy of Resources section.

There are basically two parts to the budget: the budget detail and the budget narrative. Neither section is counted as part of the overall page count of the proposal. The budget detail is the section that shows the actual monetary numbers associated with particular expenditures. The budget narrative is a written explanation or justification of the budget detail numbers. Many funding agencies provide budget forms that an applicant must fill out and submit as the budget detail. Some of these forms have spaces for an applicant to insert the budget narrative. In other cases, applicants are encouraged to include a separate narrative.

The budget should include 1) staff salaries, including what full-time equivalency (FTE) each person is working on the project; 2) fringe benefits on salaries for project personnel; 3) any travel necessary (e.g., professional conferences); 4) equipment and supplies; 5) such contractual expenses as those paid to consultants; 6) any other relevant expenses to the project (e.g., copying costs for parent training materials); and 7) indirect costs charged against the total. Some of these costs are discussed in more detail here.

There are several considerations when using grant funds to cover salary and fringe benefits. Funding usually cannot be used to cover portions of existing staff salaries, as they are already covered under the center's regular budget. However, grant funds can be used to add an additional position (e.g., reading specialist, parent coordinator) or to increase the time percentage of a part-time position. For example, Amy Hernandez, the SLP at Nuestros Niños, currently works a 20-hour week at the center, which is the equivalent of a half-time position or .50 full-time equivalency (FTE). Dr. Skye can use grant funds to increase Amy's position to 30 hours per week (.75 FTE) or more, depending on Amy's availability and whether the grant's budget can fund the salary difference. Fringe benefits costs are usually calculated as a percentage of the salary. Fringe benefit calculations are unique to each applicant agency and should be verified before developing the budget.

Items included in the budget must be relevant to the proposed project's scope of work. Travel expenses (e.g., mileage, hotel, meals, airfare) might be justifiable on Dr. Skye's budget if she wants a team of teachers to attend a state conference on early literacy in another location, but not if the conference is on a topic like childhood vaccinations, which—although probably helpful to her staff—is unrelated to her grant. Such supplies as language evaluation kits, scoring sheets, children's books, and the costs of transportation vouchers, child care, and honoraria for parents who attend trainings would all be considered appropriate expenses. Materials like paper, crayons, pencils, and markers, would not be considered appropriate because they are part of the center's standard operating budget. Notice, however, that justification could be made for additional supplies needed to stock writing centers that are part of the project's preliteracy activities, and because this would require more materials than those normally purchased for Nuestros Niños, paper, crayons, pencils and markers would be an appropriate expense.

Indirect costs refer to grant funds that are not used for direct program items or services. Indirect costs are calculated as a percentage of the total direct costs, and that percentage may be dictated by either the funding or applicant agency. In some cases, the expenses that can be covered by indirect costs are also part of an agreement between the funding source and the agency. Funding sources acknowledge that there are certain costs which are not part of the direct services provided to children, yet are associated with the necessary overall costs of running a project under the sponsorship of a center or agency. Therefore, indirect costs may be used to pay the appropriate portion of such expenses as building rent, electricity, water bills, furniture, or equipment maintenance. These funds typically go directly to the agency, not to the project director. Nuestros Niños has a standard 15% indirect cost rate that is applied to any external grant. Dr. Skye's budget totaled $134,500, which she then multiplied by 15% for an indirect cost of $20,175. Once the direct and indirect costs were added, Dr. Skye's total budget totaled $154,675.

Budget Checklist

The proposal's budget should include

❏   A budget detail that contains the items and services to be charged to the grant, broken down by categories specified by the funding agency

❏   A budget narrative

❏   Any budget forms provided by the funding agency

Proposal Submission

Before submitting the proposal, take some time to make sure everything is in order. The proposal should include the letter of intent or abstract, budget, proposal narrative, and any additional paperwork required by the funding agency. For example, every grant competition has its own required forms that must be included with the proposal, as well as specifications for appendixes. Read the RFP carefully to find out what forms are necessary and whose signatures are required on those forms. In addition, some funding sources require copies of certain agency documents, such as the following:

- Documentation of incorporation and exemption from federal income tax under Section 501(c)

- Names of and contact information for agency board of directors

- The agency's board-approved strategic plan

- The agency's nondiscrimination policy regarding staff hires

- Certain IRS forms for the most recent fiscal year

- Annual independent audit or certified financial review

- Copies of licensures or accreditations

Once the proposal sections are in order, the submission process can begin. Depending on the funding agency's requirements, proposals may be submitted electronically or in paper format. Each method has advantages and disadvantages (see Table 13.4). Electronic submissions save paper and postage or delivery service costs; however, technology glitches can occur that make the process burdensome or cause the documents to lose formatting and look less appealing than a paper submission.

The important consideration in the submission process is to avoid overlooking a requirement of the competition. Check and recheck the RFP to ensure that everything is included. Anticipate problems, usually in the very last moments of the sub-

Table 13.4.   Tips for the submission process

Electronic submission	Paper submission
Request and receive a log-in ID and password, if required by the funding agency, well in advance of grant due date.	Verify the number of copies required by the funding agency; send the required number and an extra copy or two.
Read the submission instructions carefully to avoid as many technology glitches as possible.	Double-check each and every copy to ensure that no pages are missing or stuck in the copier.
Anticipate high traffic on the agency's web site immediately prior to the submission deadline, and start early.	Read the RFP to verify whether the due date is when the proposal should be *mailed* or *received*. There is a big difference!
If you have proposal sections that you have finished early and you are sure you will not change, send them in to test potential problem areas like software compatibility.	When mailing, send the proposal by certified mail with a signature required. If you don't get confirmation of receipt within a few days, follow up to ensure the proposal's arrival.
Find out the procedures for submission of documents for which electronic versions may not be available, such as letters of support. In some cases, these documents will need to be electronically scanned.	Delivery services like FedEx, UPS, or DHL are more expensive but may be worth the cost if it is necessary to ensure delivery by a certain due date.

mittal process. Computers can freeze, files can be lost, copiers can jam, and web sites that accept proposals can work slowly when everyone is trying to submit at the last moment. Being prepared for these glitches and *submitting early whenever possible* can prevent many problems. Finally, it is helpful to print a copy of the proposal and file it where it can be easily accessed once it is funded.

PROPOSAL REVIEW

After submission, proposals undergo a review process. As mentioned earlier, many agencies use a pool of reviewers who are selected for specific panels based on their background and experience. The depth and intensity of panel reviews varies by funding agency. In some instances, the panelists read and score the proposals independently, using panel review forms. Reviewers record comments, including strengths and weaknesses, and determine scores for each section, which are then totaled for an overall score. When the panel members convene, in person or by phone, each proposal is discussed in detail. This discussion may result in a panel member's raising or lowering his or her score as other panelists point out positive and negative aspects of the proposal. Final, post-discussion scores are then tallied along with any Competitive Preference points assigned by the panelists. Some agencies conduct interviews and site visits as part of the review process. The applicants who are visited have usually written a high-scoring proposal, and the interviews and/or visits are the second part of the review process.

Top-ranked proposals are usually recommended or approved for funding. When many proposals are approved, agencies often start funding with the top-ranked proposal and continue down the list of approved proposals until they have committed all of their funds. If there were a lot of high-quality submissions to a grant competition, it is possible to have a proposal that is approved and recommended but does not receive funding. Knowing that the proposal is a strong one, an applicant can use the reviewers' comments to strengthen and then resubmit the proposal.

GRANT MANAGEMENT

The RFP often lists a date by which applicants will be notified of funding. Funding agencies usually notify grant recipients (i.e., grantees) by phone or mail. Once that phone call or letter has arrived, it is time to begin the next part of the grant process: grant management.

Running a Project Efficiently

After cheering, jumping up and down, and running happily around the room, the first thing a grantee should do is pull out the copy of the proposal and review what was written, as the time between submission and notification may have been many months and memories may be a little cloudy. The information submitted in the grant management section will come in handy. Next, the director needs to spend some time notifying others about the grant, setting up the budget, and coordinating and supervising project activities. Each of these tasks is described in more detail below.

Notification   All of the people involved in the proposal development and submission process should be notified of a grant's success. It is a sad and unfortunately common situation for people who wrote letters of support to never hear the outcome of the submission or to hear from a different source that the grant *was* funded. A lack of communication can have a negative impact on a relationship that needs to be sustained throughout the duration of the grant. So, grantees need to make a special effort to inform everyone involved.

Teachers, other staff members, and parents should be informed of the grant award and the subsequent training and interventions that they will be involved in shortly. Other organizations that agreed to a partnership in the proposal need to be notified so that activities can be coordinated and any promised resources can be accessed. People who agreed to be advisory board members or consultants need to be informed so that they can plan their future time commitments accordingly. Key leadership people in the agency need information about the grant so that they can relay it to whatever public relations or media releases the agency uses.

Setting Up and Monitoring the Budget   Once an organization has funding, it is imperative to monitor expenditures closely. Some funding agencies award the grant funds and require no subsequent information on how the money was spent. Others require that budget statements be submitted in quarterly or annual reports. Computer programs such as Excel, Quicken, or QuickBooks are very useful in tracking expenditures. Spending reports are available at the click of a mouse, allowing a project director like Dr. Skye to find out whether funding is available for an extra parent training session or more books for the family lending library, or whether she has overspent her allocated funding on language assessments.

When grant expenditures are made, the budget in the proposal should be adhered to as closely as possible. Of course, unexpected expenses will always arise. Again, the source of the funding dictates how these expenses should be addressed. A project director should check with the funding agency for explicit guidelines related to budgets, including issues like when a director can and cannot move money from one budget category to another, or what to do if there is money left at the end of a fiscal year. This could occur if a budgeted staff position was not filled immediately.

It is important that the budget be monitored regularly to make sure that expenditures are accurate, appropriate, and within planned parameters. Any expenses associated with the grant should be entered into the spreadsheet or file. Mistakes can happen; expenses can be entered inaccurately, and charges may be omitted. A center or agency that has several ongoing grants may have a different set of books for each one. Careful supervision is necessary to ensure that expenses are charged to the correct account. For example, in addition to the language development and early literacy project, Dr. Skye also has a Healthy Child Grant aimed at improving childhood nutrition. While checking over her spreadsheets one day, she noticed that the expenses for a recent parent training on nutrition had been charged to her language and literacy project's budget. Her bookkeeper, who was not involved in the day-to-day operations of Nuestros Niños, had assumed that the parent training was on early literacy activities and had charged these expenses to the wrong project. Dr. Skye's careful financial administration helped her avoid a potential budgetary shortfall later in her language and literacy grant's cycle.

Coordinating and Supervising Project Activities   The various aspects of project management outlined in the proposal must now be implemented and monitored. The project goals and objectives must be accomplished, and activities must be completed on time and within budget. A review of certain items in the proposal—the goals, objectives, and activities table; time line; personnel loading chart; and evaluation plan—can help the project director set up an effective management system. It is wise to take a little time as soon as the grant is funded to implement procedures for project data collection and progress monitoring. Many of the tables used to outline the project in the original application can be modified and used to track the progress of the project.

The proposal also provided details on projected outcomes and the evaluation measures used to report and evaluate them. During the grant's implementation, the project director should follow the procedures for outcome monitoring as delineated in the evaluation plan and create systematic checks to ensure progress on goals and objectives. Data collection is very important, as progress toward the grant's outcomes must be reported to the funding agency.

Reporting

Once the grant project is underway, various reporting activities are required. Funding agencies may require reporting anywhere from quarterly to annually.

Progress Reports   Progress reports inform the funding agency of the grant recipient's progress toward achieving the goals, objectives, and outcomes listed in the proposal. Progress reports can vary in frequency. The funding agency will specify the timing and the information to be included in the report; typically, the report includes progress on grant goals and objectives, budgetary expenditures, outcome data, and explanations of any staffing or programmatic changes.

Some funding agencies use report forms with blank spaces or tables where project data must be recorded. Others provide an outline or suggested format, and the grantee summarizes the project data in a report format. Grantees can find out what the reporting requirements are by maintaining communication with the funding agency.

Some agencies conduct site visits as part of the progress monitoring process. A representative from the funding agency may spend some time observing in classrooms, meeting with teachers and parents, or discussing programmatic issues with the project director. In other cases, teams of trained volunteers, sometimes the same volunteers who reviewed the initial proposal, conduct the site visits.

Reports for Continuation Funding   Most grant awards are for multiple years; however, the grant funds are typically distributed one year at a time. Funding agencies want to ensure that the grant has progressed adequately during the previous 12 months before committing funds for an additional year. Reports for continuation funding provide the information funding agencies need to determine whether another year of funding is warranted. This information is similar to that required in quarterly reports (e.g., progress on goals, objectives, and outcomes; budgetary information) but summarizes the grant's progress for an entire year. If adequate progress has been achieved, then funding will continue.

Sometimes an annual report can serve the same function as a report for continuation funding. Other agencies require a short application for continuation funds. Because each agency has different policies on this process, grantees should check with the funding agency to ensure that the appropriate paperwork is submitted in a timely manner. A late report could result in a funding delay for the subsequent year.

Grant Management Checklist

The educational leader in charge of the grant should be sure to

❑   Notify people associated with the grant of the funding award

❑   Set up and monitor the budget

❑   Coordinate and supervise project activities

❑   Submit reports for project outcomes and continuation funding

---

CONCLUSIONS

This chapter has provided an overview of the grant application process at the federal, state, and local levels, from both public and private funding agencies. Service providers can get detailed information on proposal development and submission requirements from the various RFPs that are available to grant writers. Grant writing is not so much an exercise in creative writing as it is in following instructions. Once funded, the grant management process is fairly straightforward, if grantees follow the guidelines set forth in the funding agency's reporting requirements.

The quotation at the beginning of this chapter indicates that a lack of funding is less problematic than a deficiency of good ideas. Like Dr. Skye, most leaders in the ECSE field have great ideas for programmatic improvements. With grant funding, those ideas can become a reality that positively affects the lives of young children and their families.

REFERENCES

Hawaii Department of Education. (2006). *Application form to participate in the Reading First Program Grant: Cohort C grant application* [application form]. Retrieved April 9, 2008, from http://doe.k12.hi.us/readingfirst/index.htm

Illinois State Board of Education. (2005). *Request for proposals (RFP): Even Start family literacy— Breaking the cycle of intergenerational poverty and illiteracy* [application form]. Springfield, IL: Author.

Office of Special Education Programs. (2003). *Research and innovation to improve services and results for children with disabilities (CFDA 84.324)* [application form]. Washington, DC: Author.

Office of Special Education Programs. (2004). *Personnel preparation to improve services and results for children with disabilities (CFDA 84.325)* [application form]. Washington, DC: Author.

Tennessee Department of Education, Division of Teaching and Learning. (2005). *Tennessee Even Start request for funding proposal, 2005–2006* [application form]. Nashville, TN: Author.

U.S. Department of Education. (2007). *Fiscal year 2007 application for new early childhood educator professional development program grants (CFDA 84.349A)* [application form]. Washington, DC: Author. Retrieved April 9, 2008 from http://www.ed.gov/programs/ededucator/applicant.html

United Ways in Greater Kansas City. (2007). *2007 program proposal* [application form]. Kansas City, KS: Author. Retrieved April 9, 2008 from http://unitedwaygkc.org/index.php?option=com_content&task=blogcategory&id=166&Itemid=280

United Way of Metropolitan Nashville. (2007). *Request for proposals, Part B: 2008–2001 investment cycle* [application criteria and forms]. Nashville, TN: Author. Retrieved April 9, 2007 from http://www.unitedwaynashville.org/rfp2008

ADDITIONAL RESOURCES

Web Sites

http://www.grants.gov

This site provides information and access to over 900 federal grant programs and contains a database that can be searched by keyword (e.g., *early childhood, early reading*).

http://www.naeyc.org

The web site for the National Association for the Education of Young Children provides a wealth of information for child care providers, much of it helpful to the grant application process.

http://national.unitedway.org/

This is the national web site for the United Way. This site has links to other non-profit organizations that may be helpful, as well as a searchable database to help volunteers and grant seekers find the nearest local chapter.

http://www.nectac.org/chouse/adjhome.asp

The National Early Childhood Technical Assistance Center's (NECTAC) Gateway to Scientific Literature web site contains information on a variety of topics, including issues related to finance.

http://www.nectac.org/topics/finance/finance.asp

NECTAC's search engine for finance provides a listing of additional resources that cover issues such as state insurance legislation, IDEA finance regulations, funding sources, and workshops and meetings.

Other Helpful Materials

The Finance Project. (2003, January). *Blending and braiding funds to support early care and education initiatives* (Financing Strategy Series). Available from http://www.financeprojectinfo.org/Publications/FP%20 Blending%20Funds%201_24.pdf; however, use a search engine to find the entire PDF.

Whaley, K., Goode, S., & deFosset, S. (2005). *Selected resources on financing early childhood systems to support inclusive options for young children with disabilities—Minibibliography.* The National Early Childhood Technical Assistance Center. Available from http://www.nectac.org/~pdfs/pubs/financemini.pdf

Legal Issues in Establishing and Managing an Early Childhood Special Education Program

Andrew W. Nussbaum

I am still learning.
Michelangelo (favorite saying)

What If? Spencer Freeman is a teacher at La Puerta de los Niños, a preschool for children with and without disabilities. He teaches a class of fifteen 3-year-old children, several of whom have either Asperger syndrome or autism. One of the children runs away from Spencer or the instructional assistants at every opportunity. Spencer has been worrying lately about the issue of liability with regard to this child, Alonzo. What if Alonzo were to slip out of the classroom and escape the building? Spencer has scheduled a team meeting to address Alonzo's behavior and has asked the center director to attend to participate in developing an intervention plan. A behavior plan will be implemented following the meeting, but what if the worst-case scenario (i.e., Alonzo gets away from the teacher and assistants and heads for a building exit) occurs?

CHAPTER OVERVIEW

This chapter describes legal issues surrounding the establishment and management of early childhood special education (ECSE) programs. Discussed are several different business structures and issues of negligence and liability.

CHAPTER OBJECTIVES

After reviewing this chapter, the reader will

- Know the possible structures of businesses

- Understand the need for insurance

- Understand the legal issues and liabilities involved in owning a business

EARLY CHILDHOOD SPECIAL EDUCATION AS A SMALL BUSINESS

ECSE programs may be part of a public school system; part of a private school or other academic institution, such as a university or community college; or a private, stand-alone facility. If a program is established as part of a public school system, a private school, or another academic or educational institution or entity, the parent entity will presumably ensure that the legal requirements for operating the program are met. For example, the parent entity will make certain that the building has met zoning, health, and occupancy requirements; that the program is properly insured; that the teachers meet certification or registration requirements; and that all the policies and procedures that should be in place for program operation are, in fact, adopted and instituted.

A private program, however, is not part of a larger entity, and the owners of that program and facility will be responsible for dealing with a great number of legal issues. A stand-alone facility is a small (or perhaps not-so-small) business as well as an educational institution, and the same decisions that need to be made in opening any small business must be made in starting an ECSE program. It is essential that the individuals starting the business consult with an attorney and a financial specialist to ensure that those decisions are in the owners' best interests. There is a plethora of publications in bookstores and libraries about establishing and operating a small business. These publications can be very useful to individuals interested in starting an early childhood program. This chapter is not intended to replace the very important need to consult with an attorney, an accountant, a financial expert, and/or an insurance professional before starting any business.

TYPES OF BUSINESS STRUCTURES

One of the first decisions that must be made when establishing a center is what type of business vehicle would best suit the owners of the business. Although state laws, not federal laws, control business formations, there are typically four types of business structures:

- Sole proprietorship

- Corporation

- Partnership

- Limited liability company or partnership

The following is a very brief overview of these structures. The choice of business structure is a crucial one and should be made only after consultation with legal and financial professionals. There are many factors that should be weighed when considering which business structure to use, including but not limited to the cost to start up the business and the source(s) of start-up funds; the cost to maintain the business and the source(s) of those funds; the tax implications of the various business structures; the impact of government regulations; and the degree of personal risk the owner(s) are willing to take.

Sole Proprietorship

A sole proprietorship is the simplest form of a business. The business is owned solely by one person, and there are no officers, no board of directors, no partners, and no stock. Most states or local jurisdictions require registering the business name if the name of the business does not include the name of the owner. This type of structure is sometimes known as a DBA, or "doing business as." Thus, the business might be officially known as "Jane Smith, dba [doing business as] Main Street Early Childhood Center." A sole proprietorship is not a separate legal entity, as a corporation would be, and the business owner is personally liable for all of the business's liabilities, debts, contracts, and taxes. The income and the debts of the business are the personal income and debts of the owner. This would include, of course, any claims or lawsuits that might be made or filed against the business, in excess of any available insurance coverage. Perhaps the biggest disadvantage of a sole proprietorship is this personal liability of the owner. In addition, federal, state, and local tax liability rests solely with the business owner, who must include the business profits as part of his or her personal tax returns. The business is not taxed as a separate entity, but it would be part of the owner's individual tax return. The tax consequence of a sole proprietorship may be an advantage or a disadvantage, depending on the owner's tax status.

Some of the advantages of a sole proprietorship are that

- It is simple and uncomplicated; there is nothing needed to formally organize the business.

- It is inexpensive to form the business.

- It is easy to start the business, easy to close the business, and easy to sell the business to someone else.

- The owner has complete control over the business, with no one else to answer to.

- The owner can decide whether to keep the profits of the business or reinvest them in the enterprise.

Some disadvantages of a sole proprietorship are that

- The owner is *personally* liable for any debts, claims, liabilities, etc., that are not covered by insurance.

- Some may view the business as less prestigious or reliable than some other forms of business.

- It may be more difficult to obtain and secure financing.

- Because the business is owned by one individual, the business ends when the owner dies, unless it is passed on to another person or persons through estate planning.

Corporation

A corporation is a legal entity separate from its owners, who are called stockholders or shareholders. Corporations are perhaps the most complex business structures. Corporations are formed or chartered by state, not federal, laws. In addition to stockholders or shareholders, a corporation generally requires officers and directors, and legal documents must be prepared and filed with the state to formally establish a corporate entity. Unlike a sole proprietorship, the income and debts of a corporation belong to the corporate entity itself, not to the individual owners. Because a corporation is a separate legal entity, its stockholders or shareholders are generally insulated from liability—the debts of the business are that of the business entity and not of the owners. One disadvantage to this structure is that the earnings or profits of the business may ultimately be taxed twice—once to the corporation, and again to the owners if the profits are paid in the form of dividends. One advantage is that raising capital or financing might be easier with a corporation because the business can sell shares of stock or bonds to potential investors to raise additional capital.

There is a special type of corporation, called a sub-chapter S corporation, that allows the owners of the corporation to be taxed instead of the business entity. Some advantages of a corporation, whether sub-chapter S or not, are that

- Personal liability of the owners/stockholders is limited.

- It presents a favorable business image.

- Financing may be easier to obtain and secure.

- The business entity survives the death of the owner.

- Shares of some or all of the stock can be sold to others.

   Some disadvantages are that

- It requires expensive and intensive paperwork to start and maintain.

- It involves more governmental regulation than other business forms.

- It may involve double taxation.

Partnership

A partnership is an entity that has a minimum of two owners and as many owners as will be efficient. In some respects, a partnership is a sole proprietorship with more than one owner. Partnerships are easier to establish than corporations and are easier to maintain and operate. Although a written agreement is not legally necessary to establish a partnership, it is preferable, and it is very important to develop a partnership agreement that spells out in specific detail the partners' roles and responsibilities. As a matter of most state laws, partners have fiduciary responsibilities to each other and to the business; setting forth how the business will be operated, and what roles the partners will play in it, is an important part of any partnership agreement.

   Some advantages of a partnership are that

- It is fairly easy to organize and put into effect.

- The business relies on the skills, expertise, and efforts of more than one person.

- The risks and expenses of the business can be shared.

- There are few governmental requirements and little governmental control over partnerships.

   Some possible disadvantages are that

- Unlike shareholders in a corporation, the partners remain personally liable for business debts and liabilities.

- It requires more paperwork than a sole proprietorship (although less than a corporation).

Limited Liability Company or Partnership

The limited liability company (LLC) and the limited liability partnership (LLP) are relatively new vehicles that have been adopted in all states and the District of Columbia. Like a corporation, LLCs and LLPs are creatures of state laws, not federal laws. These structures attempt to blend the features of partnerships and corporations. Generally speaking, they are less formal than corporations, but they offer the liability protection typically found in corporations. Owners of LLCs and LLPs are known as members, as opposed to stockholders (corporations) or partners (partnerships). Business income or profits are treated in the same manner as in partnerships—it is taxed to the individual member, not to the entity itself. Like a corporation and unlike a partnership, the organizing documents must be filed with the state. In addition, each LLC or LLP must have an operating agreement that establishes the relationships between the members and the company.

Whichever structure is chosen, it is important that an attorney prepare the documents in such a way as to meet all of the requirements required by state law. In addition, consultation with an accountant is encouraged to ensure that tax consequences are considered and that accounting and bookkeeping issues are fully explored.

INSURANCE AND LAWSUITS

If an ECSE program is established as part of another entity, that entity will presumably ensure that the program has the necessary and required insurance coverage. The owners of a stand-alone program must make certain that the business is adequately insured. All owners of a business that employs people must carry workers' compensation insurance. The specific requirements vary from state to state. Workers' compensation is designed to provide insurance coverage, on a no-fault basis, to employees who sustain on-the-job injuries that result in medical expenses, lost wages, and perhaps permanent disability. "No-fault" means that unlike negligence cases, an employee who is injured does not need to prove that the injuries were the result of any negligence or misconduct on the part of the employer. Workers' compensation cases or claims are often resolved between the employee and the insurance carrier, with minimal involvement of the business itself.

Perhaps the biggest fear of any educator or business owner is the fear of lawsuits from nonemployees, and the administrators and owners of early child care centers face the same range of potential claims, liabilities, and lawsuits as any other business. The answer to the question "Can I be sued if [fill in the blank]?" is almost always yes, no matter what is stated in the blank. The more relevant questions, therefore, might be "What happens if I am sued?" and "How can I prevent or minimize lawsuits?"

Negligence

Before addressing those questions, it might be helpful to review the most common claim or lawsuit, which involves the legal concept of negligence. The common law tort of negligence generally applies to public programs as well as private programs, although public programs may have defenses not available to a private entity such as sovereign immunity or statutory limits of liability. Negligence has been described as a "tort involving fault when one's unintentional conduct breaches a duty of care and injures another person or persons" (Russo, 2006, p. 384).

Negligence is a legal principle that consists of the following elements: 1) a duty owed to the injured person by the person who caused the injury; 2) a breach of that duty, by the failure of the person causing the injury to exercise an appropriate standard of care; 3) an injury proximately caused by the negligence conduct; and 4) the occurrence of an actual injury.

Generally, school systems, private schools, and individual administrators and teachers have a duty to act in a reasonable and prudent manner to protect persons from injury and to assist injured individuals. This entails anticipating reasonably foreseeable injuries or risks to students and taking reasonable steps to try to protect them from harm (Russo, 2006). In most situations, this duty of care extends beyond students to include parents and other parties on the premises, such as visitors, vendors, and suppliers. (Because employees have the exclusive remedy provided by workers' compensation laws, they are barred from filing suits based on negligence.) Foreseeability is a very flexible legal concept that depends on a number of factors, including the student's age and physical and mental condition and the degree of danger involved in the situation at hand. The law does not require that schools and educators guarantee that no individual will be injured or harmed, but it does require that they take reasonable and prudent measures to prevent injury caused by situations of which they are actually aware, or those that could reasonably be anticipated. The concept of foreseeability is a fairly broad one, and courts have frequently found injuries to be foreseeable even in somewhat tenuous and far-reaching situations.

For example, a court case in New Jersey demonstrates the extent to which foreseeability applies. The injured party in the case of *Jerkins v. Anderson* (2007), was a 9-year-old student in third grade. The student, Joseph, typically was met after school by his father or older brother and walked home. Joseph failed to advise his father or brother that school was scheduled to be dismissed early on June 15, 2001, and when school was dismissed, Joseph left the building without his father or brother. At around 4:00 p.m., Joseph was struck by a car when he ran into the road. Joseph and his family sued not only the driver of the automobile that struck him but the school system as well, alleging that the school and its administrators had acted negligently by failing to advise parents of the early dismissal and by failing to have in place any policy that upon dismissal, students must be released into the care of an adult. They also alleged that it should have been foreseeable that an accident such as the one that befell Joseph could have resulted from the school's negligence. Although the school's published calendars showed June 15 to be a half day, Joseph's father said he was unaware of it. The trial-level judge found that there was no duty of reasonable care for Joseph's safety and the case was dismissed. The family then appealed, and the first-level appellate court (the Superior Court of New Jersey, Appellate Division) reversed the trial court. That appellate court discussed the issue of foreseeability and noted

> In our view, the risk of harm in this matter was foreseeable. At the time of the accident, Joseph was only nine years old. When Joseph was dismissed early from school, no adult or responsible older sibling was on hand to meet him. Several hours later, he was still without supervision. Joseph was playing with a friend on the side of the road...a few blocks from the school. Joseph ran into the street and was struck by a car. It is foreseeable that a nine-year old child who is dismissed early from school without proper supervision, could thereafter run into the path of a motor vehicle on a busy thoroughfare several blocks from the school. (*Jerkins v. Anderson*, 2006).

The case was then appealed to, and ultimately decided by, the Supreme Court of New Jersey (*Jerkins v. Anderson*, 2006), which noted

> First, with respect to the relationship of the parties, parents entrust their children to the care of schools, the Court quoted previous cases that noted: "[e]ducators have '[n]o greater obligation . . . than to protect the children in their charge from foreseeable dangers, whether those dangers arise from the careless acts or intentional transgressions of others.'". . . School officials have a general duty "to exercise reasonable supervisory care for the safety of students entrusted to them, and [are accountable] for injuries resulting from failure to discharge that duty."
>
> The relationship between the school, children, and parents encompasses the school's responsibility to ensure the safety of the children in its charge. It logically flows from that relationship, particularly the caretaker role the school assumes, that school officials must reasonably supervise children throughout the school day, including dismissal time. Because "parents . . . relinquish their supervisory role over their children to teachers and administrators during school hours," and thus "transfer to school officials the power to act as guardians of those young wards,". . . school officials have a duty to students until those officials have successfully monitored the students through dismissal.

The court then discussed the question of whether there was a duty of reasonable care to be imposed on the school. In determining whether or not a duty of care should be imposed, the court considers the relationship of the parties, the nature of the attendant risk, the opportunity and capacity of the defendants to exercise reasonable care, and the public interest in the proposed solution. After reviewing each of these elements, the court found that the school did have a duty to exercise reasonable care. The case was remanded to the trial court for a new trial, at which a jury could determine whether, given the facts in the case, the school had breached its duty to adequately supervise Joseph and whether the school's negligence was the proximate cause of his injuries.

This case is but one small example of the types of negligence cases that can be filed against educational institutions of any type. Negligence in a school or child care center can occur in numerous situations, and examples of potential lawsuits are virtually limitless: A child who is inadequately supervised sustains injury when she falls while playing in the playground; a parent volunteer slips and falls on a wet floor and sustains an injury; a vendor comes into the school and is injured when an improperly secured bookshelf falls on him; a student who is improperly supervised injures another student; an employee injures a child while imposing disciplinary measures. The list could go on and on.

In the litigious society that exists today in the United States, an injury—*any* injury—is likely to result in at least a claim being made that it was caused through *someone's* negligent conduct, and more often than not, injured persons and their attorneys look for the person or entity with an ability to pay. That is often the educational setting or institution in which the injury occurred.

When a Lawsuit Occurs

When a business is sued, what happens depends on one factor: whether the business has adequate insurance. If it does, the insurance company will provide an attorney to represent the business and insurance coverage to protect the business from a monetary judgment against it. If the insurance is inadequate, however, the injured person may well end up with a judgment that exceeds that insurance coverage, and the injured party will look to the business itself to pay the rest. In the case of a corporation, the liability may ultimately rest on the business; it may rest personally on the owners if the business is a sole proprietorship or partnership. Therefore, one of the first things a business running any type of an educational center must do is to obtain insurance coverage to an adequate level, which will depend on the community in which the business is based. What may be sufficient in a small town may be woefully inadequate in a large metropolitan area. It is imperative to consult with the professionals in the area of the business to determine the necessary amount of insurance.

Preventing Lawsuits

Foreseeability and preparation are the keys to preventing lawsuits. Anticipating all of the possible ways in which someone could be injured is impractical, but anticipating as many as possible will go a long way toward preventing injuries and thereby preventing lawsuits. Make certain that policies are in place—written, if possible—to address situations of known danger. For example, policies must be in place to address procedures for dropping off and picking up students; the supervision of students during all parts of their day; the hiring of teachers and other staff; the supervision and training of teachers and staff; procedures for cleaning and maintaining the premises; procedures for dealing with accidents and injuries on the premises; and procedures for notifying parents in cases of accidents and injuries. If you can imagine a scenario in which someone could be injured, then a policy addressing that situation should be developed and implemented. Obviously, having policies and procedures in place may not prevent all accidents and injuries on the premises, but it should help to minimize those occurrences. There are consultants and other individuals who deal with risk management and accident prevention, and they can be used as resources to assist in this area.

REFERENCES

Jerkins v. Anderson, 909 A.2d 725 (2006), affirmed as modified, in 922 A.2d 1279 (N.J. 2007).
Russo, C.J. (2006). *Reutter's the law of public education* (6th ed.). New York: Foundation Press.

RESOURCES

Edwards, P., Edwards, S., & Economy, P. (2005). *Home-based business for dummies.* New York: Wiley.
Kennedy, J. (2005). *The small business owner's manual.* Franklin Lakes, NJ: The Career Press.
Lesonsky, R. (2004). *Start your own business.* Irvine, CA: Entrepreneur Media.
Thaler, J. (2005). *The elements of small business.* Los Angeles: Silver Lake Publishing.
Warner, R. (2004). *How to run a thriving business.* Valencia, CA: Delta Printing Solutions.

Early Childhood Program Evaluation

Deborah T. Carran

*The only person who is educated is the
one who has learned how to learn and change.*
Carl Rogers

What If?   Denise Rosenberg is the director of the community's largest child care center, which serves children with and without disabilities. The center has been open for 3 years, and the teaching staff is anxious to try new methods for supporting early literacy. The approach teachers would like to pursue requires the purchase of new early literacy materials and professional development. Denise has decided to look for foundation funding to support this effort. One foundation is interested but has asked for a copy of the center's latest program evaluation report before a final funding decision is made. Although Denise is not sure what a program evaluation report should involve, she is willing to put one together. She knows that there are a lot of data collected by teachers. Where should she begin?

CHAPTER OVERVIEW

This chapter will help early childhood administrators plan and implement a program evaluation by presenting a framework and model for the design and reporting of a program evaluation. Programs are facing additional pressure with the new reporting requirements instituted by the Office of Special Education Programs (OSEP). As of February 2008, states have responded to early intervention monitoring priorities for IDEA Part C and Part B programs requiring states to report child level progress data for three outcome areas (social/emotional skills, use of knowledge and skills, and appropriate behaviors to meet their needs). Selected program elements will be presented along with a model for putting them together into a finished program evaluation report. The chapter explains each stage in this cycle and includes checklists and examples. A scenario of an early childhood special education (ECSE) program to be evaluated will be used throughout the narrative.

CHAPTER OBJECTIVES

After reviewing this chapter, the reader will

- Understand the process of program evaluation and the people involved in it

- Understand how to plan and conduct an evaluation

- Understand how to analyze an evaluation

- Know how to modify a program

- Understand how to monitor changes

HISTORY AND PURPOSE OF PROGRAM EVALUATION

Evaluation in human services programs has grown from an informative to a mandatory component of many programs. The Joint Committee on Standards for Educational Evaluation defined evaluation as a "systematic investigation of the worth or merit of an object" (e.g., a program, project, or instructional material) (1994, p. 205). Unfortunately, program personnel often view evaluation as an arduous, labor-intensive, and unjustly critical process. Accountability and mandatory reporting are the intimidating components of evaluation, and many people prepare to respond defensively to any comment or recommendation made by those evaluating them. Such may be the perception of evaluation, but it is not the intent of evaluation. All programs engage in some form of evaluation, for purposes ranging from accountability to determining program outcome to finding areas for improvement. Regardless of the purpose, evaluation aids in the search for a program's value. It is this scrutiny that should be the significant feature of evaluation: to look at programs objectively for purposes of constructive analysis.

Beginning in the 1960s with the war on poverty, the U.S. government started requiring evaluations of many funded programs. Program evaluation became required by law through the work of Senator Robert Kennedy and the Elementary and Secondary Education Act of 1965 (PL 89-10). This act made program evaluation the chain attached to funding; if a program was federally funded, it must be evaluated for purposes of accountability.

Each year competitive programs are awarded millions of dollars from private foundations, government agencies, and other funding sources in the form of grants and contracts. This is a great deal of money being invested in programs. Funding sources must know whether their money is being used wisely and whether a funded program is doing what it proposed to do. Furthermore, everyone involved in a program should also want to know that all their hard work does make a difference—that they are delivering quality services, that they are reaching their target audience, that their program has an impact. So program evaluation itself is not a bad thing. All programs should be evaluated, whether required or not, and a good program evaluation requires planning from the start of the program.

The program evaluation model used in this chapter is presented in Figure 15.1. This five-stage model is a simple one of initial preparatory stages that establish a framework of evaluation questions, goals, objectives, and indicators to get a new program evaluation launched. Later stages of the model are designed to sustain the evaluation through a cycle of modification and monitoring.

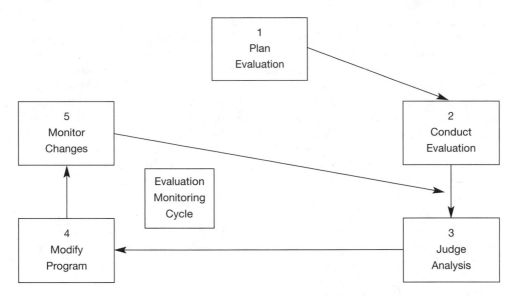

Figure 15.1.   Stages in program evaluation and the evaluation monitoring cycle.

What will become evident in the chapter is that many of the elements necessary for a high-quality evaluation are also elements of experimental research designs (Davidson, 2005; Mertens, 2005). Like a researcher, the evaluator needs to be concerned with design, validity, reliability, statistical analyses, and dissemination. The information presented in the following pages, however, should not be regarded as a plan to address the call for more rigorous and scientifically based research. Although many components of research and evaluation are similar, the use of intact groups and the lack of a comparison or control group prohibit identifying the information gained through evaluation as research. Evaluation is a way to begin to address accountability. It is methodologically limited. It is not experimental research. Done properly, however, using the model framework and guidelines presented, results will be both useful and essential. If you have your program's goals clearly in mind, the process of evaluation will be much easier.

THE EVALUATION PROCESS

There are many ways to evaluate a program. The evaluation process proposed here, as noted, is a five-step sequence (see Figure 15.1):

- Stage 1: Plan the evaluation

- Stage 2: Conduct the evaluation

- Stage 3: Judge the analysis

- Stage 4: Modify the program

- Stage 5: Monitor changes

Stage 1 is the critical first step that defines the evaluation framework with evaluation questions, goals, indicators, stakeholders, and a time line. Stage 2 is the action sequence; evaluators apply the plan and analyze the data. Stage 3 is the writing phase, during which the evaluators use the indicators to judge goals and objectives, answer the evaluation questions, and make recommendations for program changes (if warranted). Stage 4 is the planning phase for the following year's program modifications, based on the recommendations from the evaluation. In Stage 5 the modifications are evaluated to determine whether they had an impact. The evaluation is then judged, which starts the evaluation monitoring cycle again. The cycle is a feedback loop designed to facilitate ongoing program evaluation.

Ms. Juliet Enfin has been hired as the program director for a newly funded 3-year ECSE program called Talking Live Before Five. The purpose of this program is to facilitate communication skills in children with disabilities under the age of 5. A research-based intervention was selected that had been shown to be effective for improving language skills through an intense therapeutic milieu. As part of Ms. Enfin's responsibilities, she is responsible for the annual program evaluation. As this chapter presents the stages of evaluation, Ms. Enfin's progress through these same stages will help illustrate the evaluation process.

Stage 1: Plan the Evaluation

Planning and design may be *the* most important elements of the whole evaluation sequence. Results are wholly dependent on a comprehensive, valid, and reliable evaluation design. The framework for the evaluation may be viewed as a map of where you want the program to go and how you will know when it has arrived. The design elements that make up the evaluation framework are 1) the stakeholders; 2) the evaluation question(s); 3) the goal(s), objectives, and indicators; and 4) the time line. The following section describes each of these framework components and suggests ways to apply them in your evaluation.

Stakeholders   Anyone connected to your program in any way may be considered a stakeholder. Obvious stakeholders will be the individuals directly served by your program, such as children only, parents only, or families. Many programs appear to target children by providing enriched environments that focus on children's needs and progress, but these are actually family-centered approaches (Murphy, Lee, Turnbull, & Turnbull, 1995; Warfield, 1995) or full-service school models (Graue & Walsh, 1998) that target the entire family and community. To identify all stakeholders directly served by your program, answer the following questions:

- Whom was the program intended to serve?

- Describe any strict inclusion criteria for participants. (Fully explain the tool used to screen or select participants.)

- Was there an income level requirement?

- Was there a requirement that participants have a diagnostic label or minimal functional level?

- Was there a list of inclusion criteria and, for example, did participants have to have a minimum of three?

Consider other stakeholders, such as community members or kindergarten programs, who may not be directly served by the program but who have an interest in it or are affected by it. All stakeholders need to be identified so that all the accomplishments you want to come from the program can be identified. It will also be im-

Stakeholders	✏️
Children	❏
Parents	❏
Families	❏
Teachers	❏
Administration	❏
Other agency(ies) *Other schools (public/private), kindergarten*	❏
Community	❏

Figure 15.2.   Program stakeholders form.

portant to include all stakeholders when setting up the goals, objectives, and indicators of the evaluation. For example, Ms. Enfin may include as stakeholders parents of children attending the program, classroom educators, or the director from another local program. To help determine who the stakeholders are for the program, use the checklist shown in Figure 15.2, marking all that apply to the program.

The Evaluation Question   Perhaps the most critical step in planning for evaluation will be the evaluation question; what is it you want to know about your program? A good place to begin is often by defining the clients served by the program, determining whether the program was delivered properly, and asking whether the program had the intended outcomes. The evaluation question serves to focus or direct the evaluation. If you do not know where the program should be headed, will you know how to get there? Because the evaluation question serves as the guide for the entire evaluation plan, it should be written clearly and precisely. To begin composing the evaluation question for your program, answer the following items as succinctly as possible:

- Item 1: Who will be served? (Who are your clients? Who are the people you serve?)

- Item 2: What is the purpose of the program? (What is your program changing?)

- Item 3: What needs to be known about the program? (Which of the program areas shown in Figure 15.3—Descriptive, Integrity, and Outcome—need to be evaluated? Check all that apply.)

- Item 4: What is the time frame for the evaluation period?

Program areas to be evaluated		
Area:	(General Evaluation Question)	✏️
Descriptive:	(Did the program reach the target audience?)	❏
Integrity:	(Was the program properly delivered?)	❏
Outcome:	(Did the program make a difference?)	❏

Figure 15.3.   Checklist of program areas to be evaluated.

To compose her evaluation questions, Ms. Enfin answers these four items like this:

- Item 1: Who will be served? *Children from birth to age 5 with disabilities.*

- Item 2: What is the purpose of the program? *To improve language skills.*

- Item 3: What needs to be known about the program? *Did the program serve children who were deficient in language skills? Was the program delivered properly? Did children who attended the program improve their language skills?*

- Item 4: What is the time frame for the evaluation period? *One year or last year (this fiscal year)*

Once you have identified answers for these items, create evaluation questions for *each* of the program areas being evaluated (Descriptive, Integrity, and Outcome), as shown in Figure 15.3.

These are the basic elements necessary for an evaluation question. Putting this information together with a little bit of editing, an evaluation question is easily composed. Often, more than one program area (i.e., Item 3) needs to be evaluated. To use the simple evaluation template presented here, it is important to identify all of the program areas you wish to evaluate and write an evaluation question for *each* area. Having separate evaluation questions will serve to differentiate and guide the goals, objectives, and indicators under each evaluation question.

Using her answers to the four items, Ms. Enfin creates three evaluation questions—one for each program area:

- Descriptive: Did the program Talking Live Before Five, serving children from birth to age 5 with disabilities to improve their language skills, serve the target audience during the first year?

- Integrity: Was the program Talking Live Before Five properly delivered during the first year?

- Outcome: Did children improve their language skills while enrolled in the Talking Live Before Five program for one year?

Goals, Objectives, and Indicators   A goal is defined as "an end that one strives to achieve" (Joint Committee on Standards for Educational Evaluation, 1994, p. 206). Each evaluation question will have its own goal(s), defined by the evaluation question you have written. Figure 15.4 demonstrates the relationship among the evaluation framework components for the planning stage. Each component flows from the previous one.

With the evaluation questions completed, Ms. Enfin writes the goals, objectives, and indicators. She first writes the goals as actions, taking the wording for each goal directly from each respective research question. Because she has three evaluation questions, she writes three goals:

- Goal 1: The target audience for the program Talking Live Before Five will be enrolled in the program for the year.

- Goal 2: The program Talking Live Before Five will be delivered properly.

- Goal 3: The language skills of children with disabilities attending Talking Live Before Five for 6 months or more will improve.

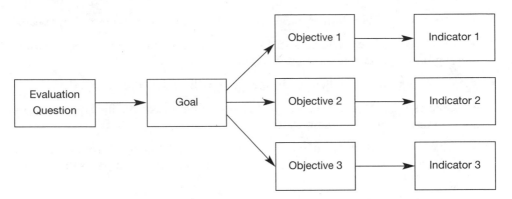

Figure 15.4.   Relationship of evaluation components in planning stage.

Objectives are used to further define goals. Objectives are defined as "something aimed at or striven for, more specified than a goal" (Joint Committee on Standards for Educational Evaluation, 1994, p. 206). Objectives tease out the specifics of goals. This is the part of the evaluation plan where the goals are defined in measurable terms; these measurable terms will determine whether the goal was met or not.

Indicators are measures, instruments, or performances that reflect an objective. For each of the objectives, an indicator is identified and paired with the objective.

Writing objectives and indicators is simple but often confusing. There are two key elements to keep in mind:

1.   Triangulation of data: Multiple objectives and indicators should be used for each goal.

2.   Direct linkage: Indicators should match objectives.

Triangulation of data is the measurement of something using more than one method, observer, or time point. If there is only one indicator for a goal and there is a problem with the measurement of the indicator, the goal cannot be supported. If you have a couple of backup indicators, however, there is the possibility of being able to support or partially support the goal. Triangulation of data, therefore, gives the program a little extra breathing room.

Direct linkage is a tool for creating objectives and indicators. Once you have determined the indicators for a goal, write the objectives that will match them. There should be a pairing of indicators and objectives.

Both triangulation and direct linkage are indicated in Figure 15.4. As is shown, determining goals, objectives, and indicators is a linear process: The evaluation questions determine the goals; the goals are better defined by multiple objectives; the objectives are directly linked to specific measurable indicators. Each goal has a minimum of three objectives, which are directly linked with matching indicators.

Following are the objectives that further elaborate Ms Enfin's program goals. Note that there are at least three objectives (i.e., triangulation) for each goal.

- Goal 1: The target audience for the program Talking Live Before Five will be enrolled in the program for the year.

    - Objective 1a: 90% of children referred and meeting eligibility requirements will enroll in the program.

- Objective 1b: There will be a 15% increase in program enrollment across years.

- Objective 1c: There will be a 15% increase in screening children for program eligibility and enrollment across years.

- Goal 2: The Talking Live Before Five program will be delivered properly.

  - Objective 2a: All children enrolled in the Talking Live Before Five program will have a 95% attendance rate.

  - Objective 2b: All children attending Talking Live Before Five program classes will receive the prescribed number of program delivery hours in the appropriate setting.

  - Objective 2c: All classroom specialists delivering the Talking Live Before Five program will complete the program training materials.

- Goal 3: The language skills of children with disabilities attending Talking Live Before Five for 6 months or more will improve.

  - Objective 3a: Children who attend the Talking Live Before Five program for 6 months or more will increase the number of spoken words and objects named.

  - Objective 3b: Children who attend the Talking Live Before Five program for 6 months or more will improve their communications skills in the classroom.

  - Objective 3c: Children who attend the Talking Live Before Five program for 6 months or more will improve their communications skills in other settings.

  - Objective 3d: Children who attend the Talking Live Before Five program for 6 months or more will have better communications skills in a school setting compared with children who do not attend the program.

For the novice evaluation planner, the process of determining goals, objectives, and indicators may seem convoluted; therefore, this section gives some hints for selecting indicators and writing objectives. To begin, examine each goal for the program areas you are evaluating (Descriptive, Integrity, and/or Outcome). One way to write objectives is to identify valid and reliable indicators, or assessments, that reflect the goal and answer the evaluation question. Keeping triangulation in mind, be sure to select more than one indicator for a goal. When you are satisfied with the indicators, write the objectives that directly link with the indicators. This may be a reverse method to write objectives, but it helps keep objectives clear. Table 15.1 shows the possible indicators that could be used to answer the questions in Ms. Enfin's evaluation.

Selecting indicators for program areas often requires creative thinking. The Descriptive area—serving the target audience—involves the number of eligible children screened and enrolled in the program during the year. These indicators mostly require reviews of records. As shown in Ms. Enfin's scenario, additional indicators are included to reflect program growth (number of children enrolled and screened in present year as compared with previous year). This is something funders like to see.

For the area of Integrity, select indicators from program records that reflect good program/intervention delivery. In Ms. Enfin's case, child attendance and documentation of staff training are good indicators that the children are present and that staff are trained in the intervention being delivered. Ms. Enfin also adds the Integrity indicator of children receiving the prescribed number of program delivery hours in the

Table 15.1.   Example of indicators that address Ms. Enfin's evaluation questions

Program area questions	Possible indicators
Descriptive: Did the program reach the target audience?	Number of enrollments Number of screenings
Integrity: Was the program properly delivered?	Attendance/children's classroom hours Training hours/staff attendance
Outcome: Did the program make a difference?	Standardized instruments Stakeholder interviews

appropriate setting to reflect that the children are receiving direct intervention, not just child care.

The Outcome program area is perhaps the easiest to write indicators for. You know what your program wants to change, and indicators of change have been reflected in the literature. A valid, reliable instrument is always a good choice for measuring outcomes; in addition, you might use interviews from stakeholders. An instrument will render a normed- or criterion-referenced score for analysis, but an interview with someone close to those served by the program has the benefit of providing a story behind the numbers. Anecdotal evidence can really draw attention to your program efforts and provide the evaluation with something others can relate to. Success stories can be put into print and given to funders.

With the indicators identified and quantified, write the objectives. As recommended earlier, there should be a direct link between each indicator and the corresponding objective. Note, for instance, Ms. Enfin's indicators:

- Indicator for Objective 1a: The number of referrals will be recorded and tracked for program eligibility and enrollment during the year.

- Indicator for Objective 1b: The number of children enrolled for 9 months or longer of this year will be compared with the number enrolled for 9 months or longer last year.

- Indicator for Objective 1c: The number of children screened for the program this year will be recorded and compared with the number of children screened last year.

- Indicator for Objective 2a: Each child's attendance will be recorded and calculated for the year.

- Indicator for Objective 2b: Each child's number of classroom hours will be recorded and calculated for the year.

- Indicator for Objective 2c: The attendance sheet from each program training module will be checked for classroom specialists' attendance.

- Indicator for Objective 3a: *Early Learning Accomplishment Profile/Learning Accomplishment Profile* (E-LAP/LAP-3) communication/language subscale will be scored at entry into program and at end of program year.

- Indicator for Objective 3b: Classroom teacher will be interviewed for report of child's level of communication at entry into program and at end of program year.

- Indicator for Objective 3c: Parent will be interviewed for report of child's level of communication at entry into program and at end of program year.

- Indicator for Objective 3d: Kindergarten teacher will be interviewed to determine child's level of communication at entry into kindergarten in comparison with children with similar disabilities.

Table 15.2 presents the entire framework for Ms. Enfin's evaluation, including goals, objectives, and indicators. It shows the relationships among these evaluation framework components.

Time Line   Having written the evaluation questions, goals, objectives, and indicators, all that remains to complete the evaluation design is to devise the time line. It is critical that the indicators be collected at the specific time necessary to answer the questions. Record reviews generally take place at the end of the year and require that the program's records have been kept properly and completely on every client (e.g., child). This is very important.

Testing to demonstrate growth in a target skill will generally be done using a pretest–posttest design. It is vital to allow as much time as possible between the pretest and posttest to ensure that the intervention has the best possible chance to be effective. The reason the objectives and indicators for Goal 3 (see Table 15.2) state that "children attending the program 6 months or more will..." is to ensure that only children who have been in the program for a minimum amount of time are included in the testing for the indicator. Children enrolled for shorter periods of time may not have a demonstrably positive outcome.

It is essential that the reporting data on children and staff (and others, as applicable), performance indicators, and academic and developmental indicators be selected and operationally defined before the program is started. Change across time will be much easier to demonstrate, and this change may then be attributed to the program. If the indicators or data collection methods change across years, there will be little to demonstrate program impact.

Based on the indicators and objective she has identified, Ms. Enfin determines when the data on each child for the indicators will be collected. She puts this information into a time line (see Figure 15.5). Figure 15.6 shows a checklist of all the instruments or forms that need to be collected or created for her program's evaluation.

Problems with Evaluations   A poorly planned and designed evaluation will be fraught with problems. It is often said of research designs, "garbage in, garbage out"; the same is true for an evaluation. It is therefore critical that the planning stage be thorough and done in concert with the program staff. Unfortunately, program evaluators do not usually know there are problems with the evaluation until the point of data analysis, or judging the analysis (Stage 3). By then it is often too late to salvage some of the goals.

Common problems encountered (Davidson, 2005; Weiss, 1998) when conducting an evaluation include

- Key components missing (e.g., not all stakeholders are involved, key program areas for evaluation are missing)

- Evaluation questions, goals, and/or objectives not aligned

- Indicators not reflective of goals and objectives

- Lack of training for key data recorders and collectors

- Interviewers biased

- Data collection time points missed

- Instrument problems (e.g., outdated forms, changes in instrumentation over the evaluation period, instrument not valid or not reliable)

- Personnel problems (e.g., turnover) resulting in lack of continuity

- Program (i.e., intervention) not delivered as prescribed

- Lack of support from program administration and lack of cooperation from program staff

- Program records not documented properly or updated in a timely manner

Problems encountered with evaluations should be noted in the report and addressed in the recommendations.

Stage 2: Conduct the Evaluation

Once the evaluation is planned and complete with stakeholders' input, framework, data collection sheets/instruments, and time line, you are ready to conduct the evaluation. This stage of evaluation involves collecting the data for the indicators at the designated times and analyzing the data in preparation for Stage 3: Judge the Analysis (writing the report).

Conducting the evaluation means following the time line for every child and making sure that the program's recordkeeping procedures are secure and being followed by all staff. Recordkeeping is a very critical aspect of evaluation and was noted previously as a common problem. Many indicators in an evaluation depend on program records. If these records are not properly maintained or frequently updated, the indicator will not be valid. This is especially critical if there is a gap in the records for a time period during a program year. Program staff must be reminded at regular intervals (e.g., at staff meetings, through e-mail) to be sure to continue recording data as they have been instructed. It may also be wise at this time to review the procedures that have been established for data recording.

During the evaluation period, the evaluator should periodically review files and procedures. Files for each client need to be reviewed to ensure data collection is complete to date (i.e., files contain the data collection sheets/instruments) and that procedures are being followed. In this way, any problems with data collection may be identified early and modifications or changes made in the procedure or instruments.

Once all of the data have been collected, the preparation for report writing begins. Analysis of quantitative and qualitative data should be done first. Results of interviews or focus groups need to be transcribed and quantitative data gathered for analysis.

If there is no assistance from a statistician or experienced evaluator, data analysis should consist mostly of descriptive or simple comparisons. Most people will be interested in your program and the results of the evaluation but may not want to wade through a highly technical section of statistics and analyses. Give readers

Table 15.2. Comprehensive framework for Ms. Enfin's evaluation

Program area	Evaluation question	Goal	Objective	Indicator
Descriptive	1. Did the program Talking Live Before Five, aimed at children with disabilities ages birth to 5 to improve their language skills, serve the target audience during the first year?	1. The target audience for the program Talking Live Before Five will be enrolled in the program for the year.	1a. 90% of children referred and meeting eligibility requirements will enroll in the program.	1a. The number of referrals will be recorded and tracked for program enrollment during the year.
			1b. There will be a 15% increase in program enrollment across years.	1b. The number of children enrolled for 9 months or longer of this year will be compared with number enrolled for 9 months or longer last year.
			1c. There will be a 15% increase in screening children for program enrollment across years.	1c. The number of children screened for the program this year will be recorded and compared with the number of children screened last year.
Integrity	2. Was the program Talking Live Before Five properly delivered during the first year?	2. The program Talking Live Before Five will be delivered properly.	2a. All children enrolled in Talking Live Before Five will have a 95% attendance rate.	2a. Each child's attendance will be recorded and the percent calculated for the year.
			2b. All children attending Talking Live Before Five program classes will receive the prescribed number of program hours in the appropriate setting.	2b. Each child's number of classroom hours will be recorded and the total calculated for the year.
			2c. All classroom specialists delivering the Talking Live Before Five program will complete the program training materials.	2c. Attendance sheet from each program training module will be checked for classroom specialists' attendance.

Outcome			
3. Will children with disabilities ages birth to 5 improve their language skills while enrolled in the Talking Live Before Five program for one year?	3. The language skills of children with disabilities attending Talking Live Before Five for 6 months or more will improve.	3a. Children who attend Talking Live Before Five for 6 months or more will improve their language skills.	3a. E-LAP/LAP communication subscale will be scored at entry into program and at end of program year.
		3b. Children who attend the Talking Live Before Five program for 6 months or more will improve their communications skills in the classroom.	3b. Classroom teacher will be interviewed for report of child's level of communication at entry into program and at end of program year.
		3c. Children who attend the Talking Live Before Five program for 6 months or more will improve their communications skills in other settings.	3c. Parent will be interviewed for report of child's level of communication at entry into program and at end of program year.
		3d. Children who attend the Talking Live Before Five program for 6 months or more will have better communications skills in a school setting compared with children who did not attend the program.	3d. Kindergarten teacher will be interviewed to determine child's level of communication at entry into kindergarten in comparison with children with similar disabilities.

Program	End of Year 1
entry data	data

Eligibility forms

Enrollment forms

Attendance forms (on going)

Attendance sheets for staff training (ongoing)

Stakeholder interviews

E-LAP/LAP pretesting

Stakeholder Interviews

E-LAP/LAP posttesting

Figure 15.5. Time line of data to collect for evaluation.

something that they understand, is easy to review, and is meaningful by presenting the descriptive results of your analysis in tables and figures. Table 15.3 presents some ideas for simple analyses and presentations of data. The Chapter 15 appendix illustrates Stages 1 and 2, showing several tables and charts made by Ms. Enfin to display her evaluation data and analyses.

Stage 3: Judge the Analysis

In Stage 3 you will pull together all of the data and determine whether or not the program has met the stated goals for the time period. It is then time to write the evaluation report and present the findings.

There are as many ways to write and present an evaluation report as there are ways of doing evaluations. The evaluation report should contain enough information for a reader to understand how the program operated, who the target audience was, what was evaluated, and what the findings showed. One way of covering all these points is to divide the evaluation report into several sections, including but not limited to 1) an executive summary; 2) a table summary of goals, objectives, and program highlights; 3) a method section; 4) results of evaluation questions; and 5) a sum-

Data collection preparation	✎
Eligibility forms	❑
Enrollment forms	❑
Attendance forms	❑
Attendance sheets for staff training	❑
Classroom teacher interview questions	❑
Parent interview questions	❑
Kindergarten teacher interview questions	❑
E-LAP instrument	❑
LAP instrument	❑

Figure 15.6. Data collection checklist.

Table 15.3.   Data elements and suggestions for analysis and presentation

Data element	Analysis/presentation recommendation
Client demographics	Frequencies of demographic characteristics for all clients
Program records	Frequencies of record variables during the time
	Table of aggregate demographic frequencies (all clients as a group)
	Bar chart of selected demographic frequencies (e.g., sex, ethnicity)
Program hours/attendance/ delivery during the year	Frequencies or mean and standard deviation for all clients
	Table of aggregate data or reported values in text of report
	Bar charts of total values at end of year or line graphs by month/ quarter
Standardized test results	Individual scores pre/post or mean and standard deviation pre/post for all clients
	Bar chart of each individual pre/post scores
	Bar chart of aggregate pre/post scores
	Statistical analysis: paired t-test of mean scores for all clients
Interviews/focus groups	Transcription included in appendices of evaluation report
	Key points summarized in table and incorporated into evaluation report

mary of findings and recommendations. Appendices should include a description of new instruments and executive summaries of each previous evaluation as well as complete transcripts of focus group or stakeholder interviews. Each of the suggested five main sections is discussed below.

Executive Summary   The executive summary is a synopsis of program results. It is generally only one page and is placed after the title page of the report. This summary is useful to administrators and other program planners. The executive summary may be presented as a narrative text, but it is often easier for reviewers to scan if items are bulleted. The executive summary may include

- A short paragraph describing the program
- The number of children/families served, hours of program provided, percent attendance of children, and number of staff employed by the program
- Program goals and whether they were met
- Recommendations

Table Summary of Goals, Objectives, and Program Highlights   The next section also allows readers to quickly review each of the program's goals and objectives and whether they were accomplished. For each objective, report whether it fell under one of four categories (having four categories of accomplishment provides some breathing room for objectives that were nearly met but fell short by a small measure):

1. Accomplished
2. Partially accomplished
3. Not accomplished
4. Not applicable

Table 15.4.   Table summary of goals and objectives

Goal and objectives	Status Year 1
1.0 The target audience for the program Talking Live Before Five will be enrolled in the program for the year.	Accomplished
Objective 1a: 90% of children referred and meeting eligibility requirements will enroll in the program.	Accomplished
Objective 1b: There will be a 15% increase in program enrollment across years.	Not applicable
Objective 1c: There will be a 15% increase in screening children for program eligibility and enrollment across years.	Not applicable

This information is presented in a table (as shown in Table 15.4 for the first goal and corresponding objectives of Ms. Enfin's evaluation).

Review each objective under each goal along with the results of the indicators and make a determination for each objective from these four categories. This is the critical point in judging the analysis. You must determine whether your program accomplished, partially accomplished, or did not accomplish the goals and objectives that were planned for the year. If the goals were written concisely and measurably, it is easy to judge if they were accomplished. In Table 15.4, for instance, it is easy to determine that 1a was accomplished. It is also understandable why 1b and 1c were marked Not Applicable, because this was the first year of the program and these two objectives are longitudinal in nature. They would be evaluated in the coming years but not during the start-up year.

More difficult to determine are the categories of Partially Accomplished and Not Accomplished. These might seem like arbitrary categories, but not necessarily. Objectives that were nearly met but narrowly missed the target should be designated as Partially Accomplished. A rule often followed is that objectives that missed the target by 25% or less should be designated as Partially Accomplished; those that missed by more than 25% should be designated Not Accomplished.

For example, Ms. Enfin's objective 2a, "All children enrolled in the Talking Live Before Five program will have a 95% attendance rate," was not exactly met. Figure 4 in the Chapter 15 appendix shows that the mean attendance rate for all eligible enrolled children was 93%. This is lower than the objective of 95%. The attendance rate of 93% was only 2% lower than the 95% objective, and any program director would consider 93% to be a wonderful attendance rate, so this objective should be reported as Partially Accomplished. This designation gives the program a sense of accomplishment and the funders a sense of wise investment. The label of Not Accomplished has ominous implications and can overshadow any feelings of success a program may have experienced; it should therefore be reserved for instances in which objectives truly were not close to being met.

After the summary table, present program highlights from the year in a bulleted list. These are things you would like others to know about the program that were perhaps not part of the evaluation.

- Was the program mentioned in a local newspaper?

- Did the program receive any awards?

- Did program staff present at a regional or national conference about the program?

- Were there some outstanding graduates of your program? Tell their story.

- Did program staff develop special materials that other programs might find helpful? Briefly describe the materials, their development, and their uses.

Also, list sources of external funding or programs that were introduced that did not cost the targeted granting agency additional money. It is important to show that the project's seed money is being used to reap more program benefits.

Method Section   To convey how the evaluation was conducted, describe the topics listed in Table 15.5. The method section should be presented in sufficient detail so that anyone reading the evaluation report will know how your program operated, whom it served, and how the evaluation was conducted. This allows readers to compare your program with other operating programs and helps them determine if your program could work in another setting. It is very important that this section is complete and sufficiently detailed.

Results of Evaluation Questions   The results section presents each evaluation question, goal, and relevant objectives. Describe each objective under each goal and question. For each objective, state the indicator and then present the results of each indicator. This is where the tables and graphs will be placed in the report. Along with the tables and graphs, write a short narrative to further describe what is being presented.

After all objectives for a question have been reported, conclude with a summary paragraph before continuing on to the next question. The summary paragraph should convey whether each objective was accomplished and whether the goal was met or not. This will answer the evaluation question. Do this for each evaluation question.

Summary Findings and Recommendations   This section follows the results section and reiterates what was concluded. This serves as the foundation for the recommendations you will make. A page or two will summarize to the reader the findings for each goal and evaluation question. Based on these findings, make your recommendations.

This is a critical section and one that the program, board, or steering committee will use for planning. The recommendations are the basis for Stage 4 in the evaluation sequence, Modify the Program. They need to be specific and, most of all, reason-

Table 15.5.   Suggested topics to include in methods section

Section of method	Include the following
Participants: children/families, staff	Participant overview Eligibility requirements Demographics of children/families Qualifications of staff
Program integrity	Location Description of program/intervention delivery Description of program management
Evaluation method	Evaluation questions, goals, objectives, and indicators Time line Analysis

able. There are many types of recommendations and several ways to formulate them. The following lists some suggestions for making program recommendations that could be implemented in the next stage.

- If the program is not reaching the target population, review what the program has been doing and suggest ways to enhance the outreach, other activities the program could sponsor, or agencies that could be partnered with to reach the population. Be wary of making recommendations that are not feasible or that will put an additional burden on program staff.

- How could program delivery be changed to make the program more effective? Think of some alternative program delivery methods or enhancements that could be made in the coming year.

- If any objectives were not accomplished or were partially accomplished, make a recommendation for what the program could do to accomplish those objectives.

- Are there organizational changes that could make the program more effective?

- Does a program component require more attention? Explain and be specific about changes that could be instituted.

- Recommend some ways to disseminate the evaluation report. Many foundation web sites publish their evaluation reports. Alternative print sources include professional publications, such as magazines or newsletters. Contact community organizations and request 15 minutes at their meeting to report on your program evaluation. This enables the local community to know more about the program and to know that your organization is accountable. One of the easiest and best ways to disseminate is through local, regional, or national professional meetings by way of paper or poster presentations.

Stage 4: Modify Program

Modifying the program is the planning and implementing stage for any or all of the recommendations that resulted from the evaluation. It is critical that modifications be planned with stakeholders and initiated before the next program year. An important part of this stage is the new evaluation plan that must be designed for the proposed changes.

Program modifications take many forms and may include any of the following:

- Change in outreach techniques

- Change in eligibility requirements for enrollment

- Change in delivery/implementation of the intervention

- Change in the intervention

- Restatement of objectives

- Different indicators selected for specific objectives

- New evaluation questions with new goals, objectives, and indicators

These are just a few of the ways in which a program can modify and change as a result of an evaluation report. There will be many others that will emerge for any particular program.

Modification plans must be discussed between program personnel and stakeholders. A good setting to begin this stage may be a meeting of the steering committee or board of directors or other meeting where stakeholders would normally be present. This type of setting is sufficiently structured to expect all stakeholders to share their views and contribute their ideas. The results of the evaluation report should be presented to the members and the meeting turned into a working forum to discuss how the program could be modified to implement the recommendations. The program director and representative staff must also be present at this meeting to serve as the experts in program/staff feasibility discussions. Notes should be recorded by a designated member and made into a summary list of program modifications that were discussed. Typing this information directly into a laptop computer greatly facilitates this process. Before the end of the meeting, the list should be typed and distributed to attendees for each attendee to prioritize the items on the list. Each stakeholder's prioritized list should then be shared with the group so that the group may reach a consensus on prioritized program modifications to be implemented during the coming year. The prioritized list should be formally approved.

The planning for the next program evaluation begins. Program evaluation is an ongoing process (Rossi & Freeman, 1993). When program modifications are made, it will be necessary to determine whether the modified program affects the objectives. A new evaluation plan will also need to be designed. Program goals and objectives may change, or they may stay the same. That depends on the changes that have been instituted. If new indicators are selected but the goals and objectives remain, only the indicator statements will change. If new evaluation questions are added, new goals, objectives, and indicators will need to be added to the evaluation plan. If existing goals and objectives are changed, this will need to be reflected in the evaluation plan.

It is critical that this stage be done before the start of the next program year. Waiting until mid-year to implement changes would endanger the program's integrity and pose a threat to internal validity.

This new evaluation plan must be as complete as the one designed for the previous year, which means specifying the elements that make up the evaluation framework: 1) the stakeholders; 2) the evaluation questions; 3) the goals, objectives, and indicators; and 4) the time line. The plan is not complete without all of these elements. With the modifications plan in place, it is time to monitor the changes by conducting the new evaluation plan.

Stage 5: Monitor Changes

There is no better way to monitor changes than through the use of a program evaluation. Program modifications are made in response to the previous evaluation, which may have prompted a different evaluation framework. This monitoring stage has now become necessary with the program modifications recommended either by the previous evaluation report or the steering committee in response to the report. A new evaluation will be used to monitor the changes by examining the impact of the changes on the evaluation questions, goals, and objectives. This stage of the evaluation is carried out just as Stage 2, Conduct Evaluation, was, except with the new evaluation plan and program modifications. The evaluation is carried out according to the time line; the data are collected and analyzed. Results are compiled and the analysis is judged (Stage 3). The results of the new evaluation report will be the monitoring tool.

As the program passes the first start-up year and moves into subsequent years with changes and new phases, your evaluation will change as well. The previous two sections of this chapter, Stage 3 and Stage 4, have provided a model for modifying your program and then monitoring the changes that were made. These are the first steps leading to the Evaluation Monitoring Cycle. The Evaluation Monitoring Cycle depicted in Figure 15.1 consists of Stages 4, 5, and 3, in that order. Stage 4, Modify Program, leads to Stage 5, Monitor Changes, in which data are analyzed; these data are then judged during Stage 3, Judge Analysis. Based on the judgment of the analysis (Stage 3), the program may again be modified (Stage 4) and monitored (Stage 5), which will produce an evaluation report that must be judged (Stage 3). The cycle is ongoing. Changes are made, changes are evaluated, and changes are judged.

This leads us back to the question of why evaluation is important. The answer? To continue to do the best job possible in serving the needs of the target population.

ETHICS FOR EVALUATION

The ethical considerations for evaluation are the same as those for research. A few important topics in the ethics of evaluation need to be highlighted and discussed.

- Participant confidentiality

- Informed consent

- Evaluator integrity

All of these topics are equally important when conducting an evaluation. Participant confidentiality ensures that no individually identifiable information will be released in the evaluation report. Notice in Ms. Enfin's scenario that individual participants are identified by letters (see Tables 1 and 2 in the Chapter 15 appendix), not by names or sensitive numbers (e.g., Social Security numbers). There must be no possible way that someone from outside the program can look at your report and determine if a specific individual was enrolled.

Participants must be informed when they enroll in the program that information will be collected during the year for purposes of evaluation reporting. They have a right to know that their data may end up in the public domain. With this knowledge, participants must have the opportunity to decline to have their data included in the evaluation report released to public domain without reprisal. Parents, families, or other participants should sign informed consent forms at the time of program enrollment.

Above everything else, those conducting and judging the evaluation must be candid and honest. It was stated at the beginning of this chapter that evaluation is intended to look at programs objectively for purposes of constructive analysis. If program reporters or data collectors are not honest, the results will not be either. Integrity is not always easy for evaluators to achieve. There is a lot invested in a program and a lot riding on the results of the evaluation report. An honest but critical evaluation may terminate or reduce program funding; a less-than-honest glowing evaluation of the same program may lead to continued funding for a program that may not be serving the needs of the population. There are two sides in evaluation, the program and funders, and the evaluator is caught in the middle. For this reason the evaluator must be above reproach. Do your job while being mindful of these ethical issues, and never lose sight of the needs of the population you are serving.

SUMMARY

The keys to a successful evaluation are good evaluation questions, useful outcomes, and scheduling. The guidelines in this chapter will help Denise Rosenberg to plan for conducting and reporting a program evaluation. Using the framework and tools provided, Denise will be able to tailor the program evaluation of the early literacy program her child care center provides and obtain results that are relevant to her and potential funders.

REFERENCES

Davidson, E.J. (2005). *Evaluation methodology basics: The nuts and bolts of sound evaluation.* Thousand Oaks, CA: Sage.

Glover, E.M., Preminger, J.L., & Sanford, A.R. (2002). *Early Learning Accomplishment Profile, Third Edition.* Lewisville, NC: Kaplan Early Learning.

Hardin, B.J., & Peisner-Feinberg, E.S. (2004). *Learning Accomplishment Profile, Third Edition.* Lewisville, NC: Kaplan Early Learning.

Elementary and Secondary Education Act of 1965, PL 89-10, 20 U.S.C. §§ 241 *et seq.*

Graue, & Walsh, (1998). *Studying children in context: Theories, methods, ethics.* Thousand Oaks, CA: Sage.

Joint Committee on Standards for Educational Evaluation. (1994). *The program evaluation standards: How to assess evaluations of educational programs* (2nd ed.). Thousand Oaks, CA: Sage.

Mertens, D.M. (2005). *Research and evaluation in education and psychology: Integrating diversity with quantitative, qualitative, and mixed methods* (2nd ed.). Thousand Oaks, CA: Sage.

Murphy, D.L., Lee, I.M., Turnbull, A.P., & Turnbull, H.R. (1995). The Family-Centered Program Rating Scale: An instrument for program evaluation and change. *Journal of Early Intervention, 19,* 24–42.

Rossi, P.H., & Freeman, H.E. (1993). *Evaluation: A systematic approach* (5th ed.). Thousand Oaks, CA: Sage.

Warfield, M.E. (1995). The cost-effectiveness of home visiting versus group services in early intervention. *Journal of Early Intervention, 19,* 130–148.

Weiss, C.H. (1998). *Evaluation* (2nd ed.). Upper Saddle River, NJ: Prentice Hall.

Chapter 15 Appendix

Program Evaluation Scenario

Ms. Juliet Enfin has been hired as the program director for a newly funded 3-year early childhood special education program called Talking Live Before Five. The purpose of this program is to facilitate communication skills for children with disabilities who are younger than age 5. A research-based intervention was selected which had been shown to be effective for improving language skills through an intense therapeutic milieu. As part of Ms. Enfin's responsibilities, she is responsible for the annual program evaluation.

Using this basic description of program activities, a program evaluation will be planned for the coming year. This process will take the reader through decisions necessary at each of the stages in the evaluation process.

STAGE 1: PLANNING THE EVALUATION

Stakeholders

To help determine who the stakeholders are for the program, use the checklist in Figure 15.2, marking all that apply to the program.

Evaluation Questions (EQ)

To compose an evaluation question, Ms. Enfin answered the four items:

- Item 1: Who will be served? *Children with disabilities ages birth to 5 years*

- Item 2: What is the purpose of the program? *Improve language skills*

- Item 3: What needs to be known about the program?

  Determine which of the following program areas will be evaluated (see Figure 15.3). Ms Enfin evaluated all three program areas:

  ✓ Descriptive: *Did the program Talking Live Before Five serve the target audience?*

  ✓ Integrity: *Was the program Talking Live Before Five properly delivered?*

  ✓ Outcome: *Did the program Talking Live Before Five make a difference?*

- Item 4: What is the timeframe for the evaluation period? *One year or last year (fiscal year)*

With the four items answered, the three evaluation questions (one question for each of the three program areas: Descriptive, Integrity, and Efficacy) may be written. Using the answers to each of the four item questions, Ms. Enfin created three evaluation questions for each of the program areas.

Evaluation Question (EQ) 1. Descriptive: Did the program Talking Live Before Five, serving children with disabilities ages birth to 5 years to improve their language skills, serve the target audience during the first year?

EQ 2. Integrity: Was the program Talking Live Before Five that serves children with disabilities ages birth to 5 years to improve their language skills, properly delivered during the first year?

EQ 3. Outcome: Will children with disabilities ages birth to 5 years improve their language skills while enrolled in the Talking Live Before Five program for 1 year?

Goals, Objectives, Indicators

Goal: An end that one strives to achieve

With the evaluation questions completed, Ms Enfin writes the *goals*, *objectives*, and *indicators*. Goals are written first as actions and come directly from the Evaluation Questions:

- Program Goal 1: The target audience for the program Talking Live Before Five will be enrolled in the program for the year.

- Program Goal 2: The program Talking Live Before Five will be delivered properly.

- Program Goal 3: Improve the language skills of children with disabilities attending for 6 months or more in the Talking Live Before Five program.

Objectives are things aimed at or striven for; they are more specific than a goal. Each of the program goals is further elaborated with at least three objectives (i.e., triangulation) for each goal.

For Goal 1 (the target audience for the program Talking Live Before Five will be enrolled in the program for the year), the following objectives were named:

- Objective 1a: 90% of children referred and meeting eligibility requirements will enroll in the program

- Objective 1b: There will be a 15% increase in program enrollment across years.

- Objective 1c: There will be a 15% increase in screening children for program eligibility and enrollment across years.

For Goal 2 (the program Talking Live Before Five will be delivered properly), the following objectives were named:

- Objective 2a: All children enrolled in the Talking Live Before Five program will have a 95% attendance rate.

- Objective 2b: All children attending Talking Live Before Five program classes will receive the prescribed number of program delivery hours in the appropriate setting.

- Objective 2c: All classroom specialists delivering the Talking Live Before Five program will complete the program training materials.

For Goal 3 (Improve the language skills of children with disabilities attending for six months or more in the Talking Live Before Five program), the following objectives were named:

- Objective 3a: Children who attend the Talking Live Before Five program for 6 months or more, will improve their language skills.

- Objective 3b: Children who attend the Talking Live Before Five program for 6 months or more, will improve their communications skills in the classroom.

- Objective 3c: Children who attend the Talking Live Before Five program for 6 months or more, will improve their communications skills in other settings.

- Objective 3d: Children who attend the Talking Live Before Five program for 6 months or more, will have better communications skills in a school setting compared to children who did not attend the program.

Indicators are measures, instruments, or performances that reflect an objective. For each of the objectives, identify an indicator and pair the objective with the indicator (direct linkage).

- Indicator Objective 1a: The number of referrals will be recorded and tracked for program eligibility and enrollment during the year.

- Indicator Objective 1b: The number of children enrolled for 9 months or longer of this year will be compared to number enrolled for 9 months or longer last year.

- Indicator Objective 1c: The number of children screened for the program this year will be recorded and compared to the number of children screened last year.

- Indicator Objective 2a: Each child's attendance recorded and calculated for the year.

- Indicator Objective 2b: Each child's number of classroom hours recorded and calculated for the year.

- Indicator Objective 2c: The attendance sheet from each program training module obtained and specialists identified for attendance.

- Indicator Objective 3a: E-LAP/LAP communication subscale scores at entry into program and at end of program year.

- Indicator Objective 3b: Classroom teacher interview for report of child's level of communication at entry into program and at end of program year.

- Indicator Objective 3c: Parent interview for report of child's level of communication at entry into program and at end of program year.

- Indicator Objective 3d: Kindergarten teacher interview to determine child's level of communication at entry into kindergarten in comparison to children with similar disabilities.

The complete Evaluation Questions, goals, objectives, and indicators written have been compiled in Table 15.3.

Timeline

Based on the indicators and objectives, Ms Enfin determines exactly when the information on each child for the indicators will be collected (see Figure 15.5). Ms. Enfin makes a list of the necessary data collection sheets/instruments for the evaluation (see Figure 15.6).

STAGE 2: CONDUCT THE EVALUATION

At this stage of the evaluation sequence, Ms. Enfin starts by making a checklist of when evaluation data will be collected from the program during the year. Figure 1 is a checklist of quarterly evaluation reviews.

Data Analysis for This Project

Once data have been collected and compiled, Ms. Enfin begins data analysis and reporting. She has chosen to present descriptive statistics of eligible enrolled children in a table (see Table 1) and then uses Excel to create two charts (see Figures 2 and 3).

Ms. Enfin then looks at some of the data indicators for program integrity using Excel to create a line graph (see Figure 4). Ms. Enfin presents the outcome data indicators of the E-LAP/LAP-3 using a table and Excel to create individual graphs for each child (see Table 2). Ms. Enfin created individual pre/post bar charts for each child. Two examples are presented in Figures 5 and 6. Ms. Enfin then prepares the qualitative data in a summary format for the report (see Table 3).

STAGES 3–5

After compiling all the data from the indicators, Ms. Enfin is ready to judge the analysis and determine whether the objectives of her evaluation have been Accomplished, Partially Accomplished, or Not Accomplished, as in Table 15.4.

Data	Q1	Q2	Q3	Q4
Record /document number of screenings	❏	❏	❏	❏
Record /document number of enrollments	❏	❏	❏	❏
Eligibility forms	❏	❏	❏	❏
Enrollment forms	❏	❏	❏	❏
Child attendance forms	❏	❏	❏	❏
Attendance sign-in forms for staff training	❏	❏	❏	❏
Classroom teacher interview	❏			❏
Parent interview	❏			❏
Kindergarten teacher interview*				
E-LAP findings	❏			❏
LAP findings	❏			❏

*Interview K teachers during Fall of Year 2 of program

Figure 1. Checklist of quarterly evaluation reviews.

Table 1. Demographic characteristics of eligible enrolled children in program, Year 1

Child	Child sex	Ethnicity	Class	Child age
A	Male	Multicultural	PreK	3.92
B	Male	White	PreK	3.53
C	Male	White	3 years old	3.12
D	Male	Hispanic	3 years old	4.15
E	Male	Multicultural	PreK	4.39
F	Male	Hispanic	3 years old	3.23
G	Male	Multicultural	3 years old	4.20
H	Male	White	3 years old	3.83
I	Female	African American	PreK	4.21
J	Female	White	PreK	4.34
K	Male	White	3 years old	3.04
L	Male	White	PreK	4.24
M	Female	White	PreK	3.77
N	Male	White	PreK	4.25
O	Male	Hispanic	3 years old	3.18
P	Female	White	3 years old	4.19
Q	Female	White	3 years old	3.68
R	Male	Hispanic	PreK	4.10
S	Female	Multicultural	PreK	4.05
T	Female	N/A	PreK	N/A.

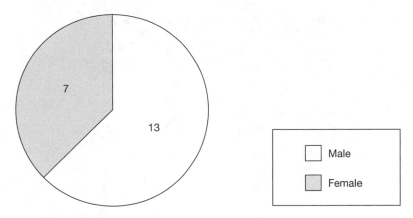

Figure 2.   Gender distribution of eligible enrolled children.

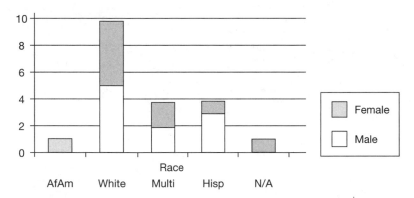

Figure 3.   Gender distribution of eligible enrolled children by race.

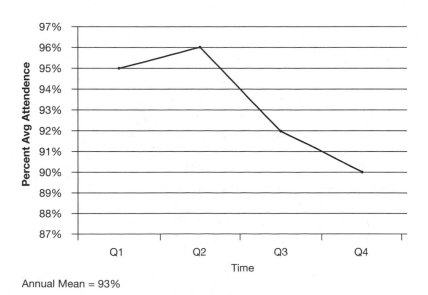

Annual Mean = 93%

Figure 4.   Average attendance of eligible enrolled children during Year 1.

Table 2.   E-LAP and LAP composite scores of
eligible enrolled children in program, Year 1

Child	Instrument	Pretest	Posttest
A	LAP	32	34
B	LAP	18	26
C	E-LAP	33	43
D	E-LAP	23	19
E	LAP	21	22
F	E-LAP	16	31
G	E-LAP	33	34
H	E-LAP	9	18
I	LAP	22	34
J	LAP	19	23
K	E-LAP	28	22
L	LAP	30	39
M	LAP	19	26
N	LAP	16	18
O	E-LAP	26	25
P	E-LAP	27	32
Q	E-LAP	22	29
R	LAP	33	35
S	LAP	10	15
T	LAP	13	39

Student T, LAP Findings

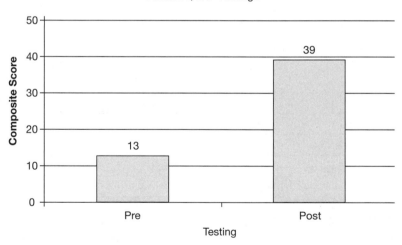

Figure 5.   Pre- and posttest LAP-3 findings for Student T.

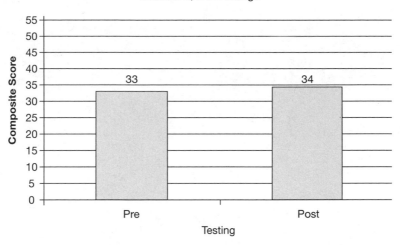

Figure 6. Pre- and posttest E-LAP findings for Student G.

Table 3. Summary of parent focus group responses

Focus group questions	Summary comments
Parents' support for children's learning in the home environment	
1. Materials in home? Selected?	Lots. Every day
2. TV/video viewing? Discuss program?	About 2 hours/day. Some videos. Discuss programs
3. Daily "teachable moments"? Important?	Yes. Everyday activities
4. Learning experiences for family? Activities?	Time to be together. Sports, picnics, beach
5. How does the program support child's learning environment?	Little things. Social skills, different cultures
Parents' roles in interactive literacy activities	
1. Talking and language development? Strategies?	Kids talking more since being in program. Now taking the time to talk and listen
2. Reading and language development? Strategies?	Very important. They love it. Many different strategies taught
3. Print understanding activities?	Everyday activities
4. Parent's role in child's literacy development?	Knew. Now really made it come to life
Taking on the parenting role	
1. Set limits/rules on child's choices?	Limits on TV. Does not always work
2. Manage problems, protect from stress?	Yes. Child behavior problems
3. Safe and healthy environment for child?	Yes
4. Learn from program to be a better parent?	Learn developmental stages, anticipate behaviors
Program	
1. Like about program?	Interactions. Child progress. My involvement
2. Hardest part of program?	Time to do everything. Staff are wonderful
3. What would you like to learn?	Child care provider
4. Worthwhile to be in program?	Yes

Providing for the Safety and Security Needs of Young Students

Sheldon Greenberg

*Any intelligent fool can make things bigger,
more complex, and more violent. It takes a touch of
genius—and a lot of courage—to move in the opposite direction.*
E.F. Schumacher

What If? At a large private preschool serving children with and without disabilities, the director, Ellen Rosenberg, is working on the professional development schedule for the coming year. She has decided to address the issue of safety at the first faculty meeting and has invited members of the board of directors to join the faculty for this important meeting. Ellen would like some ideas for specific agenda items for the meeting. She is in the process of reading several books and journal articles about school safety and is hoping that the information she finds there will help her develop agenda items on schools and the safety of young children.

CHAPTER OVERVIEW

In the years since the twin towers of the World Trade Center in New York City were destroyed by terrorist attacks, many people in education have wondered if there are steps that can and should be taken to prevent violence of any variety in their educational settings. This chapter provides a series of considerations, cautions, and recommendations to guide school administrators, teachers, law enforcement officers, parents, and others in sustaining a safe school, reducing fear, and implementing a successful school resource officer (SRO) program.

The chapter begins with a discussion about keeping perspective when considering safety. It is followed by a discussion of scope and cost associated with safety issues, principles for ensuring a safe environment for learning and interaction, and common mistakes made in regard to SRO programs. The chapter ends with a discussion on how to assess safety needs and establish responsible expectations.

CHAPTER OBJECTIVES

After reviewing this chapter, the reader will

- Know the history of school safety and violence

- Understand how to keep perspective on safety issues

- Know and understand the 10 principles for ensuring a genuine, comfortable, secure environment for learning and interaction

- Know the common mistakes that are made in SRO programs

- Understand how to assess the need and establish responsible expectations for safety

- Understand how to include students with disabilities in a safety assessment

SCHOOL VIOLENCE AND ITS EFFECTS

Statistics on school safety abound, compiled by federal and state government agencies, professional associations, researchers, and vendors. As with most statistics, they are interpreted to support the story of the storyteller. This is particularly significant in reports on the safety of children in school, with some vendors and associations spinning horror stories to support funding, and school administrations, police, and political leaders downplaying the data to reduce fear and put students and parents at ease. The data shown here (Bureau of Justice Statistics, 2007) were compiled by the U.S. Department of Justice based on agency reports and surveys:

- During 2005, older students (ages 15–18) were less likely than younger students (ages 12–14) to be victims of crime at school, but older students were more likely than younger students to be victims of crime away from school.

- From July 1, 2005, through June 30, 2006, there were 35 school-associated violent deaths in elementary and secondary schools in the United States.

- Young people are more than 50 times more likely to be murdered away from school than at school.

- The rates for serious violent victimization (rape, sexual assault, robbery, and aggravated assault) were lower at school than away from school for every Department of Justice survey year from 1992 through 2005.

- In 2005 nearly all (99%) students ages 12–18 observed at least one security measure at school. The percentage of students who observed the use of school security cameras increased from 39% in 2001 to 58% in 2005.

- During 2005 an estimated 90% of students reported observing school staff or other adult supervision in the hallway, and 68% of students reported the presence of security guards and/or police officers at their school.

On April 20, 1999, the assault on Columbine High School took place, in which two student gunmen killed 12 students and a teacher before committing suicide. This incident sparked national dialogue on school safety, initiated large federal and state expenditures on school security measures, led to rapid assignment of thousands of police officers to schools, and dramatically changed the perception of school environments from that of safe havens and sanctuaries for children to places of fear and uncertainty.

No group requires or deserves attention to safety more than young children. School administrators, teachers, police officers, parents, and others share responsibility for sustaining safe schools and creating an environment in which children can learn and interact without fear or harm. Efforts to provide such environments, however, have been inhibited by myth, misperception, and hyperbole about school crime. School safety issues abound, whether the threat is real or perceived. Whether driven by media coverage, political rhetoric, or actual offenses, school crime has become a social problem (Hanke, 1996). From maintaining safe classrooms to responding to violent acts that occur on school property, education and public safety officials face challenges and responsibilities that, a decade ago, received limited attention. Managing the behavior of students, once the primary responsibility of teachers and a task confined mainly to the classroom, has emerged into a costly and consuming effort by administrators, police officers, and others to prevent and react to myriad incidents. Incidents once considered minor and addressed as misbehavior now evoke police intervention and are often classified as crimes.

Because of this, a burgeoning school safety industry has emerged in the United States. Billions of dollars of federal, state, and local funds have been channeled to schools, police and sheriffs departments, researchers, and private consultants and vendors. As with any enterprise that affects jobs and funding, the school safety industry must perpetuate itself. Perceptions of schools as unsafe environments must be perpetuated if SROs, consultants, and administrators who oversee school safety grants are to keep their jobs. Bringing order and stability to this newly formed industry is critical if its intended goal of creating a safe learning environment is to be achieved and sustained.

The haste to respond to portrayed crime and violence in the nation's schools has resulted in new partnerships, enhanced curricula, and a perception of increased safety. To a larger degree, however, the school safety movement has led to disjointed and haphazard efforts, ineffective show-and-tell programs, and fierce competition for funding among schools and law enforcement agencies. The motives behind implementing some school safety efforts are, at best, questionable (Lewis, 2003). Ineffective reporting on school crimes by the media, overresponse by police, and calls for more school safety programs by political officials for the purpose of garnering votes are rarely questioned (Menifield, Rose, Homa, & Cunningham, 2001).

The bombardment of information on school crime and safety causes students in the nation's safest schools to believe that they are vulnerable. Among the victims of this bombardment are the nation's youngest and most vulnerable children, particularly those in special education. Already facing myriad challenges and feelings of apprehension, the sense of order, peace, security, and sanctuary important to young students in special education is diminished by the fear, confusion, and disruption caused by overattention to shootings, massacres, aggravated assaults, and other crimes.

KEEPING PERSPECTIVE

A positive learning climate in a school for young children is a composite of many things. It is an attitude that respects children. It is a place where children receive guidance and encouragement from the responsible adults around them. It is an environment where children can experiment and try out new ideas with-

out fear of failure. It is an atmosphere that builds children's self-confidence so
they dare to take risks. It is an environment that nurtures a love of learning.
    Carol B. Hillman, *Creating a Learning Climate for the Early Childhood Years*
(1989, p. 35)

There has been "an unprecedented intensification of school militarization and student criminalization"(Lewis, 2003). For the sake of security, technology, psychological profiles, and other interventions have been deployed. Schools have become
places of sophisticated surveillance and other security measures. They have become a testing ground for constitutional challenges to infringement on students'
right to privacy. They have become the workplace of police officers pulled from
other areas of service, such as patrol and criminal investigations. The logic that
drives the implementation of these safety measures may not be ideologically neutral (Lewis, 2003).

    Certainly schools exist that have a record of repeated serious crimes and related
problems. Significant intervention is needed in those schools in which genuine
crime, threat, fear, and disruption thwart people's safety and opportunities to teach
and learn. Such schools, however, are few in number, considering the 95,600 public
elementary and high schools and 29,200 private schools providing K–12 education in
the United States (U.S. Census Bureau, 2006). Statistically, schools remain among the
safest places for young children (National Education Association, 2007a). A child is
two times more likely to be the victim of a violent crime at or near home than at a
school. He or she is four times more likely to be the victim of a violent crime on the
street or in a commercial establishment, park, or parking lot than at school. Only 10%
of the nation's schools report any instance of serious crime, and 43% report no crime
at all. More than 99% of school-age children's deaths occur away from school. The
vast majority of crimes in school are property offenses; most are minor and go un-
reported. The majority of crimes against persons that occur in schools involve
threats, with no physical contact. Approximately 5% of these crimes result in physical contact in which injury is reported. The vast majority of these injuries are minor
(Hanke, 1996).

    Crime rates for students have declined. From 1992 to 2002, the victimization rate
for students ages 12–18 declined both at school and away from school. This included
victimization in crimes such as theft, violence (rape, sexual assault, robbery, and aggravated assault), and nonaggravated assault (Devoe et al., 2004). Despite this, in
general people believe that schools are becoming more dangerous. Their perception
of juvenile crime in and out of school has not diminished. This perception is due, in
part, to intense media coverage of criminal incidents (Menifield et al., 2001).

    Approximately 87% of students say their schools are safe (National Education
Association, 2007b). Generally, students who question the overall safety of schools
base their opinion on perception rather than on fact or experience (Mijanovich &
Weitzman, 2003). Students' perceptions of school safety are drawn from adults, the
media, the school system, and law enforcement agencies. Specifically, media portray-
als of the Columbine High School shootings have had more of an impact on students'
perceptions of safety than their own victimization experiences (Stretesky & Hogan,
2001). Approximately half of the elementary students surveyed in a Florida study
expressed concern about school safety (Carney, Shannon, & Murphey, 2005). However,
most of their concerns were directed at locations other than their classroom or the
school's hallways. Their concerns focused on school bathrooms and, to a much
greater extent, areas outside of the school. Young students, particularly males, who

generally do not feel safe in their neighborhood or community, expressed most concern about safety while going to and from school and outside of the school (Carney, Shannon, & Murphy, 2005).

In general, teachers are concerned about safety in and around their school. Their concern is documented in numerous studies, reports, and articles. However, much of the research based on surveys of teachers' opinions about safety is questionable and warrants challenge. In the wake of Columbine and several other heinous incidents, surveys on school safety were conducted in school systems, colleges and universities, police departments, and communities nationwide. In the haste to gather information, fulfill grant requirements, justify budget requests, and bring legitimate attention to school safety, those conducting the surveys asked dubious and leading questions. The following examples are among the types of questions that continue to appear frequently in surveys:

- Are you concerned about the presence of guns in your school?

- Is physical confrontation among students a concern in your school?

- Would you feel safer with police presence in the school?

- Do your students express concern about bullying in school?

The answers to such questions are headlined in report summaries, grant reports, and press releases.

Quality school safety programs and plans require and provide much more than surveys and questionnaires designed to justify grants and the development of sit-on-the-shelf documents. Some initiatives, such as the Safe Schools/Healthy Students initiative in Pinellas County, Florida, address capacity building, prevention, intervention, evaluation, and more, with the aim of reducing barriers to learning and creating a healthy environment that goes beyond basic safety (Armstrong et al., 2003). Teachers perceive such comprehensive efforts to be more effective than show-and-tell school safety efforts that continue to emerge.

Schools engage in a large number of activities aimed at promoting safety, from target hardening to counseling and instructional programs. Suspension (home and school based) remains a primary means of responding to student misconduct. Many of the activities in which schools are engaged to promote safety have not been evaluated, and research on their effectiveness is scarce. Nevertheless, the array of school safety practices continues to grow, with some officials questioning whether the vast number can be carried out with attention to quality (Gottfredson, 2001).

SCOPE AND COST OF SCHOOL SAFETY MEASURES

No single agency tracks or publishes accurate numbers on school violence. There is no comprehensive, mandatory federal crime reporting and tracking of incidents of school crime for grades K–12. Congress enacted the Cleary Act in 1990 to improve crime reporting on college campuses but mandated no such requirements for public or private K–12 schools. School crime and violence data consist of a jumbled collection of government reports, academic surveys, and research studies (Trump, 2007).

Since the Columbine High School incident, expenditures on school safety have skyrocketed. Total expenditures for school safety are incalculable as they involve federal, state, local, foundation, and private funds. Over $31 million in grants was awarded to 19 school districts in 14 states in 2006, funded by the U.S. Departments of Education, Health and Human Services, and Justice. This effort was designed to support schools in sustaining environments that promote healthy childhood development and prevent youth violence and drug use. Since 1999, these three departments have administered the Safe Schools/Healthy Students initiative. This initiative has provided more than $1 billion to local educational, mental health, law enforcement, and juvenile justice partnerships under the No Child Left Behind Act of 2001 (PL 107-110).

Although total dollar costs of efforts to make schools safe are difficult to calculate, the emotional costs of school violence are clear. Elementary school students who are victimized tend to miss school, shudder at the prospect of recess, and fear going to and from school. Middle and high school students who are victimized or believe that they may be victimized turn to cliques for support, hesitate to use school restrooms, and carry weapons for self-protection.

In an ideal world, school safety would focus on the needs and well-being of students above all others. It would target the needs of the most vulnerable—the youngest students, students with special needs, and students who, for a variety of reasons, are vulnerable to physical and emotional harm. It would focus on students, teachers, and staff in the most troubled schools, in which threat and risk of harm are pervasive. Unfortunately, the school safety movement and the massive industry it has created cater to a number of "publics," often detracting attention from the schools and people most in need. Much of the nation's school safety effort focuses on those more interested in relinquishing responsibility, gaining political favor, generating public relations, and pursuing funds than it does on serving vulnerable populations.

TEN PRINCIPLES FOR ENSURING A SECURE SCHOOL ENVIRONMENT

There are many stakeholders in school safety, each bearing responsibility for success and potential repercussion if efforts are not successful. Among the stakeholders with vested interest in school safety are

- Students

- Teachers

- Parents

- School staff (e.g., cafeteria workers, bus drivers, maintenance workers)

- School and police administrators

- Police officers

- Community leaders

- Politicians

- Media

- Vendors, consultants, and other providers

Administrators, principals, teachers, staff, parent leaders, and others in positions of influence have an obligation to do more than simply offer rhetoric and hype about school safety. The following guiding principles provide a foundation for rising above the crowd, disembarking from the school safety bandwagon, and ensuring a genuine, comfortable, secure environment for learning and interaction.

1. Keep perspective.

2. Maintain order.

3. Reinforce core values.

4. Let children be children.

5. Maintain an inviting environment.

6. Manage fear.

7. Embrace prevention.

8. Attend to ingress and egress.

9. Accept responsibility.

10. Engage police effectively.

Keep Perspective

People, especially young children, turn to their leaders and role models to provide perspective—to provide understanding, direction, and a vision of intended outcomes. Therefore leaders in the system, school, and classroom need to be conscious of overstating the magnitude of school safety issues. Although safety-related concerns are extreme and student behavior is out of control in some schools, these environments are rare. Few schools are in crisis, despite media hype. Here are some ways leaders can keep perspective on school violence and safety:

- Avoid labeling schools simply because it is popular to confront issues of school safety.

- Define the issues precisely. Using broad generalities to draw attention to school safety issues is a disservice to all involved.

- Cite the positives—call a safe school a safe school. Many schools, particularly elementary schools, do not have crime and security problems.

- Do not overstate a problem when one occurs. A single incident, including one of magnitude, does not create an unsafe school.

- Use only the degree of preventive and enforcement measures necessary to fix identified concerns. Limit target hardening and enforcement actions to those that are minimally required.

Maintain Order

Perception of school disorder is a major factor associated with students' and adults' negative feelings about their welfare. Such perception affects security, health, vulnerability, threats, and crime. Lack of order is a school's version of "broken windows," sending a signal to students and adults that there is little concern for safety and little hope for change. Disorder breeds further disorder. Fixing the broken windows of school disorderliness can influence positive feelings about safety (Mijanovich & Weitzman, 2003).

Among the best defenses against crime and a real or perceived decline in safety is an orderly environment. To achieve and maintain such an environment, leaders should

- Master the basics of maintaining order.

- Educate all stakeholders on how order is defined and will be maintained in the school. It should not be assumed that teachers and staff know the basics of maintaining order.

- Make it everyone's responsibility to maintain positive behavior and control deviance from behavioral standards. Responsibility for behavior management should never be relinquished to just a few people, especially police officers assigned to the school.

- Set clear standards for order and make certain that all stakeholders understand them; do not tolerate anything less.

- Make it a priority to provide support for all teachers and staff who work appropriately to uphold the standards.

Reinforce Core Values

Creating and reinforcing meaningful core values rallies people to support those values. It is not enough to say, "We value safety." Concrete steps such as the following must be taken to ensure that values guide behavior:

- Be specific in establishing values. Focus on important fundamentals, such as attitude, optimism, commitment, honor, responsibility, citizenship, respect, and prevention of violence and disruption.

- Think about how stakeholders gain familiarity with the values and their intended purpose. Let stakeholders know how they are expected to live out the values.

- Let stakeholders know when they have been successful at implementing the values.

A safe environment is not a strong value. Rather, it should be a product of the embracing of core values.

Let Children Be Children

Young children will get in fights, throw things, yell, run, go where they are not supposed to, talk back, curse, take things that do not belong to them, and test the school rules. Except for extreme cases, these actions do not constitute acts of assault, theft, trespass, or other crimes against society.

One of the sad byproducts of the school safety movement is the stripping away of opportunities for children to be children—the testing of school rules, misbehavior, confrontation, and stretching of the norm that come with youth. When a 6-year-old is suspended for having a plastic knife in her lunch bag to spread jelly on bread or an SRO is called to a classroom because a child refuses to change his seat, the school safety movement has gone too far. Those in leadership have a mandate to return the movement to a level of normalcy so that young children can be what they are supposed to be and, when necessary, be redressed for wrongdoing and learn from their mistakes without extreme consequence.

Maintain an Inviting Environment

A building that is filthy, tainted by old paint and broken fixtures, and surrounded by dirty and overgrown playgrounds and fields invites disruption, trespass, and crime. This appearance signals a lack of caring, an inability to control actions, and vulnerability. To avoid this and maintain an inviting environment, leaders can do the following:

- Fix problems that taint the school environment quickly, before they become extreme.

- Avoid using a tight budget as an excuse. Volunteers, soap and water, donated paint and supplies, and collective pressure placed on facilities managers often make a big difference in a school's appearance.

- Swiftly and harshly discipline those who destroy property, recognizing that they cause disruption, inconvenience, and cost for others.

- Tend to the schoolyard. A playground that is missing equipment, has rusted equipment, is overrun with weeds, or has been trashed invites outsiders to make themselves at home.

Manage Fear

Where fear is present, wisdom cannot be.
Lactantius

Despite the funds and resources spent on school safety and security, little has been done to evaluate the efficacy of these efforts in reducing student, teacher, and staff fear. Critics of excessive security practices in schools cite the possible negative consequences of such practices and note that these consequences may outweigh the benefits. The effect of security measures on student fear and student relationships is of particular concern (Phaneuf, 2005). Bombarding students and parents with excessive negative information, overstating threats, installing metal detectors when little or no threat exists, and holding active-shooter drills can create a climate of fear. Like a communicable disease, fear is contagious. Whether started purposefully or inadvertently, if left unchecked it spreads rapidly. The initial cause of the fear is often and quickly overtaken by the fear frenzy itself, with logic and rational thought falling victim to it along the way.

Leaders at every level of the school system play a role in managing fear in a way that does not conflict with safety planning, preparedness, prevention, or drills. Fear can be managed by continually reinforcing important values, creating a pleasant environment, and doing all that is possible to create positive experiences for students, teachers, staff, and parents. Teaching fear management to administrators and teachers is also essential.

Embrace Prevention

Our schoolchildren should never fear [for] their safety when they enter into a classroom.
President George W. Bush, October 3, 2006

As Ben Franklin said, "An ounce of prevention is worth a pound of cure." Keeping students safe requires balancing prevention method with risk. Prevention techniques used in troubled high schools should not be applied to elementary schools that have minimal risk, yet some techniques—such as metal detectors, see-through backpacks, police officers in the hallways—have been implemented in many schools that do not need them.

Administrators who espouse prevention without learning what it entails will prevent little. Expertise in prevention is readily available to schools through such sources as law enforcement and fire/EMS agencies, the National Crime Prevention Council, and the National School Safety Center. A school safety assessment should be conducted as a first step to developing a prevention plan. This assessment involves a strategic evaluation and facilities audit to identify current and potential school safety concerns. After the plan is in place, it should be assessed routinely and any necessary changes noted. Safety assessment will be further discussed later in this chapter.

To facilitate violence prevention, administrators should

- Identify risks—legitimate threats, not hype.

- Develop safety plans based on the identified risks.

- Review current policies and prevention and response practices.

- Conduct crime prevention surveys routinely (a police department's crime prevention unit should provide support in conducting a nonresidential crime prevention survey).

- Conduct fire prevention surveys routinely (different from fire drills and response planning).

- Provide appropriate target hardening (i.e., security measures), but no more than necessary based on risk assessment and legitimate threat and concern.

- Know and apply the principles of Crime Prevention Through Environmental Design (CPTED; Jeffrey, 1999).

Attend to Ingress and Egress

Students, parents, teachers, and bus drivers express concern about crime and behavioral issues that occur outside the school; in fact, many are more fearful of people and activities outside the school than those in the school building. A comprehensive safety plan should therefore address ingress and egress, or entering and exiting locations and procedures. This includes the exterior school property, school buses, parking lots, and traffic patterns. The excuse that the school does not control off-site property does not negate responsibility or need. To help keep students safe when entering and leaving school property, administrators should

- Know the safest routes to and from school and publicize them to parents and students.

- Identify concerns that students, parents, and staff have about ingress and egress and incorporate solutions into school safety plans.

- Work closely with local law enforcement agencies to provide concentrated patrols along roadways of ingress and egress at peak periods.

- Provide support to bus drivers, including training, meetings, electronic communication, and the presence of administrators and teachers during pickup and drop-off periods.

Accept Responsibility

School safety is unique to each school, and responsibility for it resides with each school. Tending to the well-being of students, particularly the most vulnerable (young students, students with special needs), is a local matter, the responsibility of administrators, teachers, staff, parents, and students in the school. It is also the responsibility of neighborhood leaders and businesses that support or are located near the school. Responsibility cannot be relinquished to the central administration, police department, or other entity, and excuses cannot be rendered because the school superintendent and police chief have not provided what the principal, teachers, or PTA president want or need.

Engage Police Effectively

With little exception, the most visible (and among the most costly) effort to improve and maintain school safety is the placement of full-time and part-time law enforcement officers (e.g., police officers, deputy sheriffs, state troopers) in public schools. Having an SRO assigned to a school on a full-time or part-time basis is not an effective engagement of the police in preventing and addressing safety and security. Police presence in schools means little unless it is well-planned and purposeful and the right persons are involved. If not managed well, such an assignment may be counterproductive. It is critical for school administrators and teachers to know when, where, and how to engage police officers as part of a school safety effort. This is discussed in the following section.

SCHOOL RESOURCE OFFICERS

Typically, an SRO is a law enforcement officer assigned to serve as a liaison between the police department and the school. SROs may be assigned to a particular school on a full-time basis or to several schools. The SRO may fulfill multiple roles, such as police officer, advisor, counselor, and teacher (Maryland Association of School Resource Officers, 2007). SROs range from carefully selected, dedicated officers committed to the citizenship, education, and well-being of young people to volunteers who simply seek an easy job with favorable working hours. Their assignments range from developing and playing a role in delivering law-related education and working to implement school safety plans to standing duty at entrances and in cafeterias.

In the late 1990s, there were approximately 12,000 full-time SROs assigned to schools. Since then, the number of SROs has grown considerably. SROs are funded by federal grants, school districts, and law enforcement agencies. The U.S. Department of Justice, Office of Community Oriented Police Services (COPS), awarded approximately $700 million to over 2,600 law enforcement agencies to support the hiring of SROs ("Cops In Schools" funding initiative) (McDevitt & Paniello, 2005). The exact number of officers assigned to schools is unknown because funding sources and types of placement (full time, part time, overtime) vary.

SRO programs are expensive. Budgets can range from $80,000 for a single officer in a school in a small community to millions of dollars for SROs and SRO supervisors in a large city. In a metropolitan area, in which police salaries tend to be higher than in smaller and rural communities, the cost of a single SRO can exceed $125,000 (Finn, 2006). This includes items such as salary and benefits, uniforms and other ancillary costs, vehicles, and percentage of supervisory time.

For law enforcement agencies and the communities they serve, there are few efforts more valuable or meaningful than having police officers work closely with teachers and others to develop young people as citizens, ensure a safe learning environment, and establish schools as integral components of viable, sustainable communities. When an SRO program is planned and managed well, its value is incalculable. When implemented for the wrong reasons or managed poorly, few programs could be more costly or carry more severe consequences, such as embellishing the seriousness of incidents and possibly criminalizing minor infractions.

The concept of placing police officers in schools evolved long before the Columbine High School incident. In the 1970s, police officers were working in schools nationwide and were engaged in delivering an integrated law-related education curriculum. For instance, the Law-Related Education Program in Schools of Maryland, housed at Wilde Lake High School in Columbia, Maryland, was part of the national effort begun in 1978 by the U.S. Department of Justice. Police officers assigned to high schools on a full-time basis worked with teachers in different subject areas to incorporate public safety. The expectation at that time was that they would work with teachers across the curriculum to develop students as citizens. Their role focused almost solely on supporting the educational process and helping students mature. By the early 1980s, most of the experimental law-related education programs ended due to diminished federal support and declining local and state budgets.

Expectations of police officers, deputies, and troopers in schools have changed since that era. Despite rhetoric about having officers engage in teaching and counseling, the primary expectation is that they will prevent and resolve crime and disruption. The change in focus from education to security and enforcement is a byproduct of the Columbine High School incident and several other well-publicized heinous school crimes.

There is much discussion and debate over the role and responsibilities of SROs. The perspectives and needs of principals, law enforcement administrators, and SROs themselves are, at times, conflicting. Depending on the jurisdiction and school, SROs see their role as preventing and handling crimes, developing informants, providing classroom lectures, teaching, monitoring hallways, counseling, patrolling school property, and serving at the discretion of principals. Expectations for SROs and the SRO program and the rationale behind these expectations need to be clear (Lambert & McGinty, 2002). The National Association of School Resource Officers (NASRO; Lambert & McGinty, 2002) suggests that SROs provide three primary functions:

- Law enforcement

- Classroom instruction of law-related education

- Counseling on law-related matters

The results of some surveys tend to support SROs as a panacea to help school personnel successfully manage behavior, teach, and counsel. They call for SROs to engage in maintaining order in the classroom, assisting in assessing student suspensions, minimizing truancy, monitoring student projects in the community, and encouraging students to engage more fully in the learning process (Benigni, 2004). Much of the survey input comes from school administrators, law enforcement administrators, and SROs, most of whom have a great deal to gain politically by appearing responsive to school crime and violence and fiscally by obtaining grant funds. As federal grant support for SRO programs declines, law enforcement executives warn that SRO programs are in jeopardy unless increases are allotted to local law enforcement budgets (Telvock, 2005). Table 16.1 provides 25 common mistakes associated with SRO programs.

Criminalizing Disruption and Misbehavior

Behavioral issues once managed by teachers in the classroom, with support from school administrators, are now often assigned to SROs for resolution. Police officers in schools are sometimes called upon to intervene in cases of verbal defiance, romantic

Table 16.1. Common mistakes associated with school resource officer (SRO) programs

1. Establishing unrealistic expectations for the SRO program (e.g., systemwide expectations; those of the police department, individual schools, stakeholders)
2. Having an ill-defined purpose to the program
3. Lacking a clear mission for the SRO
4. Failing to conduct an assessment to determine if placement of an SRO is necessary
5. Failing to check for underlying or hidden motives of those making the decision about SROs
6. Accepting validity of need based on unsubstantiated or overstated claims of problems or concerns in the school
7. Placing too many or too few SROs in a school
8. Placing officers in the SRO program or a school based solely on volunteerism
9. Lacking a well-defined selection criteria for SROs
10. Assuming that principals and assistant principals have the time, orientation, skill, and commitment to carry out the stated safety plan
11. Allowing law enforcement officers to work at the discretion of school officials
12. Assigning officers to work with school counselors without adequate training and/or clear definition of their role and responsibilities; this creates high potential for negative liability
13. Having SROs perceive their primary role as developing informants within the school
14. Allowing the SRO program to negate responsibility of beat patrol officers to police the schools
15. Lacking a law-related education curriculum or program
16. Placing officers who lack teaching skills or training in the SRO program
17. Using SROs as security officers
18. Allowing SROs to intervene in classroom management, relieving teachers and administrators from their responsibility
19. Allowing SROs to intervene in student behavior issues outside the classroom that should be handled by teachers and school administrators
20. Failing to adequately supervise SROs (i.e., by police supervisors)
21. Failing to adequately monitor SRO workload
22. Allowing SROs to be sole reporters of their need, workload, and success
23. Allowing school administrators to be sole reporters of SRO need, workload, and success
24. Ignoring the safety of the school's external environment
25. Requiring rigid SRO work hours, including lack of flexibility and use of overtime to engage SROs in covering school events

quarrels, student harassment, tardiness, loitering, and littering. They assume responsibilities that go beyond the role of SRO, monitoring morning ingress and afternoon
egress through school entrances and providing cafeteria duty, hallway duty, and recess management. In troubled schools, such intervention may be merited. In general,
however, involving police officers in routine matters of classroom management is a
misuse of the SRO program.

Relinquishing such responsibilities to police officers increases the risk of negative liability. Police tend to criminalize inappropriate behavior, looking for violation
of law and relying on arrest to achieve peace, order, and prevention of future infringement. This is their culture; it is what they know. It is among their primary
means of recourse for resolving a crisis that involves a breach of rules. Being assigned
as an SRO does not change the police officer's culture or commitment and approach
to enforcement. Student behavior that was once handled as misbehavior by a teacher
may be elevated to serious, and possibly, criminal offense by an SRO.

Lack of and Need for Law-Related Education Curriculum

Opportunities abound to engage SROs in learning programs at every grade level.
Their involvement in supporting the school's curriculum has incredible potential to
positively influence students, particularly in early childhood. SROs can relate real-
world experiences to an array of subjects. In a math class, for instance, a police officer might relate the concepts of angles and fractions to radar enforcement. Police experiences in the community can support lessons in history, civics, and science. Police
knowledge of law and reporting systems can be used to support reading and writing
skills. In most school systems this potential is unfortunately wasted, with SROs at
best serving only as occasional guest lecturers in classrooms. In educating the youngest
children (ages 3–6), SROs can engage in learning with regard to safety habits (e.g.,
crossing streets, bicycling, getting in and out of cars, avoiding play in unsafe areas),
dealing with emergencies in the home, protecting oneself against strangers, and the
importance of respect and courtesy.

Incorporating law-related education across the curriculum and engaging SROs
in the learning program offer numerous benefits, including these:

- Increased real-world application of course content

- Greater sense of curiosity and inquiry among students

- Increased student focus on and interest in science, math, and technology

- Exposure to important subject matter

- Citizenship building

- Increased partnership between teachers and SROs

- Improved professionalism of SRO program

- Better use of SRO time

ASSESSING SAFETY NEEDS AND
ESTABLISHING REASONABLE EXPECTATIONS

In assessing and responding to a school's safety needs, it is important to fit the solution to the needs. Schools are challenged to identify appropriate programs and strate-

gies related to safety and security. A 2002 report from the Northwest Regional Educational Laboratory stated that safety and security decisions—at the system and school level—are often based on promising practices that are not supported by quality assessment, research, or other knowledge base. As a result, decisions to adopt safety and violence prevention programs are based on personal preference and experience (Atkinson, 2002).

Security technology is emerging rapidly, is employed as a first resort in school safety initiatives, and too often fails to deliver on its promises. According to Mary Green, Security Specialist, Sandia Labs, U.S. Department of Energy, metal detectors are appropriate in only 2%–5% of schools because they are so personnel intensive. Biometric devices, which allow access based on fingerprint, handprint, or iris identification, are complex, costly, and difficult to maintain. Identification badges, which have the potential to enhance school safety, require motivating students and staff to wear or carry them. Many people perceive security cameras and related technology as an intrusion to personal rights (Colgan, 2005).

No principal, superintendent, chief of police, or sheriff should commit a resource officer to a school—or conduct any other major school safety initiative—without an assessment of the school's environment. The outcome of the assessment should be an overview of risk, a determination of what is needed to address the identified risk, and a well-defined set of tasks and expectations. No police or sheriff's department should enter into a relationship with a school without knowledge of the school's principal and assistant principals and their intent or motive and style of operation. No school should enter into an agreement with a law enforcement agency without similar knowledge of the agency's administrators.

In assessing a potential partnership, being aware of any underlying motives is as important as knowing the people involved. If the motive to create an SRO program or other prevention or intervention effort is to take advantage of available grant funds, appease politicians or others, or simply provide parents with the perception that protection is being provided, the effort is likely to fail and should be avoided. Although every safety and security initiative has a public relations or marketing component, none—particularly those focusing on the well-being of children—should exist simply to fund, market, or appease.

Assessing risk, needs, and tasks requires asking tough questions and seeking balance between need and solutions. Are the right approaches to assessment being used? Some assessment tools are based on the assumption that schools are unsafe and are used only to confirm these assumptions. What do stakeholders know about safety— the facts? Do those involved need to better understand safety and security issues before participating in assessing needs? When and how will success be realized? Who is in charge of safety initiatives? Are identified problems schoolwide or isolated to a handful of students, a few classes, or a wing of the building? How flexible are the initiatives if needs change? Are new policies needed? Is negative liability being created? Who will determine when to end the safety initiatives, and on what basis?

A safety assessment should also consider such issues as

- An inordinately high number of calls for police service at the school, both crime and noncrime related

- Crime patterns and practices within the school

- Disorder and behavioral patterns and practices within the school

- Areas of the school in which most concerns are centered

- Inability of area police patrol officers to provide adequate response

- Special needs of the student population (number of students who have disabilities, number of students who commit repeat offenses, limits imposed by overcrowding)

- Use of safety programs on an experimental or trial basis rather than permanence

- Potential relevance of implemented model to other schools

- Identified fear, with well-defined or well-documented cause

- Law-related education programs or curricula in which police can play a multifaceted, well-integrated role (i.e., beyond an occasional, simple lecture)

- Time frame to accomplish the desired tasks, following which the program will be reassessed or ended

- Expectation for safety initiatives or programs by school system executives, principals, assistant principals, counselors, parents, students, and others

- Background and experience of school administrators and/or others who will oversee the program or interact routinely with the SROs

Based on a thorough assessment, a plan should be developed that sets forth how prevention and intervention activities—including the SRO program—should be implemented in the school. As part of the assessment and planning effort, school administrators should establish a contract between the school and a participating law enforcement agency. No administrator should implement an SRO effort without such a contract, which should be distinct from the school safety plan. Assistance in providing assessments is readily available from school systems, the National School Safety Center, National Crime Prevention Council, and professional associations.

FOCUSING ON STUDENTS WITH DISABILITIES IN THE ASSESSMENT

Safety assessments should give special attention to students who have disabilities. There are approximately six million students with disabilities attending schools in the United States. Ignoring or minimizing this population in developing safety plans, emergency response, and prevention and exclusion policies and practices can result in failure, injury, and negative liability (Ramirez, Peek-Asa, & Kraus, 2004).

Cognitive and physical constraints may compromise students' ability to respond to threats and hazards. Students with disabilities are at greater risk of injury than students without disabilities, and students with multiple disabilities are at greater risk than those who have a single disability (Atkinson & Kipper, 2004). Students with mobility and communication disabilities often experience fear, sometimes to the extreme. They may be targeted for bullying, theft, and other forms of victimization. They may not comprehend the sudden change, rapid movement, and apprehension common during fire drills and active-shooter exercises. Their responses to confusing or frightening events may cause disruption and cause them to become labeled as a problem by teachers, administrators, and police officers.

The Individuals with Disabilities Education Act Amendments (IDEA) of 1997 (PL 105-17) support students with disabilities, define their rights, define the school's responsibilities toward them, and establish parameters on how their needs must be met. Every assessment and resulting plan of action should address the needs of these students and ways in which traditional systemic barriers will be overcome (Rehm, 2002).

CONCLUSIONS

Every school in the United States will be free of drugs,
violence, and unauthorized presence of firearms and alcohol
and will offer a disciplined environment conducive to learning.
Goals 2000: Reforming Education to
Improve Student Achievement, April 30, 1998

School safety is not an urban issue. Nor is it a suburban, rural, small-town, wealthy community, poor community, East Coast, West Coast, or Southern border issue. Since the 1999 shootings at Columbine High School, school safety has become a societal issue.

School safety and the well-being of the nation's most vulnerable children is a primary responsibility of every teacher, school administrator, police officer, parent, and community leader. Part of this responsibility is keeping perspective, focusing on what matters, and putting the needs of children before internal and external politics, funding, personal advancement, or public relations.

The number of heinous incidents that have occurred in schools in the United States remains slight. The likelihood of another Columbine-like incident occurring remains extremely small. Students are at risk of being victimized by many other things—from falls to traffic accidents—during the course of their day.

There is a proliferation of certain crimes and disorder in the most troubled schools. This cannot be denied. Too many teachers and staff members live each day in fear in these schools. They face challenges, turmoil, and risks that were not part of their personal commitment to serve young people. In these schools, too many students have their daily routine, opportunities, and happiness stifled by apprehension and victimization. They miss out on opportunities to learn, participate in school events, interact with others, and enjoy simple privileges because of fear of harm due to crime, disruption, and bullying. Concerns for safety in troubled schools are legitimate and warrant immediate and intensive interdiction.

Most schools in the United States, however, are not troubled by illegality and disorder. They are relatively free of extreme strife due to drugs, violence, and the unauthorized presence of firearms and alcohol. They have the opportunity to provide an environment conducive to learning. They are safe, free of wanton crime and disruption, and able to focus on providing quality educational opportunities to all students. However, politics, media coverage, individual and organizational greed, and lack of information has led officials in the safest schools to characterize their institutions as places of high threat. Rather than focus on appropriate measures necessary to balance risk and safety, they overreact. They turn their schools into fortresses, complete with metal detectors, surveillance cameras, and full-time police officers roaming hallways. They convey distrust of students, treat minor acts of misbehavior as serious incidents and, on occasion, with the support of police officers, criminalize noncriminal events.

School safety, at its extreme, has become ingrained in the culture of public education but not necessarily in a way that meets the best interests of young people. Despite research to the contrary, students in grades 3–12, parents, and teachers perceive that schools are becoming havens for an increasing number of violent episodes (National Center for Education Statistics, 1996). It will take a new generation of exceptional, forthright, inspired school and police administrators to undo the harm done to the public educational system by those who have chosen to jump on the school safety bandwagon. It will take this group of exceptional leaders to change distorted views of the safety of the nation's schools and overcome those whose selfish and politically expedient missions, under the guise of school safety, undermine student well-being.

REFERENCES

Armstrong, K.H., Massey, O.T., Boroughs, M., Bailey, R., & LaJoie, D. (2003). Safe Schools/ Healthy Students initiative: Pinellas County, Florida. *Psychology in the Schools, 40*(5), 489–501.

Atkinson, A. (2002). *Guide 5: Fostering school law enforcement partnerships* (pp. 3–47). Portland, OR: Northwest Regional Education Laboratory.

Atkinson, A.J., & Kipper, R.J. (2004). Individuals with Disabilities Education Act. In *The Virginia School Resource Officer: Resource Guide.* Richmond, VA: Governor's Office for Safe and Drug-Free Schools and Communities. Retrieved July 18, 2008, from http://www.dcjs.virginia.gov/ forms/cple/sroguide.pdf

Benigni, M. (2004). The need for school resource officers. *FBI Law Enforcement Bulletin, 73*(5), 23–26.

Bureau of Justice Statistics. (2007, December 2). *School crime rates stable: Children more likely to be murdered away from school than at school.* Available from www.ojp.usdoj.gov/bjs

Carney, S., Shannon, D., & Murphy, C. (2005). An examination of school violence and safety in South Florida elementary schools. *Journal of School Violence, 4*(3), 21–35.

Colgan, C. (2005). The new look of school safety: Emerging security strategies begin with collaboration and motivation. *American School Board Journal, 102*(3), 3–6.

Devoe, J., Peter, K., Kaufman, P., Miller, A., Noonan, M., Snyder, T.D., & Baum, K. (2004, November). Indicators of school crime and safety: 2004 (executive summary). *Educational Statistics Quarterly, 6*(4), iii–iv.

Finn, P. (2006). School resource officer programs: Finding the funding, reaping the benefits. *FBI Law Enforcement Bulletin, 75*(8), 1–14.

Gottfredson, G. (2001). What schools do to prevent problem behavior and promote safe environments. *Journal of Educational and Psychological Consultation, 12*(4), 313–344.

Hanke, P. (1996). Putting school crime into perspective: Self-reported school victimizations of high school seniors. *Journal of Criminal Justice, 24*(3), 207–226.

Hillman, C.B. (1989). *Creating a learning climate for the early childhood years* (p. 35). Bloomington, IN: Phi Delta Kappa.

Individuals with Disabilities Education Act Amendments (IDEA) of 1997, PL 105-17, U.S.C. §§ 1400 *et seq.*

Jeanne Clery Disclosure of Campus Security Policy and Campus Crime Statistics Act (Clery Act) of 1990, PL 101-542, 20 U.S.C. § 1092(f).

Jeffrey, C. (1999). *CPTED: Past, present, and future.* Position paper before the 4th annual International CPTED Association Conference. Mississaugua, Ontario, Canada, September 20–22, 1999.

Lambert, R., & McGinty, D. (2002). Law enforcement officers in schools: Setting priorities. *Journal of Educational Administration, 40*(3), 257–273.

Lewis, T. (2003). The surveillance economy of post-Columbine schools. *The Review of Education, Pedagogy, & Cultural Studies, 4*(25), 335–355.

Maryland Association of School Resource Officers. (2007). *What is an SRO?* Retrieved August 19, 2007, from http://www.masro.com

McDevitt, J., & Paniello, J. (2005). *National assessment of SRO programs: Survey of students in three large new SRO programs.* Washington, DC: National Institute of Justice.

Menifield, C., Rose, W., Homa, J., & Cunningham, A. (2001). The media's portrayal of urban and rural school violence: A preliminary analysis. *Deviant Behavior, 22,* 447–464.

Mijanovich, T., & Weitzman, B.C. (2003). Which "broken windows" matter? School, neighborhood, and family characteristics associated with youths' feelings of unsafety. *Journal of Urban Health: Bulletin of the New York Academy of Medicine, 80*(3), 400–415.

National Center for Education Statistics. (1996). *How safe are the public schools: What do teachers say?* (Issue Brief). Washington, DC: U.S. Department of Education.

National Education Association. (2007a). *School safety.* Retrieved September 4, 2007, from www.nea.org/school_safety

National Education Association. (2007b). *What research says: Issues in education.* Retrieved January 9, 2008, from http://www.nea.org/schoolsafety.html

No Child Left Behind Act of 2001, PL 107-110, 115 Stat. 1425, 20 U.S.C. §§ 6301 *et seq.*

Phaneuf, S. (2005, November). *School security, student fear and school climate: Results from a national study.* Paper presented at the annual meeting of the American Society of Criminology, Royal York, Toronto. Retrieved August 11, 2007, from http://www.allacademic.com/meta/p90384_index.html

Ramirez, M., Peek-Asa, C., & Kraus, J. (2004). Disability and risk of school-related injury. *Injury Prevention, 10,* 21–26.

Rehm, R. (2002). Creating a context of safety and achievement at school for children who are medically fragile/technology dependent. *Advances in Nursing Science, 24*(3), 71–84.

Stretesky, P., & Hogan, M. (2001). Columbine and student perceptions of safety: A quasi-experimental study. *Journal of Criminal Justice, 29*(5), 429–443.

Telvock, D. (2005, March 18). School resource officer funding under threat. *Leesburg Today,* p. 1.

Trump, K. (2007, May 17). Testimony before the hearing on Protecting Our Schools: Federal Efforts to Strengthen Community Preparedness and Response. Washington, DC, Committee on Homeland Security of the U.S. House of Representatives. Retrieved July 18, 2008, from http://www.schoolsecurity.org/news/TestimonyTrump.pdf

U.S. Census Bureau. (2006). Section 4: Education. *Statistical Abstract of the United States: 2006* (pp. 204–294). Retrieved July 18, 2008, from http://www.census.gov/prod/2005pubs/06statab/educ.pdf

Appendices

Maryland State
Department of Education
Division of Special Education/
Early Intervention Services

Sample Individualized Education Program (IEP): Max Entering Kindergarten

☐ Draft   ☑ Approved   ☐ Amended:

Name:
Agency: The Howard County Public School System
IEP Team Meeting Date: June 1, 2007

I. STUDENT AND SCHOOL INFORMATION

Name:

Address:

Grade: Kindergarten

Unique Student Identification Number (State):

Student Identification Number (Local)

Date of Birth: 8/4/2001

Age: 6

Race: Black or African American (not of Hispanic Origin)

Student identified as Limited English Proficient: ☐ Yes   ☑ No

Student's native language: English

Residence County: 13

Residence School: Phelps Luck Elementary

Service County: 13

Service School: Waterloo Elementary

Which jurisdiction is financially responsible?: Howard

Is the student currently under the care and custody of a state agency?:

☐ Yes   ☑ No

Parent/Guardian 1

Name:

Home Phone: (410) 555 - 1111   Cell: ( )   -

Email:

Parent native language, if not English: English

Interpreter needed?: ☐ Yes   ☐ No

Gender: Male

Parent/Guardian 2

Name:

Home Phone: ( )   -   Cell: ( )   -

Email:

Parent native language, if not English:English

Interpreter needed?: ☐ Yes   ☐ No

Case Manager: Kimberly A Kallini

IEP Team Meeting Date(s): 1/26/2007, 1/23/2008, 6/3/2008

IEP Annual Review Date: 6/3/2008

Maryland State
Department of Education
Division of Special Education/
Early Intervention Services

Sample Individualized Education Program (IEP): Max Entering Kindergarten

Name:
Agency: The Howard County Public School System
IEP Team Meeting Date: June 3, 2008

If yes, name of state agency:

Does the student require a parent surrogate?: ☐ Yes ☐ No

Parent Surrogate Name:

Surrogate Phone: ( )   -

Parent was provided a copy of the Procedural Safeguards Parental Rights document?

☐ Yes ☐ No

Projected Annual Review Date: 6/3/2009

Most Recent Evaluation Date: 1/26/2006

Projected Evaluation Date: 1/26/2009

Primary Disability: Speech or Language Impairment

Areas affected by disability: Reading, Expressive/Receptive Language

IEP Team Participants

Name	Position	Name	Position
Kimberly A Kallini	IEP Case Manager	Anne Hickey	IEP Chair
	Parent/Guardian		Parent/Guardian
A. Principal	Principal/Designee	L. Davis	General Educator
			Guidance Counselor
			Social Worker
Kimberly A Kallini	Special Educator		
	School Psychologist		
Karen B Favinger	Speech/Language Pathologist		
	Agency Representative		

Maryland State
Department of Education
Division of Special Education/
Early Intervention Services

Sample Individualized Education Program (IEP): Max Entering Kindergarten

Name:
Agency: The Howard County Public School System
IEP Team Meeting Date: June 3, 2008

Academic: Reading

(Document student's academic achievement and functional performance levels In academic areas, as appropriate.)

Source(s): Early Childhood Curriculum Data

Curriculum-based Assessments

Observation

Instructional Grade Level Performance: General Reading Processes:

Phonemic Awareness: Shows interest in rhyming words, but is unable to consistently identify rhymes

Phonics: Identifies K and O (uppercase) out of the context of his name, but has difficulty identifying the other letters in his name as well as the lowercase letters

Fluency: Identifies his name in print when given a field of names to choose from

Vocabulary: Uses increasingly more age appropriate vocabulary and labels pictures and finds details in pictures

Comprehension: Relates events in stories to real-life events spontaneously. Answers simple "wh" questions given visual supports. Responds to simple questions in the classroom about a book and describes drawings to his classmates.

Writing: Uses drawings and letter-like symbols to express personal ideas

Maryland State
Department of Education
Division of Special Education/
Early Intervention Services

Sample Individualized Education Program (IEP): Max Entering Kindergarten

Name:
Agency: The Howard County Public School System
IEP Team Meeting Date: June 3, 2008

Controlling Language: Consistently uses 4 to 5 word sentences to communicate in class to request, comment, make choices, socialize with peers and participate in class-room activities. Uses several grammatical structures with a verbal model

Listening: Follows one and two step directions with familiar concepts

Speaking: Imitates medial sounds in phrases and is beginning to use final sounds in spontaneous speech

(Consider private, state, local school system, and classroom based assessments, as applicable.)

Summary of Assessment Findings (Including dates of administration):

Does this area impact the student's academic achievement and / or functional performance? ☑ Yes ☐ No

II. PRESENT LEVELS OF ACADEMIC ACHIEVEMENT AND FUNCTIONAL PERFORMANCE

What is the parental input regarding the child's educational program?

The parent(s) provided input at the IEP meeting and the information was used in the development of the IEP.

What are the child's strengths, interest areas, significant personal attributes, and personal accomplishments? (Include preferences and interests for post-school outcomes, if appropriate.)

Student is eager to please his teachers and enjoys classroom activities and peer interactions.

Sample Individualized Education Program (IEP): Max Entering Kindergarten

Name:
Agency: The Howard County Public School System
IEP Team Meeting Date: June 3, 2008

How does the child's disability affect his involvement in the general education curriculum?

Student's speech and language impairment interferes with his interactions with others, his acquisition of vocabulary and his comprehension.

For preschool age children, how does the disability affect the child's participation in appropriate activities?

Communication (required)

Does the student have special communication needs? ☐ Yes ☑ No If yes, describe the specific needs.

Assistive Technology (AT) (required)

Consider the AT device(s) and service(s) that are needed to increase, maintain or improve functional capabilities of a student with a disability.

Was assistive technology considered? ☑ Yes ☐ No

Does the student need an AT service(s)? ☐ Yes ☑ No

Does the student need an AT device(s)? ☐ Yes ☑ No If yes, list AT Device(s).

Document basis for decision(s):

Instructional and Testing Accommodations

Instructional and testing accommodations were considered and no instructional and testing accommodations are required at this time.

Discussion to Support Decision:

Sample Individualized Education Program (IEP): Max Entering Kindergarten

Name:
Agency: The Howard County Public School System
IEP Team Meeting Date: June 3, 2008

III. SPECIAL CONSIDERATIONS AND ACCOMMODATIONS

☑ Supplementary Aids, Services, Program Modifications and Supports were considered and none are required at this time.

Discussion to support decision(s):

IV. GOALS

Reading Basic Skills

Goal: Student will identify and manipulate sounds in spoken words, develop knowledge of letters, and communicate effectively in a variety of situations.

By: 6/3/2009

Evaluation Method: Classroom-Based Assessment, Observation Record, Report Card

With: 80% Accuracy

ESY Goal? Decision Deferred

Objective 1: Student will discriminate and produce rhyming words and alliteration by repeating rhyming words, repeating phrases and sentences with alliteration, discriminating rhyming words from non-rhyming words.

Objective 2: Student will use grammar concepts and skills that strengthen oral language by using complete sentences to respond to questions by using:

- pronouns (he, she, him, her, they)
- articles (a, the)
- auxilliary verbs (is, am, are)

Maryland State
Department of Education
Division of Special Education/
Early Intervention Services

Sample Individualized Education Program (IEP): Max Entering Kindergarten

Name:
Agency: The Howard County Public School System
IEP Team Meeting Date: June 3, 2008

Objective 3: Student will speak clearly enough to be heard and unerstood in a variety of settings by:

- producing the following sounds:

  - sh, ch, l in sentences; k, g, p, b, m in conversation

- producing medial and final consonants (or sound approximations) in:

  - sentences
  - connected speech

Objective 4: Student will identify and label

- all upper-case letters
- all lower-case letters

Progress Toward Goal

Progress Report 1   Progress Code:

Date   Description:

Progress Report 2   Progress Code:

Date   Description:

Progress Report 3   Progress Code:

Date   Description:

Progress Report 4   Progress Code:

Date   Description:

363

Maryland State
Department of Education
Division of Special Education/
Early Intervention Services

Sample Individualized Education Program (IEP): Max Entering Kindergarten

Name:
Agency: The Howard County Public School System
IEP Team Meeting Date: June 3, 2008

Progress Report 5

Date

Progress Code:

Description:

How will the parent be notified of the student's progress toward the IEP goals? IEP Progress Reports will be sent during report time frame.

How often? quarterly

Reading Comprehension

Goal: Student will use a variety of strategies to understand word meaning, increase vocabulary and understand what has been read,   By: 6/3/2009

Evaluation Method: Classroom-Based Assessment, Observation Record, Report Card   With: 80 % accuracy

ESY Goal? Decision Deferred

Objective: Student will demonstrate understanding by answering questions related to a book, picture, event, or activity including:

- what
- who
- where
- when

Objective: Student will develop and use appropriate vocabulary when telling about activities and events including:

- nouns
- verbs
- spatial concepts/location
- adjectives such as: soft, hard, long, short

Maryland State
Department of Education
Division of Special Education/
Early Intervention Services

Sample Individualized Education Program
(IEP): Max Entering Kindergarten

Objective:

Objective: Student will:

- predict what will happen next in stories
- recall stories that have been read by using visual cues
- sequence a 3-4 part story that has been read

Progress Toward Goal

Progress Report 1   Progress Code:

Date   Description:

Progress Report 2   Progress Code:

Date   Description:

Progress Report 3   Progress Code:

Date   Description:

Progress Report 4   Progress Code:

Date   Description:

Progress Report 5   Progress Code:

Date   Description:

Maryland State
Department of Education
Division of Special Education/
Early Intervention Services

Sample Individualized Education Program (IEP): Max Entering Kindergarten

Name:
Agency: The Howard County Public School System
IEP Team Meeting Date: June 3, 2008

How will the parent be notified of the student's progress toward the IEP goals? IEP Progress Reports will be sent during report time frame.

How often? quarterly

V. SERVICES

Special Education Services

| Service Nature | Location | Number of sessions | Length of time | Service Description | | | | Provider(s)/ agency | Summary of service |
				Frequency	Begin date	End date			
Classroom Instruction	In General Education		7hrs 30 mins	Weekly				P Special Ed Teacher O Instructional Assistant.	7 hrs. 30 min. Weekly
Speech/ Language Therapy	In General Education		30 mins	Weekly	8/25/2008			P Speech/ Lang. Path.	30Min. Weekly

Begin date for Speech/Language Therapy: 8/25/2008

Key: P = Primary; O = Other

Discussion of service(s) delivery: Special instruction will be delivered during language arts and content as appropriate.

Note: For service delivery that will occur as recheck periodically or only once, length of time fields in this table must contain 0. A detailed description of the services, including frequency of contacts, type of contact (direct or indirect), amount of time per contact, and fading schedule (if applicable) will be described below.

Maryland State
Department of Education
Division of Special Education/
Early Intervention Services

**Sample Individualized Education Program
(IEP): Max Entering Kindergarten**

Name:
Agency: The Howard County Public School System
IEP Team Meeting Date: June 3, 2008

VI.   PLACEMENT DATA

Least Restrictive Environment (LRE) Decision Making & Placement Summary

(A student with disability is not removed from general education in an age-appropriate instructional setting solely because of needed modifications to the general curriculum.)

What placement option(s) did the IEP Team consider? Inside General Education (80% or more)

If removed from the general education environment, explain reasons why services cannot be provided in the general education environment with the use of supplementary aids and services:

Document basis for decision(s): Services can be delivered in the general education classroom.

Total time in school week: -   Total time outside of General Education: =   Total time in General Education:
32 hrs. 30 minutes   0 hours minutes/week   32 hours 30 minutes/week

Special education placement (ages 3-5): Least Restrictive Environment: INSIDE GENERAL EDUCATION (80% or more)

Average 100%/day

In selecting the LRE are there any potential harmful effects on the student or quality of services he or she needs?   ☐ Yes   ☑ No

367

**Maryland State
Department of Education
Division of Special Education/
Early Intervention Services**

Sample Individualized Education Program (IEP): Max Entering Kindergarten

Name:
Agency: The Howard County Public School System
IEP Team Meeting Date: June 3, 2008

Are the services in the student's home school (the school the student would attend if not disabled)? ☑ Yes ☐ No   Because Max will enter Kindergarten as a 6 year old, the school age LRE codes were Used.

If no, is placement as close as possible to the student's home? ☐ Yes ☐ No

Is special transportation needed? ☐ Yes ☑ No

Are personnel needed to assist the student during transportation? ☐ Yes ☑ No

Document basis for decision(s) (including consideration of theamount of time and distance involved in travel):

Provide an explanation to the extent, if any, the student will not participate with non-disabled peers in academic, non-academic, and extracurricular activities?

SSIS Resident County: Howard   SSIS Resident School: Phelps Luck Elementary

SSIS Service County: Howard   SSIS Service School: Waterloo Elementary

Child Count Eligibility Codes:

(1) Eligible student with a disability served in a public school or placed in a nonpublic school by the public agency to receive FAPE

Sample Individualized Education Program (IEP)

☐ Draft ☑ Approved ☐ Amended:

Name:
Agency: The Howard County Public School System
IEP Team Meeting Date: June 1, 2007

STUDENT AND SCHOOL INFORMATION

Name:

Address:

Grade: Preschool, ages 3-5

Unique Student Identification Number (State):

Student Identification Number (Local)

Date of Birth: 8/10/2004

Age: 2

Race: White, Not of Hispanic Origin

Student identified as Limited English Proficient: ☐ Yes ☑ No

Student's native language: English

Residence County: 13

Residence School: Bellows Spring Elementary

Service County: 13

Service School: Bellows Spring Elementary

Which jurisdiction is financially responsible?: Howard

Is the student currently under the care and custody of a state agency?:

☐ Yes ☑ No

Parent/Guardian 1

Name:

Home Phone: ( ) -   Cell: ( ) -

Email:

Parent native language, if not English: English

Interpreter needed?:   ☐ Yes ☑ No

Gender: Male

Parent/Guardian 2

Name:

Home Phone: ( ) -   Cell: ( ) -

Email:

Parent native language, if not English:English

Interpreter needed?: ☐ Yes ☐ No

Case Manager: Joanna A Hicks

IEP Team Meeting Date(s): 6/1/2007

IEP Annual Review Date: 6/1/2007

Maryland State
Department of Education
Division of Special Education/
Early Intervention Services

Sample Individualized Education Program (IEP)

Name:
Agency: The Howard County Public School System
IEP Team Meeting Date: April 03, 2008

If yes, name of state agency:

Does the student require a parent surrogate?: ☐ Yes ☑ No

Parent Surrogate Name:

Surrogate Phone: ( ) -

Parent was provided a copy of the Procedural Safeguards Parental Rights document?

☑ Yes ☐ No

Projected Annual Review Date: 6/1/2008

Most Recent Evaluation Date: 6/1/2007

Projected Evaluation Date: 6/1/2010

Primary Disability: Speech or Language Impairment

Areas affected by disability: Expressive/Receptive Language, Fine Motor, Social/Emotional

IEP Team Participants

Name	Position	Name	Position
Joanna A Hicks	IEP Case Manager	Jacqueline K Klamerus	IEP Chair
	Parent/Guardian		Parent/Guardian
J. Klamerus	Principal/Designee	Not Applicable	General Educator
Joanna A Hicks	Special Educator		Guidance Counselor
	School Psychologist		Social Worker
Jennifer L Perry	Speech/Language Pathologist	Diana Burch	Pals Teacher
	Agency Representative		
K. Jones	Community Preschool Teacher		

Sample Individualized Education Program (IEP)

I. MEETING AND IDENTIFYING INFORMATION

Initial Evaluation Eligibility Data

(Only required for student's initial evaluation to determine eligibility)

Identify area(s) impacted by the student's suspected disability: Fine Motor, Expressive/Receptive Language, Social/Emotional

Discussion to support decision: Areas of need were determined by parent information and screening information.

Is a determinant factor for the student's lack of academic progress the result of:

a) a lack of an appropriate instruction in reading, including essential components of reading instruction?   ☐ Yes   ☑ No

b) lack of instruction in math?   ☐ Yes   ☑ No

c) limited English proficiency?   ☐ Yes   ☑ No

Does the student require specially designed instruction in order to make adequate progress in school?   ☑ Yes   ☐ No

Eligible as a student with a disability?   ☑ Yes   ☐ No

Document basis for decision(s): Nicholas displays a moderate speech-language impairment in the areas of language and articulation.

Indicate primary disability:

371

Maryland State
Department of Education
Division of Special Education/
Early Intervention Services

Sample Individualized Education Program (IEP)

Name:
Agency: The Howard County Public School System
IEP Team Meeting Date: April 03, 2008

☐ Autism	☐ Developmental Delay	☐ Mental Specific Retardation	☐ Visual Learning Disability	☐ Impairment	☐ Deaf
☐ Emotional Disturbance	☐ Orthopedic Impairment	☐ Speech or Language Impairment	☐ Deaf-Blindness	☐ Hearing Impairment	☐ Other Health Impairment

☐ Traumatic Brain Injury

Mutiple Disabilities (Identify the cognitive disability and at least one sensory/physical disability):

Cognitive: ☐ Autism ☐ Mental Retardation ☐ Traumatic Brain Injury

Sensory/Physical: ☐ Deaf ☐ Deaf-Blindness ☐ Orthopedic Impairment ☐ Visual Impairments

Date of parent consent for initial evaluation: 6/1/2007

Date of initial evaluation: 6/1/2007

Date of initial IEP development: 6/1/2007

Date of parent consent for initiation of services: 6/1 /2007

Date of implementation of initial IEP: 8/10/2007

Reason(s) for delay: ☐ Student not available ☐ Parent requested delay ☐ Other, explain:

If the parent fails to respond or refuses consent to the initial provision of special education and related services, the public agency shall not provide special education and related services to the student and will not be considered in violation of the requirement to make RAPE available in accordance with 34 CFR 300.

Is this student transitioning from Infants and Toddlers (Part C) to Pre-School (Part B) and will be receiving services? ☑ Yes ☐ No

Sample Individualized Education Program (IEP)

II. PRESENT LEVEL OF ACADEMIC ACHIEVEMENT AND FUNCTIONAL PERFORMANCE

Academic: Early Childhood Skills

(Document student's academic achievement and functional performance levels in academic areas, as appropriate.)

Source(s): Observation, Assessment Report, Parent Information

Instructional Grade Level Performance:

- Physical Development. He has begun to develop pre-writing skill. His imitation of various strokes modeled for him is very light and not always oriented in the proper direction. He will make circular scribbles but does not yet make a circle from a model. Grasp on his crayon or pencil is still immature. He has not yet developed the use of scissors.

- Personal and Social. He is inconsistent in his social and play interactions with adults and other children. He may respond to a greeting or simply ignore attempts to gain his attention; will initially participate in adult directed activities but may become distracted or ignore continued play during the activity. When frustrated or unable to engage in his preferred task, he often will whine, lay on the floor, and refuse to interact socially. When involved in simple one on one interactive games and preferred activities, he can be very engaging and responsive to social praise and encouragement.

- Communication. He follows routine and novel directions throughout his day and demonstrates understanding of various basic concepts. Expressively, typically uses one word or sign to communicate his wants and needs. His vocal utterances often contain sound errors that affect both consonants and vowels. His speech is characterized by final consonant deletion and neutral vowels. Recently, his parents have seen an increase in drooling as well as an open mouth posture.

(Consider private, state, local school system, and classroom based assessments, as applicable.)

Summary of Assessment Findings (Including dates of administration): LAP-D and PLS administered April 2007, indicate age level skills in gross motor, concept development, and receptive language. Articulation, expressive language and fine motor are mildly to moderately delayed.

Does this area impact the student's academic achievement and / or functional performance? ☑ Yes ☐ No

| Maryland State
Department of Education
Division of Special Education/
Early Intervention Services | **Sample Individualized Education Program (IEP)** | **Name:**
Agency: The Howard County Public School System
IEP Team Meeting Date: April 03, 2008 |

What is the parental input educational program?

Parents are concerned about ability to clearly communicate wants and need, the social impact of his language delay on interactions with others, and general social development in groups

What are strengths, interest areas, significant personal attributes, and personal accomplishments? (Include preferences and interests for post-school outcomes, if appropriate.)

Gross motor, receptive language, preacademic concepts

How does disability affect his involvement in the general education curriculum?

He is not of school age, see participation in appropriate preschool activities.

For preschool age children, how does the disability affect participation in appropriate activities?

Disability affects preschool activities that require communication and social interactions with adults and peers.

III. SPECIAL CONSIDERATIONS AND ACCOMMODATIONS

Communication (required)

Does the student have special communication needs? ☐ Yes ☑ No

(If yes, describe the specific needs.)

Sample Individualized Education Program (IEP)

Name:
Agency: The Howard County Public School System
IEP Team Meeting Date: April 03, 2008

Assistive Technology (AT) (required)

Consider the AT device(s) and service(s) that are needed to increase, maintain or improve functional capabilities of a student with a disability.

Was assistive technology considered? ☐ Yes ☑ No

Does the student need an AT service(s)? ☐ Yes ☑ No

Does the student need an AT device(s)? ☐ Yes ☑ No   If yes, list AT Device(s)

Document basis for decision(s): Nicholas is able to communicate verbally.

Instructional and Testing Accommodations

☐ Instructional and testing accommodations were considered and no instructional and testing accommodations are required at this time.

Discussion to Support Decision: not eligible to participate in thd Maryland School Assessment Program designed for student in grade 3 to 10.

Supplementary Aids, Services, Program Modifications And Supports

Service Nature	Service Description Anticipated Frequency	Begin Date	End Date	Provider(s)
Visual Tactile Cues	Activities requiring verbal response	8/29/2007	6/1/2008	Speech/Lang. Path.
Sensory Strategies	As needed (OT consult)	8/29/2007	6/1/2008	Occupational Therapist Classroom staff

Clarify the location and manner in which Supplementary Aids, Services, Program Modifications and Supports to or, on behalf of, the student will be provided:

Visual tactile cues will be used during speech therapy sessions and activities requiring a verbal response. Sensory strategies will be used aas needed to increase or maintain engagement

Maryland State
Department of Education
Division of Special Education/
Early Intervention Services

Sample Individualized Education Program (IEP)

Name:
Agency: The Howard County Public School System
IEP Team Meeting Date: April 03, 2008

Communication

Goal: will speak clearly enough to be understood by familiar listeners.

Evaluation Method: Observation record, SLP report

ESY Goal? Decision Deferred

Objective 1: Using a least to most prompt hierarchy, will product target sounds (p,m,b,n,w,k,g,t) in: initial position of words, final position of words, two syllable words containing varied consonants (e.g. bunny)

By: 6/1/2008

With: 70% of the time

Objective 2: will use two word sentences to label request, negate, protest and greet

Objective 3:

Objective 4:

Progress Toward Goal

Progress Report 1	Progress Code:
Date	Description:
Progress Report 2	Progress Code:
Date	Description:
Progress Report 3	Progress Code:
Date	Description:
Progress Report 4	Progress Code:
Date	Description:

Sample Individualized Education Program (IEP)

Name:
Agency: The Howard County Public School System
IEP Team Meeting Date: April 03, 2008

Progress Report 5   Progress Code:

Date   Description:

How will the parent be notified of the student's progress toward the IEP goals? Report card, IEP progress report

How often? quarterly

Physical Development and Health

Goal: will use an adult grasp on writing tools imitate strokes in the proper direction   By: 6/1/2008
using an appropriate amount of pressure, draw a circle after a model and use scissors
independently to snip across paper.

Evaluation Method: Observation record, Report card   With: 80% of the time

ESY Goal? Decision Deferred

Objective 1: will use a tripod grasp when using drawing and writing tools

Objective 2: will use an appropriate amount of pressure when coloring or using a
pencil

Objective 3: will imitate the drawing of horizontal linse, vertical and circular scribbles.

Objective 4: will place scissors correctly on his hand and orient them to paper to
snip on a line and cut across the paper.

Progress Toward Goal

Progress Report 1   Progress Code:

Date   Description:

Sample Individualized Education Program (IEP)

Name:
Agency: The Howard County Public School System
IEP Team Meeting Date: April 03, 2008

Progress Report 2   Progress Code:

Date   Description:

Progress Report 3   Progress Code:

Date   Description:

Progress Report 4   Progress Code:

Date   Description:

Progress Report 5   Progress Code:

Date   Description:

How will the parent be notified of the student's progress toward the IEP goals? Report card, IEP progress summary

How often? quarterly

IV. GOALS

Personal and Social Development

Goal: will spontaneously greet, engage in group games and activities,   By: 6/1/2008
indicate ownership, and complete activities structured by an adult.

With: 80% of the time

Evaluation Method: Observation record, report card

ESY Goal? Decision Deferred

Page 11 of 15

Maryland State
Department of Education
Division of Special Education/
Early Intervention Services

Sample Individualized Education Program (IEP)

Name:
Agency: The Howard County Public School System
IEP Team Meeting Date: April 03, 2008

Objective 1: will spontaneously greet and say Goodbye to familiar adults

Objective 2: will use the word "mine" to indicate ownership or peers

Objective 3: will participate in circle and simple interactive games with help

Objective 4: Begin to obey and respect simple rules

Progress Toward Goal

Progress Report 1   Progress Code:
Date   Description:

Progress Report 2   Progress Code:
Date   Description:

Progress Report 3   Progress Code:
Date   Description:

Progress Report 4   Progress Code:
Date   Description:

Progress Report 5   Progress Code:
Date   Description:

How will the parent be notified of the student's progress toward the IEP goals? report card, IEP progress summary

How often? quarterly

Sample Individualized Education Program (IEP)

Name:
Agency: The Howard County Public School System
IEP Team Meeting Date: April 03, 2008

V. SERVICES

Special Education Services

Service Nature	Location	Number of sessions	Length of time	Frequency	Begin date	End date	Provider(s)/ agency	Summary of service
				Service Description				
Speech/ Language Therapy	Outside General Education	31	30 mins	Yearly	8/27/2007	6/1/2008	P Speech/ Lang. Path.	15 hrs. 30 min. Yearly
Speech/ Language Therapy	In General Education	31	30 mins	Yearly	8/27/2007	6/1/2008	P Speech/ Lang. Path.	15Hrs. 30Min. Yearly
Classroom Instruction	In General Education		2hrs	Weekly	8/27/2007	6/1/2008	P Special Ed Teacher	2Hrs. Weekly

Key: P = Primary; O = Other

Discussion of service(s) delivery: Instruction will be provided within classroom activities

Note: For service delivery that will occur as recheck periodically or only once, length of time fields in this table must contain 0. A detailed description of the services, including frequency of contacts, type of contact (direct or indirect), amount of time per contact, and fading schedule (if applicable) will be described below.

Maryland State
Department of Education
Division of Special Education/
Early Intervention Services

Sample Individualized Education Program (IEP)

Name:
Agency: The Howard County Public School System
IEP Team Meeting Date: April 03, 2008

Least Restrictive Environment (LRE) Decision Making & Placement Summary

A student with disability is not removed from general education in an age-appropriate instructional setting solely because of needed modifications to the general curriculum.

What placement option(s) did the IEP Team consider?

The team discussed the community preschool program where Nicholas' parents plan to enroll him. The IEP can be implemented there.

If removed from the general education environment, explain reasons why services cannot be provided in the general education environment with the use of supplementary aids and services:

Articulation needs require direct instruction in a structured setting

Document basis for decision(s): Clinical opinion of speech-language pathologist

Total time in school week: 15 hrs. minutes – Total time outside of General Education: hours 30 minutes/week = Total time in General Education: hours minutes/week

Special education placement (ages 3–5): Least Restrictive Environment: IN REGULAR EARLY CHILDHOOD SETTING (at least 80%)

Average %/day

In selecting the LRE are there any potential harmful effects on the student or quality of services he or she needs? ☐ Yes ☑ No

Are the services in the student's home school (the school the student would attend if not disabled)? ☑ Yes ☐ No

If no, is placement as close as possible to the student's home? ☑ Yes ☐ No

Maryland State **Department of Education** **Division of Special Education/** **Early Intervention Services**	**Sample Individualized Education Program (IEP)**	**Name:** **Agency:** The Howard County Public School System **IEP Team Meeting Date:** April 03, 2008

Is special transportation needed? ☐ Yes ☑ No

Are personnel needed to assist the student during transportation? ☐ Yes ☑ No

Document basis for decision(s) (including consideration of the amount of time and distance involved in travel):

Provide an explanation to the extent, if any, the student will not participate with non-disabled peers in academic, non-academic, and extracurricular activities?

Nicholas will not participate with non-disabled peers during pull-out speech therapy sessions to address articulation. During all other activities, he will participate with peers.

SSIS Resident County: Howard   SSIS Resident School: Bellows Spring Elementary

SSIS Service County: Howard   SSIS Service School: Bellows Spring Elementary

Child Count Eligibility Codes:

(1) Eligible student with a disability served in a public school or placed in a nonpublic school by the public agency to receive FAPE.

Maryland State
Department of Education
Division of Special Education/
Early Intervention Services

Sample Individualized Education Program (IEP)

Name:
Agency: The Howard County Public School System
IEP Team Meeting Date: April 03, 2008

VII. AUTHORIZATION(S)

Consent for Initiation of Services (initial IEP only)

I have received a copy of the Evaluation Report informing me in writing of the reasons for this action.

The special education and related services will be provided as described in the IEP. I understand that the IEP will be reviewed periodically but not less than annually.

I understand that records will not be released without my signed and written consent except under the provisions of the Family Education Rights and Privacy Act (FERPA). This law allows the release of educational records to a public school or educational agency.

I understand that my consent is voluntary and that I may revoke consent at any time. Should I revoke consent it is not retroactive.

I understand that the public agency will submit information that will be used for the special services information system. This system will be used by the MSDE and other State Agencies, as appropriate, to enable funding of programs and assure my child's rights to any needed assessment.

I have been informed of the determination(s) of the IEP team in my native language or other mode of communication.

I have been informed of my rights, as explained in the Procedural Safeguards - Parental Rights document, I have received.

I give consent for my child/student to receive special education and related services.

Parent Signature: _____ Date: _____

**Maryland State
Department of Education
Division of Special Education/
Early Intervention Services**

Maryland Individualized
Family Service Plan (IFSP)

Maryland Individualized Family Service Plan (IFSP)

Part I :   Child and Family Information

Part XI: Child Development Status and Family Information

Part III: Child/Family Outcomes Related to Development

Part IV: Early Intervention Services

Part V: Service Linkages

Part VI: Transition Information

| Child Name: | Referral Date: 02/28/2007 |
| | Annual Evaluation: April 03, 2008 |

PART I: CHILD AND FAMILY INFORMATION

Child Address:
City State Zip:
Date of Birth:
Phone Number:
Home School:
Was the Child Adopted?　No
Is the Child Currently in Foster Care?　No
Race:　Other
Gender:　Male
Hospital of Birth:　Harbor Hospital Center
Gestation:

Parent(s)/Guardian/Surrogate

Mother
Name:
Address:
City/State/Zip:
Primary Phone:
Secondary Phone:
Cell Phone:
Email:
Is this Person the Primary Caregiver:

Father
Name:
Address:
City/State/Zip:
Primary Phone:
Secondary Phone:
Cell Phone:
Email:
Is this Person the Primary Caregiver:

Service Coordinator Information
Name:
Agency:
Address:
City/State/Zip:
Home Phone:
Work Phone:
Email:

Referral ID:

Interim Service Coordinator Information
Name:
Agency:
Address:
City/State/Zip:
Home Phone:
Work Phone:
Email:

PART II: CHILD DEVELOPMENT STATUS AND FAMILY INFORMATION

Present Levels of Development

Cognitive
Date of Procedure: 03/07/2008
Chronological Age: 29 month(s)
Age Level/Age Range: 30m to 33m
Qualitative Description: ELAP: 30-33 mos

Communication
Date of Procedure: 03/07/2008
Chronological Age: 29 month(s)
Age Level/Age Range: 30m
Qualitative Description: ELAP: 30 mos; follows routine directions fairly consistently. When new concepts or novel directions are asked of him, he often demonstrates off-task/distraction behaviors, most likely due to a lack of understanding. He has begun to combine words into phrases, but he does not consistently use this skill across all settings.

Social-emotional
Date of Procedure: 03/03/2008
Chronological Age: 29 month(s)
Age Level/Age Range:
Qualitative Description: ELAP: 33 mos.; has some difficulty demonstrating ease in familiar social settings. He doesn't consistently engage in familiar music or imitation activities and typically refuses to participate in that setting, but perform the skills at home.

Adaptive
Date of Procedure: 03/10/2008
Chronological Age: 29 month(s)
Age Level/Age Range: 24m
Qualitative Description: ELAP: 24 mos

Referral ID:

Gross Motor
Date of Procedure: 03/10/2008
Chronological Age: 29 month(s)
Age Level/Age Range: 30m
Qualitative Description: ELAP: 30 mos

Fine Motor
Date of Procedure: 03/07/2008
Chronological Age: 29 month(s)
Age Level/Age Range: 30m to 33m
Qualitative Description: ELAP: 30-33 mos

Hearing
Date of Procedure: 03/07/2008
Chronological Age: 29 month(s)
Qualitative Description: hearing wasn't formally evaluated. He localizes to environmental sounds,answers questions and repeats words and sounds.

Vision
Date of Procedure: 03/07/2008
Chronological Age: 29 month(s)
Qualitative Description: vision wasn't formally evaluated. He visually tracks adults walk across the room, locates small items on the floor, and points to details in pictures in books.

Health
Date of Procedure: 03/07/2008
Chronological Age: 29 month(s)
Qualitative Description: is reported to be verv healthy and only suffers from occassional colds. His doctor, routinely monitors health.

Primary Health Care Provider
Name:
Phone Number:

Immunization
DtaP/DT: Received
IPV: Received
Hib: Received
MMR: Received
HepB: Received
Varicella: Received
Comments:

Referral ID:

Family's Concerns, Priorities, and Resources

Strengths
- Pleasant temperament, happy child loving, sense of humor
- Strong pre-academic concept knowledge (labels colors, shapes, numbers, letters)
- Recent progress with expressive language skills and uses word combinations

Needs
- Further language development (expressing his wants/ thoughts with language, paying attention to and understanding questions posed and responding appropriately)
- comfort in social situations (interaction with other children)
- potty training
- eating well with utensils

Family's Concerns, Priorities, and Resources
Stated their current concerns with development to be continuing to build expressive and receptive language skills. Their current priorities include supporting communication and social interaction skills.
Family resources include the following: Nanny, grandparents, and an aunt and uncle.

Was this Information Gathered as a Result of a Family Assessment?
This information was gathered as a result of a family directed assessment

Natural Enviroments
Childs home. Library, Toddler play group

What are the daily routines of the child and family? Are there other routines that the family would like to establish?
Up at 8a - milk and breakfast
Play time - usually morning activity (i.e. library story time, I&T playgroup, teacher's visit, gym class)
Lunch followed by playtime/learning time (books, craft etc)
Nap 2-4p
Playtime, park etc
Dinner 6:30p
Nighttime routine - Bath, milk, 1/2 hrTV, brush teeth, story, bedtime

What barriers prohibit the provision of services in the child/family's routines and activities?
Currently, work on a full-time basis from Monday through Friday while is cared for by his nanny in the family home. The Infant and Toddler staff will try to best accommodate the family's work schedule as well as have visits with nanny.

What will need to change in order for this service to be provided within the family's routines?

Not applicable.

Eligibility Status

Atypical development

Social-Emotional

PART III: CHILD/FAMILY OUTCOMES RELATED TO DEVELOPMENT

Outcome

family would like him to continue to develop language so that he can follow directions and communicate with adults and peers.

Strategies/Activities

- Family training model
- Repeat key words and phrases frequently
- Vocally highlight important words
- Select target vocabulary
- Share printed information about language development

Criteria

will follow directions containing an object and a location (e.g. put the cup on the table) and directions containing basic concepts (e.g. big, wet).

He will use verb+ing to describe actions.

He will use 2-3 word phrases to comment, label, request, greet, and protest.

Timeline

3rd birthday- October 2008

Person(s) Involved

Parents

Date Achieved

Outcome

family would like him to understand and respond to simple requests, or directions, and understand age appropriate concepts.

Strategies/Activities

- Parents will be given strategies, written handouts, and modeling of activities.
- Family will make sure they have visual attention and that he is in close proximity when giving him verbal directions.
- Total communication strategies will be used.

Referral ID:

- Family will use a prompt hierarchy to assist when he does not respond to verbal directions.
- Family will model language to promote development of new skills.
- Play activities and daily routines will be used as times to teach and reinforce concepts.

Criteria
- will follow basic directions (put it in, give it to me, sit down, etc)
- will consistently point to body parts, articles of clothing, and familiar objects and pictures when named.
- will respond by looking when asked "where" an object is placed.
- will sort and match objects, by attributes.

Timeline

October 2007- 6 month review

April 2008- Annual review

Person(s) Involved

Parents and caregivers

Date Achieved

04/03/2008

Outcome

family would like him to use words to communicate.

Strategies/Activities
- Be on physical level
- Hold toys/objects up to your mouth as your say the name of the object
- Model total communication (pictures, signs, vocalizations, words)
- Repeat key words and phrases frequently
- Vocally highlight important words
- Select target vocabulary
- Share printed information about language development
- Demonstrate song book
- Repetition of songs and finger plays for motor, sound, and word imitation
- Use of modeling, sabotage, and prompting to facilitate language
- Wait time or prompts for interactions
- Sound bag to facilitate speech sound production

Criteria
- will consistently imitate motor actions, familiar songs and fingerplays, environmental sounds (such as wee, uh-oh, boom) and beginning sounds.
- will communicate at least 5 wants and needs

Timeline
October 2007- 6 month review
April 2008- Annual review

Person(s) Involved
Parents and careaivers

Date Achieved
04/03/2008

Outcome
parents would like him to demonstrate greater comfort in social situations.

Strategies/Activities
- Infant and Toddler Staff will discuss and demonstrate how to use a prompting hierarchy when teaching new skills
- Infant and Toddler Staff will discuss and model strategies to facilitate interactions between and peers during social interactions (i.e. modeling appropriate language and actions, pairing up with a strong peer, use of motivating materials)
- Staff will provide parents with resources regarding community playgroups for toddlers, including biweekly EB playgroup Staff will provide onsite support (including observations, feedback, and one-on-one support) in community settings upon parent request.
- Staff will share information and resources regarding behavior management strategies and social developmental milestones

Criteria
will:
1. Verbally greet familiar adults and peers in a variety of social settings with an adult prompt as needed.
2. Participate in large group activities in community settings (including performing fingerplays and movement activities).
3. Engage in parallel play with a peer for 10 minutes with a familiar adult at a distance.
4. Verbally respond to questions and use words to communicate his wants and needs with familiar adults and peers in community settings.
5. Use words to defend possessions ("no" "my turn" "mine")
6. Participate in a back and forth game with a peer for at least 3 turns with adult facilitation.

Timeline
By third birthday

Person(s) Involved

Date Achieved

Referral ID:

Outcome

parents would like him to engage in imitation games or activities.

Strategies/Activities

- Infant and Toddler Staff will discuss and model strategies to support skill development during play, including prompting hierarchies, wait time, and sabotage.
- Staff will provide information and suggestions concerning age-appropriate toys and activities
- Staff and parents will collaborate and plan appropriate play activities to be embedded within daily routine
- Staff will discuss and demonstrate how to use a prompting hierarchy and "shape up" approximations/attempts when teaching new skills
- Incorporate objects into play, such as twist caps, spoon, stacking toys

Criteria

On 4 out of 5 opportunities, will:

1. Imitate simple motor actions during play or song activities (clap hands, stomp feet, blow kiss, etc.)
2. Imitate simple 1-step actions on an object (pat doll, drop block, move bean bag up in the air, etc.)
3. Combine two objects in play and imitate simple actions with items (stir spoon in bowl, put spoon baby's mouth, use hammer to bang toy nails down, stack blocks on cup)
4. Imitate 2-3 step play actions (move figurine up ladder and down slide; move animal figurine to water trough, food trough, and in the barn)

Timeline

6-month review (10/10/07)
Annual review (4/10/08)

Person(s) Involved

Date Achieved

04/03/2008

Outcome

parents would like for him to demonstrate greater comfort when exploring new places, new equipment, and new people.

Strategies/Activities

- A coaching model will be used with parents
- Daily sensory activities providing vestibular and proprioceptive inputs for self-regulation (increase engagement and attention to activities)
- Increase tolerance to vestibular input to expand on play schemes
- Provide variety of activities to build confidence for motor tasks

Referral ID:

Criteria

will:

1. greet familiar and non-familiar adults and/or peers by waving, smiling, or vocalizing.
2. engage in adult directed activities for 5-10 minutes
3. explore new toys/materials/equipment with minimal assistance
4. use climbing equipment and swings with confidence

Timeline

6 month review
Annual Review - April 2008

Person(s) Involved

Date Achieved

Outcome

parents would like him to have a smooth transition to appropriate services on his third birthday.

Strategies/Activities

- Early Intervention Specialist will explain the process and timeline for transition, review the transition booklet, and answer the family's questions.
- Information concerning both community and school program options will be provided to the family.
- Family will be encouraged to observe possible program options.
- Assessments will be scheduled and completed and results reviewed with the parents at an IFSP meeting.
- A transition meeting will occur when is 27 to 33 months of age.
- With parental written consent, the assessment report will be used to determine if is eligible for services following his third birthday.
- If eligible, the team and parents will develop an Individual Education Plan to meet needs, and conduct a meeting to approve the IEP.
- An IEP meeting will be scheduled prior to third birthday.

Criteria

- family will have an opportunity to review the process and explore program options.
- Part C and Part B paperwork will be completed within timeline.
- Parent satisfaction with a smooth transition process.

Timeline

By third birthday

Person(s) Involved

Date Achieved

Referral ID:

PART IV: EARLY INTERVENTION SERVICES

Occupational

Frequency: 2 x Only
Intensity: 45 minutes
Basis: Individual
Financial Responsibility: Local School System
Provider Agency: HCPSS
Provider Name:
Location: Home
Reimbursement Source:
Service Initiation Date: 08/24/2007
Projected Duration: 04/2008
Service Ending Date: 04/03/2008
Location Justification:

Special Instruction

Frequency: 4 x Monthly
Intensity: 45 minutes
Basis: Individual
Financial Responsibility: Local School System
Provider Agency: HCPSS
Provider Name:
Location: Home
Reimbursement Source:
Service Initiation Date: 04/24/2007
Projected Duration: 10/2007
Service Ending Date:
Location Justification:

Speech/Language

Frequency: 6 x Only
Intensity: 45 minutes
Basis: Individual
Financial Responsibility: Local School System
Provider Agency: HCPSS
Provider Name:
Location: Home
Reimbursement Source:
Service Initiation Date: 04/30/2007
Projected Duration: 10/2007
Service Ending Date:
Location Justification:

Referral ID:

Assistive Technology and Transportation

Does this plan include any services provided in a Judy Center? No

Does this plan include assistive technology? No

Type of Assistive Technology:

Provider Name:

Phone Number:

Does this plan include transportation? No

Type of Transportation:

Is any special equipment needed for transporting the child? No

Provider Name:

Phone Number:

PART V: SERVICE LINKAGES

Family

Agency: Howard County Family Support and Resource Center

Person Involved:

Person Title: Parent Kesource Coordinators

Person Phone:

Added: Friday, March 23, 2007

Child Care/Enrichment:

Medical Health:

Counseling:

Income Assistance:

Other: Family Support Center

Payment Source:

Strategies: Contact information was shared with family for them to use at their discretion.

PART VI: TRANSITION INFORMATION

Transition Planning Meeting Date:

Consideration of Part B Special Education:

Referred to Community Services:

Results of the IEP Eligibility Meeting:

Transition Activity

Activity:

Person(s) Responsible:

Timelines:

Referral ID:

Practitioner Rating Scale

Practitioner: **Date:**

Evaluator/title:

To Evaluator: Please use the following scale (circle the appropriate number) to evaluate the practitioner you have supervised. Please share your evaluation with the practitioner as part of the overall evaluation process.

0 —————— 1 —————— 2 —————— 3 —————— 4 —————— 5

Cannot   Needs   Satisfactory   Excellent

determine   improvement

1.	Ability to evaluate a child's developmental or academic strengths and needs	1	2	3	4	5
2.	Knowledge of the professional literature in early childhood special education	1	2	3	4	5
3.	Ability to develop and maintain good working relationships with families	1	2	3	4	5
4.	Ability to develop and maintain good working relationships with colleagues	1	2	3	4	5
5.	Ability to teach children new skills and support development of new schemata	1	2	3	4	5
6.	Ability to supervise the work of paraprofessionals/volunteers	1	2	3	4	5
7.	Ability to support positive behavioral outcomes	1	2	3	4	5
8.	Ability to develop high-quality IFSPs or IEPs in a timely fashion	1	2	3	4	5
9.	Effective written communication skills	1	2	3	4	5
10.	Effective oral communication skills	1	2	3	4	5
11.	Ability to plan and implement effective interventions	1	2	3	4	5
12.	Ability to collaborate (e.g., team planning) effectively with team members	1	2	3	4	5
13.	Ability to monitor child progress and use empirical data to modify the child's program	1	2	3	4	5
14.	Ability to serve as a consultant to and resource for other practitioners	1	2	3	4	5

		1	2	3	4	5
15.	Considers all feedback	1	2	3	4	5
16.	Uses good clinical judgment (e.g., critical thinking and action in new situations)	1	2	3	4	5
17.	Plans for and maintains an orderly and developmentally appropriate environment	1	2	3	4	5
18.	Seeks appropriate professional development opportunities	1	2	3	4	5
19.	Learns from mistakes	1	2	3	4	5
20.	Maintains a positive attitude toward teaching, children, families, colleagues, and other aspects of the program	1	2	3	4	5
	Totals					
	Final score (Add the scores from each column and dvide by 20.)					

Please complete this section during the mid-term evaluation conference with the practitioner.

1. Strengths:

2. Suggestions for improvement:

3. Suggestions for professional development:

Supervisor's signature

Date

Practitioner's signature

Date

Practitioner Evaluation Form

Practitioner observed:
Observer/title:

Time/setting:
Date:

Please rate the practitioner on the following:	Strongly disagree				Strongly agree
1. **Application of knowledge** (e.g., practitioner can use knowledge and skills appropriatelyl in academic and other professional situations	1	2	3	4	5
2. **Collegiality** (e.g., the degree to which practitioner interacts collaboratively with colleagues, families, and others in the educational setting)	1	2	3	4	5
3. **Content/knowledge** (e.g., how well practitioner understands important concepts and has developed skills critical to teaching young children with disabilities and their families)	1	2	3	4	5
4. **Cross-cultural competence** (e.g., in verbal, written, and nonverbal communication, practitioner indicates an understanding and respect of multiple cultures)	1	2	3	4	5
5. **Effective nonverbal communication** (e.g., practitioner uses appropriate gestures and facial expressions to exchange ideas in a clear and culturally suitable fashion)	1	2	3	4	5
6. **Effective verbal communication** (e.g., practitioner uses appropriate oral language to exchange ideas in a clear and culturally suitable fashion)	1	2	3	4	5
7. **Family centeredness, sensitivity** (e.g., in verbal, written, and nonverbal communication, practitioner is respectful of families and supports family self-sufficiency)	1	2	3	4	5
8. **Initiative** (e.g., degree to which practitioner is proactive relative to teaching, collaboration, professional development, seeking feedback, timely completion of administrative tasks)	1	2	3	4	5
9. **Openness to feedback** (e.g., practitioner's willingness to consider supervisor, family, and peer comments regarding performance/knowledge)	1	2	3	4	5
10. **Professionalism** (e.g., practitioner's timeliness, professional behavior, clinical judgment, collegial interactions)	1	2	3	4	5
Total					
Average rating across attributes (Divide total of ratings for all categories by a factor of 10.)					

Please use page 2 for additional comments.

The practitioner's areas of professional/personal strength:

Areas this practitioner might consider for professional development:

Additional comments:

Please sign this form after it has been shared with the practitioner. One copy of the completed/signed form should be given to the practitioner, and one copy of the completed/signed form should be kept in the practitioner's personnel file for use in planning individual/group professional development activities.

Practitioner/title

Date

Observer/title

Date

Routines-Based Intervention Rating Scale for Home-Based Services

Home visitor/title:	Start time:
Observer/title:	End time:
	Date:

Instructions:
- Observe the home visitor while he or she is engaged in providing family-centered intervention to a young child and his or her family member(s).
- Rate the home visitor using the following scale (Circle the ratings that apply):
  + = Correctly demonstrated
  − = Incorrectly demonstrated
  ND/NA/NO = Not demonstrated/Does not apply/No opportunity to observe
- Review and discuss observations with the home visitor. Add any additional comments or note corrections.
- Both the observer and the home visitor sign the form in the appropriate spaces.

The home visitor:

1.	Is attired appropriately for the community/setting	+	−	ND NA NO
2.	Greets family members in a culturally appropriate manner	+	−	ND NA NO
3.	Inquires about family's well-being	+	−	ND NA NO
4.	Washes up prior to the intervention portion of the home visit	+	−	ND NA NO
5.	Makes sure the family's basic needs are met (e.g., food, shelter, clothing, utilities)	+	−	ND NA NO
6.	Reviews the most important outcome(s) in the child's individualized family service plan (IFSP)	+	−	ND NA NO
7.	If outcome(s) achieved, disconcontinued; if not achieved, collaborates with family to review/revise strategies	+	−	ND NA NO
8.	Reviews noteworthy events, successes, concerns, and changes in family routines from last visit	+	−	ND NA NO
9.	Develops family routines-based strategies to support achievement of priority outcome(s)	+	−	ND NA NO
10.	Follows the family's lead in discussions, as appropriate	+	−	ND NA NO

Rating Scale for Home-Based Services

		+	–	
11.	Explains clearly and coaches family in implementation of any proposed interventions	+	–	ND NA NO
12.	Prepares written instructions/diagrams/handouts for proposed activities	+	–	ND NA NO
13.	Identifies additional information/services needed by the family (e.g., food stamps, child care)	+	–	ND NA NO
14.	Develops strategies for obtaining needed community-based information/services	+	–	ND NA NO
15.	Conveys a positive attitude about the child and family	+	–	ND NA NO
16.	Listens empathically to family's recent successes and concerns	+	–	ND NA NO
17.	Communicates clearly	+	–	ND NA NO
18.	Includes all family members (e.g., siblings, grandparents), as appropriate	+	–	ND NA NO
19.	Summarizes visit orally and in writing (i.e., for the family); makes plans for follow-up (e.g., phone, visits)	+	–	ND NA NO
20.	Ensures that written materials are culturally sensitive and in the family's preferred language or literacy level	+	–	ND NA NO
	Total marks in each column			

Comments regarding strengths of home visitor:

Comments regarding areas of improvement for home visitor:

Suggestions for professional development:

Please sign this form after it has been shared with the home visitor. One copy of the completed/signed form should be given to the home visitor, and one copy of the completed/signed form should be kept in the home visitor's personnel file for use in planning individual/group professional development activities.

_____   _____
Practitioner/title   **Observer/title**

_____   _____
Date   **Date**

Index

Page numbers followed by *f* indicate a figure and by *t* indicate a table.